GRAMMATICAL THEORY IN
WESTERN EUROPE
1500–1700

GRAMMATICAL THEORY IN WESTERN EUROPE

1500-1700

The Latin Tradition

G. A. PADLEY

Professor of Linguistics
Laval University, Quebec

CAMBRIDGE UNIVERSITY PRESS

CAMBRIDGE

LONDON · NEW YORK · MELBOURNE

Published by the Syndics of the Cambridge University Press
The Pitt Building, Trumpington Street, Cambridge CB2 1RP
Bentley House, 200 Euston Road, London NW1 2DB
32 East 57th Street, New York, NY 10022, USA
296 Beaconsfield Parade, Middle Park, Melbourne 3206, Australia

First published 1976

Printed in Great Britain at the
University Printing House, Cambridge
(Euan Phillips, University Printer)

Library of Congress Cataloguing in Publication Data
Padley, G. A. 1924–
  Grammatical theory in Western Europe, 1500–1700
  Based on the author's thesis, Oxford.
  Bibliography: p. 268.
  Includes index.
   1. Grammar, Comparative and general–History. 2. Linguistics–History. I. Title.
P151. P3   415   75-44573
ISBN 0 521 21079 8

To Peter and Barbara Spiers

CONTENTS

ACKNOWLEDGMENTS

Among those scholars to whose encouragement this work owes its genesis and growth, I am especially indebted to Mrs Vivian Salmon of Edinburgh University, without whose initial advice and stimulus my steps might well not have been guided towards a fascinating subject. I am also grateful to her for penetrating criticism of the work in its original form. This first version, submitted for an Oxford doctorate, attempted to cover a somewhat wider field than the final study, including a survey of the Latin tradition in grammatical theory as reflected in English and French vernacular grammars of the period 1500–1700. This section of the work, more especially, owed a good deal to Professor E. J. Dobson of Jesus College, Oxford, who kindly put his detailed knowledge of editions of the early English orthoepists and grammarians at my disposal. While my research was in progress, much of what I had to say on English grammar was however anticipated, on a much broader canvas, first by E. Vorlat's 'Progress in English Grammar 1585–1735' (University of Louvain doctoral thesis, 1963), and later by Ian Michael's *English Grammatical Categories and the Tradition to 1800* (Cambridge, 1970). A fuller treatment of the implications of the Latin tradition for European vernacular grammar would have involved a discussion of German, Dutch, Italian and Spanish grammatical practice, but this was of course precluded by the limited scope of a doctoral dissertation.

In reshaping the work for publication, I had to bear in mind that it was the Latin section that was potentially of most interest to readers, giving as it does a survey of works that are little known or have not hitherto been treated. It is this section, much expanded by additional research and placed in the context of contemporary cultural developments, that I now offer as a contribution to the history of linguistics. It will, I hope, play its part in bridging the scandalous gap in that history between medieval grammatical endeavours and the eighteenth century.

All historians of grammatical theory owe a deep debt to Professor R. H. Robins of London University, and it is with special pleasure that I thank him for kindly reading the typescript in its final version. Thanks are also due to Professor Dr Herbert Brekle of Ratisbon for reading it through, and to my colleague Dr John Gallup of Laval University, from whose wide knowledge of medieval grammar and philosophy I profited on numerous occasions. The staffs of the Bodleian, the British Library and the Bibliothèque Nationale gave as always their ungrudging assistance.

Finally, a very special word of thanks to Evelyn Broy of Windsor, Ontario, for her unfailingly cheerful competence in preparing the typescript.

G. A. P.

Quebec
January 1976

ABBREVIATIONS

SHORT TITLE	FULL TITLE
Baebler, J. J., *Beiträge*	*Beiträge zu einer Geschichte der lateinischen Grammatik im Mittelalter* (1885)
Bolgar, R. R., *The Classical Heritage*	*The Classical Heritage and its Beneficiaries* (1954)
Caspari, F., *Humanism and the Social Order*	*Humanism and the Social Order in Tudor England* (1954)
De Wulf, M., *Medieval Philosophy*	*Medieval Philosophy Illustrated from the System of Thomas Aquinas* (1922)
Fischer, K., *Descartes*	*Descartes and his School* (1887)
Formigari, L., *Linguistica*	*Linguistica ed empirismo nel seicento inglese* (1970)
Funke, O., 'Frühzeit'	'Die Frühzeit der englischen Grammatik', *Schriften der literarischen Gesellschaft Bern*, IV (1941), pp. 1–91
'Weltsprachenproblem'	'Zum Weltsprachenproblem in England im 17. Jahrhundert', *Anglistische Forschungen*, 69 (1929), pp. i–v, 1–163
García, C., *Contribución*	*Contribución a la historia de los conceptos gramaticales: la aportación del Brocense* (1960)
Graves, F. P., *A History of Education*	*A History of Education during the Middle Ages and the Transition to Modern Times* (1914)
Howell, W. S., *Logic and Rhetoric*	*Logic and Rhetoric in England, 1500–1700* (1956)
Jellinek, M. H., *Geschichte*	*Geschichte der neuhochdeutschen Grammatik von den Anfängen bis auf Adelung* (1913–14)

Kukenheim, L., *Contributions* — *Contributions à l'histoire de la grammaire grecque, latine et hébraïque à l époque de la Renaissance* (1951)

Esquisse — *Esquisse historique de la linguistique française et de ses rapports avec la linguistique générale* (1962)

Lily, W., *L* — Lily's Latin grammar of 1527

L' — Lily's Latin grammar of 1566

Mullally, J. P., *Peter of Spain* — *The Summulae Logicales of Peter of Spain* (1945)

Poldauf, I., 'Problems of English grammar' — 'On the History of Some Problems of English Grammar before 1800', *Prague Studies in English*, LV (1948), pp. 1–322

Robins, R. H., *Short History* — *A Short History of Linguistics* (1967)

Rossi, P., *Francis Bacon* — *Francis Bacon: from Magic to Science* (1968)

Sahlin, G., *César Chesneau du Marsais* — *César Chesneau du Marsais et son rôle dans l'évolution de la grammaire générale* (1928)

Salmon, V., *Francis Lodwick* — *The Works of Francis Lodwick* (1972)

'James Shirley' — 'James Shirley and Some Problems of Seventeenth-Century Grammar', *Archiv für das Studium der neueren Sprachen*, 197:4 (1961), pp. 287–96

'Language-planning' — 'Language-planning in Seventeenth-Century England', in *In Memory of J. R. Firth*, ed. C. E. Bazell *et al.* (1966), pp. 370–97

Steinthal, H., *Geschichte*, II — *Geschichte der Sprachwissenschaft bei den Griechern und Römern mit besonderer Rücksicht auf die Logik*, 2nd ed., vol. II (1891)

Thurot, C., *Extraits* — *Extraits de divers manuscrits latins pour servir à l'histoire des doctrines grammaticales au moyen âge* (1869)

Vorlat, E., 'Progress' — 'Progress in English Grammar 1585–1735' (1963)

Watson, F., *The English Grammar Schools to 1660* — *The English Grammar Schools to 1660: Their Curriculum and Practice* (1908)

xii

There is nothing so trivial as a Grammar, and scarce
any thing so rare as a good grammar.   – G. Miège

Alle diese Typen . . . aus dem Unbewusstsein in das
Bewusstsein zu heben – und das ist doch die Aufgabe
des Grammatikers – ist ein gewaltiges Unternehmen,
das auch den hellsten Köpfen, selbst Männern wie
Aristoteles, nicht auf den ersten Anlauf gelingen
konnte.   – B. Delbrück

INTRODUCTION

Though the present century has seen a vast expansion of linguistic teaching and research, there was until recently a tendency to regard such studies as originating in the work of the nineteenth-century comparatists or even, as far as the synchronic approach is concerned, with twentieth-century scholars such as Ferdinand de Saussure. The majority of linguists were unaware not only of the long and distinguished history of their subject, but also of the relevance to present-day theory of much earlier speculation about language. More particularly in the English-speaking world, an unbroken European tradition of some two thousand years was until the immediate postwar period largely ignored. Now, thanks to the work of R. H. Robins and a few other scholars, and in some measure to N. A. Chomsky's *Cartesian Linguistics*, which has stimulated interest in certain aspects of seventeenth-century theory relevant to contemporary trends, the history of linguistics is beginning to find a place in the university curriculum. This increased awareness of the importance of a knowledge of the linguistic theory of past centuries coincides with a movement away from the 'structuralist' classification of phonological and morphological data which has been for some decades a major preoccupation of linguistic scholarship, more particularly in the United States, and towards an interest in syntactic questions. The time would accordingly seem ripe for a study of the grammatical theory of those centuries immediately preceding our own era, which prepares the way for, and indeed in many respects anticipates, a good deal of what is customarily regarded as a specifically twentieth-century contribution to linguistics.

The period 1500–1700 is a crucial one in the history of western civilization. At its beginning, European thought is still in many respects medieval. At its end, that scientific revolution which more than anything else has shaped our modern world is already under way. A period of transition, it has its own particular contribution to make to the development of thought about language, a contribution which has however been almost completely neglected by linguistic historians. The ancient world has been ably treated in R. H. Robins' *Ancient and Medieval Grammatical Theory in Europe* and his *Short History of Linguistics*, and the newly awakened interest in medieval theory has been catered for by studies such as G. L. Bursill-Hall's *Speculative Grammars of the Middle Ages*. There has also been no lack of attention to the linguistic history of the eighteenth and nineteenth centuries, but as far as grammar is concerned, studies of this period have generally assumed that modern pre-structuralist theory, more particularly as applied to universal grammar, begins with the Port-Royal *Grammaire générale et raisonnée* of 1660. In the history of linguistics a whole period – that separating medieval speculative grammar from Port-Royal – is missing, leaving a gap which it is the aim of the present work to fill.

Much energy has in the last few decades gone into the synchronic study of various languages, but until quite recently there has been a marked absence, at any rate in English, of monographs on individual grammarians of previous centuries,[1] and even more of any consideration, outside the works of Robins and Bursill-Hall, of the broad sweep of grammatical theory over a long period of time and within a common tradition. The only extensive study embracing the classical languages in the post-medieval period is L. Kukenheim's *Contributions à l'histoire de la grammaire grecque, latine et hébraïque à l'époque de la Renaissance*, which is a history of grammar within the cultural context rather than a treatment of grammatical theory, and in any case does not go beyond 1540. As for works on vernacular grammar, they are either inaccessible to the majority of English-speaking students because they exist only in German, or they do not treat their subject within the wider context of the historical development of grammatical theory. M. H. Jellinek's *Geschichte der neuhochdeutschen Grammatik* falls short of the English-speaking student's needs in both these respects, while the scattered researches of O. Funke, including articles on Bullokar's and Ben Jonson's English grammars, on Paul Greaves' *Grammatica Anglicana* and on early English grammars in general, have not been translated. Those full-length accounts of vernacular grammar which do exist in English – I. Poldauf's

---

[1] V. J. Flynn's facsimile edition (1945) of Lily's Latin grammar is an honourable exception. In recent years, of course, the Scolar Press reprints have greatly contributed to a wider knowledge of sixteenth- and seventeenth-century English grammarians.

article 'On the history of some problems of English grammar before 1800' and E. Vorlat's 'Progress in English Grammar 1585–1735' – are unsatisfactory in that they do not link the grammatical doctrines they discuss to the long Latin tradition in which they are rooted. E. Vorlat in particular, while aiming to show 'the interdependence among the early English grammarians', makes no attempt to demonstrate their dependence on a common European mainstream of theory, but presents grammatical notions almost in isolation as if they were the original inventions of the authors concerned. Not until 1970, in Ian Michael's *English Grammatical Categories and the Tradition to 1800*, do we have a work exempt from this criticism. This is not to disparage the excellence of these works as presentations of vernacular grammar as such. It is simply that they do not, by and large, take into account the derivative nature of much vernacular theory. Nor could they be expected to do so, for no full, coherent account of the vernacular grammarians' antecedents in the Latin tradition of grammatical theory exists. E. Vorlat has no difficulty in demonstrating the commonplace that Bullokar derives from Lily, but she cannot and does not situate Lily himself within the tradition from which he springs. A consideration of that tradition is an essential preliminary to the study of vernacular theory, and it is all the more surprising that it has never been undertaken, especially in view of the importance of the period 1500–1700 as a transition between medievalism and the rationalistic eighteenth century. Existing studies are few, and for the most part confined to a single author. P. A. Verburg's important *Taal en Functionaliteit* is in Dutch and hard to come by; C. García's study of the Spanish classical scholar Sanctius (*Contribución a la historia de los conceptos gramaticales: la aportación del Brocense*) has not been translated and is in many respects unsatisfactory; and V. Salmon's interesting articles on Shirley's Latin grammars, though they are models of the way in which items of grammatical doctrine can be linked to the wider tradition underlying them, treat aspects of the theory of only one particular grammarian.

In undertaking to supply the lack of an overall study of the Latin tradition between 1500 and 1700, I cannot claim to have read – nor indeed have I attempted to read – every grammatical work published in the period. The broad lines of theory are laid down by the great grammarians of the time – a Scaliger, a Ramus, a Vossius – the host of minor authors being largely imitators whose work is none the less

3

of interest as an indication of the extent to which the doctrines of the great find common acceptance. Rather than aiming at bibliographical completeness, this study sets out to give a general view of the direction taken by grammatical theory from 1500 to 1700, and to determine what it owes to previous tradition both classical and medieval. The necessity for such a study has been underlined by the publication of Chomsky's *Cartesian Linguistics*, which reawakened interest in the Port-Royal Grammar but at the same time posited for it origins which an examination of its sources in the Latin tradition show to be demonstrably false. The discussion surrounding the merits and demerits of Chomsky's arguments has served to highlight the need for research into Port-Royal's antecedents in the immediately preceding centuries, into the linguistic history of a period which constitutes 'too significant a topic to be ignored as it has been'.[1] Not only does earlier theory need to be scrutinized for the origins of the Port-Royal Grammar and of much modern linguistic doctrine, but any such scrutiny must take into account the cultural context from which that theory springs. Any other approach must inevitably lead to precisely the kind of distortion of linguistic history which Chomsky himself – in a book otherwise containing valuable insights – has inadvertently perpetrated. To consider sixteenth-century grammatical theory divorced from its basis in the Revival of Learning with its mixed Renaissance/Medieval Scholastic inheritance, or seventeenth-century theory apart from its roots in rationalist and empiricist thought, would be to treat them as independent entities removed from their underlying causes. A grammatical tradition inevitably reflects a cultural one, whether stable or in a state of change.

[1] R. Lakoff, Review of C. Lancelot and A. Arnauld, *Grammaire générale et raisonnée*, ed. H. Brekle, Stuttgart-Bad Cannstatt, 1966, in *Language*, 45 (1969), p. 364.

1. THE HUMANIST TRADITION

THE CULTURAL BACKGROUND

The early sixteenth-century grammarians were heirs to a stable tradition, that represented by the culture of Greece and Rome, and any evaluation of their grammatical practice must be made against the background of the rediscovery of classical learning. The penetration of this New Learning into western Europe is usually dated from the fall of Constantinople in 1453 and the flight of Greek scholars to Italy. Some authorities however attach less importance to this event, seeing the migration of scholars as simply a continuation of an already existing trend.[1] They point out that Greek studies were already flourishing in Italy by the early fifteenth century, Manuel Chrysoloras for instance, professor of Greek at Florence, having been sent to Venice as early as 1393, and Theodore Gaza, first teacher of Greek at Ferrara,[2] having fled Thessalonica before its capture by the Turks in 1430. Whichever of these viewpoints one accepts, until the end of the century the New Learning was largely confined to Italy, with such milestones as the establishment of Aldus Manutius' press in Venice, the publishing of Vergil in Florence in 1472, and the formation in 1500 of a 'New Academy' for the dissemination of Humanist learning. In France, though Paris had its professorship of Greek by 1458, it was not until the reign of Francis I (1515–47), to whom Guillaume Budé dedicated his Humanist educational treatise *De l'institution du prince* (1516), that the Collège de France with its chairs of Greek, Latin and Hebrew was set up. In 1526 the establishment of the royal press, with Robert Estienne as first printer, ensured the spread of Humanist ideas, though both press and college were for some time overshadowed by the enormous prestige of the University of Paris, whose long-established monopoly of Scholasticism and medieval logic constituted a major obstacle to Humanist studies.

[1] v. D. Bush, *The Renaissance and English Humanism*, University of Toronto Press, 1939, p. 1.

[2] His Greek grammar was published by the Aldine press in Venice in 1495.

One important consequence was that the early Italian Humanists' campaign to purge the schools of such medieval grammatical 'barbarities' as Alexander of Villedieu's *Doctrinale* received little support in Paris, and it was not before Budé's death in 1540 that French Humanism was firmly established. Reluctant to yield place in Paris, Scholastic learning disappeared yet more slowly in Germany, in spite of the efforts of fifteenth-century wandering scholars, and though a chair of Poetry and Eloquence had been set up at Erfurt by 1494, it was not until the end of the first quarter of the following century that scholars of the stature of Reuchlin and Melanchthon were produced.

This slow development of Humanism, its co-existence over quite a long period of time with Scholasticism, is important for its effect on grammatical theory, for it means that many grammarians received a Scholastic training and retained elements of medieval practice in their works. English Humanism in particular was slow to discard entirely the medieval world-view. At the time when Humphrey Duke of Gloucester was giving the initial impetus to Humanist studies,[1] Scholasticism was still very much the dominant force in the universities, and though by the middle of the fifteenth century Englishmen were already visiting the centres of learning in Italy and bringing back with them increasing numbers of manuscripts and translations, it was some time before the results of this activity began to be felt in education. Grocyn, Linacre, and Latimer, who went to Florence around 1488, introduced Greek studies into Oxford on their return, Grocyn becoming the first lecturer in the language, and the Spanish scholar J. L. Vives, whose *De tradendis disciplinis*[2] enumerated the tasks of Humanism and allotted to each discipline its place in the scheme of scholarly enquiry, was teaching at Oxford in 1524. Further, Bishop Fox's Corpus Christi College (1517) was founded with the express intention of encouraging Humanist learning. At Cambridge, Humanism owed its appearance to the efforts of Bishop Fisher, who became Chancellor of the University in 1504, and above all to the Dutch scholar Erasmus. The latter, after studying Latin and Greek in Paris, making the acquaintance of Colet and More and following the lectures of Grocyn and Linacre at Oxford in 1499, spent four

---

[1] V. H. H. Green, *A History of Oxford University*, London, 1974, p. 33, notes that Humphrey gave the University 129 manuscripts in 1437, 17 in 1442, and 134 in 1444.

[2] *De disciplinis libri XII; septem de corruptis artibus; quinque de tradendis disciplinis*, 1531.

years at Cambridge as Professor of Divinity, lectured on Greek, and aided Colet in the foundation of his new school of St Paul's. The teaching of Greek at Cambridge was suppressed for a time as a result of Wolsey's antagonism to Fisher, but Sir Thomas Smith was giving Greek lectures in 1533, and in 1540 a regius professorship was founded whose second incumbent was Roger Ascham, author of *The Scholemaster*.[1]

F. Caspari[2] distinguishes four periods in the development of the New Learning in England: that of the nascent Humanism of the late fifteenth century; the period that, beginning in the last decade of that century with the return from Italy of Grocyn, Colet, and Linacre and ending in the 1530s, sees the publication of More's *Utopia* and Elyot's *Governour*; the period of the separation from Rome and the confiscation and redistribution of monastic property, accompanied by a partial secularization of education; and finally, from 1558, the age of Elizabeth. He follows R. Weiss[3] in holding that for most of the fifteenth century Humanism was a means rather than an end in itself, an aid to an improved Latin style and to the art of letter-writing. It was only in the second of the periods enumerated by Caspari that Humanism became a truly vital force in England, and it was in this period that it was put on a firm footing and began to spread into the schools. By the age of Elizabeth, the convergence of the aims of Humanist education and the needs and demands of the gentry as an emergent governing class had made a knowledge of Latin a prerequisite for social advancement. But one must accept Caspari's view, again echoing Weiss, that in England at any rate the forms of Humanism were simply grafted onto an essentially medieval intellectual and social framework:

In contrast to their Italian contemporaries, the early English humanists – most of them churchmen – did not perceive any fundamental difference between scholasticism and humanism, and they did not adopt a humanistic philosophy . . . the transition from the old to the new learning was gradual when it actually came – as it did in the theology and pedagogy of John Colet, for instance . . . traditional theology and humanistic learning continued to exist side by side, often in the same persons . . . the break between the two was less radical than it had been in Italy . . .[4]

[1] v. F. P. Graves, *A History of Education during the Middle Ages and the Transition to Modern Times*, New York, 1914, pp. 163–4.
[2] *Humanism and the Social Order in Tudor England*, University of Chicago Press, 1954, pp. 16–19.   [3] *Humanism in England during the Fifteenth Century*, Oxford, 1941.
[4] F. Caspari, *Humanism and the Social Order*, pp. 19–20.

In England as compared with Italy, as Weiss points out, Humanism was subordinated to medieval culture rather than opposed to it, producing a situation of compromise in which even the chief Humanist scholars, Grocyn, Colet, More, Linacre, 'disclose alongside with strong humanistic elements some very solid scholastic foundations'.[1] Undoubtedly true of England, this generalization can be extended to northern France and Germany, and even partially to Italy, the co-existence of Scholastic and Humanist traits being a striking feature of many of the grammars considered in this study.

Not only in this matter of the greater tenacity of medieval Scholasticism did the Humanist movement in northern Europe differ from its counterpart in Italy. In the north, more particularly in the Protestant areas, the Renaissance 'took on more of a social and moral color'.[2] The classical revival had the more immediately utilitarian aim of extracting a new meaning from the Scriptures and furnishing material for religious polemic, as well as providing the tools for a return to original Christian sources via the study of the New Testament in the original Greek. In England as elsewhere, the New Learning became bound up with the cultural and political aspirations of the wealthy bourgeois, legal, and upper mercantile classes. It soon became apparent that the road to preferment lay, for the ambitious, through an ability to write and speak Ciceronian Latin. But at a deeper level than this, the 'establishment' of the day began to realize that there was a social and political parallel between the values of Greek and Roman literature and philosophy, and the needs of the state and its newly emergent administrative classes.

During the sixteenth century therefore, and particularly in England, as Caspari notes,[3] English Humanists sought in Plato and Aristotle, Cicero and Quintilian, at once a justification of the hierarchy of 'order and degree' in the state, and a means of improving and consolidating the position of the gentry. What nineteenth-century England sought to accomplish by means of the Public Schools, sixteenth-century educators sought in some measure to achieve through the Grammar Schools and a Humanist pedagogy. Schools, of which Colet's foundation of St Paul's was the first, were set up on Humanist principles to educate the increasingly wealthy

---

[1] R. Weiss, *Humanism in England*, p. 183.
[2] F. P. Graves, *A History of Education*, p. 141.
[3] *Humanism and the Social Order*, p. 1.

class of lawyers, merchants and gentry which was in process of taking over the administration of the state. There were obvious parallels between this new civil governing class, with its demand for a new type of education, and the needs and ideals of the Greek and Roman aristocracy with which Humanist educators invited them to identify themselves. This alliance between Humanist ideals and the needs of an ambitious upper middle class vastly favoured the spread of the New Learning in England, and indeed in northern Europe in general, in the early decades of the sixteenth century. There was however a price to pay. Pure scholarship tended to be subordinated to wider interests such as the cult of eloquence, or the good of the state. Scholars were under pressure to train textual critics, to undertake Biblical exegesis, to train logicians and lawyers, to educate the new administrative class.

The first pressing task of early Humanism was to transcribe, comment upon, and hand on to its successors the corpus of classical knowledge, and the second was to devise an adequate pedagogy. In accordance with the temper of the age, it was concerned more particularly with memorizing and imitation. Rather than a training in original thought, it proposed a model of elegance. The first task of the Florentine *Accademia Platonica* in the mid-fifteenth century had been the revival of Plato's philosophy, and to that end Marsilio Ficino (1433–99) had translated into Latin the works of both Plato and Plotinus. As time went by, however, this academy and its numerous progeny abandoned the wide interests which had characterized them at first, and increasingly put emphasis on philological studies, devoting themselves to the writing of elegant Latin and, eventually, almost solely to the improvement of the Italian vernacular. Characteristic of Italian Humanism is the emphasis placed on rhetoric and the study of orators, involving a close study of Cicero's *Epistles*, and of such contemporary aids as Valla's *De elegantia*, and the *De copia* and *De conscribendis epistolis* of Erasmus. It should however be noted that not only in Italy but throughout western Europe the sixteenth century offers many examples of grammatical treatises which continue to make a distinction between that *grammatica methodice et horistica* whose end is the establishment of normative rules, and the *grammatica exegetice sive enarrativa et historica* devoted to philological and rhetorical considerations. Everywhere, Renaissance grammar remains to a large extent bound up with rhetoric. But the continuance of Italian scholars in particular in this tradition, together with such external factors as the sack of Rome in 1527 and the authoritarianism of the Church, meant that little of note was produced by them in the early sixteenth century. Even elsewhere, however, the impulse toward the imitation of Greek and Roman models was eventually exhausted, the demand for the products of a Humanist education slackened, and Humanism began, by about 1530, to outlive its usefulness. Scholars had the choice between stagnating in philological byways and breaking new ground. Outside those byways, the ideas underlying the great movement of thought which characterizes the transition from sixteenth-century, and still to some extent medieval, modes of enquiry to those of the empirical, rationalist seventeenth century, were already germinating.

Kuno Fischer[1] sees in the Renaissance a trend of thought which moves 'from the religious-philosophical view of the world to that of the natural-philosophical'. This trend, which is more particularly associated with seventeenth-century empiricism and its manifestations such as the Royal Society in England, has its starting-point in Italian Neo-Platonism, of which Italian nature-philosophy is a direct development. These trends are rooted in a desire to explain phenomena by natural causes, a desire which ultimately leads to the dethronement of Aristotle in favour of Plato. In the universities Aristotle still reigns supreme, but elsewhere Plato's influence is increasingly felt, particularly in political theory, as in More's *Utopia*, and as in Erasmus' prescriptions for the education of a Christian prince.[2] By the time of the French scholar Peter Ramus, it is France and England, rather than Italy, that are the centre of Platonic studies. As Caspari has demonstrated, the English Humanists were all indebted to Platonic philosophy, but used it in conjunction with ideas taken from Aristotle's *Politics* and *Ethics*, and from Cicero and Quintilian. It is worth noting that, like so many products of the Renaissance, Florentine Neo-Platonism was deeply rooted in medieval thought:

. . . the Platonism of the Florentine Academy was not only of Renaissance origin, but derived a great deal of its motive force, both on the philosophical and the religious side, from the mediaeval traditions onto which it was

---

[1] *Descartes and his School*, translation from the German of the 3rd ed. by J. P. Gordy, London, 1887, p. 96.
[2] v. F. Caspari, *Humanism and the Social Order*, pp. 9–15.

grafted . . . Renaissance thought of this type kept the mediaeval objective of a synthesis between religion and philosophy, but aimed at achieving this through Neo-Platonic mysticism rather than through Aristotelian logic . . . Renaissance Neo-Platonism is in some ways a return to that closer relationship between religion and philosophy which characterized the pre-Thomist mediaeval thinkers.[1]

This Neo-Platonic movement had as its concomitants on the one hand a rejection of Aristotelian logic, which was too firmly allied to Scholasticism to find favour with the Humanists, and on the other an attempt to wrest Aristotle from the control of the Church and study him for his own sake in the original texts. Hence the rejection of logic, by early Humanists such as Valla, in favour of rhetoric. The culminating point of the tendency is the fierce anti-Aristotelianism of Peter Ramus (1515–72) and his followers.

Here, it is necessary to make a distinction between the rejection of Aristotle's logic and the readiness of Renaissance grammarians to incorporate parts of his linguistic theory into their work, whether these concepts come to them via the medieval *Grammatica speculativa*, or through Greek sources such as Theodore Gaza's grammar of 1495. The whole of Aristotle's *Organon* was available to scholars, either in Boethius' version or in new translations, by the second half of the twelfth century, and certain of his linguistic ideas were thus quite early incorporated into Scholastic grammar.[2] According to G. L. Bursill-Hall, 'it would perhaps not be too much to say that the impact of Aristotle on the medieval schoolmen of the twelfth and thirteenth centuries was the single most important factor in producing the change in direction of the grammatical thought of that period . . . Aristotelian thought is all-pervasive in grammar, certainly up to the end of the Middle Ages.'[3] Though his influence is no longer all-pervasive, Aristotle still overshadows Renaissance grammatical theory, whether we consider the Greek elements in the system of Linacre, the reapplication of Aristotelian theory (in a not always post-Scholastic idiom) by J. C. Scaliger, or the violent antagonism of the Ramists.

Given the importance of Aristotle for grammatical theory over such a long period of time, it will be appropriate to consider at the

[1] F. A. Yates, *The French Academies of the Sixteenth Century*, The Warburg Institute, University of London, 1947, pp. 2–3.

[2] v. W. and M. Kneale, *The Development of Logic*, Oxford, 1962, p. 225.

[3] *Thomas of Erfurt Grammatica Speculativa: An Edition with Translation and Commentary*, London, 1972.

outset the thoughts on grammar which are scattered among his logical and philosophical treatises, particularly in the rather perfunctory first four chapters of the *De interpretatione*. Unlike most present-day linguistic scholars, Aristotle makes meaning rather than form the basis for his classifications, a view which has its counterpart in Renaissance grammar. His definition of words as 'symbols or signs of affections or impressions of the soul' is a mentalistic one.¹ He appears to make a distinction between lexical and grammatical meaning:² 'A noun or verb by itself much resembles a concept or thought which is neither combined nor disjoined. Such is "man" for example . . . unless in addition you predicate being or not being of it.'³ Implicitly, he makes a distinction between the *word*, a meaningful linguistic unit, and the *part of speech*, that same unit provided with an additional grammatical meaning or function in the sentence, a distinction that the medieval doctrine of *dictio* and *pars orationis* was to render explicit. A further indication of his concern with semasiological criteria rather than with formal structure is his division of the word-classes into 'full' ones with independent lexical meaning apart from any grammatical function, and 'conjunctions' without meaning aside from such function. He recognizes that nouns (and hence presumably all other words too) receive their meaning by arbitrary convention, and in the ancient controversy as to whether words have meaning by nature (φύσις), or by imposition (θέσις), he takes the latter standpoint.⁴ Further, in order to mark them off from verbs, he defines nouns as making no reference to time.⁵ Here, Aristotle must have in mind the grammatical meaning of the noun, for he was no doubt well aware that a word such as *day* signifies time. This supposi-

---

¹ H. P. Cooke, *Aristotle: The Organon*, London and Cambridge, Mass., 1938, p. 115 (*De interpretatione*, cap. 1). Cf. L. Bloomfield, *Language*, New York, 1933, p. 142: 'Adherents of mentalistic psychology . . . believe that, prior to the utterance of a linguistic form, there occurs within the speaker a non-physical process, a *thought, concept, image, feeling, act of will,* or the like . . . The mentalist, therefore, can define the meaning of a linguistic form as the characteristic mental event which occurs in every speaker and hearer in connection with the utterance or hearing of the linguistic form . . . For the mentalist, language is *the expression of ideas, feelings, or volitions.*'

² As indeed does Bloomfield (*Language*, p. 264), who readily accepts that 'each linguistic form has a constant and specific meaning'. What he rejects is the positing of any kind of mental 'image' behind this meaning.

³ H. P. Cooke, *Aristotle*, p. 117 (*De interpretatione*, cap. 1).

⁴ v. R. H. Robins, *A Short History of Linguistics*, London, 1967, pp. 17–19.

⁵ H. P. Cooke, *Aristotle*, p. 117 (*De interpretatione*, cap. 2): 'A noun is a sound having meaning established by convention alone but with no reference whatever to time' (Ὄνομα μὲν οὖν ἐστὶ φωνὴ σημαντικὴ κατὰ συνθήκην ἄνευ χρόνου).

tion is made all the more probable by his definition of the verb as that which προσσημαίνει χρόνον – 'consignifies time' or 'signifies time in addition'.[1] Here, the reference can only be to grammatical meaning. Aristotle additionally defines the verb as indicating an affirmation, as predicating something about the logical subject of a proposition and linking it with its attribute.[2] This second part of his definition was ignored by the classical grammarians, not to reappear until the Middle Ages, and the criterion of the consignification of time was not in general, outside Greek grammar, treated as a primary distinction marking off verb from noun. The grammatical concept of consignification however, before being progressively lost sight of in the seventeenth century, played an important role in medieval and some Renaissance grammars.

Aristotle's ideas linger in the grammatical treatises of the age, but his position as the intellectual basis for much of Scholasticism made him suspect in many Humanist quarters. In Protestant areas especially, the Reformation prompted a search for a method of scientific enquiry independent of Scholasticism and Catholic philosophy. In England, Sir Thomas Wilson's *Rule of Reason* (1551)[3] and Everard Digby's *Theoria analytica* (1579) proposed new theories of or new approaches to knowledge some decades before Bacon's epoch-making proposals. Already Digby, basing himself on the Neo-Platonic theory of the correspondence between the mind of man and the world of nature, discusses the question of the obtaining of knowledge through the senses, a question which was so deeply to preoccupy thinkers of the seventeenth century.[4] Such enquiries as Digby's however spring from theological preoccupations, and have little in common with Bacon's inductive approach. Wilson's *Rule of Reason*, which attempts to apply Scholastic logic to utilitarian ends, had considerable success, being reprinted in 1552, 1553, 1567 and 1580. The appearance of Ramistic logic in England in the 1570s put an end to such attempts to refurbish Scholastic logic, but it is worth noting that the advent of what may be termed sense realism occurs much earlier than is generally supposed. The originators of this approach are usually thought to be Bacon and Comenius, but

---

[1] *Ibid.* p. 119 (*De interpretatione*, cap. 3): 'Ῥῆμα δέ ἐστὶ τὸ προσσημαῖνον χρόνον.
[2] *Ibid.* p. 119 (*De interpretatione*, cap. 3): καὶ ἐστιν ἀεὶ τῶν καθ' ἑτέρου λεγομένων σημεῖον.
[3] *The Rule of Reason, Conteinyng the Arte of Logique, Set Forth in Englishe.*
[4] v. M. H. Carré (ed.), *De Veritate by Edward, Lord Herbert of Cherbury. Translated with an Introduction,* University of Bristol, 1937.

tendencies toward an earlier realism are discernible in the work of the English schoolmaster Richard Mulcaster (1530–1611), author of the important educational works *Positions* (1581) and *Elementarie* (1582). His Sensualist theories had little effect on the educational methods of his day, but must surely have influenced later realists such as Bacon.[1]

The importance of empirical and naturalist influences in the sixteenth and seventeenth centuries must however be weighed against the actual state of education. In the universities, for instance, the Scholastic tradition, both in subject-matter and pedagogical method, was long to reign supreme. It is true that in 1550 Duns Scotus' texts were publicly burnt in England, and that supporters of Ockhamist trends had to move from Oxford to London, but in general the universities remained strongholds of a rigid Aristotelianism.[2] It is against this background that Humanists waged their campaign for the establishment of the New Learning, and grammatical studies too had to fight vested interests surviving from the medieval period. Men like Valla and Vives campaigned for the abandonment of medieval grammatical treatises such as Alexander of Villedieu's *Doctrinale* and Évrard of Béthune's *Graecismus*,[3] for the adoption of a Latin purged of medieval 'barbarisms', for a standard of eloquence based on 'usus' rather than the logicians' 'causae', and for the replacement of the old dialectic grammars or *grammaticae speculativae* by works of Humanists such as Despauterius and Melanchthon. The movement for the reinstitution of classical Latin eloquence, begun by Petrarch, was carried forward by Laurentius Valla, professor of rhetoric in Rome, whose *De linguae Latinae elegantia* (1471), printed a large number of times, is at the basis of the veritable cult of eloquence and Ciceronianism pursued by the Humanists. His attempt to purify contemporary Latin finally resulted in a victory for philological over legal studies in Italy.[4] The tradition of eloquence thus established was very much at the heart of Humanist education. Sir Thomas Elyot, author of *The Boke Named the Governour* (1531), the great

[1] v. F. P. Graves, *A History of Education*, pp. 250, 253–4.

[2] v. P. Rossi, *Francis Bacon: From Magic to Science*, translated from the Italian (Bari, 1957) by S. Rabinovitch, London, 1968, pp. 39–40.

[3] The *Doctrinale*, a prescribed text in the universities, first appeared in 1199, saw a final Paris edition in 1527, and was printed for the last time in 1588. Both it and the *Graecismus* (1212) were verse treatises.

[4] v. R. R. Bolgar, *The Classical Heritage and its Beneficiaries*, Cambridge University Press, 1954, pp. 270–1.

popularizer of Humanism in England, proposed that the noble child whose education he discusses should be able to speak, read, and write elegant Latin before the age of seven. Gradually facilities for the training of the *homo trilinguis*, the Humanist versed in Latin, Greek and Hebrew, begin to appear: Corpus Christi College, Oxford (1517), and, in the same year, the *Collège des trois langues* at Louvain, in which Erasmus took an interest. 1528 saw the establishment in Spain of the *Collegium trilingue Complutense*, while France as already noted received in 1529 its 'noble et trilingue académie', the *Collège des lecteurs royaux* (the present *Collège de France*).[1] By the middle of the century there were Jesuit colleges in seven Italian cities, including Rome, Florence, and Venice, whose pupils received instruction in the grammars of Despauterius and the fourth-century Donatus.[2]

Grammatical studies were no exception to the general Humanist aim of restoring the lost classical past, in that they sought to go back beyond medieval conceptions to the grammars of Donatus (*c.* 350) and Priscian (*c.* 500). The approach of the early Humanists is consciously modelled on these two major Roman grammarians, who had of course been available to the Middle Ages but whose doctrine, or rather selected portions of it, had been rethought and reshaped in Scholastic terms. Much of late fifteenth- and early sixteenth-century grammar is a restatement of Donatus and Priscian, often a word-for-word reproduction. In view of the overriding importance of these authors as sources for Renaissance grammarians, a few remarks on their availability are in order.[3] Donatus' *Ars maior* was neglected during the Middle Ages, while his *Ars minor*, a short work in question-and-answer form treating only of the eight parts of speech, became the standard Latin text for schools. It was already printed in Harlem before 1447, the first French edition dates from 1460,[4] and from then on editions were legion. The *Ars maior* appeared for the first time in the 1476 edition of Diomedes' grammar, omitting the introductory section on letters and syllables, which was not printed until 1503.[5]

---

[1] v. L. Kukenheim, *Contributions à l'histoire de la grammaire grecque, latine et hébraïque à l'époque de la Renaissance*, Leyden, 1951, p. 1.

[2] v. R. R. Bolgar, *Classical Heritage*, p. 357.

[3] The Roman grammarian Varro, either not known to or not followed by the majority of early Humanist grammarians, will be mentioned where appropriate in the treatment of individual Renaissance authors.

[4] L. Kukenheim, *Contributions*, p. 83, note 1.

[5] H. Keil, *Grammatici Latini*, Hildesheim, 1961 (a reproduction of the Leipzig edition of 1857–74), vol. IV, p. xxxviii.

H. Keil[1] mentions six editions of Priscian (of whose eighteen books the last two, dealing with syntax, tended to be published separately as the *volumen minus*) between 1470 and 1503. Before printing became general scholars had access to numerous manuscripts. Neither Donatus nor Priscian is original, Donatus having used the same sources as Charisius and Diomedes, without adding anything of his own,[2] while Priscian names as his authority and bases his grammar on the second-century Greek grammarian Apollonius Dyscolus.[3]

In grammar, as in rhetoric, the Humanist aim, consonant with the training of a new ruling class, is the inculcation of correctness and eloquence. But as V. Salmon points out, to hold that the Humanists, in their reaction against the logical minutiae of Scholasticism, minimized the importance of grammar, is an over-simplification:

On the one hand were teachers like Erasmus and Vives, Ascham and Mulcaster, who pleaded for the minimum of grammar-learning; on the other were men like Melanchthon, who warned school-teachers against attempting to teach Latin without first making the child thoroughly acquainted with the grammar. As the sixteenth century progressed, the grammarians increased their hold.[4]

So much so that, as Mrs Salmon remarks, by about 1600 a few enterprising teachers were planning revolution. But the immediate aim of the early Humanist grammarians was undoubtedly the establishment of norms of correct grammar for rhetorical ends, as is amply demonstrated by the common definition of grammar as an *ars recte loquendi*, an art of correct speaking. In this pedagogical aim, their endeavours coincided with the needs both of the new administrative classes and of the state that offered them preferment. Early Humanism is above all literary and normative.

THE HUMANIST GRAMMARIANS

The work of the more important of the late fifteenth-century grammarians and those sixteenth-century authors who remain closely dependent on Roman tradition forms a coherent whole, a

---

[1] *Ibid.* vol. II, pp. xxiii–xxiv.

[2] Cf. C. Thurot, *Extraits de divers manuscrits latins pour servir à l'histoire des doctrines grammaticales au moyen âge*, Paris, 1869, p. 60.

[3] 'Cuius auctoritatem in omnibus sequendam', notes Priscian (H. Keil, *Grammatici Latini*, III, p. 24).

[4] V. Salmon, 'Joseph Webbe: Some Seventeenth-Century Views on Language-teaching and the Nature of Meaning', *Bibliothèque d'Humanisme et Renaissance*, XXIII (1961), pp. 324–40.

unified body of doctrine. From the 1470s to about 1540 Latin grammarians stay by and large within this tradition. In considering these grammarians, I shall make no attempt at an exhaustive treatment aiming to include every author who wrote a Latin grammar in this period. In addition to the great names, such as Linacre and Melanchthon,[1] I shall however treat a few minor ones, the common run of grammarians being often a more trustworthy index to general trends – in particular the trend to conservatism – than spectacular innovators.

As the guiding force behind the early Humanist movement it would be difficult to overestimate the importance of the Roman Laurentius Valla, the ablest representative of the Neo-Latin Renaissance. He was the first to attack the medieval system, proposing the replacement of logic by rhetoric, and advocating the necessity of submitting ecclesiastical documents, including the Vulgate, to philological criticism. His *De linguae Latinae elegantia*, written *c.* 1440 and printed in 1471, is at once an exposition of Latin and a return to the classical approach to the reading and writing of Latin and the study of authors. He gives as his grammatical sources Donatus and Priscian, who represent for him the last trustworthy authorities before the barbarous products of medievalism. Even these authorities, however, he corrects wherever he feels necessary. Among medieval grammarians he condemns in particular 'Hisidorus indoctorum arrogantissimus' (Isidore of Seville) and 'Eberardus' (Évrard of Béthune, author of the thirteenth-century *Graecismus*).[2] His *Elegantiae*, in the rhetorical tradition of the Italian Renaissance, is largely concerned with matters of style and usage. The grammatical material is haphazardly arranged and incidental to the main aim, which is to improve the quality of written Latin. The work of Valla's fellow-Humanist Nicolaus Perottus acquired a wide reputation after the 1473 edition of his *Rudimenta grammatices*, first published *c.* 1464. His grammar is more carefully codified than that of Valla, and it is clear that he has closely followed Donatus and Priscian, particularly the latter, from whom the definitions of the word-classes and their accidents are usually copied word for word. Perottus' work was widely diffused both within Italy and abroad. Very similar to it in

---

[1] I have not been able to see a copy of the grammar of Nicolaus Clenardus, or Cleynaerts (1495–1542), who taught Latin in Spain at Braga and Granada.

[2] *De linguae Latinae elegantia*, Venice, 1471, f. 32^r.

conception is Sulpitius' *Grammatica* of 1475.[1] It too is normative and is similarly an elementary teaching grammar rather than an exposition of theory. Again the chief influence is that of Priscian, from whom almost all word-class definitions are taken, but though Sulpitius follows the Ancients closely his work still shows vestiges of medieval doctrine. His importance, together with Valla and Perottus, is as a model for Humanist grammatical reformers. It is of course usually impossible to tell whether a sixteenth-century author receives Roman theory direct from the newly printed versions of Donatus and Priscian or via these early Italian writers, but their value as models can hardly be overestimated. No less than thirty-four editions of Valla's *Elegantiae* were published in France, Germany and Italy between 1501 and 1544, and a copy of it was among Fleming's books in Lincoln College, Oxford.[2] An edition of Perottus' *Rudimenta* with English passages replacing the Italian ones appeared at Louvain in 1486, and John Anwykyll's *Compendium totius grammaticae* (Oxford, 1483) was an abridgment of Perottus and Valla together with elements from Alexander of Villedieu's *Doctrinale*. This work is proof that Valla and Perottus were well known in Oxford at this date.[3] Sulpitius was published by Wynkyn de Worde in 1499, and all three of these scholars are named in the foreword to Whittinton's *Vulgaria* of 1520.

Among these early Humanists, mention should be made of the important Spanish scholar Nebrija (1444–1522), whose works continued to be printed until as late as 1869. Antonio Martínez de Cala, surnamed Nebrissensis after his birthplace Nebrija or Lebrija, travelled to Italy when still only nineteen to study the New Learning, and was probably there from 1463 to 1470. He returned to Spain determined to introduce the new doctrines into the University of Salamanca, and in 1481 his *Introductiones Latinae* appeared,[4] the first edition running into more than a thousand copies and being reprinted the following year. It quickly became the standard authority in Spain, especially after the addition of an erudite commentary to the Salamanca edition of 1495, and was published in France and Italy until the middle of the sixteenth century. A translation of the

[1] Reference is here made to the Nuremberg edition of 1482.
[2] v. R. Weiss, *Humanism in England*, p. 168.
[3] v. *ibid.* p. 169. Anwykyll was grammar master at Magdalen College School, Oxford.
[4] A revised form, differing from the *editio princeps* chiefly in being partly in hexameters, appeared in Venice in 1491.

Spanish version was published in England as late as 1631 under the title *A Briefe Introduction to Syntax*.[1] Nebrija was the founder of Humanistic studies in Spain, though it should be noted that Perottus' *Rudimenta* had been published there as early as 1475.[2] The *Introductiones* is a straightforward grammar for didactic purposes, the essence of Nebrija's grammatical doctrine being contained in the commentaries. Use is made here of an annotated edition of 1509[3] for the latter, reference otherwise being made to the unannotated Saragossa edition of 1533.[4] In the foreword to this edition, Nebrija recommends the study of the Roman grammarians Sergius, Phocas, Diomedes, Servius, Asper, Rhemnius and Caper, mention of Donatus and Priscian being of course superfluous. Nebrija's immense work contains little that is original, but the reinstatement of classical learning and pre-medieval grammatical theory was in itself a Herculean task, and it would be a mistake to expect originality at this early date. He laid the foundations of Spanish classical scholarship, and his example was widely followed. The *Introductiones Latinae* had already been reprinted four times by 1500, and there is no doubt that it set the logical and semantic tone of grammar for his successors.

In Italy by the time of Aldus Manutius' grammar[5] the new approach is well established. His *Rudimenta* stays close to Roman tradition, the definitions of the word-classes being very largely repeated word for word from Donatus, with the exception of verb and pronoun, where Priscian is preferred. There is however a medieval legacy in the comparatively large space devoted to syntax.

In Flanders, the University of Louvain had been founded in 1426 and the school of the *Lilium* or *Lis* in 1437. A product of this school, Johannes van Pauteren (alias Despauterius), published in 1510 and 1511 three works[6] aimed at replacing Alexander of Villedieu's *Doctrinale*, still reigning in the schools, by a clearer exposition. The immediate outcry from those who thought his new rules contrary to

[1] For these details I am indebted to I. González-Llubera's introduction to his edition of Nebrija's *Gramatica Castellana*, Oxford University Press, 1926.

[2] v. *ibid.* p. xxiv, note 2.

[3] *Aelii Antonii Nebrissensis ars nova grammatices cum eiusdem uberrimis commentariis*, Lyons, 1509. (Nebrija's preface, reprinted with the text, refers to 'tertiam hanc aeditionem'.)

[4] *Grammatica Antonii Nebrissensis iampridem solicite revisa*, Saragossa, 1533. (This and the work cited in the note immediately above will be referred to in succeeding notes as *Introductiones* (1533) and (1509) respectively.)

[5] *Aldi Manutii Romani Rudimenta grammatices Latinae linguae*, Venice, 1501. (The *Institutiones grammaticae*, also first published 1501, follows the *Rudimenta* closely.)

[6] *Ars versificatoria, De accentibus et punctis,* and *De carminum generibus.*

the usage of the Church[1] obliged him to publish in 1512 an *epistola apologetica* in his defence. In his *Ars versificatoria* he had railed against those 'indocti homines' who, though but sparrows to Aristotle's nightingale, rushed in the name of Aristotle to Alexander's defence. In 1514 however the Synod of Mecheln [Malines] ordered his work to replace the *Doctrinale* in the schools, and his grammar came to be widely used not only in Flanders but also in France. These preliminary skirmishes with Alexander were followed in 1514 by the appearance of the *Rudimenta*,[2] and in 1537 Robert Estienne published the whole of Despauterius' grammatical output in Paris under the title *Commentarii grammatici*.[3] This grammar, which runs to over six hundred pages, and whose sources are given as Perottus, Sulpitius, Manutius and Nebrija, was to dominate Latin teaching in France for a long time to come,[4] replacing the *Doctrinale*[5] and exerting an influence analogous to that of Lily's grammar in England.

Similar to the position occupied by Nebrija in Spain and Despauterius in France is that of Philip Melanchthon (1497–1560)[6] among German Latinists. As a scholar he ranks with Erasmus, having by the time he was seventeen received a thorough Humanist training not only in Greek, Latin, Hebrew and Biblical exegesis, but also in history, law, medicine, logic and mathematics. He was certainly one of the most learned scholars of his day, helped in establishing Humanism at the Universities of Heidelberg and Tübingen, and became in 1518 Professor of Greek at the University of Wittenberg, where he turned to theology and became an associate of Luther. Generally known as a theologian and a Reformer, he probably had an even greater influence on education though that influence was confined to Germany.[7] He became Protestant Germany's leading authority on schools and universities, his endeavours earning him the title *Praeceptor Germaniae*. His educational schemes were at once

---

[1] v. C. Thurot, *Extraits*, p. 494.

[2] Here consulted in a Paris (2nd) edition of 1527.

[3] Dated 1537 on title-page. At the end of the volume the date of printing is given as 1538. Despauterius' various works had already been printed in France by Josse Bade since 1512.

[4] Until the eighteenth century, according to G. Sahlin, *César Chesneau du Marsais et son rôle dans l'évolution de la grammaire générale*, Paris [1928].

[5] Described as 'barbarum, insufficiens et falsum'. R. R. Bolgar, *The Classical Heritage*, p. 341, notes that the use of Despauterius' grammar in place of the *Doctrinale* 'could not under any circumstances have occurred before 1512'.

[6] *Melanchthon* is a Greek rendering of the name *Schwarzerd*.

[7] v. F. P. Graves, *A History of Education*, pp. 155–7.

Humanist, Germanic and Protestant, and he has been called 'the most complete type of the reconciliation of humanism with Protestant and Germanic consciousness'.[1] With Erasmus he was the leading exponent of the *pietas literata*, the Humanist educational movement, though it has been held that he narrowed the field of classical knowledge that Erasmus had prescribed.[2] In the best Humanist tradition he lectured on Vergil, Terence and the rhetorical works of Cicero, and advocated a thorough training in grammar and style.[3] His *Grammatica Latina*, of which the *Orthographia* and *Etymologia* appeared in 1525 and the *Syntaxis* and *Prosodia* a year later, became the most widely diffused grammatical work in Protestant Germany. It was frequently reprinted until the middle of the seventeenth century and continued to appear well into the eighteenth. Author of a Greek grammar, Melanchthon consulted a whole series of Greek sources, including Apollonius Dyscolus and Gaza. He was also familiar with Linacre's *De structura*, as is shown by the approving foreword to the Leyden edition of 1541. The editions of Melanchthon's work used here are the *Grammatica Latina* (i.e. the *Etymologia*) in Robert Estienne's edition of 1527,[4] the *Syntaxis* in his edition of 1528,[5] and a 1550 edition from the same press combining both *Etymologia* and *Syntaxis*.[6]

In England, Melanchthon's counterpart as a Humanist with a European reputation is Thomas Linacre (*c.* 1460–1524) whom F. Caspari[7] regards as the connecting link between the first and second periods of English Humanism. Before him there were no real philological works by Englishmen, the treatises of Holt, Stanbridge and Whittinton being more concerned with normative rules than with the philological approach. He accompanied his uncle and teacher William of Selling on an embassy to the Pope in 1485–6, was introduced to Politian in Florence, and followed the Greek instruction given by Chalcondyles to the sons of Lorenzo de' Medici. A year later he went to Rome with Grocyn and Latimer, and moved on to Venice. In Florence he was at the very centre of Italian Humanism

---

[1] W. H. Woodward, *Studies in Education during the Age of the Renaissance 1400–1600* (*Contributions to the History of Education II*), Cambridge University Press, 1906, p. 214.

[2] v. R. R. Bolgar, *The Classical Heritage*, p. 349.

[3] v. J. E. Sandys, *A History of Classical Scholarship*, vol. II, Cambridge University Press, 1908, p. 265.   [4] *Grammatica Latina Philippi Melanchthonis*, Paris, 1527.

[5] *Syntaxis Philippi Melanchthonis*, Paris, 1528.

[6] *Grammatica Phil. Melanchthonis Latina*, Paris, 1550.

[7] *Humanism and the Social Order*, p. 23.

and Neo-Platonism, and in Venice equally, as an honorary member of Aldus Manutius' Academy, he must have been in touch with some of the leading minds of the day. He was probably the guest of Manutius at the time the latter was occupied in printing Theodore Gaza's famous Greek grammar, and thus may be assumed to have had first-hand knowledge both of that work and of the early Italian Humanists' endeavours. Manutius brought out Linacre's translation of Proclus' *Sphere*, and there is ground for supposing that the English scholar helped to produce the Aldine edition of Aristotle (1495–8).[1] He translated into Latin parts of Aristotle and Galen, and in the 1490s took a degree in medicine at the University of Padua. He was Thomas More's *studiorum praeceptor* in 1504, became tutor to Prince Arthur and Princess Mary, and in 1509 was appointed physician to Henry VIII. While lecturing on medicine at Oxford he also taught Greek and Latin, assisted Grocyn with the education of More, Erasmus and Colet, and published three Latin grammars – two short works for teaching purposes and an exhaustive treatment containing the main body of his doctrine. The first of these, the *Progymnasmata grammatices vulgaria* of *c.* 1512, was written at Colet's suggestion for St Paul's School but proved unsuitable. Linacre reissued it however, virtually unchanged, as *Rudimenta grammatices* (dated *c.* 1522 in the introduction to Thomas Hayne's *Grammatices Latinae compendium* of 1640), intended for the instruction of Princess Mary. Both these grammars were written in English, with French translations provided for parts of the *Rudimenta*, but a Latin version, which I have used here, was produced by the Scot George Buchanan.[2] Linacre's main grammatical treatise, the *De structura* published posthumously in 1524,[3] quickly became a leading authority, being prescribed along with Priscian in both English and Continental universities.[4] It consists of six books, no less than five of which deal with syntax.[5] With Grocyn and Colet, Linacre was one

---

[1] For details, v. P. S. Allen, 'Linacre and Latimer in Italy', *The English Historical Review*, LXXI (1903), p. 515. v. also J. E. Sandys, *History of Classical Scholarship*, II, p. 226.

[2] *Rudimenta grammatices Thomae Linacri ex Anglico sermone in Latinum versa, interprete Georgio Buchanano Scoto*, Paris, 1533.

[3] *Thomae Linacri Britanni de emendata structura Latini sermonis libri sex*, London, 1524.

[4] O. Funke, 'Die Frühzeit der englischen Grammatik', *Schriften der literarischen Gesellschaft Bern*, IV (1941), p. 45, lists no less than nine continental reprints between 1527 and 1557. Melanchthon produced a corrected edition (Paris, 1533).

[5] Books I *De octo partibus* (fols. 1–34); II *De partium enallage* (35–48); III *De constructione nominis et pronominis* (49–77); IV *De constructione verbi et participii* (77–113); V *De non declinatarum constructione* (i–xxii); VI *De constructionis figuris* (xxii–lxxviii).

of the founders of Greek studies in England. A man of immense erudition, he is obviously well read in the Ancient grammarians. He frequently cites Donatus and Priscian, together with Servius and Diomedes, and refers to the Stoics and Apollonius. He is well versed in Gaza, and knows the works of his predecessors Perottus, Sulpitius and Manutius. Valla in particular he cites at length. Among Latin grammarians working in England it is Linacre who, together with Lily, has the greatest influence on the growth of English vernacular grammar.

Though Linacre's *De structura* was without doubt the most erudite Latin grammatical work of its date in England, it was much too large and unsuited to didactic purposes ever to pass into general use. The chief Latin grammars which appeared in print in England before 1500 have been listed by F. Watson.[1] The list includes Alexander of Villedieu's *Doctrinale*, John Anwykyll's *Compendium totius grammaticae* (Oxford, 1483), Donatus' *De octo partibus orationis*, Wynkyn de Worde's *Introductorium linguae Latinae* (1495 and 1499), Perottus in the Louvain edition of 1486, and Sulpitius. Of T. Rood's and R. Pynson's Latin grammars (1481 and 1496) only two leaves of each work are extant. The school which showed the greatest interest in furthering grammatical studies was Magdalen College School, Oxford, where Anwykyll was Informator or Schoolmaster *c.* 1481–7. He was succeeded in 1488 by John Stanbridge, who became famous for his methods of grammar teaching and published grammatical works – including the *Vulgaria* (1508), a Latin and English vocabulary – of pedagogical interest. His pupil Robert Whittinton also published various school grammars, of no interest for grammatical theory. Encouraged at Magdalen College School, Humanist studies received a further impetus from Colet's foundation of St Paul's which owed much to Erasmus. John Colet (*c.* 1467–1519), a close friend of Erasmus, studied at Oxford under Grocyn and Linacre. He was in Italy from *c.* 1493 to 1496, being especially attracted by Neo-Platonism and the attempt to reconcile classical learning with Christian doctrine. His chief interest remained theology, and he became Dean of St Paul's in 1505, appointing William Lily, a pupil of Stanbridge, first high master of his new school, with John Ritwyse as 'surmaister' or usher.

---

[1] *The English Grammar Schools to 1660: Their Curriculum and Practice*, Cambridge University Press, 1908, pp. 232–3.

Linacre's *Progymnasmata grammatices vulgaria* of *c.* 1512 intended for use in this school had, as noted above, been rejected by Colet. The standard school grammar of Tudor England was not to be Linacre's but that of Lily, which it would be no exaggeration to describe as *the* school grammar, for it reigned supreme from about 1515 to 1758, at which date it was transmuted into the *Eton Latin Grammar*, its influence continuing well into the nineteenth century and even beyond. Lily had been in Rome at the same time as Colet and Linacre as a pupil of Sulpitius,[1] and on his return to England he wrote a number of separate texts which were combined posthumously and published with added material as 'Lily's Grammar'. The first published work, the *Absolutissimus de octo orationis partium constructione libellus*, was written at the request of Colet. It was amended by Erasmus, which led to its being popularly ascribed to him, and consisted of a short syntax in Latin. Perhaps because of the ascription to Erasmus[2] it was published all over Europe, the first edition appearing in 1513. Between then and 1595 it underwent almost two hundred editions, though only four of them were in England.[3] Prior to this in date of composition is the *Rudimenta grammatices*, which originally appeared in 1509–10,[4] though the earliest extant edition dates only from 1527. It consists of a very short syntax in English, usually published together with an accidence (Colet's *Aeditio*) also written in English. This is the work adopted by Wolsey for his school at Ipswich and published in 1529, with other material possibly by Wolsey himself, as *Rudimenta grammatices*. It is described in the title as being intended not merely for Wolsey's school, but for those of the whole of England.

In the 1540s a new edition appeared, based on Colet's *Aeditio* in English and Lily's syntax in Latin, with a royal injunction commanding exclusive use of Lily's grammar in the schools. It is really two separate grammars, one in Latin and one in English. V. J. Flynn has found records of about one hundred different editions, and notes that in 1587 the Stationers' Company was reckoning with an annual printing of ten thousand copies.[5] From its first appearance onward this work was the official Latin grammar of England, the use of all

---

[1] v. V. J. Flynn's introduction to his facsimile ed., *A Shorte Introduction of Grammar by William Lily*, New York, 1945, p. iii.
[2] O. Funke, 'Frühzeit', p. 50, quotes Erasmus as recognizing Lily's authorship.
[3] v. V. J. Flynn, *Shorte Introduction*, p. vi.
[4] For the establishment of this date v. O. Funke, 'Frühzeit', p. 49.
[5] *Shorte Introduction*, p. x, note 4.

others in the schools being at least in theory illegal. The royal injunction was repeated by later sovereigns, and the publishing of the grammar in England became a monopoly of the King's Printer. In the foreword to the 1549 edition[1] Edward VI enjoined the use of 'one kynd of grammar', the 'tendernes of youth' being unable to 'suffer the endless diversitee of sundry schoolemaisters'. In this way, a powerful impetus to uniformity in grammar was introduced. Since it is prescribed by the Canons Ecclesiastical of 1604, Lily's grammar is presumably still technically the 'authorized version' for England. The foreword to the 1557 edition, *A Short Introduction of Grammar Generallie to be Used*, extols the virtues of 'one Grammar'. There is only 'one bestnes', and Lily's grammar is manifestly thought to represent it. The first fifty pages of this edition consist of an introduction to Latin grammar by Colet, written in English. The remaining one hundred and twenty-five pages, written in Latin by Lily, constitute the main grammar. In 1566 Lily's grammar underwent a *quasi*-final revision, and after the definitive edition of 1574 it suffered no further changes until its appearance as the *Eton Latin Grammar* in 1758. It is the 1566 edition that is reproduced by V. J. Flynn, it being of particular interest historically as that used by Shakespeare, Ben Jonson, Milton, Dryden and other literary figures. S. Blach's reprint of 1908–9[2] reproduces both that edition and the *editio princeps* of 1527. In the present study, Reginald Wolf's London edition of 1557 is used in preference to the same printer's 1549 edition, of which the available copy proved to be imperfect. The two editions are however identical, apart from the inclusion in that of 1549 of a foreword by Edward VI. Where the 1527 and 1566 editions consulted by Flynn and Blach vary substantially from that of 1557, this is noted. Following Funke's precedent,[3] the 1527 edition will be referred to here as *L*, that of 1566 as *L'*. They are both consulted in Blach's reprint, which uses for *L* the Peterborough Cathedral copy, printed (though Blach indicates 'kein Druckort') in Antwerp

[1] Presumably the first, since there is no real evidence for the 1540 edition posited by Flynn. E. J. Dobson, *English Pronunciation 1500–1700*, amends his second edition (Oxford, 1968), following R. C. Alston's *Bibliography of the English Language*, and gives Lily's 1549 edition as the first one.
[2] 'Shakespeares Lateingrammatik. Lilys Grammatica nach der ältesten bekannten Ausgabe von 1527 und der für Shakespeare in Betracht kommenden Ausgabe von 1566 (London, R. Wolfius)', *Jahrbuch der deutschen Shakespeare-Gesellschaft*, 44 (1908), pp. 65–117; 45 (1909), pp. 51–101.
[3] In his article 'Die Frühzeit der englischen Grammatik'.

by M. Hellenius.[1] All editions from 1557 on are in the style of the 1566 edition, and the differences between it and the 1557 edition are in fact slight, consisting of little more than the addition to Colet's *Aeditio* of a section on letters and syllables.

In a 'lytell proheme' prefacing his section of *L*, Colet disclaims any originality. His *Aeditio*, intended for the 'new schole of Poules', is purposely concise in consideration for the 'tendernes and small capacyte of lytel myndes'.[2] His section of the grammar is meant as a bare outline for beginners, so his definitions should not perhaps be taken as closely reflecting his grammatical theory. They are illuminating however as illustrating what he felt bound to retain as essential, and what he thought could safely be jettisoned in the interests of clarity and economy. Both Colet's and Lily's sections are indeed meant to form a practical teaching grammar, not a disquisition on grammatical theory. On the whole Lily follows Donatus closely, with an admixture of Priscian. Linacre's influence is also perceptible, and he is mentioned by Lily in flattering terms. Lily's most interesting contribution to grammatical theory lies in his system of *signs*, with its structural implications. But the time was not ripe for the development of such a system, and the widespread use of his grammar ensured in fact the continuation of the more semantic elements in his approach to the end of the century and beyond. By about 1540 the Humanist impetus to the production of normative grammars based on the practice of the Ancients had in any case more or less spent itself. The official status accorded to one such grammar is an indication that a plateau had been reached, that contemporary theories were regarded as definitive. The genesis of Lily's grammar has been dealt with at some length both because of its central importance to grammatical studies in England, and because its continuous presence for two centuries and more ensured that certain elements in its presentation became accepted doctrine for minor grammarians. No such grammarian with an eye for his career could afford to publish a grammar, until at any rate the end of the sixteenth

[1] *Ioannis Coleti . . . aeditio, una cum quibusdam G. Lilij Grammatices rudimentis.* For the 1566 ed. Blach uses the Bodleian copy, which was not available at the time the notes for this study were compiled. Blach's edition is however an exact replica, apart from the missing folios 13–14 of the English section, which he supplies from the Bodleian copy of the 1572 edition. The edition is dated 1566 at the end of the volume, but Lily's section, which stands first, is dated 1567.

[2] S. Blach, 'Shakespeares Lateingrammatik', *Jahrbuch der deutschen Shakespeare-Gesellschaft*, vol. 44, p. 73.

century, without paying ritual tribute in his foreword to the *Regia grammatica*, together with a declaration of his intention to stay fairly close to it. The inhibiting effect of the royal injunction must have been considerable.

As an example of the lip-service paid in England to Lily one may cite John Stockwood's *Rules of Construction* (1590),[1] which are in the growing pedagogical tradition that a grounding in vernacular grammar is 'as it were the foundation of all the rest of Grammar building, the which being laid, they shall be the better able to proceed to the understanding of Latin Authors'.[2] The work is simply an annotated version of the rules of concord in Colet's section of Lily's grammar – what came to be known as the *English Rules* – and is in effect a Latin grammar written in English. Stockwood's *Disputatiunculae*[3] is also intended as an adjunct to Lily, as the reference to the *Regia grammatica* on the title-page makes clear, and consists largely of a collection of quibbles on the aptness (which is of course confirmed) of Lily's definitions of the parts of speech. Stockwood's practice does not bear out his statement that 'philosophi rerum naturas, Grammatici linguam potius [spectant]'.[4] His chief aim is to give flattering assent to the doctrines in the *Regia grammatica*. If the nouns *Styx* and *Lethe*, being feminine, appear to contradict Lily's statement that all names of rivers are masculine, then they cannot be names of rivers but must refer to stagnant waters. The only activity left to minor English grammarians of the period is approving annotation of the received text.

One could multiply references to lesser grammarians on both sides of the Channel. Suffice it to mention four authors whose works taken together cover the whole spread of the sixteenth century, and thus mirror faithfully the tendencies operating in conservative grammatical tradition throughout the period. The *Grammaticae institutiones* (1510) of Johannes Brassicanus of Tübingen are, as might be expected at this date, closely modelled on Donatus and his commentator Servius with occasional borrowings from Priscian, and in fashionable reaction against the medieval tradition still very much in evidence in Germany. His grammar opens with the customary

---

[1] *A Plaine and Easie Laying Open of the Meaning and Understanding of the Rules of Construction in the English Accidence*, London, 1590.
[2] *Ibid.* foreword.
[3] *Disputatiuncularum grammaticalium libellus*, London, 1598 (2nd ed.).
[4] *Ibid.* fol. 48ᵛ.

diatribes against medievalists who claim that no one can be a grammarian without a knowledge of metaphysics.[1] Grammars constructed 'ex modis significandi & metaphysica' are dismissed as the 'clacking of old women,[2] the *modi significandi* in particular being condemned as a 'barbarorum inventum'. Both in his insistence on a return to previously neglected Roman tradition, and in his retention none the less of certain aspects of medieval theory, he is a representative early Humanist grammarian.

The fashion for publishing trilingual or quadrilingual grammars is illustrated by Jean Drosay's *Grammatica quadrilinguis* (1544),[3] which treats the three classical languages and French. A simple teaching grammar, it gives no definitions of the word-classes, but otherwise follows Roman tradition closely, with a great deal of superfluous semasiological classification hardly appropriate to language teaching. The continued ascendancy of the classical languages over the vernaculars, and the contemporary attempt to raise the status of the latter, is illustrated by Drosay's insistence that French resembles Hebrew in its 'manières de signifier'.

The continental grammarians were of course not subject to the rule of Lily, and were free to break new ground. The title of Corradus' *De lingua Latina* (1575)[4] is inspired by the Roman linguist Varro's work of the same name, and the author is unusual in his constant appeal to Varro as his final authority, a fact which may owe something to the grammar's Italian provenance. The conservative nature of his Humanism is illustrated by his claim to follow the *latinitas* of Varro's day and the 'gravissima veterum auctoritas'. His compatriot Emmanuel Alvarus, Jesuit author of a Latin grammar late in the century,[5] is a rare example of a grammarian who names his sources, which are given as Varro, Quintilian's *De institutione oratoria*, Probus, Diomedes, Donatus and Priscian, the latter being singled out for special praise. There are obvious traces in this grammar also of Varro's scheme of word-class definition in terms of the presence or absence of case or tense. The major criteria are however semantic rather than formal ones, and in this Alvarus is typical of the general

[1] 'Sine metaphysices cognitione.'
[2] 'Mera deliramenta & aniles quaculationes.'
[3] *Grammaticae quadrilinguis partitiones*, Paris, 1544.
[4] *De lingua Latina*, Bologna, 1575. (The title-page bears reference to a 'prior editio' whose printing was unsatisfactory.)
[5] *Emmanuelis Alvari e Societate Iesu, De institutione grammatica*, 2nd ed., Milan, 1595.

trend. He is included here partly because he is yet another illustration of the late sixteenth- and early seventeenth-century predilection for Varro, and partly because, as a Jesuit with a Scholastic training, he shows certain medieval and Aristotelian features. But these minor grammarians within the established Roman tradition must speak in the name of many. The great innovators of the sixteenth century – Scaliger, Ramus, Sanctius – will form the subject of the next chapter.

HUMANIST GRAMMATICAL THEORY

In general the early Humanist grammarians follow Donatus and Priscian closely, and it would serve no useful purpose to repeat here, except when necessary explanations are called for, notions of Roman grammar already treated in R. H. Robins' *Ancient and Medieval Grammatical Theory in Europe*[1] and his *Short History of Linguistics*.[2] Those who wish to read the Roman grammarians in the original texts are referred to H. Keil's monumental *Grammatici Latini*.[3] Nor do I propose, other than in dealing with certain specific points as they arise, to give a résumé of medieval grammatical theory. The reader will find all the information he needs in Robins' two works and in G. L. Bursill-Hall's *Speculative Grammars of the Middle Ages*[4] and his edition of Thomas of Erfurt's *Grammatica speculativa*.[5] Attention will however be drawn to noteworthy departures from Roman tradition, more especially where they are of importance for later developments in grammatical theory, and to features which show a continuance of medieval traditions.[6] Pre-1500 Humanist grammar contains little of note. The presentation and interpretation of Roman practice was in itself a sufficiently arduous task, hardly leaving scope for innovation. In any case, the whole bias of the age is towards the imitation and memorizing of classical models deemed perfect precisely because they are classical. Where the earlier Humanist authors are occasionally of interest is in their anticipation of a trend which gathers force as the years go by, and in their

[1] London, 1951. [2] London, 1967.
[3] Leipzig, 1857–74. Reprinted 1961.
[4] The Hague and Paris, 1971. [5] London, 1972.
[6] Donatus' and Priscian's definitions of the word-classes, together with some of the more important medieval definitions, have been brought together in an appendix at the end of this volume. The reader may also consult G. L. Bursill-Hall's 'Medieval Grammatical Theories', *The Canadian Journal of Linguistics*, 9:1 (1963), pp. 40–54.

continued use of certain medieval Scholastic features. Ostensibly returning to Ancient models and abjuring medieval practice, they none the less sometimes find themselves accommodating Ancient doctrine to Scholastic theory. In general however both they and the grammarians of the early decades of the sixteenth century stay close to Ancient precedent. What innovations there are consist of an emphasis on neglected Varronian or Greek sources, rather than the heralding of a new approach.

The problems confronting these authors are those their Roman predecessors had to face: how to reconcile in a common grammatical scheme the morphological and structural facts of the Latin language and the semantically based criteria used to describe them. From their models they inherited a mixed approach in which both formal and semasiological criteria were employed, in striking contrast to the methods of present-day descriptive linguists, who assume that the utterances they classify are meaningful but, once this assumption has been made, base their analysis on purely formal relationships and oppositions. Here, the early Humanist grammarians go beyond Roman practice, but in the opposite direction to that followed by modern structural linguists, towards ever more semasiological definition. Particularly in the work of Nebrija, and of the later grammarian Melanchthon, is this flight from formal to semantic criteria evident. The semantic approach to grammar is not an invention of the seventeenth century, but the harvest from seeds set at the very outset of the New Learning.

The approach is however highly normative. In accordance with the newly refound emphasis on rhetoric and on oratorical rather than dialectical training, grammar is commonly defined as the art of writing and speaking correctly.[1] The importance of legal studies in Italy had quite early inclined Humanist grammatical treatises to practical, rhetorical ends, in sharp contrast to the tradition of logical speculation at the University of Paris. It was customary for an *ars dictaminis* or *ars dictandi* to be appended to grammatical works,[2] and the whole grammatical output of the Italian Renaissance is coloured by rhetorical preoccupations and questions of usage. Perottus defines grammar not only as an *ars recte loquendi, recteque scribendi*, but also, following what had always been an aim of the Ancients, as an

---

[1] Both Perottus and Lily e.g. describe it as a 'recte scribendi atque loquendi ars'.
[2] Perottus adds a treatise *de modo epistolandi*.

art which is to be learnt in the pages of poets and prose writers.[1] He
thus returns at least in part to that view of grammar as the servant of
literary studies held by the medieval school of Orleans before its
eclipse by the purely logical studies of Paris. Sulpitius' *Grammatica*
has a similarly normative definition of grammar as a *rectae loquelae,
rectae scripturae scientia,*[2] with the added literary aim of *verba inter-
pretandi,*[3] and has Perottus' division of grammar into the four sections
littera, syllaba, dictio and *oratio.* By the time of Aldus Manutius the
new approach is well established. Grammar is determined not by the
application of medieval categories of logic, but 'by usage, reason and
authority'. It falls into the Ancients' two divisions of *methodice* and
historice, the first being *finitiva* or strictly normative and dealing with
the rules of correct speech, the latter *enarrativa* and concerning itself
with the explanation of authors.[4] A similar division of grammar is
Brassicanus' *methodica* and *exegetice.* Of particular interest in view of
the seventeenth-century reversal of this trend is his statement that
the criteria of what constitutes good Latin must be based not on
ratio but on *exempla,* a statement which clearly establishes the primacy of usage over reason.

The four sections of grammar established by Perottus and Sulpitius are mandatory by the early part of the sixteenth century. The
first two parts of grammar set up by the Humanists, *littera* and
syllaba, will not concern us here, since only in the very widest sense
of the term can they be considered relevant to grammatical studies.
One may however note in passing that Roman and Humanist
grammarians regarded the written letter, rather than the sound, as
the minimal unit of linguistic construction. Among the Humanists,
only Despautarius makes a groping attempt at some kind of phonetic
theory, distinguishing the unit of sound as an *elementum* – 'Litera
scribitur: elementum profertur.'[5] It is true that he ties this in with
the physics of his day, with its elements earth, air, fire and water, but
his approach none the less constitutes an early step forward. If in the
sixteenth century there is no possibility of a science of phonetics, let
alone anything approaching phonemic theory, there is equally

---

[1] An *ars scriptorum et poetarum lectionibus observata.*
[2] *Sulpitii Verulani Grammatica,* Nuremberg, 1482, p. [1].
[3] Thus in the 1490 (Rome) edition, *De arte grammatica opusculum compendiosum.*
[4] *Rudimenta,* pp. [1–2].
[5] *Rudimenta Despauterii secundo aedita in treis partes divisa,* Paris, 1527, f. 15ᵛ. As Despauterius remarks, this distinction is rarely observed.

nothing resembling the doctrine of the morpheme. Renaissance grammar is word-based, but here again it is Despauterius who furnishes what might well, if taken up by others, have resulted in an embryonic morphemic theory. Humanist grammarians based an art of prosody on the study of syllables, without however treating them as potential meaning-bearing entities. In Despauterius' treatment of the *syllabicae adiectiones* (the inseparable pronominal particles *-met*, *-te*, etc.) as syllables whose meaning is made known only in composition,[1] we may however perhaps see the beginnings of a distinction between bound and free morphemes.

The parts of grammar *dictio* and *oratio* deal respectively with the word-classes and their paradigms, and – often rather summarily – with sentence-structure. The early Humanist grammarians' approach to the *oratio* or sentence, repeatedly expressed in terms of Priscian's criterion of the expression of 'perfect sense' which ultimately goes back to Dionysius Thrax,[2] is basically semantic. There is of course no question of any definition in terms remotely resembling those of present-day structural linguistics, which treats the sentence simply as a structure which does not form part of another linguistic structure.[3] The Greco-Roman requirement that the *oratio* express a 'complete thought'[4] was in vogue for centuries, existing long before the general extension of semasiological definition and the identification of the grammatical sentence with the logical proposition in the seventeenth century. In defining the sentence in these terms, Brassicanus and Corradus are representative of many.

As with the sentence, so with the word, the definitions of these early Humanist grammarians set the tone of grammatical theory for a very long time to come. The definition of the word presents difficulties in any system of linguistic analysis, morphemes being in many respects easier to establish. Representative of modern approaches is R. H. Robins' treatment of sentences as free linguistic forms (i.e. not dependent on or forming part of other linguistic structures), and of

---

[1] *Ibid.* f. 16ᵛ.

[2] v. H. Steinthal, *Geschichte der Sprachwissenschaft bei den Griechern und Römern*, 2nd ed., Berlin, 1891, ii, 209.

[3] Modern linguists regard the sentence as a potentially complete utterance, without specifying that it is the *sense* that is complete. R. H. Robins, *General Linguistics: An Introductory Survey*, London, 1964, p. 191, simply defines it as 'the upper limit of structural statement at the grammatical level'. He adds that it is 'meaningful within the situation in which it is uttered', but its linguistic status as a sentence is established without reference to its meaning.

[4] Priscian adds a syntactic requirement, that it be an 'ordinatio dictionum congrua'.

words as minimal sentences or, in Bloomfield's classic definition, minimum free forms.[1] If in modern grammatical analysis words are further assigned to word-classes, it is 'on the formal basis of *syntactic behaviour*, supplemented and reinforced by differences of *morphological paradigms*, so that every word in a language is a member of a word class'.[2] Thus, the definition that is appropriate to the word *per se* is not appropriate to that same word functioning grammatically as a member of its class or – to use the traditional designation – as a part of speech. Medieval grammarians were well aware of this, and made a careful distinction between the *vox* or unit of expression, the *dictio* or meaning-bearing lexical element (i.e. the word *per se*), and the *pars orationis* or word functioning grammatically as a part of speech.

The term *dictio* in Priscian's system would seem however to occupy to at least some extent the position occupied by the term *pars orationis* in medieval grammar. He calls *vox inarticulata* the element of expression considered separately from its meaning, and *vox articulata* the same form plus 'some sense in the speaker's mind'.[3] This distinction between presumably formal *voces* and meaning-bearing ones has obvious relevance in twentieth-century linguistics to F. de Saussure's view of the word as consisting of a formal *significant* and a semantic *significate*.[4] In Priscian's system, however, it is only in construction with other *voces* in an utterance that the *vox articulata* achieves the status of a *dictio*, which attains its full meaning only by virtue of its relationship to other *dictiones* in a linguistic structure. In what seems at first sight a very modern definition, Priscian further defines the *dictio* as, following Dionysius Thrax, a minimal unit of structure, a *pars minima orationis constructae*. But he does not see it in modern linguistic terms as simply a formal unit of syntactic structure, but as part of a meaningful whole, receiving its grammatical status by virtue of its relation to the 'complete sense' of the whole sentence. It is a minimal unit with respect to this larger semantic unit, *quantum ad totius sensus intellectum*.[5] The minimal meaning-bearing unit of modern linguistics is however not the word, but the morpheme. Roman grammar, having no morphemic theory, does not

---

[1] *General Linguistics*, p. 194.   [2] *Ibid.* p. 227.

[3] H. Keil, *Grammatici Latini*, II, 5: 'cum aliquo sensu mentis eius, qui loquitur'.

[4] *Cours de linguistique générale*, 5th ed., Paris, 1955, pp. 97–100, 158–9. De Saussure uses the terms *signifiant* and *signifié*.

[5] Keil, *Grammatici Latini*, II, 53.

recognize any meaningful element below the level of the word. Apart from monosyllabic words, syllables can have no meaning. To signal meaning – *aliquid significare* – is the property of the *dictio* alone.

Priscian's distinction between meaningful and non-meaningful *voces* is in line with that made between *vox* and *dictio* by medieval grammarians, who use him as a source. It is not the unit of expression *vox* that interests the *Grammatica speculativa,* but the *vox significativa* or *dictio*[1] considered as a linguistic sign – 'the *vox* as such is not the province of the grammarian; it interests him only in so far as it is a sign, for grammar is concerned with the signs of things'.[2] This again approaches modern doctrines of the linguistic sign such as that of de Saussure. The *vox significativa* or *dictio* can however play a role in the sentence as a *pars orationis* only by virtue of an added *modus significandi activus*[3] which confers on it a grammatical meaning. For medieval grammarians *vox, dictio* and *pars orationis* are thus seen not to be synonymous terms. Typical Humanist grammatical practice blurs these medieval distinctions *vox + significatio = dictio*: *dictio + consignificatio* (grammatical function) = *pars orationis*. It is true that Manutius defines the word (*dictio*) in the Roman grammarian Diomedes' terms as a *vox articulata cum aliqua significatione,*[4] reflecting precisely the medieval and Saussurean view of words as linguistic signs with both formal and semantic facets. But though repeating the common Roman definition of the *littera* (present-day linguists, dealing with the spoken sound rather than the written letter, would say the *phoneme*) as a *pars minima vocis*, a minimal unit of structure on the phonetic level of discourse, he does not take the logical step of defining the *dictio* in Priscian's terms as a *pars minima orationis constructae*, a minimal unit on the syntactic level.[5] Despauterius does in fact take this step, defining the word as a *pars minima orationis*, but he too, rather than treating it as in fact a minimal unit of syntax,

[1] Cf. Thomas of Erfurt's *Grammatica speculativa*, cap. vi: 'dicitur dictio . . . per rationem signandi, voci superadditam'. The edition used here is that of L. Vivès, Paris, 1891, reproduced in mimeographed form by M. Doyon, Quebec, 1962. This edition is simply a reprint of Wadding's version of 1639, ascribed to Duns Scotus and printed as part of the latter's complete works.

[2] *Ibid.* cap. vi: 'vox inquantum vox, non consideratur a Grammatico; sed inquantum signum, quia Grammatica est de signis rerum'.

[3] Cf. *ibid.* cap. vi: 'pars orationis . . . est per modum significandi activum, dictioni superadditum'.

[4] *Rudimenta*, p. [5].

[5] As noted above, for present-day linguists the minimal meaningful unit is the *morpheme*, at a lower level of analysis than the word.

stresses its semantic aspect as a *pars aliquid significans*. If I have treated this question at some length, it is because here, at the very outset of the period under study, the shape of future developments is determined. In defining the word-class (*pars orationis*) as simply a mental concept, Sulpitius initiates a line of thought, in fact a distortion, of primary importance for the development of grammatical theory in the sixteenth and seventeenth centuries. As already noted,[1] among twentieth-century linguists even a behaviourist and anti-mentalist such as L. Bloomfield makes a distinction between lexical and grammatical meaning.[2] But increasingly as the sixteenth century advances, grammarians ignore grammatical function and put the emphasis on lexis and nomenclature.

In classifying the parts of speech, the early Humanists similarly foreshadow later developments in grammatical theory by tending to increase the semasiological element of their Roman models at the expense of the formal one. Nowhere at this early date is the general preference for semantically based definition more marked than in the work of Nebrija, whose statement in his Castilian grammar that the diversity of the parts of speech is founded on a similar diversity in the *maneras de significar*,[3] explicitly rejects formal criteria. By *manera de significar* he would seem to mean, not the medieval *modus significandi*, but something approaching Priscian's 'informing force and meaning'[4] of each part of speech. It is interesting to note that the definitions of the word-classes in Nebrija's elementary teaching grammar, the *Prima puerorum praeexercitamenta*, are much more formally based than those in the main body of his work. He stresses however that the simplified definitions there given[5] are not strictly speaking definitions, but merely indications of the *proprietates* of the word-classes.[6]

Given the priority accorded to criteria based on meaning, it is not surprising to find these early grammarians upholding the semantic primacy of noun and verb which forms an important part of Aristotelian doctrine. Particularly interesting is Nebrija's partial definition of the noun (subject) as that without which, in accordance with the

---

[1] p. 12, note 2, above.   [2] *Language*, p. 264.
[3] E. Walberg (ed.), *Gramatica Castellana. Reproduction phototypique de l'édition princeps* (*1492*), Halle, 1909, p. [73].
[4] 'Vis et significatio uniuscuiusque partis.'
[5] E.g. the definition of the noun as 'quod declinatur per casus: et non significat cum tempore', *Introductiones* (1533), p. [34].
[6] *Introductiones* (1509), p. [38].

teaching of 'all logicians', an *oratio* remains incomplete. As early as 1481 the notion of the logical proposition, so important for seventeenth-century grammatical theory, is already being transferred from dialectics to grammar. By the end of the sixteenth century, under the influence of Scaliger and Sanctius, Aristotelian criteria are increasingly in use even by grammarians who otherwise stay within the conservative Humanist tradition. Corradus for instance regards noun and verb as the two natural word-classes supplied by 'nature herself', the verb expressing *universi sermonis vim,* and noun and verb together forming a complete *oratio* without requiring help from any other word-classes – a view he describes as Platonic.[1] All other word-classes receive the Aristotelian status of *syncategoremata,* that is to say of words that consignify with the two principal parts of speech, but cannot function apart from them.[2] Where the later sixteenth-century grammarians differ from their Humanist predecessors is in the greater attention paid to Varro's *De lingua Latina,* which represents a much earlier stratum of Roman grammar than Donatus and Priscian. Corradus for instance divides his word-classes in Varronian fashion into those with case and/or tense, and those which show neither.

It is Varro's definition of the noun as having case but not tense that may be thought to lie behind Linacre's treatment of it as a case-marked word signifying something without at the same time consignifying time.[3] The time reference used to distinguish verb from noun owes however more to Greek tradition than to Varro's formal approach,[4] and is ultimately Aristotelian. Present in neither Donatus nor Priscian, it is a traditional element in Greek grammar,[5] occurring in Theodore Gaza's important work of 1495 with which Linacre was no doubt familiar. Linacre's definition preserves the Aristotelian grammatical notion of consignification, presenting a parallel to Aristotle's definition of the verb as that which consignifies time.[6] Besides maintaining an important grammatical distinction, Linacre's

[1] *De lingua Latina,* p. 105.

[2] Corradus notes however that the pronoun can replace the noun as subject of a sentence, for then the noun 'hanc vim suam communicat etiam pronomini'.

[3] *Rudimenta,* p. 37: 'quae casibus inflecta, significat aliquid sine ulla temporis assignificantia'.

[4] Formal, that is, if Varro's criterion is morphological markers of case and tense rather than the semantic relations involved.

[5] There are traces of it in Roman grammar, as in Charisius' definition of the noun as 'cum casu sine tempore significans rem' (H. Keil, *Grammatici Latini,* IV, 152).

[6] *De interpretatione,* cap. 3: τὸ προσσημαῖνον χρόνον. For this work I have used H. P. Cooke's edition of the *Organon,* London and Cambridge (Mass.), 1938.

approach is an indication of the influence of Greek studies in England, where Greek features were often preserved long after they had disappeared elsewhere.

More revealing of the temper of the age is Despauterius' definition of the noun, in his preliminary *Minutissima*, and hence to be taken as indictating the essentials of the word-class for beginners, as signifying in Priscian's terms 'substance together with common or proper quality'.[1] The terms *substantia* and *qualitas* as used by the Ancient grammarians do not constitute an exact parallel with the logicians' use of the terms substance and accident.[2] For Priscian *qualitas* does not indicate the philosophical notion of accident, but lexical content, which is why he is able to define the pronoun as signifying substance without definite quality.[3] The fact that later grammarians misunderstood this and equated *qualitas* with accident is responsible for a whole new development in the theory of substantive and adjective in the seventeenth century, which saw *qualitas*, thus wrongly interpreted, as the distinguishing mark of the adjective alone. Priscian defines adjectives as being added to other nouns (i.e. substantives) in order to indicate their quality, but nowhere does he define the substantive as that which signifies only substance, or the adjective as that which separately signifies quality. His adjective 'makes manifest' the quality already present in the substantive.[4] The seventeenth-century grammarians were no doubt helped towards this misconception by the medieval cleavage of the word-class *nomen* into the separate sub-classes *substantivum* and *adiectivum*,[5] which paved the way for their notion of the substantive as indicating a *thing*, and the adjective as indicating a *quality* of a thing. Despauterius still connects *qualitas*[6] with the lexical difference between

---

[1] *Rudimenta*, f. 3ᵛ. In the *tertia pars* of this work, Despauterius gives Donatus' definition with its formal reference to case. The definitions in that section are curiously less semantic than those of the supposedly more elementary *Minutissima*.

[2] For a discussion of the philosophical notions of substance and accident, v. below, pp. 58–9.

[3] 'Substantiam sine aliqua certa qualitate.' Priscian's definition of the noun as signifying 'substantiam cum qualitate propria vel communi' is repeated from Apollonius.

[4] H. Keil, *Grammatici Latini*, II, 58: 'adiectiva . . . aliis appellativis, quae substantiam significant . . . adici solent ad manifestandam eorum qualitatem'. For an interesting remark on the inability of the Ancients to envisage quality as other than 'substantialized', or substance as other than qualitatively determined, v. H. Steinthal, *Geschichte*, II, 255.

[5] Priscian uses the term *nomen substantivum* solely for the word *qui*, which he regards as indicating substance without quality.

[6] Cf. Aristotle, *Categories*, cap. 8: 'By "quality" I mean that in virtue of which men are called such and such' (H. P. Cooke, *Aristotle: The Organon*, p. 63).

37

common and proper nouns. Later, in the expository *tertia pars* of his grammar, he takes up the traditional Roman definition of the noun as signifying a *corpus* or a *res*,[1] terms which he explains, following Charisius, as referring to things which respectively can and cannot be perceived by the senses,[2] i.e. as equivalent to the modern *concrete/abstract* dichotomy. A further development along these lines, important for later trends in grammatical theory, is Corradus' equating of *corpus* with *substantia* and *res* with *qualitas*. To those nouns (i.e. abstract nouns and adjectives) which signify *res* and *qualitates*,[3] he then opposes a category of *nomina substantiae* or concrete nouns which signify *corpora*. Later grammatical notions often are thus seen to have their roots in sixteenth-century reinterpretation of Roman grammar.

It is however Melanchthon who is in many respects the forerunner of seventeenth-century attitudes, more especially in his rigorous exclusion of formal elements from definitions, in a major departure from the Roman use of mixed formal and semasiological criteria. His description of the noun as 'a part of speech signifying a thing, not an action' constitutes the entire definition. Of Donatus' *Nomen est pars orationis cum casu corpus aut rem proprie communiterve significans* there remains only *Nomen significat rem*. Again, the simplistic division of phenomena into *things* and *actions*, usually thought to be a specifically seventeenth-century trait, is already represented in a grammar dating from the end of the first quarter of the preceding century. Melanchthon's definition also foreshadows the direction grammatical theory is in general to take – towards ever vaguer, more semantically based definitions, and away from strictly grammatical categories. To Aristotle's grammatical *consignification* of tense marking off verb from noun, he prefers the *signification* of action. In this he is doubtless at fault, for the noun *ambulatio* and the verb *ambulare* both signify actions, and there is nothing in his system to keep them grammatically apart. In Colet's *Aeditio*, this process is taken a step further. Though he divides the parts of speech into declinable and in-

---

[1] For Priscian, *corpus* and *res* (Thrax's σῶμα and πρᾶγμα) seem to have the meanings 'person' and 'thing'. M. H. Jellinek, *Geschichte der neuhochdeutschen Grammatik von den Anfängen bis Adelung*, Heidelberg, 1913–14, ii, 79, note 1, calls *res* a clumsy translation of πρᾶγμα.

[2] *Rudimenta*, f. 17ʳ. Cf. Keil, *Grammatici Latini*, IV, 153, where Charisius refers to *res* 'corporales, quae videri possunt', and 'incorporales . . . quae intellectu tantum modo percipiuntur'.

[3] *De lingua Latina*, p. 109.

declinable, this formal criterion no more forms part of word-class definition than it does with Melanchthon. His noun is simply 'the name of a thing that may be seen, felt, heard or understand [*sic*]'.[1] It no longer *signifies* something, a concept which implies a linguistic sign divisible into signifying and signified facets. It is an item of nomenclature, a witness to the belief that to each separate entity in the world of things there corresponds a name.[2] Here again, a typically seventeenth-century preoccupation, the urge to undertake a conceptual classification of the universe with a one-to-one correspondence between names and things, has its counterpart in sixteenth-century grammar. Lily's section of the grammar is more conservative. His definition of the noun as signifying without any *difference* of tense or person[3] is obviously inspired by Linacre. It is however significant that he removes the formal reference to case and replaces *assignificantia* by *differentia*, thus eliminating the notion of consignification. He and Colet further illustrate the decline in rigour in the use of grammatical terms.

All the early Humanist grammarians repeat the medieval innovation of dividing the noun-class into substantive and adjective. Perottus and Sulpitius introduce into their definitions the formal criteria of the possible number of 'articles' (*hic, haec, hoc*) that can precede each sub-class, and the presence or absence of variable gender terminations. These formal distinctions had been pointed out by the Ancients,[4] but not made the basis of definition. Perhaps the need to provide beginners with a ready means of distinguishing adjectives from substantives[5] led to this unusual departure from the semasiological approach, which was taken up by Humanist grammarians in general. Substantive and adjective are however defined by Nebrija not according to these formal criteria but in the philosophical terms of the signification of substance or accident.[6] This medieval definition he calls the 'true' one, dismissing the definition based on the preceding 'articles' as nothing but a means of

[1] *A Short Introduction of Grammar* (1557), p. 7.
[2] Donatus' *corpus aut res* has disappeared on the surface, but it lives on, via Despauterius, in Colet's distinction between what can be 'seen, heard and felt' and what can only be understood.
[3] *Brevissima institutio* (i.e., Lily's separately paginated section of the Colet–Lily grammar) (1557), p. 8.
[4] E.g. Charisius (Keil, *Grammatici Latini*, I, 487).
[5] The paradigms were printed with one or more of the 'articles', as appropriate, preceding the nominative form in each declension.
[6] *Introductiones* (1533), p. [80].

recognition *per quaedam signa*.[1] Of great interest as a forerunner of late seventeenth-century theory is his description of the noun as *signifying* substance or *connoting* accident,[2] which may be set beside the Port-Royal view, based on J. C. Scaliger, that the adjective signifies the accident but connotes the substance of the substantive with which it is constructed. The concept of connotation is taken from medieval logic, and sows the seeds of later grammatical theory's dichotomy opposing concrete nouns on the one hand, and adjectives and abstract nouns on the other.[3] Though well known to logic, between Nebrija and Port-Royal this concept is lost sight of in grammar.

The medieval definitions of substantive and adjective in terms of the signification of substance or accident are adopted by early Humanist grammarians in preference to Roman models,[4] either alone or in conjunction with Perottus' and Sulpitius' definitions according to preceding 'articles'. This preference, illustrated both in Despauterius and in Linacre, is usually expressed in terms of syntactic dependence or independence within the *oratio*, that is to say, though the grammarians do not use the expressions, in terms of the medieval *modus per se subsistentis* and *modus adiacentis alteri*.[5] Melanchthon continues the use of Aristotelian notions of substance and accident by treating the substantive as 'that which subsists by itself', and the adjective as 'that which inheres in a subject',[6] where *subiectum* is a logical term, not a grammatical one. It is no doubt logical and philosophical considerations that lie behind this augmentation of the simple definition (the only one there given) of his 1527 edition, couched in terms that would not be repugnant to present-day structural linguists. In this definition, which arises of course from the medieval one, the adjective is defined as that to which the words *man, woman* and *thing* can be added, the substantive as that to which

---

[1] *Introductiones* (1509), p. [40]. Nebrija's use of the terminology of *signs* long before Lily popularized it is noteworthy.

[2] *Ibid.* p. [11]: 'significans substantiam seu accidens connotans'.

[3] Cf. C. Prantl, *Geschichte der Logik im Abendlande*, vol. III, Leipzig, 1867, p. 386, for a discussion of William of Ockham's *termini connotativi* which require an *expositio* (clarification) of the type *white = that which has whiteness*, in which a concrete term is explained by means of the corresponding abstract term.

[4] It should however be noted that the medieval approach is implicit in Priscian's treatment of nouns adjective as 'quae sumuntur ex accidentibus substantiae nominum' (Keil, *Grammatici Latini*, II, 60).

[5] Cf. Linacre's definition of the adjective in the *De structura* (i, 2^v) as 'quod sine altera, cui adhaereat, consistere in oratione non potest'.

[6] *Grammatica* (1550 ed.), p. 17. Cf. *Grammatica speculativa*, cap. X.

they cannot so be added. It becomes widespread in the elementary grammars of the period, and is obviously intended as a teaching aid for beginners rather than a contribution to grammatical theory. The medieval definition in terms of syntactic dependence or independence which it implies survives long in sixteenth-century grammar, sometimes, as in Colet, shorn of its semantic implications ('that standeth by him selfe' and 'that requireth to be joyned with an other word'),[1] sometimes, as in Colet and Alvarus, accompanied by a formal requirement as to endings or preceding 'articles'.[2] In the form in which it is given by Colet, it is based simply on a syntactic distinction such as those employed by modern structural linguists, who assign the adjective to its word-class purely on the basis of the position it occupies in the utterance.[3]

In setting out the various divisions of the noun-class, the grammarians reflect the Roman confusion of semantic and formal criteria. There are however attempts to bring order out of the chaos, as in Linacre's division of nouns into those determined formally (*a vocibus*), i.e. derived forms, comparatives and superlatives, and those classified semantically according to the categories of reality (*a rebus sumpta*), e.g. common and proper nouns. In his attempt to separate formal and semasiological criteria in this way, he would appear to be indebted to Theodore Gaza.[4] His use of formal distinctions does not however deter him from additionally defining comparison in purely semantic terms as signifying 'the excess of some quality',[5] a definition which becomes the standard one for Humanist grammar.[6] It is often accompanied by the Roman explanation of the comparative as analysable into *magis* plus the positive form, an explanation which is of interest as offering a parallel to N. A. Chomsky's theory of 'surface' linguistic structures which represent as it were an abbreviation of 'deep' structures. On this view, Roman and Humanist grammar's *brevior = magis brevis* is a transformational procedure, and

---

[1] *A Short Introduction* (1557 ed.), p. 7. Lily's definition in the *Brevissima institutio* is similarly based on the medieval one.

[2] Both criteria of definition being used by e.g. Colet, O. Funke ('Frühzeit', p. 73) is not entirely right in opposing formally defining Italians to semasiologically defining Englishmen.

[3] E.g. C. C. Fries, *The Structure of English*, New York, 1952, p. 82.

[4] v. O. Funke, 'Frühzeit', p. 74.

[5] *Rudimenta*, p. 38. Cf. Roman grammar's limitation of comparison to those nouns adjective 'quorum significatio augeri, minuive potest'.

[6] As e.g. in Despauterius' *Rudimenta*, f. 4ʳ. The superlative is defined in similar terms.

shows that from a very early date linguists were aware that a logical restatement of items of discourse was possible. Similar to Linacre's distinction is that made by Corradus between formal criteria *in vocibus* and semasiological ones *in significationibus*,[1] though he leaves no doubt of his preference for the latter. Drosay also makes an effort to keep apart formal and semantic considerations by pointing out in each word-class those features which are *secundum vocem*, and those which are *secundum rem*, but he is unusual in the primacy he gives to form. His observation that gender would be superfluous if adjectives, with their marks of syntactic congruence with substantives, did not exist,[2] antedates Sanctius' announcement of this fact by more than forty years, and Ramus' formally based approach by fifteen. Apart from scattered insights such as these, the bias of grammar is however increasingly semasiological. Where formal terminations are mentioned, they are not seen as central to the discussion. Their recognition as meaning-bearing signs is inhibited, as in Roman grammar, by the lack of a theory of the morpheme. The only Humanist grammarian who seems to be on the way to such a theory is, as already noted, Despauterius.[3] In his discussion of *figura* or the formation of compound words, his insistence that each element must be *intelligibilis* and *prioris sensus capax*[4] again seems to constitute a first step towards morphemic theory. Had he been able to link this in a coherent treatment with his earlier remarks concerning those syllables whose meaning is expressed only in composition, he might have laid the foundations of such a theory. As it is, his linguistic analysis is word-based, like that of all other grammarians both Humanist and Ancient, though one may note in passing at least one present-day linguist's contention that for 'inflecting' languages such as Latin a word-based grammar is more satisfactory than a morpheme-based one, in that it 'frees us from the difficulties of morphological segmentation and the invocation of a whole battery of "empty morphs"'.[5]

In accordance with the general drift towards a semantically based grammar, Humanist grammarians continue to append to their treat-

---

[1] *De lingua Latina*, p. 143.

[2] *Partitiones*, p. 53: 'si adiectiva non essent, generibus opus non esset'.

[3] v. p. 32 above.

[4] *Rudimenta*, f. 4ᵛ.

[5] J. Lyons, *Structural Semantics: An Analysis of Part of the Vocabulary of Plato*, Blackwell, Oxford, 1963, p. 11.

ment of the noun the traditional *regulae generales* listing names of
trees, rivers, etc., with their plethora of extra-linguistic *nomina
patronymica, nomina ad aliquid, nomina quasi ad aliquid,* and so on.[1]
Their tendency to add to the Ancients' *casus* the further grammatical
'accident' *declinatio* seems to spring however from a desire to keep
apart semantically determined case relationships and the formal
differences exhibited by the paradigms. Corradus' Varronian bias
leads him to treat all items of formal variation under the same heading, with Varro's distinction between 'casus obliqui' (*albus, -i, -o*)
and 'casus recti' (*albus, -a, -um*), and his 'constant' natural declensions (*mensa, mensae*) and 'inconstant' voluntary ones (*ovus,
ovile*).[2] Apart from these Varronian features, the grammarians'
debate is centred on whether a semantically determined difference
in case calls for a corresponding difference in form and, arising out
of this, on the propriety of following certain of the Ancients by
instituting a seventh case. Linacre sets the tone of the debate by
defining the nominative both syntactically and semantically, as
preceding a finite verb and signifying 'the thing absolutely, as it is',
and the oblique cases semantically in terms of the signification of
possession, acquisition, etc. Lily defines nominative and accusative
as constituting replies to the questions *who?, whom?* and the other
cases according to the 'tokens' which correspond to them in English,
the genitive e.g. being known 'by this token Of'.[3] These are obviously intended as aids to the student in determining when to use a
particular Latin case rather than as analyses of English structure,
but they are seized upon by later grammarians as evidence of a case
system in the vernacular. They are the only structural note in what
is otherwise a wholeheartedly semasiological approach, but constitute no proof that in using them Lily was really conscious of the
analytical character of English as opposed to Latin. Nor is this use of
signs original to Lily. Nebrija had already recognized the status as
signa of the 'articles' used to mark gender and case in Latin paradigms,[4] the early Italian vernacular grammarians had treated
prepositions as *segni dei casi,* and Linacre had noted that certain
French prepositions are *articuli sive notae* of case.[5] In view of the

---

[1] Typical in this respect is Sulpitius' *Opusculum.*
[2] *De lingua Latina,* pp. 89, 92–3. For a discussion of Varro's treatment of inflection and
derivation v. R. H. Robins, *Short History,* p. 50.
[3] *A Short Introduction* (1557), p. 8.   [4] *Introductiones Latinae* (1509), p. 40.
[5] *Rudimenta,* p. 39.

seventeenth-century Port-Royal Grammar's treatment of case and particle-plus-noun as semantically equivalent structures, these antecedents are not without interest.

Early Humanist treatment of the pronoun calls for little comment. It continues to regard it in Roman fashion as an almost complete semantic substitute for the noun,[1] and to be dominated by Priscian's dichotomy of *pronomina demonstrativa* denoting things present to the speaker and *pronomina relativa* denoting absent ones. Grammarians differ seriously only in their acceptance or rejection of Priscian's fifteen-pronoun system with its exclusion of certain words such as *quis* which are counted as nouns because they signify both substance and (indefinite) quality. Linacre however gives in his *Rudimenta* a definition which moves away from the idea of noun substitution and puts the emphasis on deixis and anaphora: 'it signifies a thing as pointed out, referred to, or possessed, with some definite distinction of person'.[2] The link with the Greek (Apollonian) tradition followed by Priscian, in which the pronoun cannot indicate the thing as such but only *tanquam demonstratam*, is obvious. In the *De structura*, however, in contrast to medieval doctrine, Linacre has the pronoun additionally signify *individuam maxime essentiam*,[3] in line with his idea that it signifies reality with sharper definition than the noun itself.[4] Lily's grammar too follows the general evolution away from the concept of noun substitution, the pronoun retaining in the 1557 edition only the deictic and anaphoric function of 'a parte of speache muche like to a Noune: which is used in shewing or rehersing'.[5] Interesting as illustrating two widely divergent paths taken by grammatical theory in the sixteenth century are the approaches of Stockwood and Alvarus. The latter's 'certam finitamque personam adsignificat'[6] continues medieval Aristotelianism in an unbroken tradition. His use of *adsignificat* rather than *significat* per-

[1] Brassicanus e.g. repeats, without acknowledgment, Servius' remark that 'nomina plenas faciunt elocutiones, pronomina semiplenas' (Keil, *Grammatici Latini*, IV, 409).

[2] p. 40: 'rem significat tanquam demonstratam, relatam, aut possessam cum aliqua certae personae differentia'.

[3] Following Priscian's view of the pronoun as signifying 'substantiam meram, vel substantiam sine qualitate', the *Grammatica speculativa* (cap. xii) has it signify 'aliquam essentiam indeterminatam'.

[4] i, 7: 'certius aliquid quam proprium nomen significat'.

[5] *A Short Introduction* (1557), p. 14. Lily's Latin definition in the *Brevissima institutio* (1557), p. 34, similarly repeats Melanchthon's 'qua in demonstranda aut in repetenda re utimur' (*Grammatica*, 1527 ed., f. 25ʳ).

[6] *De institutione*, p. 114. This reverses the traditional view of the noun as *consignifying* and the pronoun as *signifying* person.

44

petuates the notion of a part of speech as comprising, in addition to
its lexical signification, a consignified grammatical function. As a
Jesuit, he had no doubt received a Scholastic training. By contrast,
Stockwood's approach is lacking in rigour and indicates the trend to
lexical nomenclature. His pronouns 'are not things, nor do they
signify any thing, but they are persons', with persons defined as
affectiones or *qualitates* of *res* or *corpora*.[1] The inference to be drawn is
clear: *nomen* = *res*; *pronomen* = *rei affectio* = *persona*. Once again there
is illustrated the growing tendency to confound the real world and
the linguistic symbolization of it.

In defining the verb the Roman grammarians used in part formal
criteria (the absence of case endings), in part semasiological criteria
with formal implications (the presence of tense and person), and in
part the wholly semasiological criterion of the signification of action
or the undergoing of action.[2] Linacre defines it formally as inflected
for mood and tense, semantically in terms of *actio* and *passio* and the
Aristotelian reference to time.[3] Though he does not say this, one
assumes by analogy with his definition of the noun that he sees tense
as grammatically *consignified* by the verb. The definition of the verb
according to *actio* or *passio* is of course based on philosophical abstractions, though grammarians could equally well have founded their
analysis on the formal terminations of the various moods, tenses and
voices. One consequence of this was that these abstractions were
assumed to be equally valid for languages other than Greek and
Latin, regardless of the formal and syntactic structures exhibited by
those languages.[4] This kind of assumption, made by seventeenth-
century universal grammarians and language-planners, rests on
previous Humanist and Roman grammatical practice in using extra-
linguistic criteria in classifying the parts of speech. During the sixteenth and seventeenth centuries it is precisely this extra-linguistic
feature of the expression of *actio* or *passio* that gains in importance,
until finally the verb is seen wholly in these terms.

Here again, as in so many respects, it is Melanchthon who is the
forerunner of seventeenth-century developments. Following the
logical sequence promised by his definition of the noun as that which
signifies 'a thing, not an action', he has the verb signify 'to act or be

---

[1] *Disputatiunculae*, f. 27ᵛ.

[2] Thus Donatus. Priscian adds a reference to mood.

[3] *Rudimenta*, p. 41.   [4] v. R. H. Robins, *General Linguistics*, p. 228.

acted upon'.[1] This constitutes the entire definition, which is bare of all formal criteria[2] and of any reference to person or tense. Devoid of any grammatical criterion, referring to lexical content alone, it would be equally appropriate to many nouns. Melanchthon perhaps realized this, for he later states that the noun contains *rerum nomenclaturam* (itself a description highly significant of the trend away from properly grammatical classification), the verb *actio* and *passio* together with *discrimina* of tense and person. These *discrimina* are not however considered to be part of the essence of the verb, whose role is the signification of *actio* and *passio*.[3] Melanchthon's approach is remarkable, so early in the century, for its almost completely semasiological character. Colet and Lily by contrast retain certain formal elements, defining the verb as declined with mood and tense, and betokening doing, suffering or being.[4]

This last definition illustrates a Humanist innovation, namely the addition to Roman grammar's *actio* and *passio* of the signification of *esse* as one of the verb's distinguishing features. This innovation stems no doubt from the prominence given to the verb *to be* in medieval grammatical systems.[5] In the sixteenth century the medieval division of the verb into *substantivum* and *adiectivum*[6] is not infrequent, and is already found in Perottus and Sulpitius. This dichotomy was unknown to Roman grammar, though the former of the two terms is found in Priscian, who having already translated the Greeks' ὕπαρξις ('existence') by *substantia*, took their ὑπαρκτικὸν ῥῆμα ('verb of existence') to be a *verbum substantivum*. This was an unfortunate translation, for it led on the one hand to a discrepancy between the value of the word *substantivum* as applied to nouns and to verbs, and on the other to the twelfth-century grammarians' use of the term *verbum substantivum* to refer to a verb signifying substance. When

---

[1] *Grammatica* (1527 ed.), f. 26^r. The noun signifies 'rem, non actionem', the verb 'agere aut pati'.

[2] The dichotomy *declinable/indeclinable* is not used by Melanchthon in defining the word-classes.

[3] He is perhaps influenced by Greek sources here (cf. H. Steinthal, *Geschichte*, ii, 267). One should note however his contradictory statement (*Grammatica*, 1527 ed., f. 28^r) that tense distinctions constitute 'propria verborum natura'.

[4] *A Short Introduction* (1557), p. 17. An exception to the general tendency to semasiological treatment is again Drosay, who distinguishes *secundum vocem* the formally based dichotomies personal/impersonal, regular/irregular, perfect/defective, simple/composite and primary/derivative (*Partitiones*, pp. 58, 60).

[5] The *Grammatica speculativa* (cap. xxvi), while having the verb in general signify *per modum esse*, has the verb *sum* signify *esse generale specificabile*.

[6] Cf. *Grammatica speculativa*, cap. xxvi.

medieval grammarians isolated this verb as signifying 'purum esse rei'[1] and as functioning as a copula, all other verbs (signifying *actio* and *passio*) received in contrast the appellation *adiectiva*, thus forming a neat parallel to the corresponding division of the noun. The term *verba adiectiva* is in general use by the thirteenth century, Peter of Spain's *Summulae logicales* (*c.* 1250) foreshadowing the *Grammatica speculativa* in this respect. Despauterius' definition of verbs adjective as those which add something to the meaning of the substantive (verb) seems to be based on this mistaken analogy between *verbum adiectivum* and *nomen adiectivum*. His resolution, in medieval fashion, of the verb into *sum* plus the present participle (*amo = sum amans*)[2] shows however on what this idea of the *verbum adiectivum* as adding a component of meaning to the *copula* in order to form the complete verb is based. It becomes comprehensible in the light of his consequent definition of the *verbum substantivum* as 'per quod alia verba declarantur aut coniugantur'.[3] Once again certain celebrated later theories, such as the seventeenth-century Port-Royal Grammar's similar analysis of the verb based on predication and the linking of the predicate to its logical subject by means of the *copula*, are seen to have been anticipated in medieval and early Humanist grammar.

The increased importance of the *verbum substantivum* leads grammarians to classify it separately when treating voice, as in Linacre's triple division into *verbum substantiae* ('sum'), *verba absoluta* (intransitives, 'quae per se sensum absolvunt') and *verba transitiva*, the latter then undergoing the Roman classification into active, passive, deponent, *commune* and *neutrum*. In an attempt to bring order into the Roman confusion of imperfectly overlapping formal and semantic distinctions, Linacre classifies separately those voices (active, passive, *neutrum*) recognized by their *significatio*. Formally derived forms such as the inchoatives can then be included here 'vocis ratione' as *declinata*, and transitive and intransitive verbs are distinguished 'constructionis ratione'.[4] The traditional class of *neutra* followed by an

---

[1] Thus Remigius of Auxerre. v. J. J. Baebler, *Beiträge zu einer Geschichte der lateinischen Grammatik im Mittelalter*, Halle, 1885, p. 58.

[2] Cf. J. P. Mullally, *The Summulae Logicales of Peter of Spain*, Notre Dame University (Indiana) dissertation, 1945, p. xci: 'In defining a categorical proposition, Peter of Spain says that every such proposition is composed of . . . a subject, a predicate, and a copula . . . But if a categorical proposition always includes a copula, the verb "is" must be included in every verb as its root . . . The statement "A man thinks" should be resolved into "A man is thinking" . . .'

[3] *Rudimenta*, f. 12ᵛ. In Stockwood's *Disputatiunculae* (ff. 41ᵛ–42ʳ) *scribo* is regarded as a contraction of *sum scribens*.   [4] *De structura*, I, 9ʳ.

accusative 'cognatae significationis' (*vivo vitam*) are kept separate from the *absoluta*. In a similar attempt to disentangle formal matters and semantic ones, Despauterius contrasts *verba activi generis*, formally marked as active, with *verba activa* recognized as active only by the application of semantic criteria. Sensory verbs like *video*, widely held by grammarians to signify *passio*, present a difficulty, but Despauterius resolves it by declaring them *verba activi generis* signifying *passio* 'per modum agendi'.[1] Thus do the methods of medieval grammar linger on in the works of the Humanists, with Despauterius, the professed enemy of Scholasticism, pressing into service both the concept of the *modus significandi* and the *Grammatica speculativa*'s dictum 'non sit idem dicere, Verbum Activum, et Activi generis'.[2] Nearer the end of the century Corradus' treatment of voice, discarding such purely grammatical considerations, takes to an extreme the Roman and Humanist inclination to semantic, extra-linguistic classification. Verbs are classified by him according as their action passes from man to beast (*equitare*), from man to inanimate object (*arare*), or from man to nothing (*lacrimare*). Equally superfluous grammatically is the statement that *vivere* pertains to animals, *esse* to all things, and *fulminare* to hidden powers. This tendency to define words in terms of observed phenomena rather than in linguistic terms is a constant feature of Humanist grammar.

The primacy of mood over tense is a typical feature of Ancient and Humanist grammar. Linacre refuses to follow those of the Ancients who add such items as a *modus participialis* or a *gerundi modus* to the five moods universally accepted. He restricts the term *modus* to the notion expressed by the Greek ἔγκλισις, to 'voluntas, vel affectio animi per vocem significata' or, as he prefers to say, 'adsignificata vel consignificata'.[3] His definition is therefore close to the 'diversae inclinationes' of Priscian (equally Greek in origin and repeated by most Humanist grammarians) with a typical added insistence on the grammatical *consignification* of mood. The emphasis is however, in spite of his 'per vocem consignificata', on semantic definition, the optative e.g. being that which signifies 'rem ut optatam'.[4] The number of moods is brought up to six by the addition of a *modus potentialis*, found neither in Roman nor in medieval grammar, signifying 'potentiam aut debitum'. This new mood – Linacre appears to be the

---

[1] Cf. on this type of medieval distinction J. J. Baebler, *Beiträge*, p. 160.
[2] Cap. xxvi.   [3] *De structura*, I, 11ᵛ.   [4] *Rudimenta*, p. 42.

first to introduce it – is justified on grounds of economy as expressing singly and by itself an *affectio animi* expressed in Greek by two separate procedures.[1] Linacre overlooks the fact that it does not represent an economy for Latin, and that its institution on the grounds that it represents a separate *affectio animi* leaves the way open, since it is accompanied by no formal difference, to a flood of moods limited only by the number of *affectiones* that can be invented. Formally, the potential is identical with the subjunctive and optative, an indication that Linacre makes grammatical distinctions in the same way as Nebrija, 'ratione significationis'.[2]

Moods are defined by Colet in singularly non-grammatical fashion as 'the maner of spekynge'[3] and described, subjunctive and optative apart, in purely semantic terms. The indicative 'sheweth a reason true or false', the optative 'wisheth or desireth' but is preceded by an 'adverbe of wishing' and recognized in English by such *signs* as 'wold God', and the subjunctive is a syntactically dependent form preceded by a conjunction. The infinitive is used 'whan with another verb I declare my doynge', is known by the sign *to*, and is defined in the usual Roman and Humanist terms as being without person or number.[4] The potential mood, absent from *L* and no doubt inserted into later editions in imitation of Linacre, is known by the signs *may*, *can*, etc.[5] Lily follows Linacre in cumulating a number of modal distinctions under one formal *vox*,[6] but his formally identical subjunctive, potential and optative 'discernuntur significatu & signis',[7] the optative being distinguished by its *adverbium optandi*, the subjunctive by its preceding conjunction. Lily's use of English *signs* to facilitate learning has led him to put an emphasis on similar *signa* in Latin, and to introduce a syntactic, structural criterion that is almost wholly absent in Linacre.

Tenses are still, in the sixteenth century, subservient to mood, of

---

[1] By ἄν+indicative, and ἄν+optative.

[2] Nebrija, *Introductiones* (1533), p. [11]. Cf. p. [12]: 'non vocum sed significationum diversitas faciat distinctos modos'. Linacre remarks however (*De structura*, I, 15ᵛ) that 'Modi, si vocum discrimen spectes, quatuor tantum sunt'.

[3] In *L* (S. Blach, 'Shakespeares Lateingrammatik', *Jahrbuch der deutschen Shakespeare-Gesellschaft*, vol. 44, p. 87).

[4] *Ibid.* (vol. 44, p. 87), and *A Short Introduction* (1557), pp. 17–18. Signs like 'wold God' represent a deliberate attempt to provide English with *adverbia optandi* corresponding to Latin *utinam* etc.   [5] *A Short Introduction* (1557), p. 18.

[6] Cf. V. Salmon, 'James Shirley and Some Problems of Seventeenth-Century Grammar', *Archiv für das Studium der neueren Sprachen*, vol. 197, 4 (1961), p. 291, on this tendency in Lily.   [7] *Brevissima institutio* (1557), p. 42 (my italics).

which they are 'partes quaedam'.[1] Though nominally at least differences in meaning are tied to differences in form – 'ut sensu differunt, ita declinatu interesse debent'[2] – Roman semantically based definitions are followed closely. The definitions of the participle also in general continue the Roman view of it as participating in the nature of both noun and verb, a view which can be expressed in purely semantic terms.[3] The parts of speech other than noun, verb, pronoun and participle continue to be treated as indeclinables, and regarded by some grammarians (e.g. Melanchthon) in Aristotelian fashion as *syncategoremata* or *consignificantia*.[4] The adverb is defined following Roman practice as modifying the meaning of the verb, and an extensive number of semantically determined sub-classes is usually set up. Melanchthon describes these *significationes* as 'actionum circunstantiae', with the adverb consequently defined as the expression of 'actionis aut passionis circunstantiam', in logical sequence to his view of the verb as indicating *actio* or *passio*. This definition, peculiar to Melanchthon among the earlier Humanists, is perhaps of Greek origin, with affinities to Apollonius' treatment of the adverb as expressing 'certain modalities' of the verb and, by its relation to them, completing their sense.[5] It is increasingly copied by later grammarians, as in Colet's 'parte that accompanyeth the verbe, and declared [*sic*] the maner and the circunstans of the doynge or the suffryng of the verbe'.[6]

In defining the preposition, sixteenth-century grammarians hesitate between Priscian's purely formal definition[7] and Donatus' semantic one in terms of its effect on the meaning of the noun with which it is constructed.[8] Donatus' definition is however sometimes rejected as applying only to inseparable prepositions.[9] Linacre makes

---

[1] Thus Corradus, *De lingua Latina*, pp. 191 and 243.

[2] Brassicanus, *Grammaticae institutiones*, f. lvii^r.

[3] Cf. Diomedes' 'verbi et nominis, vim participet' (Keil, *Grammatici Latini*, I, 401).

[4] Note Priscian's 'Graeci proprium dicunt esse praepositionis, ut nihil certum per se positae sine aliis partibus orationis significare possint' (H. Keil, *Grammatici Latini*, III, 29). Cf. also J. J. Baebler's remark (*Beiträge*, p. 80) that certain medieval grammars attribute to prepositions only an *imperfecta significatio*, treating them as *syncategoremata*.

[5] Cf. V. Brøndal, *Les parties du discours* (French translation by P. Naert), Copenhagen, 1948, p. 54. [6] In *L* (S. Blach's edition, vol. 45, pp. 51–2).

[7] H. Keil, *Grammatici Latini*, III, 24. [8] *Ibid.* IV, 389.

[9] The *Grammatica speculativa* (cap. xlii) applies Donatus' definition – 'significationem aut mutat aut conplet aut minuit' – to bound forms on the level of signification (*materialiter*), thus recognizing it lexically as a morpheme, but refuses it grammatical function as a preposition, holding it to fall 'in vim dictionis, cum qua componitur'. Melanchthon similarly refuses to count bound forms as prepositions.

a fresh departure, in which all reference to the prepositive character of the word-class disappears, defining it as signifying 'circumstantiam aut habitudinem rei in loco, ordine, aut causa'.[1] There is an obvious parallel between Melanchthon's definition of the adverb as expressing *actionis circumstantiam* and this one of the preposition as expressing *circumstantiam rei*, i.e. as performing for the noun a function similar to that which Melanchthon's adverb performs for the verb. Here again, one may note that the seventeenth-century's *thing/action* dichotomy, and its tendency to treat grammatical categories as reflections of these two abstractions or as modes of them, is already in place before the middle of the sixteenth century. Melanchthon's own definition of the preposition resembles Linacre's. He regards it as properly speaking an *article* linking the verb to a noun signifying 'aliquam facti circunstantiam'.[2] Already before these Humanist authors, medieval theorists had rejected the Roman definitions as inadequate, and efforts had been made to replace them, Petrus Heliae e.g. having the preposition signify 'circunstantias rerum'.[3] The *Grammatica speculativa* added to this a linking function, treating the preposition as being in 'construction with a case inflected word, linking and relating it to an action'.[4] Melanchthon's definition[5] is clearly this medieval one transposed into the language of the Humanists, and here once more we see Scholastic tradition modifying the Roman doctrine sixteenth-century grammarians are professedly transmitting.

Syntax receives on the whole scant attention. Even where voluminous studies are made of it, authors usually do little more than repeat material culled from Priscian's two final books, relaying the traditional teaching on the three concords[6] and the endless minutiae of case government inherited from medieval tradition. Despauterius' syntax,[7] with its division into *syntaxis praeceptiva* (giving norms to be

---

[1] *Rudimenta*, p. 43.

[2] The word *articulus* has obviously here the sense of the Greek term ἄρθρον, that is to say *link* or *joint*. Melanchthon gives the example *ad musas currere*, in which *ad* functions 'tanquam articulus'.

[3] v. C. Thurot, *Extraits*, p. 154.

[4] R. H. Robins' translation (*Short History*, p. 80) of the *Grammatica speculativa*'s 'significans per modum adiacentis alteri casuali, ipsum contrahens, et ad actum reducens' (cap. xli).

[5] *Grammatica* (1527 ed.), f. 41^r: 'Praepositio est propemodum articulus verbo nomen adiungens, quod aliquam facti circunstantiam significat'.

[6] The agreement of adjective with substantive, nominative subject with verb, and relative with antecedent.   [7] *Commentarii*, pp. 185ff.

followed), *permissiva* (detailing acceptable variants), and *prohibitiva*, may be taken as typical. It defines the government of one word by another in the semantic terms of 'quae confuse significans declaratur per alteram', and takes as its norm the usage of the learned. The explanations are tortuous and semantically based. Worthy of note however is Despauterius' use of the terms *suppositum* and *appositum*, the former indicating the noun in the nominative case preceding the verb, the latter the case-marked noun governed by the verb.[1] After an early utilization, copied from rhetoric and not sustained, of the terms *subiectum* and *declarativum*,[2] medieval grammar used solely, in reintroducing the notion of predication, these words *suppositum* and *appositum*. Petrus Heliae (*c.* 1150) once uses them to indicate subject and predicate,[3] and they occur in Alexander of Villedieu's *Doctrinale*.[4] The word *suppositio* had a further use in medieval logic, where it indicated the function of a term in discourse,[5] but *suppositum* and *appositum* were kept rigorously apart from the logical terms *subiectum* and *praedicatum* (with which grammarians were of course familiar), and continued in use in the sixteenth and seventeenth centuries, particularly in the works of Ramus, Sanctius and Vossius. The terms *subiectum* and *attributum* are however used in 1575 by Corradus, an isolated example of a Humanist grammarian using them thus early – much earlier than their occurrence in Vossius noted by V. Salmon.[6]

Much of seventeenth-century doctrine concerning the proposition is already present quite early in the sixteenth century, as witness Melanchthon's definition of the noun as that which 'sine verbo, non absolvit orationem integram', and of the verb similarly as requiring a noun subject in order to function in an *oratio*, the whole then constituting an 'integrae sententiae explicatio'.[7] This treatment of noun and verb as essential to a (logical) sentence would seem to owe something to Aristotelian logic, and to invalidate I. Poldauf's contention that in Melanchthon's grammar, as in those of Scaliger and Sanctius, 'Latin definitely ceases to be regarded as a means of logic, but becomes an independent system of expressions and

---

[1] *Ibid.* p. 200.
[2] v. M. H. Jellinek, *Geschichte*, II, 465.
[3] v. C. Thurot, *Extraits*, p. 217.   [4] v. J. P. Mullally, *Peter of Spain*, p. lv.
[5] v. V. Salmon, 'James Shirley', p. 294. For further discussion of this question v. W. and M. Kneale, *The Development of Logic*, pp. 248–51.
[6] 'James Shirley', p. 293.
[7] *Syntaxis Philippi Melanchthonis*, Paris, 1528, f. 2ᵛ.

symbols.'[1] Precisely similar in tenor is L. Kukenheim's remark that 'already Nebrija and Melanchthon are trying to rid themselves of logic and take account of the form of words'.[2] These views no doubt stem from Melanchthon's preliminary definition of *etymologia* as that which concerns 'discrimina casuum in dictionibus', that is to say, as his examples make clear, formal derivation. But he also defines it, following Cicero's rendering of Greek *etymologia* by the Latin expression *veriloquium,* as the indication of 'dictionum proprietates',[3] the semantic properties of words. His grammar is characterized by a strong semasiological bias, and he is even less given than most of his contemporaries to defining in formal terms. The views of Poldauf and Kukenheim need reassessing, especially in the face of W. H. Woodward's contrary opinion that it was precisely at the time of Melanchthon's dominance of the Humanist educational movement that 'grammar of the logically complete type' began to achieve its hegemony in the schools.[4]

The only Humanist author to discuss syntax at any great length is Linacre, who devotes five of the six books of his *De structura* to construction. His treatment perpetuates the use of the terms *transitiva* and *intransitiva constructio,* found in Priscian and common in medieval grammar. The *De structura* has a further refinement by which syntax is divided into that which depends on *personae ratio* and that which does not.[5] *Persona* seems to mean here the syntactic use of any case or personal distinction, and recalls Linacre's attribution of person to all declinable word-classes. This introduction of the notion of person into syntax to indicate relations of concordance or government is a medieval contribution,[6] based perhaps on the important place occupied by person in the *De constructione* appended to the grammar of Priscian, the only Roman author to deal at length with syntactic questions. Here again, in Linacre's treatment, we have an example of a Humanist grammarian retaining a strong medieval influence.

More interesting for present-day readers in view of later develop-

[1] 'On the History of Some Problems of English Grammar before 1800', *Prague Studies in English,* LV (1948), p. 47.
[2] *Contributions,* p. 132: 'déjà Nebrija et Mélanchton essayent de se défaire de la logique et s'attachent à la forme des mots'.
[3] *Grammatica* (1527 ed.), f. 2r.
[4] *Studies in Education during the Age of the Renaissance 1400–1600,* p. 120.
[5] This procedure is also followed by Drosay, who probably used Linacre as his source.
[6] The *constructio impersonalis* is however absent from the *Grammatica speculativa,* which has no doctrine of the *syncategoremata.*

ments in Sanctius and the Port-Royal Grammar, which raise questions that present-day transformational grammar treats in terms of a logical 'deep structure' underlying the 'surface structure' of actual discourse, is Linacre's further division of syntax into the two varieties *Justa* and *Figurata*, the latter including elliptic structures.[1] From a perusal of these sections, it emerges that the *constructio justa* is regarded as the statement in full of utterances only partially actualized in the surface structure exhibited by the *constructio figurata*. Linacre is not alone as an example of sixteenth-century awareness of deep and surface structure, for Despauterius treats e.g. the neuter adjective *triste* standing alone as being semantically equivalent to *tristis res*, and his expansion of *amo* into the logically more complete *sum amans* has already been noted. Linacre is however the only early Humanist to give the matter an extended treatment comparable to, and even surpassing, that of Sanctius. His *Rudimenta*[2] already gives the common expansion, cited by Sanctius, of *pluit* into *Deus pluit* or *pluvia pluit*, but a more interesting precedent is Book II of the *De structura*, which deals at great length with what Linacre, using a Greek term, calls the *Enallage* of the parts of speech, that is to say their interchangeability in discourse.[3] According to this an adjective (*recens*) can replace an adverb (*recenter*) and, more germane to the deep/surface structure question, an adverb can act as the semantic equivalent of the structure relative-plus-preposition, a conjunction can replace pronoun-plus-preposition, and noun-plus-verb may substitute for verb.

Linacre's treatment of substitution implies a recognition of an underlying mental structure which can be variously actualized by items of discourse. This recognition is made explicit by the treatment in Book VI (*De constructionis figuris*), which describes the *constructio justa* as that which faithfully reproduces the *sensum animi* or mental discourse, while ellipse is presented as the absence of an element which is essential to that *legitima constructio* 'in sensu'.[4] In this section Linacre gives examples of 'defective' structures in figurative construction, and contrasts them with structures in which the underlying *sensus* is given in full. By these procedures, *Parisii* must be restated as

---

[1] *De structura*, III, 50ʳ.   [2] P. 65.
[3] Ἐναλλαγή means *interchange*.
[4] Cf. f. xxiiᵛ, 'ad sensum animi prodendum, iusta se habet partium inter se constructio', and the definition of ellipse on f. xxiiiʳ as 'dictionis ad legitimam constructionem necessariae in sensu defectus'.

Parisii homines, Ianuarius as *Ianuarius mensis*, and *eo Romam* as *eo ad Romam*.[1] Similarly, *Cicero erat brevis staturae* becomes *Cicero erat homo brevis staturae*, while other structures require that *officium* or *res* be understood:

Tuum est mihi ignoscere = *Tuum officium est mihi ignoscere*;

Non est humani iudicii = *Non est res humani iudicii*.[2]

Intransitive verbs like *vivo* and *curro* require the addition of an *accusativus cognatae significationis*, giving such underlying structures as *vivo vitam* and *curro cursum*. Of particular interest in view of the expansions of impersonal verbs suggested by Sanctius and the Port-Royal authors are the resolutions of *sedetur* into *sessio sedetur*, and of *curritur* into *cursus curritur*.[3] Linacre devotes nearly forty pages to ellipse, dealing with each part of speech in turn. Suffice it to mention finally his resolution of *me authore* into *me enti authore* on the grounds that this structure 'nisi participio subaudito consistere non potest', and his anticipation of Sanctius' resolutions of the type *mittas* = *fac ut mittas*.[4] In this treatment of ellipse Linacre precedes Sanctius by some sixty years and the Port-Royal Latin grammar by over a hundred. In spite of his remark that syntax is 'in vocibus, non in rebus',[5] a matter of formal rather than semantic congruence, his approach is in fact based on the interchangeability of structures which differ on the level of oral discourse but are semantic equivalents on the level of the mental discourse of the underlying linguistic system.

The aim the early Humanist grammarians set themselves was, as I have said, the restatement of Donatus and Priscian in the original terms, shorn of the accretion of Scholastic dialectics which, though based these two authors and especially Priscian, was the hallmark of the medieval *Grammatica speculativa*. Rather than give a complete résumé of this restated Roman theory, I have chosen certain topics which contain the germ of future developments, indicate the persistence of medieval ways of thought, or illustrate a general trend. Many Renaissance grammars are encyclopaedic in extent. Linacre's and Melanchthon's chief works each consist of nearly four hundred pages, while Despauterius' *Commentarii grammatici* runs to nearly seven hundred. Searching out the kernel of theory involves working

---

[1] Ff. xxv^r, xxv^v, xxxiv^v. [2] Ff. xxv^r, xxvi^v.
[3] Ff. xxvi^r, xxvi^v. [4] Ff. xxxiii^v, xxx^r.
[5] Bk. III, f. 50^v.

through an immense amount of trivia, in which grammatical rules, stylistic directives and examples from authors are almost inextricably mingled. What emerges from all this is an overwhelming tendency, even greater than that of the Roman models, toward the use of semasiological criteria in analysing linguistic structure. Certain topics discussed have been chosen to illustrate this, and to give an idea of the grammarians' inability to reconcile the demands of a formally-based grammar with those of a meaning-based one. Increasingly, as formal criteria are abandoned, the concept of the linguistic sign, with its twin facets of form and meaning, is lost sight of. Correspondingly, the notion of consignification, of a grammatical function existing in a word over and above its lexical meaning, is suppressed, word (*dictio*) and part of speech (*pars orationis*) becoming synonymous terms. Both these concepts, the doctrine of the *sign* and the idea of the *consignification* of a grammatical meaning, were essential to medieval grammar, which anticipates much of present-day theory in this respect. 'Grammatica est de signis rerum', said the *Grammatica speculativa,* 'grammar is concerned with linguistic signs.' By the time of Lily's 'the noun is the name of a thing' even the notion of signification is being blurred. Grammar now deals directly with *things,* or rather, given the interest in nomenclature that is to become almost an obsession of seventeenth-century thought, with their *names.*

A good deal, in fact, of what has hitherto been regarded as the specifically seventeenth- or even eighteenth-century contribution to grammatical theory is found to be already present in these earlier authors, more particularly in Melanchthon. In his work the logical proposition is already being taken as the norm for the grammatical *oratio,* the seventeenth-century *thing/action* dichotomy is already in place in the definitions of noun and verb, and the treatment of the latter solely in the semantic, extra-linguistic terms of the signification of *agere* or *pati* anticipates Vossius' identical definition of the 'essence' of the verb by over a century. Even late sixteenth-century 'innovations' such as Sanctius' treatment of ellipse, with its implied recognition of a 'deep' and a 'surface' structure to language, a *verbum mentis* underlying the *verbum oris* of actual discourse, are given full-length treatment in Linacre's *De structura* as early as 1524. Apart from these seminal features, the early Humanist grammarians remain none the less conservative, and indeed the foundations laid by them continue in use to the end of the century and beyond. As early as 1540 however, with the publication of Scaliger's grammar, a whole new approach, to be continued a few decades later by Sanctius, begins to make itself felt.

Already by the middle of the sixteenth century it was becoming evident that Humanism was losing ground. By 1530 the new pedagogy was well founded, and the first, urgent task of restoring the Latin language to its pristine purity and establishing reliable texts, of producing a vast body of material that could be easily memorized, had been largely completed. Even before the death of Melanchthon in 1560, the demand for a Humanist education was proving somewhat limited. Humanism, though in a vast burst of energy it had assembled and presented to the age the considerable corpus of Ancient literature and put forward an ideal of education for the new administrative classes, had not solved the problems of methodology which, as learning crossed new frontiers, were becoming increasingly acute.[1] The only body of knowledge it offered, at a time when the scope of human enquiry was being dramatically increased, was that embraced by classical Antiquity. Humanism having fulfilled its programme and exhausted the then existing notions of philology and normative grammar, purely linguistic studies were about to give way to philosophical and theological preoccupations. In northern Europe the slackening of the demand for the products of Humanist education, coupled with the advance in status of the vernacular languages, left Latin and Greek studies in the cultural byways, as mere mental disciplines always in danger of declining into philological dilettantism. Those linguists who wished to remain in the forefront of scientific enquiry were obliged to break new ground. In this respect the publication in 1540 of J. C. Scaliger's *De causis linguae Latinae* marks a new departure.[2] Scaliger and those grammarians who follow him still emphasize to a marked degree the claims of usage. But from now on grammar, even when professedly based on usage, must be made to square with reason, conform to a *ratio*, and follow a method.

[1] v. W. H. Woodward, *Studies in Education during the Age of the Renaissance*, pp. 242–3.

[2] It should be noted however that P. A. Verburg (*Taal en Functionaliteit*, Wageningen, 1952, p. 163) sees Scaliger as the originator of an isolation of Latin philological studies which was not to end before the latter part of the nineteenth century.

2. THE BREAK WITH TRADITION: SCALIGER, RAMUS, SANCTIUS

By 1540,[1] Humanism was well on the way to completing the task it had set itself. Classical studies were flourishing, chairs of Greek and Latin had been endowed, and both languages had been codified with copious examples from the best authors. After this date a fresh approach in grammatical studies was required, and it was supplied by three grammarians of first rank: J. C. Scaliger (*De causis linguae Latinae*, 1540), P. de la Ramée, alias Ramus (*Grammatica*, 1559) and F. Sanctius (*Minerva*, 1587). These three authors make what is virtually a new departure in grammar, seeking to establish philosophical bases for the study of language.

SCALIGER

Julius Caesar Scaliger (1484–1588), a classical scholar bearing the Latinized name of the Della Scala family, left Italy in 1525 to become physician to the bishop of Agen, and gained fame as an opponent of Erasmus' views as to what constituted good Latin prose. Trained like Linacre in medicine, he approached the Renaissance ideal of the all-round scholar, being zoologist, grammarian, literary critic (his *Poetice* was widely read) and botanist, and publishing commentaries not only on Hippocrates but also on the botanical writings of Aristotle. Since his *De causis* attempts to apply Aristotelian methods of classification to language, these methods will be outlined here before proceeding to an analysis of Scaliger's contribution to linguistic studies.

Aristotle's world-view is hylomorphic,[2] that is to say it avoids the Platonic dualism between matter and idea[3] by regarding matter as

---

[1] The date chosen by L. Kukenheim as the end point of his *Contributions à l'histoire de la grammaire grecque, latine et hébraïque à l'époque de la Renaissance*.

[2] *The Shorter Oxford English Dictionary* defines hylomorphism as: (*a*) the doctrine that primordial matter is the First Cause of the universe; (*b*) the Scholastic theory of matter and form.

[3] Cf. K. Fischer, *Descartes and his School*, p. 24: 'The opposition of idea and matter, of the intelligible and material worlds, of the natures of thought and sense, is peculiar to Platonic philosophy, and is grounded in its entire nature.'

having a potentiality for assuming form, and form as expressing itself through matter:

Form must be conceived as dwelling in stuff, as a formative force, i.e., as energy; and stuff must be conceived as containing form potentially in itself . . . And the world-process itself can only be conceived as a motion, in which stuff forms itself, form completes itself, potentiality actualizes itself.[1]

Hence the Aristotelian view of an object as consisting of basic matter, the *substance*, together with what gives the object its particular form, that is to say *accident*. This doctrine is fundamental to Scholastic philosophy,[2] which holds that abstractions such as quantity and thickness must have a subject in which they inhere, the *substance*, which exists in and by itself without need of support, as an *ens per se stans*, and acts as the support of the *accidents*, which can have no existence apart from it.[3] These philosophical concepts are transferred to medieval grammar, where they form the basis for the distinction between the substantive signifying *per modum per se stantis*, and the adjective signifying *per modum inhaerentis alteri*.[4] Closely dependent on them is Aristotle's system of ten *categories* or *predicaments*,[5] comprising one concept of substance and nine of accident, which are of central importance in Scholastic logic. This system offers ten separate criteria according to which phenomena may be classified:

substance	the undergoing of action (*passio*)
quantity	time when
quality[6]	place where
relation	position (*situs*)
action	*habitus*.[7]

They constitute what W. S. Howell describes as 'those words which name the possible scientific conceptions men may have as to the

[1] *Ibid.* p. 25.
[2] v. M. De Wulf, *Medieval Philosophy Illustrated from the System of Thomas Aquinas*, Harvard University Press, 1922, p. 55.
[3] Aristotle means by substance 'that which is neither asserted of nor can be found in a subject' (*Categories*, v), that which underlies (ὑποκεῖσθαι) all things. v. H. P. Cooke, *Aristotle: The Organon*, pp. 17, 25.   [4] v. *Grammatica speculativa*, cap. x.
[5] In the *Categories*, first treatise of the *Organon*.
[6] By quality Aristotle means 'that in virtue of which men are called such and such' (*Categories*, viii). v. H. P. Cooke, *Aristotle: The Organon*, p. 63.
[7] This term, difficult to translate, may perhaps be rendered by *possession*. It refers to things which do not form a permanent feature of the phenomenon in question.

nature of reality',[1] and enter into a good deal of extra-linguistic grammatical classification both medieval and Humanist. Important for Renaissance grammatical theory is Aristotle's statement that every simple expression signifies (σημαίνει) either substance or quality or one of the other categories. In his *Topics* Aristotle regarded all logical propositions as making a statement about accident, genus, property, or definition (involving questions of difference and species), and from this doctrine Scholastic logic draws its five *predicables* of genus, species, difference, property and accident, defined by Howell as 'those words which define and delimit the boundaries of scientific statements'.[2] Known in English logical treatises as 'the common words', the five predicables, together with the ten predicaments, form the basic tools of Aristotelian and Scholastic logic.[3] For the first seventy years of the sixteenth century this logic, based on Aristotle as interpreted by Classical, Christian and Arab commentators, was the recognized authority.

Scaliger was to restore to grammatical studies the Aristotelian concepts of *substance* and *accident, etc.*, and to apply them to language in a way that had not been done since the time of the medieval *Grammatica speculativa*. All this is duly noted by P. A. Verburg in his book *Taal en Functionaliteit*,[4] but R. G. Faithfull, in reviewing this work, makes the added point that Scaliger's contribution was above all 'a theory of linguistic function in terms of hylemorphic[5] assumptions... it has not been observed by modern philologists that his specific contribution was to take the basic cosmological assumptions of Greek thought, which were explicit in the form of the aetiological doctrine of the Four Causes, and apply them to language as if it were a substance'.[6] This doctrine of the Four Causes, which according

---

[1] *Logic and Rhetoric in England, 1500–1700*, Princeton University Press, 1956, p. 19.

[2] *Ibid.* p. 19.

[3] For this brief exposition of Aristotelian logic I am much indebted to W. S. Howell's *Logic and Rhetoric.* v. also W. and M. Kneale, *The Development of Logic*, p. 23.

[4] Wageningen (1952), p. 163.

[5] G. L. Bursill-Hall (*Speculative Grammars of the Middle Ages*, The Hague and Paris, 1971, pp. 48–9) points out that hylomorphic theory, with its terms *materia, forma, substantia* and *accidentia*, was used by the Modistae in establishing the oppositions between the four declinable parts of speech. But cf. p. 39, where he argues that for the Modistae 'the metaphysical device of the contrast of matter and form . . . is, however, a terminological distinction which is not to be correlated with reality', and p. 48, n. 73 for his view that 'matter and form were as much grammatical devices as metaphysical distinctions in the hands of the Modistae'.

[6] Review of P. A. Verburg, *Taal en Functionaliteit* (1952), in *Archivum Linguisticum*, 7:2 (1955), pp. 146, 147. Cf. F. de Saussure, *Cours de linguistique générale*, Paris, 1964,

to Aristotle underlie all things,[1] is of course recalled by Scaliger's title: *De causis linguae Latinae*. The first two causes reflect Aristotle's preoccupation with substance and accident: the *causa materialis*, or underlying matter, and the *causa formalis* which imposes form upon it. The third cause, the *causa efficiens*, refers to the imposer of the form, be he artisan, artist or God, and the end to which this imposition takes place constitutes the fourth cause or *causa finalis*.[2] Scaliger, with a possible debt to Linacre,[3] takes this doctrine and applies it to language. As Faithfull points out, he identifies the *causa materialis* with what is now called phonetics, and the *causa formalis* with the semantic aspect of language.[4] Here, of course, he is making no advance on medieval doctrine, with its *dictio* consisting of phonetic *vox* plus semantic *significatio* and its use of the terms *materialiter* and *formaliter*, though he has the merit of re-emphasizing it. As in the case of his medieval precedents, Scaliger's approach is of interest to the modern reader for its relevance to F. de Saussure's doctrine of the linguistic sign. It is worth noting, however, that de Saussure thought it necessary to warn the student against the errors occasioned by treating language as if it were a substance.[5] In his use of the other two causes, Scaliger is no longer restating medieval theory but is breaking new ground: 'by identifying the *causa efficiens* with the speaker in the person of the original word-maker – the Greek λογοδαίδαλος – and the *causa finalis* with what is felt . . . he established in principle a genetic and functional view of language.'[6] It is true that he makes no explicit statement of the doctrines involved, but in his use of them he 'came near to writing the book which Aristotle might have written had he left us a *De grammatica*'.[7]

p. 169: '*la langue est une forme et non une substance* . . . toutes les erreurs de notre terminologie, toutes nos façons incorrectes de désigner les choses de la langue proviennent de cette supposition involontaire qu'il y aurait une substance dans le phénomène linguistique'.
[1] Cf. *Grammatica speculativa*, cap. xlvi: 'res cognoscitur per suas causas . . . ergo per suas causas habet definiri'. The notion of *causae* was of importance in medieval grammar, as witness the *causae inventionis* of William of Conches, who taught grammar at Chartres *c.* 1120–*c.* 1154. G. L. Bursill-Hall (*Speculative Grammars*, p. 28) notes that medieval grammarians looked to the *causae* to 'provide them with the most profound knowledge about the parts of speech, *i.e.* once these were found, it would then be possible . . . to determine the proper grammatical function of a word'.
[2] These four terms are those used in Scholastic logic.
[3] Linacre is one of the few Humanist grammarians mentioned by Scaliger in his preface.
[4] It should be noted that *formalis* refers to form-giving *meaning*, not to what we would now call formal *structure*.
[5] *Cours de linguistique générale*, p. 169: 'la langue est une forme et non une substance'.
[6] R. G. Faithfull, review of *Taal en Functionaliteit*, p. 147.   [7] *Ibid.* p. 148.

Scaliger, then, is the first grammarian since the medieval Modistae to take elements of Aristotelian philosophy and deliberately build a theory of grammar on them.[1] He patently regards himself as breaking new ground, but it is interesting to note that, working in large part within the framework of Aristotle's thought, he frequently chooses to express himself by means of the vocabulary and categories of medieval grammar. Though he looks to Aristotle to dissipate the darkness surrounding contemporary grammatical practice,[2] his system represents a return to the methods of the *Grammatica speculativa* rather than a new departure. His definition of grammar as a 'scientia loquendi ex usu' does not however at first sight differ from the normative, usage-based definitions of his Humanist predecessors. What is new is his insistence that grammar is a science, not an art, and his pointing out for the first time that its object is primarily the spoken word and only secondarily the written one. It follows that the interpretation of authors is no concern of the grammarian. As with other sciences, the aim of grammar is the seeking out of *rationes*. Though the grammarian bases his findings on an examination of the details of usage, the true object of his study is the *communis ratio* of language.[3] Scaliger defines discourse – he uses the word *sermo* – as a 'dispositio vocum articulatarum',[4] an arrangement of meaning-bearing signs in a construction whose purpose, the expression of a pre-existent sequence in the mind ('ad interpretandum animum'),[5] reflects Aristotle's view of speech as the representation of mental experiences. Accordingly, he attributes to the *vox* or word the facets *formatio* and *compositio* (i.e. formal structure) and *veritas* (i.e. meaning), and reintroduces the medieval distinction between logician and grammarian, with *veritas* as the province of the former and *formatio* and

[1] Cf. G. L. Bursill-Hall's remark (*Speculative Grammars*, p. 296) that Thomas of Erfurt's *principia construendi* are based on Aristotle's four causes. Scaliger is thus seen to precede by more than two centuries the Aristotelian approach in J. Harris's *Hermes* (1751), whose 'use of the Aristotelian distinction between matter and form (ΰλη and εἶδος) with reference to the phonic substance and the semantic function of speech foreshadows the important doctrine of *innere Sprachform* set out in the work of W. von Humboldt early in the nineteenth century', which in turn 'may be likened in some degree to the *langue* of de Saussure's later *langue–parole* dichotomy'. (R. H. Robins, *Short History*, pp. 155, 175.)

[2] *De causis linguae Latinae*, Lyons, 1540, end of volume.

[3] *Ibid.* cap. lxxvi, p. 136.

[4] *Vox articulata* is the term used in Roman grammar to indicate the meaning-bearing *vox* (i.e. the word or *dictio*) taking part in a grammatical construction.

[5] *De causis*, cap. iv, p. 8.

compositio the concern of the latter.[1] If the grammarian concerns himself with meaning, the *forma* of language, it is only as a service to the logician, and Scaliger strikes a curiously modern note in his remark that the grammarian does not necessarily have to know the meaning of a linguistic form. Since *veritas* is equated with Aristotle's *forma* and linguistic structure with his *materia*, it is evident that Scaliger is indeed treating language as in the Aristotelian sense a *substantia*, of which meaning is the *forma* or accident. More specifically, the province of the grammarian is syntax (= *materia*), treated in medieval fashion as the surface actualization of underlying mental concepts,[2] an approach which is illustrated by the basing of prepositional structures on a pre-existent structure in the mind. Those concepts which receive priority in this mental syntax must be balanced by a corresponding order in the construction of discourse: 'conceptam animo sententiam primo loco exponi deberet in oratione'.[3] Discourse must repeat a structure in the order in which it 'occurs to the intellect'. In other words, the *verbum oris* of discourse and the *verbum mentis*[4] of the underlying mental structure should ideally be congruent.

Alongside this assumption, there is a further one that language, and hence mental concepts, are a faithful reflection of natural phenomena. Truth is arrived at when there is an exact coincidence of speech with things – 'Veritas est orationis aequatio cum re cuius est nota'[5] – and it is in this light that Scaliger's use of the term *veritas* for logical meaning must be seen. This again is a return to medieval notions, in this case to the Thomistic definition of truth as an *adaequatio rei et intellectus*, a conformity of things with the understanding. Of central importance here is the treatment of *orationes* as *notae rei*, as a series of linguistic signs with extra-linguistic referents. Scaliger does not however follow the Platonic doctrine of a natural affinity between word and object, but holds that names are imposed by arbitrary convention, 'ut libuit inventori'.[6] But though names do

---

[1] *Ibid.* cap. i: 'Itaque orationem eiusque partes duo artifices diversis modis contemplantur. Dialecticus sub ratione veritatis . . . grammaticus sub figurationis & compositionis modo, quam vocarunt constructionem, tamquam materiam.'

[2] The *Grammatica speculativa* (cap. xlv), quoting Aristotle in support, treats *orationes* as 'notae passionum earum, quae sunt in anima', and the purpose of discourse (*oratio*) as 'propter exprimendum mentis conceptum'.

[3] *De causis*, cap. clii, p. 301.

[4] Scaliger does not himself use these terms, but they are implicit in his treatment.

[5] *De causis*, cap. i.   [6] *Ibid.* cap. lxviii, p. 120.

not have their origin in the nature of the things named – 'a rerum natura non fluxerint' – words must none the less, as 'signs of things', *imitate* the nature of those things.[1] In this matter Scaliger's theory is of particular interest as a link between the Thomistic doctrine of the natural conformity between the understanding and phenomena, and the seventeenth-century language-planners' demand for a language which, in the interests of scientific thought, should closely mirror the universe. He explicitly states that the understanding is the mirror of things – 'Est enim quasi rerum speculum intellectus noster'[2] – and since he defines the *vox* or word as a 'sign of those notions that are in the mind',[3] it is obvious that he regards language itself as the reflection of phenomena. These notions or *species* are introduced into the mind via the senses,[4] and here again Scaliger represents a link between medieval (and ultimately Aristotelian) ideas concerning the obtaining of knowledge through the senses and the presence of *species* in the mind, and on the one hand seventeenth-century Sensualist doctrine, and on the other Port-Royal's view of words as signs of concepts in the mind.[5] Unlike the Port-Royal authors, however, Scaliger accepts medieval notions of epistemology unchanged, positing between the *species impressae* (the mind's passive registration of sense impressions) and *expressae* (the resultant mental concepts of phenomena) the intervention of an active principle, the *intellectus agens*, whose office is to render actually intelligible the potentially intelligible impressions received from the senses. In this respect, the linguistic sign is very much the mind's own creation, and it is in this type of theory that Chomsky might well have been advised to seek the creative principle he needs for his theory of language use.[6] Certainly, Scaliger's definition of the word as a 'nota unius speciei quae est in animo',[7] a sign of a mental concept, is of capital importance for later grammatical theory, more particularly as represented by the universal grammars of the seventeenth and eighteenth centuries. Since the phenomena of the real world are the same for all

[1] *Ibid.* cap. lxxv, p. 132: 'voces rerum signa sunt, earum quoque naturam imitantur'.
[2] *Ibid.* cap. lxvi, p. 138.
[3] *Ibid.* cap. i: 'est enim vox nota earum notionum, quae in anima sunt'.
[4] *Ibid.* cap. lxvii, p. 139: 'rerum notiones a rebus in mentem primum per sensus . . . profectae sunt'.
[5] Cf. *ibid.* cap. lxvi, p. 140: 'Sicut igitur imagines rerum sunt notiones intellectui: ita voces sunt notionum illarum notiones.'
[6] For a fuller discussion of this aspect of medieval doctrine concerning the linguistic sign, and its relevance to Port-Royal theory and to Chomsky's views, v. pp. 243–4 below.
[7] *De causis*, cap. lxvi, p. 140.

men, the *species* received from sense impressions will in turn be identical in all minds, even though the words which are signs of them differ from one language to another. It follows that the term *equus* represents at one and the same time an immutable phenomenon, an equally immutable *species in intellectu*, and a potentially variable *nomen in voce*. The inescapable conclusion is that Scaliger sees language as the superficial and variable actualization of an underlying and unchanging mental structure that is the same for all men everywhere. Once again, important aspects of seventeenth-century theory are anticipated quite early in the sixteenth.

Besides being signs of mental concepts, words are still however for Scaliger ultimately *notae rerum*, and as such must mirror phenomena and their modes and causes. This insistence that language reflects the real world gives a resultant grammatical dichotomy in which noun and verb signify the causes of things, while conjunction, adverb and preposition signify the modes of operation of those causes. This classification 'ex rebus'[1] – a term which will be used again in the seventeenth century by Campanella – is in actual fact based on the Aristotelian world-view rather than on things themselves, and results in a noun–verb dichotomy in which in medieval fashion nouns signify things permanent and verbs things in a state of flux. Scaliger is however careful to point out that whereas the noun can signify a thing in temporal movement ('rem fluentem', e.g. *dies*, *annus*), it cannot signify that movement ('rei fluxus') as such. Put in other terms, the noun *signifies* time, while the verb *consignifies* it by means of an added grammatical *modus significandi*.[2] As Scaliger emphasizes, repeating medieval doctrine, 'aliud est significare, aliud consignificare'[3] – lexical meaning is one thing, grammatical consignification another. One consequence, then, of his treatment of language as the mirror of phenomena, or rather of Aristotle's classification of them, is that he becomes the first Humanist grammarian to reintroduce the medieval view of noun and verb as signifying respectively *per modum permanentis* and *per modum fluxus*.[4] All word-classes are however required to play their part in reflecting the 'universus rerum ambitus, modusque', the real world and its modes

---

[1] *Ibid.* cap. lxxii, p. 125.

[2] Scaliger notes (*ibid.* cap. cli, p. 299) that *heri* signifies time, whereas *amavi*, with an added *modus significandi tempus*, signifies 'non tempus, sed actionem amandi cum tempore'.

[3] *Ibid.* cap. lxxvi, p. 136.

[4] v. *Grammatica speculativa*, cap. viii.

of being or movement, prepositions for instance being treated as expressions of movement or quietus.

Having established that linguistic classification must be congruent with the Aristotelian categories imposed on phenomena, Scaliger turns to the *rationes atque necessitates* of inflection, and to those accidents that are common to several word-classes. In accordance with Aristotle's requirement that the universally valid be treated before the particular, these matters are discussed at the outset, before the consideration of each separate part of speech. Dealing first with person,[1] an accident of all word-classes, Scaliger holds that since words are *rerum signa* reflecting the nature of things, and adverbs and conjunctions equally partake, as *voces*, in this mirroring of the universe, they too must have person. Unlike the principal word-classes however, which *signify* things and *consignify* person, they signify modes of things and are themselves consignified 'sub persona'.[2] In this discussion of accidents we find raised for the first time in a grammar the question of what features the Latin language ought on a rational basis to contain. Since ideally every word-class should possess the same accidents, the verb, which apart from its signification of reality *sub tempore* denotes the same thing as the noun, might reasonably be expected to show gender. To the gender indication in *mulier alba* there ought therefore logically to correspond a similar indication in *mulier albescit*.

Passing to the consideration of the separate word-classes, Scaliger defines the noun as marked for case and signifying a thing without any indication of time,[3] but with a continued insistence that the noun's essence consists in the signification of *res permanentes*. The formal case reference supplies one of the 'necessary differences' which serve to mark off the word-classes from each other. But since the noun definition as it stands applies equally to the pronoun, Scaliger additionally characterizes the noun as signifying a thing *primo* or *sine medio*, thus bringing in the Apollonian and Priscianic view of the pronoun as referring primarily to the noun it replaces, and only secondarily and indirectly to the *res ipsa* signified by the

---

[1] Scaliger dismisses (cap. lxxiii, p. 129) the traditional view of person as a *substantia rationalis*. Charisius and Diomedes, followed by some Humanist grammarians, define it in these Apollonian and ultimately Stoic terms (v. Keil, *Grammatici Latini*, I, 168 and 334, and cf. H. Steinthal, *Geschichte*, II, 315).

[2] *De causis*, cap. lxxv, pp. 131–2.

[3] *Ibid.* cap. lxxvi, p. 135. This is the Aristotelian definition plus a reference to case.

latter.[1] In listing the accidents peculiar to the noun, a truly medieval zeal is shown in the establishment of a hierarchy to the detriment of formal criteria. Case, a mere formal difference, is classed as inferior to *species*, the accident governing the semantically determined sub-classes of the noun, which effects a change in *modus significationis*.[2] A clear priority of the semantic over the formal is established, enabling Scaliger to rule that an accident need not be indicated formally, as witness the three structures *homo curro*, *homo curris*, *homo currit*, where the formally unvaried nouns are of first, second and third person respectively, but the phonetic *facies* remains unchanged while the semantic *vis* is modified.[3] This smacks of special pleading, for these nouns have person by virtue of the formally marked verbs with which they stand in syntactic relationship. The emphasis on semantic content similarly leads Scaliger to treat an adjective such as *felix*, with a single gender-marking termination, as a single *vox* if *materia* (phonetic form) is taken into account, but as three separate words (respectively masculine, feminine and neuter) if *forma* (meaning) is considered.[4] These Aristotelian terms *materia* and *forma*, common in Scholastic logic, are equivalent in Scaliger's system to de Saussure's *significant* and *signifié*. They are yet another illustration of Scaliger's application to language of notions from Aristotle's philosophy, as if language, like the real world with which he supposes it to be congruent, were itself made up of substance and accident, of matter and form.

It is however in the consideration of the semantically determined sub-classes of the noun that Scaliger's Aristotelian framework is most evident. Since all that exists in the universe is either absolute or relative,[5] he begins with an overall division of nouns into relative and absolute, then further classifies each section in Aristotelian fashion into its *genera* and *species*. The *genera* of absolute substantives are five, according as they signify substance, quantity, quality, time or place. The various classes coincide to some extent with those of Roman grammar, though Scaliger rejects *generalia* and *specialia*, prominent in medieval treatises, as more appropriate to dialectics, and the Romans' *corporalia* and *incorporalia* as a merely secondary classification. The relative nouns are either substantive (*servus*) or

---

[1] Since person is in Scaliger's system an accident of all word-classes, it is of course not available as a 'necessary difference' distinguishing the pronoun.
[2] *De causis*, cap. lxxvii, p. 138. [3] *Ibid*. cap. lxxvii, pp. 136–7.
[4] *Ibid*. cap. lxxix, pp. 144–6. [5] *Ibid*. cap. xciii, p. 181.

adjective (*libertinus*). They do not however signify substance, but *essentia referendi*, and are always marks of accident. They include such nouns as *nepos* and *filius*, which the Ancients had classed as adjectives because they depend for their lexical signification on the implied existence of complementary terms (*avunculus, pater*) with which they stand in a binary relationship.[1] Formal variation in the noun is recognized by a class of *mobilia*, which in addition to the formally variable adjectives caters for word derivation. The latter is however treated in terms of semantic *affectus*, according as derivatives decrease the signification of their base forms, retain it, or augment it.

The verb is not only, following medieval practice, a mark of flux, but it also signifies *things that are* in such a way that it additionally signifies *being in itself*. While the noun can only signify *a thing which is*, the verb, as in the statement *Caesar est*, indicates *ipsum esse*. Here again, since Scaliger and medieval grammar both derive their criteria from Aristotle, he arrives at a Modistic dichotomy in which the noun signifies *per modum entis*, the verb *per modum esse*. In his remark that in the utterance *Caesar est clemens* the verb does not 'signify something' but is a 'link, by means of which clemency is predicated of Caesar',[2] there is both a recognition of the substantive verb's[3] function as a copula,[4] and a return to the Aristotelian view of the verb as making an affirmation about something. The importance of Scaliger as a precursor of Port-Royal theory would seem obvious, and there is little doubt that he is one of its sources. Rejecting the traditional definition of the verb as signifying *agere* or *pati*, the performing or the undergoing of an action – and here again he provides the model for the Port-Royal authors – he further defines it, following Aristotle, as a 'nota rei sub tempore', indicating like the noun a *res* (*curro = cursum*), but adding a time reference (*curro* = not simply *cursum*, but 'cursum nondum expletum').[5] Though *actio* and *passio* are excluded from the definition, the 'universus Verborum ambitus' is divided into verbs expressing them. The active verbs, indicating

---

[1] *Ibid.* cap. xcvii, p. 187.

[2] *Ibid.* cap. xc, p. 220: 'nota coniunctionis, qua clementia in Caesare praedicetur'.

[3] Scaliger rejects however (cap. cxii) the term *verbum substantivum*, on the grounds that this verb signifies both substance and accident.

[4] Cf. cap. cxii, where the verb in *Caesar est albus* is described as 'quasi nexum, & copulam . . . qua albedo iungeretur Caesari'.

[5] *Ibid.* cap. xciii, p. 179. Cf. Diomedes' distinction between *tempus principalis*, indicated by such nouns as *heri*, and *tempus verborum* = grammatical tense (Keil, *Grammatici Latini*, I, 335).

'id, quod facit passionem', signify both *actionem* and *actionis modum*. The passives however, which do not indicate 'id, quod recipit passionem', signify *passionem* but not *passionis modum,* which seems to imply a distinction between the semantic notion of *actio* and *passio* and the grammatical consignification of them, between, in medieval terms, *significatio* and *modus significandi*.[1]

Of the accidents or *affectus* only four – *tempus, modus, persona* and *numerus* – are essential to the nature of the verb, the two latter more especially in syntactic agreement with the noun. That Scaliger follows the traditional view of the moods as *inclinationes animi* is shown by his exclusion of the infinitive on the grounds that 'nullam animi inclinationem ostendit'.[2] The imperative he calls a 'nota animi inclinati ad eliciendum actionem aut passionem ab alio' – an almost Bloomfieldian definition according to the response elicited from the hearer. The definition could equally well apply to the optative, except that the imperative elicits the response of 'personam inferiorem', the optative that of 'personam potentiorem'. The subjunctive, curiously, is not so named because it is subordinated but because it subordinates, Scaliger holding that in the sentence *Si pugnaris, vinces* 'victoria pugnae subiungitur'.[3] This is of course a logical subordination, not a grammatical one. As the touchstone in determining mood is the semantic one of the *inclinatio animi,* any number of them – *promissivus, minativus, narrativus, precativus, coniunctivus, dubitativus, potentialis* – can be set up. The infinitive is not of itself a mood, but takes on the mood of the verb with which it is constructed.

Even in the matter of formal derivation a semantic bias is given to the treatment by a broad division of derived verbs into those which modify the *modus significationis* of the primary verb and those which do not. To the former class belong the derivatives with aspectual features such as the inchoatives, iteratives, etc. The reference to the verb's ability to vary not only in gender, conjugation, mood, meaning and number, but also in case,[4] is presumably meant to cover the gerunds, though in cap. cxliii Scaliger classes them with the participle, which is traditionally defined as partaking of the nature of both noun and verb, just as 'ex Equa & Asino fit Mulus'.[5] Presumably, if Scaliger is consistent, it must then signify both flux and

---

[1] *Ibid.* cap. cx, pp. 220–1.   [2] *Ibid.* cap. cxiiii, p. 237.
[3] *Ibid.* cap. cxiiii, p. 236.   [4] *Ibid.* cap. cxxvi, p. 254.
[5] *Ibid.* cap. lxxii, p. 124.

permanence.[1] He notes however that 'plus habet Verbi, quam Nominis', being a verb by *significatio* but a noun by *modus significationis*.[2] It is of course open to argument whether he means by *modus significationis* what medieval grammar means by *modus significandi*. If one has understood his preliminary remarks on noun and verb correctly, he must mean that the participle signifies *res quae fluunt* after the grammatical manner of those *species dictionis* which signify *res permanentes*. More light is shed on this problem by the treatment of the pronoun, which resembles the noun in both *significatio* and *modus significationis* but differs from it in *modus significandi*.[3] This would suggest that *modus significationis* and *modus significandi* are not for Scaliger synonymous terms. It is interesting to note that Thomas Aquinas uses *modus significationis* to make purely semantic distinctions, classifying words e.g. as poetic, or having a poetic or metaphorical use in a given context, the term *modus significandi* being properly grammatical.[4]

All word-classes other than verb and noun are parts of speech only by virtue of these two *principales partes* – 'ab his duabus ducerentur & ad haec reducerentur'.[5] Scaliger accordingly elicits the definition of his pronoun 'ex vi nominis', and defines it as a noun substitute 'paene totum nomen'. Noting however that the definitions of the Ancients in this sense do not permit a valid distinction between noun and pronoun, Scaliger finds this distinction in the Apollonian view of the pronoun as referring first to its noun and only indirectly to reality (it is a *notarum nota*), and in the medieval concept of the *modus significandi*. Almost identical with the noun in *significatio*, it differs from it in its three functions or *modi*.[6] In the first *modus*, it indicates

---

[1] The *Grammatica speculativa*, however, while agreeing that the participle is so called 'quasi partem Nominis, et partem Verbi capiens', emphasizes that it is wrong to describe it as signifying simultaneously *per modum entis* and *per modum esse*. It has the *modi significandi accidentales* of noun and verb, not their *modi significandi essentiales* (cap. xxxvi).

[2] *De causis*, cap. cxxvii, p. 255. In the *Grammatica speculativa* the participle signifies, like the verb, *per modum esse*. Scaliger's distinction here would seem to imply signification *per modum entis*.

[3] *Ibid.* cap. cxxvii, pp. 255, 258.

[4] In the Commentaries on the *Sententiae* of Peter Lombard (Lib. I, Distinctio 22, Q. 1, Art. 2) it is evident that Aquinas' two uses of the term *modus significationis* are to be understood in this lexical sense. In the *Summa theologica* (1ᵃ pars, Q. 39, Art. 6), however, the context makes clear that *modus significationis* and *modus significandi* are synonyms with grammatical force.

[5] *De causis*, cap. cx, p. 220. Cf. Priscian's 'aliae partes orationis non a sua vi, sed ab adiunctione, quam habent ad nomen vel verbum, vocabulum acceperunt' (H. Keil, *Grammatici Latini*, II, 551).

[6] Sulpitius (*Opusculum*, p. [5]) also has a reference to *modus* in the pronoun, but he means by it 'varia declinationis forma'.

'rem praesentem loquenti' or 'praesentem ei quicum loquitur' (*ego, tu*), but 'nullo nomine subintellecto', indicating *res ipsa* 'statim per speciem intellectui . . . non per nomen'.[1] This would seem to fly in the face of his earlier assertion that the pronoun refers first of all to *ipsum nomen* and only secondarily to *res ipsa*, but it is presumably intended to keep this use of the pronoun apart from that in the third *modus*, in which pronouns act not merely as noun substitutes, but function together with a noun 'ut ipsum repraesentant', as in *Ego Caesar*.[2] In the second *modus*, they are used as noun substitutes 'ut relativa'. One may compare here the *Grammatica speculativa*'s view of the demonstrative pronouns as indicating things present *ad sensum* or *ad intellectum*. The former type of pronoun signifies directly that which it points out. The second 'hoc quod demonstrat non significat, sed aliud'.[3]

For Scaliger the division into substantive and adjective is not an *affectio* or *differentia* of the noun as such, but in its quality as *dictio*.[4] It is therefore equally available to the pronoun, where there is a distinction between pronouns like *is* in 'is color' which signify *per modum substantiae*,[5] and those like *meus* which signify *per modum accidentis*. Scaliger fails to make a valid distinction between *is* in pronominal and in adjectival function, and perpetuates the confusion of semantic and formal criteria that caused the Ancients to regard their *nomina ad aliquid* (*pater, filius, servus*, etc.) as adjectives[6] signifying possession but only *con*signifying substance. It is by an identical semantic process, ignoring formal markers,[7] that Scaliger comes to the conclusion that *meus* is an adjective: 'significat possessionem, & consignificat substantiam'.[8] He has sub-classes of *relativa substantiae* and *relativa accidentis*, with a medieval insistence that the classification

---

[1] *De causis*, cap. cxxvii, p. 259. Cf. Priscian's view of *ego* and *tu* as *demonstrativa*, of *ille* etc. as *relativa*.

[2] How this differs in *modus significandi* from nominal structures such as *Caesar victor* is not explained.

[3] Cap. xxii.   [4] *De causis*, cap. cxxvii, p. 260.

[5] Scaliger points out that in 'is color' *is* signifies both substance and accidence, but is not by grammatical function an adjective (per *modum* accidentis): 'tametsi color in corpore est, tamen non indicatur quatenus est in corpore' (*De causis*, cap. xxvii, p. 259).

[6] So also the *Grammatica speculativa* (cap. xii), which placed these nouns under its nineteenth *modus adjacentis*.

[7] Scaliger does however have a later note to the effect that 'Primitiva substantialia sunt, Derivata accidentalia' (cap. cxxx – first of two sections so numbered – p. 276).

[8] *De causis*, cap. cxxvii, p. 259. One may compare here Priscian's remark (H. Keil, *Grammatici Latini*, II, 588) that the possessives 'qualitatem ipsius possessionis non declarant, nisi adiungas nomen'.

rests on grammatical function, on the *modus significandi*. Though *qui, is* and the other *relativa substantiae* may well *signify* accident, they consignify substance *per modum substantiae*. *Qualis* is similarly a *relativum accidentis* by grammatical function: 'significat accidens ut est in substantia'.[1] Scaliger is perhaps inhibited from classing certain pronouns as completely adjectival (e.g. *qui*, as in the *Grammatica speculativa*) by memories of Priscian's view of them as signifying 'substantiam infinitam'.

As we have seen, Scaliger resembles Linacre in counting person as an accident of both noun and pronoun. The *modus personarum* is not however the same in the two word-classes. Whereas in the noun all cases except the vocative can express all three persons, each *pronomen primitivum* can signify one person only.[2] The Ancients were therefore in error in holding that the noun only consignifies person, while the pronoun signifies it, or that the pronoun determines 'certam personam' whereas the noun does not.[3] 'Aliud est significare, aliud consignificare' says Scaliger, quoting from medieval grammar and underlining a truth lost sight of in most sixteenth-century and virtually all seventeenth-century grammars. Since it has the *significatio* of a noun and substitutes for it, 'ego' *signifies* person. But since it is not *variable* for person, it only *consignifies* first person, and on these grounds Scaliger seems ready to deny the accident *person* to the pronoun.[4]

Noun and verb are for Scaliger *partes principales* forming a proposition, and he accordingly reinstates the Aristotelian view of the verb as signifying 'aliquid, quod significato nominis adiiciatur'.[5] Pronoun and participle are then treated as close in definition to these two. Adverbs are treated as 'modi, qualitatesque temperandae' of verbs,[6] adverbs of time differing from verbs in not signifying time 'propter modum significandi'. Similarly, prepositions declare the *modi* of nouns, or those *causarum modi* which the nouns, being *nota causarum naturae*, cannot signify.[7] Conjunctions are justified on the rational grounds that those things which in the real world are a unified whole must so be represented in language. With the principal

---

[1] *Ibid.* cap. cxxvii, p. 259. One should note however that the *Grammatica speculativa* (cap. xii) counts both *qui* and *qualis* as *adiectiva*.

[2] *De causis*, cap. cxxxiii, p. 278.

[3] Cf. *ibid.* cap. cxxvii, p. 260, where Scaliger points out that nouns in the vocative signify 'certam personam', but *ille, ipse*, etc., 'non certam'.

[4] *Ibid.* cap. lxxvi, p. 136.   [5] *Ibid.* cap. cxlii, p. 288.

[6] *Ibid.* cap. lxxii, pp. 125–6.   [7] *Ibid.* cap. lxxii, p. 125.

word-classes signifying *causarum natura*, and adverb and preposition (regarded as a *species media* between the main classes and the rest) *causarum modi*, the 'universus rerum ambitus, modusque' is thus linguistically covered. There remain, outside this scheme, those words (the interjections) signifying 'animorum affectus'. Syntax receives no separate treatment but, in so far as it is discussed, is dealt with as it arises in the consideration of each word-class.

The use Scaliger makes of Aristotelian features may now be briefly recapitulated. Following Aristotle, he is a mentalist for whom words represent concepts in the mind which in turn correspond to phenomena in the world of things. He returns to the medieval notion, implicit in Aristotle, of the linguistic sign with its twin facets of form and meaning, its *significant* and *significate*. In discussing these two facets, he uses the Aristotelian philosophical concepts of *materia* (substance) and *forma* (accident), in the sense 'phonetic structure' and 'semantic content'. This use of these terms was however current in Scholastic grammar, the *Grammatica speculativa*[1] noting that the definition of verbal voice (*genus*) according to first personal endings in *-o* (active) and *-or* (passive) 'non est formalis, sed materialis'.[2] Allied to this is the use of the concepts of substance and accident, of primary importance in the Aristotelian world-view. The *dictio* or word, partly *materialis* and partly *formalis*, parallels the substance/ accident dichotomy in the real world. Further, as a linguistic sign, it is a *rerum nota*, with a correspondence to things in the universe. All things, since words constitute their *notae*, must have their exact parallel in language, which thus mirrors the world, ideally covering the whole sum of phenomena, the *universus rerum ambitus*. Aristotle's cosmology being founded on causation, the principal word-classes (noun and verb) must signify *causarum natura*, while adverb and pre-position signify *causarum modi*. The hierarchy of being is reflected in a linguistic hierarchy, words corresponding to the *res*, and word-classes to the *species*, of the real world. The division of phenomena into *res permanentes* and *res fluentes* has its corresponding division in language where, in medieval fashion, the noun signifies permanence and the verb flux. Scaliger's treatment of noun and verb as principal word-classes, and of the rest as *syncategoremata*, parts of speech only by

[1] Cap. xxx.
[2] This example is taken at random. The use of the terms *materialiter* (formally) and *formaliter* (semasiologically) is fairly frequent in the *Grammatica speculativa*.

virtue of these two, is equally Aristotelian, as is the view that the verb, apart from the signification of flux as opposed to permanence, differs from the noun only in the consignification of time. More important in view of later grammatical theory, particularly that of the Port-Royal Grammar, is Scaliger's reintroduction, via the medieval notion of the use of the verb 'to be' as a copula,[1] of the Aristotelian concept of predication. As so often happens, grammatical features whose origin has customarily been attributed to Port-Royal are in fact present, at least in germ, in much earlier work.

Similarly, Scaliger takes from Aristotle his system of *classification* of phenomena and applies it to language. What is common to several word-classes (e.g. *person*) is treated before the discussion of each separate word-class, in accordance with the Aristotelian logical principle of arguing from the general to the particular. Seventeenth-century thought, led by Bacon, proceeds rather by the method of induction, passing from the observation of particular cases to the general law governing them, but Scaliger is writing long before this revolution in scientific thought. Everything in his system must be classified, following Aristotle's predicables, into *genera, species, differentiae* (marking off the word-classes from each other) and *accidentia*, with an attempt to achieve an exact symmetry by providing every word-class with the same accidents. A semasiological hierarchy is established, *casus* being inferior to *species*, a 'materiae affectio' (formal difference) being inferior to a semantic distinction. In this way, Scaliger confirms the primacy of semasiological criteria over formal ones already established by the early Humanists. In turn, the *genera* of, for example, the substantive are classified according to their signification of substance, quantity, quality, time and place, i.e. according to the Aristotelian categories or predicaments. *Actio* and *passio*, as predicaments corresponding, like all the others, to realities in the universe, play an important part in the discussion of the verb. The doctrine that everything in the real world is *absolute* or *relative* must have its counterpart in a series of absolute and relative categories in language. Once again, with Scaliger, 'Grammatica est de signis rerum', and all *res* together with their logical classification must be provided with their counterpart in grammar.

[1] When Scaliger notes that every verb can be resolved into the verb 'to be' plus participle (*amat = est amans*), he is simply repeating medieval and early Humanist tradition as it is given for instance in the works of Despauterius (v. p. 47 above).

The break with tradition: Scaliger

Scaliger is the first grammarian of importance to diverge seriously from what had been up to 1540 the general trend – the presentation of the Roman grammatical tradition in its original form unalloyed by the reinterpretations of the Schoolmen. By 1540 this Humanist trend is losing its impetus and being challenged by the forces of rationalism. Scaliger sets out to found a rational system based on pre-Scholastic Aristotelian philosophy, but since the *Grammatica speculativa* is also based on Aristotle, it is often difficult to determine what in Scaliger's work is taken direct from Aristotle and what he owes to the *Modistae*. In this respect he is still very much a man of the Renaissance. What is new is his preoccupation with methodology, and here Scaliger stands at the beginning of a trend which ultimately leads to the Port-Royal Grammar and the 'philosophical grammars' of the seventeenth and eighteenth centuries. Since he defines the end of grammar as 'recte loqui', but examines each point of received doctrine afresh with the aim of instituting a 'communem rationem loquendi' professedly based on usage,[1] he stands at a crossroads in Renaissance thought. His Aristotelian interests involve him in medieval questions such as the nature of the linguistic sign; he is caught up in the Renaissance cult of usage; and he looks ahead to the seventeenth century in his search for a *ratio*, a philosophical basis on which to build his grammar. In reading his work, one has the impression that language is a system, over and above the vagaries and intricacies of usage. For the first time in a Humanist grammar, *usus* gives ground to *ratio*, the customary normative inventory of facts gives place to a recognition that behind discourse (de Saussure's *parole*) there lie pre-existent mental operations, the *causae*, which condition the linguistic system (de Saussure's *langue*). One begins to see how much the Port-Royal Grammar, with its emphasis on 'les opérations de notre esprit', owes to Scaliger.[2]

Though it was a weakness of Scaliger's system that it limited philosophical speculation to one language, Latin, thus contributing to the isolation of classical philological studies, it remains true that his hylomorphic approach had an influence far outside Latin scholarship, his philosophically based system being taken over by vernacular philologists, particularly in their diachronic study of the Romance

---

[1] *De causis*, cap. clxxvi, p. 136.
[2] It is however highly probable that Scaliger is indebted to Linacre at several points.

languages.[1] Certainly, he may be considered a forerunner of the seventeenth-century attempts to produce a grammar based solely on philosophical principles. That this movement had its roots in the preceding century is equally demonstrated by the *Quaestiones grammaticae* (1584) of the German Nicodemus Frischlin, who requires grammarians to be well versed in Aristotle: 'scire enim, est rem ex suis causis cognoscere'.[2] The approach is obviously based on Scaliger, whom Frischlin follows closely throughout. The interest of his work, in view of later developments in grammatical theory, lies in those parts of Scaliger's doctrine he chooses to underline or amplify, more particularly his insistence on the status of the word as a 'nota earum notionum, quae sunt in anima',[3] a 'nota unius speciei, quae est in animo'.[4] This last definition repeats the medieval doctrine, to which we shall return later, of (innate?) *species* within the mind. For the present, it may be underlined that the notion of 'innate ideas' in the mind, far from beginning with Descartes, is already present in medieval philosophy and, by implication, in the work of Scaliger, whom the Port-Royal authors name as one of their sources. N. Chomsky, in his eagerness to establish Cartesian antecedents for the Port-Royal Grammar,[5] has overlooked an entire medieval and Humanist tradition that lies behind this grammar. But this is a matter to which we shall return when discussing Port-Royal and late seventeenth-century mentalist attitudes. Suffice it to point out here that these views of Scaliger and Frischlin antedate by a century or so the Port-Royal doctrine of words as signs not of immediate reality, but of intermediary concepts in the mind. At the same time, Frischlin is careful to maintain Scaliger's distinction between grammarian and logician, the former considering an utterance 'sub modo constructionis' (i.e. formally and syntactically), the latter 'sub ratione veritatis'.[6] This distinction is also destined to be jettisoned by the seventeenth century, which increasingly equates grammar with logic. This insistence on the part of Frischlin and Scaliger leads us

---

[1] v. R. Faithfull, review of *Taal en Functionaliteit*, p. 148. Hylomorphic assumptions were, as Faithfull remarks, replaced by genetico-functional assumptions in nineteenth-century linguistics, assumptions which finally brought about the breakdown of the Scaligerian system.

[2] *Quaestionum grammaticarum Libri XII*, Venice, 1584, preface.

[3] *Ibid.* p. 2. [4] *Ibid.* p. 72. This is Scaliger's definition.

[5] v. his *Cartesian Linguistics: A Chapter in the History of Rationalist Thought*, New York, 1966.

[6] *Quaestionum grammaticarum*, pp. 2–3.

however quite naturally to a consideration of the next major figure in the history of grammatical theory, and to a period when it seemed, for a time at any rate, as if a grammar based on purely formal principles might well be set up.

RAMUS

At the time Scaliger wrote his *De causis*, and indeed for many years to come, Aristotle was firmly entrenched in the universities as *the* authority on philosophy and logic. In 1585 Oxford University required all bachelors and undergraduates to 'lay aside their various Authors . . . and only follow Aristotle and those that defend him'. According to P. Rossi, who cites this observation by Anthony à Wood,[1] the regulation was directed less against the Scotists and Ockhamist Nominalists who still pullulated at Oxford, than against the rabidly anti-Aristotelian followers of Peter Ramus, who however never achieved at Oxford the footing they had at Cambridge. It none the less illustrates the continued importance of Aristotle in the university curriculum, though from the time of Roger Bacon on there had been sporadic attempts by scholars such as Valla and Vives to break out of the Aristotelian straitjacket. Usually considered as the archetype of this rebellion is Pierre de la Ramée (1515–72), who in accordance with general practice among scholars of the day Latinized his name to Ramus. He published in Paris, for so long a centre of Scholasticism, a number of works aimed at purifying and revivifying the teaching of the liberal arts. *Dialecticae partitiones*, a logical treatise, appeared in 1543 and an attack on Aristotle, the *Aristotelicae animadversiones*, in the same year. The important *Dialectique*, the first work on logic in the French language, appeared in 1555, and a Latin version, the *Dialectica*, in 1556. Ramus also turned his attention to grammar, producing in the *Scholae in liberales artes* (1559)[2] a closely argued justification of his grammatical theory, and in his *Grammatica*[3] (also 1559) a practical embodiment of the theory without explanatory material.[4] The latter

[1] Anthony à Wood, *The History and Antiquities of the University of Oxford*, ed. J. Cutch, Oxford, 1792–6, II, 226; v. P. Rossi, *Francis Bacon*, p. 40.

[2] *P. Rami Scholae in liberales artes*, Basle, 1578, is the edition used here.

[3] Consulted here in *Petri Rami . . . Grammatica. Aliquot in locis aucta et emendata*, Frankfurt, 1576.

[4] A concise version of the *Grammatica* in question and answer form, the *Rudimenta grammaticae Latinae*, also appeared in 1559.

was translated into English in 1585, and Ramus acquired a following in Puritanical circles in Britain,[1] more particularly in Scotland and at Cambridge. His *Grammaire*, an attempt to apply his theories to the vernacular, appeared anonymously in 1562, followed by a second edition a decade later. All three grammars were frequently reprinted during the remainder of the century, but without noteworthy changes. Reference will be made here to the *Scholae*, supported where necessary by the *Grammatica*.[2]

In 1536 Ramus achieved great notoriety by defending a thesis at the University of Paris – the stronghold of Aristotelianism – contending that 'quaecumque ab Aristotele dicta essent commentitia esse' ('all Aristotle's doctrines are false'). Later commentators have however exaggerated his anti-Aristotelianism, for in actual practice Ramus tended to adaptation rather than outright rejection of Aristotle. But there can be no doubt that his rash and truculent attitude, together with the charges of obscurity made against the philosopher in the *Aristotelicae animadversiones*, earned him bitter enemies among the 'establishment'. A royal decree of 1544, describing him as 'rash, arrogant, and impudent', forbade him to teach philosophy,[3] but thanks no doubt to his powerful patron the Cardinal of Lorraine he later held posts at the University's Collège de Presles, and as professor of eloquence and philosophy at the newly founded Collège des Lecteurs Royaux. This college encountered bitter opposition from the University. In northern Europe Humanism, increasingly allied as it was to movements for the moral improvement of society, had come to be identified to a large extent with Protestantism and religious reform. More particularly in the German-speaking countries, the Renaissance and the Reformation were 'but different phases of the same movement'.[4] Ramus taught at a time of internecine religious conflict, and was ultimately forced to admit publicly his adherence to Protestantism. In opposition to all this, monolithic and seemingly immovable, were the reactionary forces of Scholasti-

---

[1] v. O. Funke, 'Grammatica Anglicana von P. Gr[eaves]. (1594)', *Wiener Beiträge zur englischen Philologie*, LX (1938), p. xiii.

[2] In treating the background to Ramus' theories I am above all indebted to P. A. Duhamel, 'The Logic and Rhetoric of Peter Ramus', *Modern Philology*, XLVI (1949), pp. 163–71; F. P. Graves, *Petrus Ramus and the Educational Reformation of the Sixteenth Century*, New York, 1912; and the already cited W. S. Howell, *Logic and Rhetoric*, W. and M. Kneale, *The Development of Logic*, and P. Rossi, *Francis Bacon*.

[3] This decree was revoked in 1547.

[4] v. F. P. Graves, *Petrus Ramus*, pp. 5–8.

cism and Aristotelianism in the University. Ramus finally paid the price of his views when he was assassinated by the mob at the time of the St Bartholomew massacre.

At the period when Ramus began to take an active part in the polemics of the day, the Humanist movement was beginning to degenerate into mere Ciceronian formalism, and the time was ripe for intellectual and educational reform. Ramus accordingly undertook a programme of revivification of the traditional liberal arts of grammar and rhetoric, set out to put logic on a new basis, and campaigned for the teaching of Latin and Greek by literary rather than Scholastic logical methods.[1] In the quest for a renewal of the bases of learning, a fundamental theme runs through the works of Humanist thinkers such as Valla – with his penchant for exegesis – and Erasmus:

The demand for a less 'quibbling' form of discourse reflected a yearning for integral texts and simple faith exemplified in England by Tyndale, Colet, and More, but also expressed by Ramus and most critics of Scholasticism who said that scientific and religious renovation were inseparable, for the renewal of contact with nature through experiment coincided with a return to the true word of God.[2]

These words of P. Rossi well express the moral and religious preoccupations of Protestant Humanists such as Ramus, preoccupations which in turn led to an emphasis on practical problems of rhetoric and education reflecting the needs of contemporary society. Religious persuasion required a new plain rhetoric and a practical logic, and it is not surprising that in England, in response to the needs of a whole new class of lawyers and public propagandists and in conjunction with the drive for plain speaking in the pulpit, rhetoric became in the seventeenth century a major subject in the schools. Ramus devoted less effort to rhetoric than to the reform of logic. One of his chief concerns was to halt the widespread mutual contamination of logic and rhetoric. In discussing Renaissance communication theory it is important, following W. S. Howell, to keep in mind 'the conviction of Renaissance learning that logic and rhetoric are the two great arts of communication, and that the complete theory of communication is largely identified with both'.[3] Ramus, in his search for criteria in delimiting the boundaries of each art or science, seeks above

---

[1] v. R. H. Robins, *Short History*, p. 102.   [2] P. Rossi, *Francis Bacon*, p. 63.
[3] *Logic and Rhetoric*, p. 4.

all to keep these two apart, to ensure that what is taught in rhetoric is not repeated in logic, and vice-versa.

In spite of his anti-Aristotelian reputation, it is interesting to note that he claims to base his criteria for keeping the sciences separate from each other on Aristotle. He lays down that nothing should be included in a science (or *art*, as he calls it) unless it is universally true and unless it is homogeneous with the other components of the science. Further, all classification within a science should proceed from the general to the particular. *Generalia* must not be treated *speciatim*, nor *specialia generatim*, a rule already meticulously applied, as we have seen, by J. C. Scaliger. These requirements are in fact a development of the three laws, rendered by Latin commentators as *de omni*, *per se*, and *universaliter primum*, given in Aristotle's *Posterior Analytics*, where however they are applied to the predicates of logical propositions.[1] They lie behind Ramus' celebrated three rules – the rule of truth and certainty, the rule of justice, and the rule of wisdom – which were indefatigably applied by his followers in deciding what to include in or exclude from a particular science. Earlier in the century J. L. Vives had already posited a reform of the 'corruption of the arts'. Ramus' more thoroughgoing attempt strictly required each branch of learning to stay within its own bounds and not contaminate others. The result of his application of these principles was not altogether a happy one. In practice, he saw logic as the chief means of choosing and arranging material for public speaking,[2] with the result that rhetoric came increasingly to be regarded – and condemned by seventeenth-century empiricists – as a mere added ornament to the matter under discussion. Ciceronian rhetoric as commonly practised had consisted of the five operations invention (i.e. discovery of the subject matter), arrangement, style, memory and delivery. Invention and arrangement were also traditional operations of logic, but with Ramus' insistence on no two arts teaching the same body of knowledge, and the consequent confinement of these two topics to logic, rhetoric tended to be limited to style and delivery.[3] Though Ciceronian rhetoric continued to exert an influence

---

[1] v. W. S. Howell, *Logic and Rhetoric*, pp. 41–2. These concepts may be rendered as *universality, homogeneity*, and *primacy of the general*.

[2] Cf. *Dialectique de Pierre de la Ramée*, Paris, 1555, pp. 3–4: 'Aristote a voulu faire deux Logiques, l'une pour la science, l'autre pour l'opinion, en quoy il a tresgrandement erré . . . Dialectique ou Logique est une & mesme doctrine pour apercevoir toutes choses.'

[3] Ramus divided the *artes logicae* into *dialectica* (i.e. logic), consisting of *inventio* and *dispositio*, and *retorica*, consisting of *elocutio* and *pronuntiatio*.

right to the end of the period 1500–1700, the existence of a separate art of oratory was thus increasingly in doubt. On the other hand, by his reduction of the arts to a few principles Ramus 'made logic readily available to, and employed by, a large group of people and filled the world with logic-choppers',[1] so that even Bacon, in his *Temporis partus masculus,* cries out against 'that most dangerous of all literary corroders who constricts and distorts reality with his narrow method and his summaries'.

As the history of grammatical theory is so closely bound up with that of logic, it is important to know something of the developments that took place in logical studies during the period under consideration. In spite of the Humanists' reaction against the primacy of logic, to which they preferred rhetoric and the rule of usage, there was no sudden break between the Middle Ages and the Renaissance as far as logic was concerned. Treatises such as Peter of Spain's *Summulae logicales* were still being studied in the seventeenth century.[2] The subject was so closely identified with Latin studies that writers of early logical treatises in the vernacular felt obliged to apologize for the use of their native tongue. Ralph Lever, in the 'forespeache' to his *Arte of Reason,*[3] argues that 'English men have wits, as wel as other nations have', but in his anxiety to prove his point and avoid 'straunge and inckhorne termes' (i.e. Latin loanwords), he goes to the opposite extreme of inventing native English compounds such as *witcraft* for logic, and *backset* for predicate. This work, almost ready for the press in 1551, and Thomas Wilson's *Rule of Reason* of the same year, are the first English vernacular logics. They are traditional works based on Aristotle, and would not have been disowned by the Scholastics the Humanist tradition was supposedly in revolt against. As W. and M. Kneale have pointed out,[4] the Humanists' objection to medieval logic (as opposed to grammar) was not so much to its content as to its quibbling aridity and the barbarity of the Latin in which it was couched.

Scholastic logic was much concerned with the problem of definition and division, that is to say with scientific method, a question which was to become of central importance in the seventeenth-century

---

[1] P. A. Duhamel, 'Logic and Rhetoric of Peter Ramus', p. 171.
[2] v. W. and M. Kneale, *The Development of Logic,* p. 298. For some of the details given here I am indebted both to this work and to W. S. Howell, *Logic and Rhetoric.*
[3] *The Arte of Reason, Rightly Termed, Witcraft, Teaching a Perfect Way to Argue and Dispute,* London, 1573.   [4] *Development of Logic,* p. 300.

enquiries of Bacon and Descartes and which, in view of the post-1540 attempt to make grammar fit into a *ratio* or method, is important in any consideration of grammatical theory. The twin poles of this Scholastic system, which constitute the organizing principle of Aristotle's *Topics*, were invention, and judgment or disposition. Chiefly responsible for popularizing this bipartite division of logic was Rudolph Agricola (1443–85), professor of philosophy at Heidelberg and author of the influential *De inventione dialectica*, who 'was instrumental in inducing logicians of the sixteenth century to adopt Aristotle's *Topics* rather than other treatises of the *Organon* as guide to the main divisions of logical theory'.[1]

Invention concerns itself with the discovery of subject matter, judgment or disposition with its arrangement. Somewhat illogically – and Wilson's *Rule of Reason* is no exception to this – judgment was usually treated by Scholastic logicians before invention. W. S. Howell finds this procedure no mere accident, but an indication that the society which practises it 'is satisfied with its traditional wisdom and knows where to find it'. The great changes in thought which occur between 1500 and 1700 are in part 'a shift from the preponderant emphasis upon traditional wisdom to the preponderant emphasis upon new discoveries'.[2] The Humanists had performed the immense task of assembling the accumulated wisdom of the Classical Age, and performed it well. But as the end of the sixteenth century drew nearer, men were increasingly reluctant to base their thinking about the universe on this accumulated wisdom, preferring the more empirical basis of the direct observation of reality. Ramus' concern however, at his particular point in time, was to ensure that training in invention and arrangement should be the province of logic alone, without help from rhetoric, and that questions of method should be discussed solely under the heading of arrangement. Much of his criticism of Aristotle turns on the fact that the latter did not respect the boundaries of the sciences, nor always follow the rule that the general be taught before the particular. Where Ramus strikes a more modern note is in his insistence that invention must precede arrangement, the collection of data being an essential prerequisite to the exercise of judgment, an insistence that paves the way for later

[1] W. S. Howell, *Logic and Rhetoric*, p. 16.
[2] *Ibid.* pp. 23–4. Note the distinction in Aristotle's *Topics* between dialectical reasoning from generally accepted opinions, and demonstrative reasoning from primary premises.

empiricism with its emphasis on the collection of facts on which to base induction. More remarkable is the complete absence from his system of the Aristotelian predicaments and predicables. The place occupied in traditional systems by the five predicables as criteria for delimiting the boundaries of the sciences is usurped in Ramus' system by his 'three rules'.

In his *Aristotelicae animadversiones*, Ramus praises Plato for the simplicity and practical nature of his dialectic, a simplicity which the later corruption of the arts had destroyed. Here again, in his Platonism and in his emphasis on practicality, Ramus strikes a seventeenth-century note. Marsilio Ficino's translation of Plato, begun in 1463, had already, via the Italian academies, spread Platonic ideas abroad. But it is Ramus who, according to R. R. Bolgar, 'deserves credit for having been the first Western thinker to claim a technical understanding of Platonism'.[1] Certainly, there are distinctly Platonic features in Ramus' thought, he himself for instance attributing to Plato the typically Ramistic system of division into dichotomies. The *Aristotelicae animadversiones* declares that 'the art of dialectic should proceed from the imitation and observation of the dialectic of nature',[2] logic being an *imago naturalis dialecticae*, and that it is precisely the failure to imitate nature that constitutes a major defect in Aristotelian thought.[3] Nature, method and practice, the *natura, ratio, exercitatio* of the *Dialecticae partitiones*, are cardinal tenets of Ramus' system. On the level of logic these correspond to the faculty of reason (there is a 'natural logic' in the mind), the establishing of rules, and the formation of habits in accordance with these rules.[4] The aim of the natural sciences is the study of nature. Ramus' Platonism (perhaps via Platonism's offspring Italian nature philosophy) and his anti-Aristotelianism both point to the seventeenth-century preoccupation with natural phenomena as the basis for intellectual inquiry. Science is founded on experience – 'experientia quidem artem genuit' – says Ramus in the *Scholae*. Rules are based on observation.

We should expect to find these precepts of Ramus reflected in his treatment of grammar, and this is indeed the case. At a time when

---

[1] *The Classical Heritage*, p. 288.
[2] *Aristotelicae animadversiones*, Paris, 1543, f. 3ᵛ: 'ars enim dialectica debet ab imitatione & observatione naturalis dialecticae proficisci'.
[3] *Ibid.* f. 4ᵛ: 'in commentariis autem Aristotelis nihil est ad naturae monitionem propositum . . . ars igitur dialectica in commentariis Aristotelis nulla est'.
[4] *Scholae*, preface. v. P. Rossi, *Francis Bacon*, p. 174.

medieval methods and textbooks, including Alexander's *Doctrinale*, still held almost complete sway in Paris, when Valla's *Elegantiae* was almost unknown and the only Humanist grammatical work to have made any headway was Despauterius' *Rudimenta*, Ramus' grammar must have appeared revolutionary. It is curious that, though every other aspect of Ramus' thought, particularly his logic and his importance for education, seem to have been treated by scholars at one time or another, his grammatical achievement has been allowed to sink into oblivion. When it *is* mentioned, as for example by O. Funke,[1] it is in connection with his imitators Paul Greaves and Ben Jonson, who attempted to apply his grammatical theories to the English vernacular. The revolutionary qualities of Ramus' grammar consist however not so much in its strict application of Aristotelian principles to the methodology, as in the uncompromisingly formal approach of the grammatical theory, an approach which has led some to label him the father of structuralism.

In accordance with his dicta that every art must have its proper and practical aim (logic e.g. is the 'art de bien disputer')[2] and that the most general statements in its description must precede the less general, he begins by defining grammar in Scaliger's terms as 'ars bene loquendi',[3] the art of speaking well. The next most general statement in the hierarchy is that grammar consists of the two parts *etymology* (i.e. morphology) and *syntax*, and so Ramus continues, multiplying dichotomies as he moves further from the general and nearer to the particular. The philological preoccupations reflected in the ancient subdivision *grammatica exegetice* are significantly absent from his grammar.[4] The grammarian's material is not to be found in the poets, and even the use of prose authors can result in 'falsa testimonia' through a bad choice of examples.[5] The importance of usage is established, Ramus following Quintilian's view that 'nec lex est loquendi, sed observatio'. His quotation of Quintilian's definition of usage as founded on the common agreement of the learned (the *consensus eruditorum*) is however supported by his insistence, contrary to his earlier emphasis on the spoken language, that the precepts of good Latin are to be sought in the writings of Cicero

---

[1] v. Funke's article 'Grammatica Anglicana von P. Gr[eaves]. (1594)', cited above, and his 'Ben Jonsons *English Grammar* (1640)', *Anglia*, LXIV (1940), pp. 117–34.
[2] *Dialectique*, p. 1.   [3] *Scholae*, col. 8.
[4] Cf. *ibid.* col. 13, where he explicitly rejects this subdivision.
[5] *Ibid.* col. 5.

and Varro. Finally, that 'nobilissima bibliotheca' Priscian's grammar is to be studied for the excellence of the authors it cites, though its grammatical doctrines must be revised in the light of Aristotelian logic.[1]

True to his view that the aim of science is the study of nature, Ramus insists that the material for linguistic analysis must be taken from usage. The intellectual framework within which the subject matter is considered must however be based on *ratio*, and he quotes Varro to the effect that whereas the individual speaker must follow usage, the latter must follow reason. The relationship between what goes on in the mind (mental 'affections'), and actual utterance or discourse, was to be, as V. Salmon points out in her review of N. Chomsky's *Cartesian Linguistics*, a topic of discussion among linguists and logicians for centuries. As she mentions, these two concepts of internal discourse (*verbum mentis*) and external discourse (*verbum oris*) were already well known in the sixteenth century, predating by over a hundred years the Port-Royal Grammar's preoccupation with such matters. The roots of these concepts are of course already present in medieval theory, and indeed go back to Priscian's *mentis conceptum* and beyond him to the Greeks. Without going so far as to establish a dichotomy between language as a mental system and its actualization in discourse (de Saussure's *langue–parole* dichotomy), Ramus notes that *ratio* (reason) is one thing, and *sermo* (discourse) another, though reason is expressed in speech.[2]

Ramus holds that grammar in common with other sciences must be treated according to the logical criteria *de omni, per se*, and *universaliter primum*. The latter requirement, the treatment of the universally valid at the outset, is violated by traditional grammarians, who instead of dealing first with the general and then with its *species subiectae*, set up the three parts *etymologia, prosodia* and *orthographia*. Ramus recommends instead a binary division into *etymologia* and *syntaxis*, prosody and orthography being not separate parts, but rather running through the whole of grammar 'ut sanguis & spiritus per universum corpus'. Those grammatical features which are common to all word-classes should be set forth at the beginning of a grammar, not repeated for each separate part of speech. Similarly,

---

[1] *Ibid.* cols. 9–10.
[2] v. V. Salmon, review of N. Chomsky, *Cartesian Linguistics*, New York, 1966, in *Journal of Linguistics*, 5 (1969), pp. 174–5.

features such as gender or declension which are common to a group of word-classes should be treated as *generales* to that group rather than *speciales* to each individual word-class. The similarity to Scaliger's Aristotelian approach is apparent. Equally Aristotelian is Ramus' division of the word-classes into the two *genera* κατηγόρημα and σύνδεσμος, the former divided into the *species* noun and verb and the latter into the *species* adverb and conjunction, thus giving a four-word-class system, prepositions and interjections receiving a subordinate status as *adverbia vel adjectiva* of the other classes. The traditional systems of from five to ten word-classes are rejected as not conformable to Aristotle's logic. Further subclassification of the parts of speech must equally follow the dictates of *universaliter primum*, though Ramus admits that only by the application of analogy can the rules of grammar be brought completely under the sway of this *lex catholica*.[1]

Ramus' division of the word-classes is thus seen to be semantically based and to depend, together with the framework of his grammar, on Aristotle. Equally semasiological is the somewhat inept definition of the word (*vox*) as a 'mark by which something is named'.[2] The semantic basis of these preliminary classifications is all the more surprising in view of the uncompromising formalism of the rest of the grammatical system. It depends, it is true, on the Aristotelian and medieval notion of the consignification of a grammatical meaning elicited 'ex iis non quae significantur, sed quae adsignificantur',[3] an approach identical with that of Scaliger. The latter had noted that the grammarian, unlike the logician, is concerned with matters of formal structure, but had then proceeded to write a grammar conceived almost entirely in semantic terms. Where Ramus makes a completely new departure is in his insistence that grammatical meanings are determined formally by morphological elements ('e vocum ipsarum finibus'), and in his declared intention to reject any grammatical feature which is not signalled by these elements. At the same time, however, he notes that the grammarian who knows

---

[1] *Scholae*, col. 6.

[2] *Grammatica*, p. 5: 'nota qua unumquodque vocatur'. Cf. R. H. Robins, 'Some considerations on the status of grammar in linguistics', *Archivum linguisticum*, II (1959), p. 100: '. . . the two fundamental entities of grammar, the word and the morpheme, can be established without any reference to semantic meaning, except in so far as in all linguistic analysis . . . we must assume, or know somehow, that the material we are dealing with is all meaningful discourse'.

[3] *Scholae*, col. 5.

no logic is more likely to fall into serious error than the logician who does not know his grammar.[1] The formally determined grammatical categories must be classified within a rigorous logical framework. The Roman grammarians' proliferating series of semantically based *nomina propria* and *appellativa*, etc., and their basing of categories such as mood on a *mentis conceptum* or *inclinatio animi*, are rejected as incompatible both with this logical approach and with the requirement that grammatical meanings must be formally signalled.

In accordance with this rigorous approach, Ramus retains only the categories number, gender, comparison, case, person and tense, all of which have corresponding formal markers in noun or verb. On this purely formal basis he sets up two *genera* of the *vox* or word, the *genus numeri* and the *genus sine numero*. The traditional division of the parts of speech into declinables and indeclinables he rejects on the grounds that adverbs 'flecti possunt in nomina' (*cras/crastinus*). This Varronian view of inflection as including derived forms clearly provides an insufficient basis for distinguishing the word-classes, and Ramus prefers to it number as the feature most obviously present in some parts of speech but absent in others.[2] In the *Grammatica*, however, he finds that his division into *voces numeri* and *voces sine numero* does not entirely fit the facts of word inflection. As certain words which he wishes to term *voces numeri* are formally invariable, he has to introduce a further dichotomy of *voces numeri finitae* inflected 'certis finibus' (*doctus*, *legit*) and invariable *voces infinitae* (*nequam*, *amare*).[3] This division cuts right across one of his major dichotomies, that of *voces numeri nominales* and *verbales*, and it is difficult to see how he can justify on other than semasiological grounds the inclusion of the *voces infinitae* in the noun and verb classes, shorn as they are of the formal markers necessary for the status of *voces numeri*.

Ramus defends the dichotomy of his system of *voces numeri* and *sine numero* by likening it to Aristotle's system of κατηγορήματα and σύνδεσμοι,[4] and regrets that the Roman grammarians (apart from

---

[1] *Ibid.* col. 8.

[2] *Ibid.* col. 60. It is tempting to see as Ramus' source Priscian's statement that certain grammatical distinctions are made 'in finalibus literis', in the noun 'casuum differentia *et numeri*', in the verb 'temporis et personarum differentia *et numeri*', where number is clearly seen to be the common denominator. (H. Keil, *Grammatici Latini*, II, 405, my italics.)

[3] *Grammatica*, p. 14. Here Ramus diverges from Priscian (H. Keil, *Grammatici Latini*, II, 172), for whom *numerus finitus* indicates the singular, *numerus infinitus* the plural.

[4] Aristotle's dichotomy, however, is one between semantically self-sufficient and semantically dependent word-classes, whereas Ramus' is a formally based one.

a hint in Priscian's reference to *syncategoremata*) did not retain it.[1] Then, as a good logician, he proceeds to enumerate the species of his *genus numeri* as 'ut Aristoteli placuit', noun and verb, or rather a *numerus nominalis* and a *numerus verbalis*, the former including both pronoun and participle.[2] Subordinate to the *essentialis differentia* of number marking off noun and verb from the other word-classes, are the *speciales differentiae* distinguishing noun from verb, on the one hand gender and case, on the other tense and person. The signification of person is thus the province of the verb alone, and is entirely excluded from noun and pronoun.

Though he approves of Aristotle's division of the parts of speech into noun, verb and *syncategoremata*, Ramus rejects his definition of the noun as φωνὴ σημαντικὴ κατὰ συνθήκην ('vox significans ex arbitrio sine tempore'), the question of signification *ex arbitrio* or *naturā*, the centuries-old φύσις/νόμος controversy being meaningless. The *differentia* proper to the noun is *genus*, not, as in Aristotle, the absence of consignification of tense. Ramus accordingly defines the noun as a *vox numeri cum genere et casu*,[3] a definition according to formally marked accidents which represents a completely new departure both from the Ancients' view of it as signifying a *res* and the medieval view of it as signifying *res permanentes* 'per modum entis'. His definition of gender as a 'differentia nominis secundum sexum' is on the face of it semasiological, but the *differentia* is in practice indicated formally by the presence before the noun in declension of *hic*, *haec* or *hoc*.[4] A usage almost universally condemned by major Humanist grammarians is thus resurrected by Ramus, at a loss for formal markers. With the adjective he is on safer ground, and it is gender which provides him with his criterion for distinguishing it from the substantive: 'Substantivum est nomen generis simplicis aut summum duplicis. Adiectivum est nomen trium generum, vel in uno fine [*felix*] . . . vel in duobus [*fortis*] . . . vel in tribus [*bonus*].'[5] He is not of course the inventor of this definition. His originality lies in his using it unaccompanied by either the semasiological definitions of the Ancients or those in terms of substance and accident or syntactic

---

[1] *Scholae*, col. 61. [2] *Ibid.* col. 63.

[3] *Ibid.* col. 64.

[4] Ramus is however avoiding the question here, for the 'articles' *hic haec* are assigned by grammarians to nouns of common gender on semasiological grounds.

[5] *Grammatica*, pp. 14–16. The three genders indicated *confusē* in the ending of a single-termination adjective can only be known by reference to the substantive with which it is congruent. Here Ramus' system breaks down.

dependence of the medieval grammars. Case is formally defined as a 'specialis terminatio nominis', declension as a 'flexio nominis secundum casus'.[1] Declensions are *parisyllaba* or *imparisyllaba*, according to agreement or disagreement in number of syllables between nominative singular and dative plural, the pronouns being treated as irregular *adiectiva parisyllaba*.[2] It is difficult to square this with Ramus' definition of the adjective as a 'nomen trium generum' indicating a 'differentia secundum sexum' by means of formal endings. It also seems strange that he does not avail himself of the pronoun's idiosyncrasies of declension in order to classify it as a separate part of speech.

The other principal *vox numeri*, the verb, has the *speciales differentiae* tense and person and is hence a *vox numeri cum tempore et persona*.[3] It is tense that constitutes the primary *differentia* of the verb, as with Aristotle, the reader having been duly warned in the preface to the *Scholae* that moods are 'nil nisi barbara inertium'. Priscian's description of mood as a 'diversa inclinatio animi' is rejected as being a definition of the human will rather than of a grammatical feature of the verb.[4] His chief argument against including it is the plurality of meanings indicated by any one modal form, the fact that the semantic fields of imperative and optative overlap, and that wishes and commands are equally expressed by the future indicative. In the doctrine that calls *amet* imperative when standing alone, optative after *utinam* and subjunctive after *cum*, he sees only an 'absurda & explodenda confusio'.[5] He therefore dismisses mood from his system and concentrates on tense, repeating with due acknowledgment Varro's symmetrical arrangement according to aspect, with parallel ranges of *perfecta* and *infecta*.[6] This dismissal of mood leaves him however with a number of formal distinctions unaccounted for. In the present *infecta* he therefore sets up a 'praesens primum' *amo/amor*, a 'secundum' *amem/amer*, and a 'tertium' *amarem/amarer* (with a similar arrangement in the past tenses), and gives a first future *amabo/amabor* and a

---

[1] *Ibid.* p. 21. [2] *Ibid.* p. 28; *Scholae*, cols. 99, 104.

[3] Diomedes arrives by semasiological means at an identical conception of the verb as a part of speech whose *vis* (a semantic concept) 'temporibus et personis administratur'. In the absence of either *tempus* or *persona*, 'verbi vis dissolvatur' (H. Keil, *Grammatici Latini*, I, 334). This idea is found also in Servius' and Sergius' commentaries on Donatus (*ibid.* IV, 411 and 502), and it is tempting to think that Ramus was aware of it and simply transposed it into formal terms. Certainly there are references to Diomedes elsewhere in the *Scholae*.

[4] *Scholae*, col. 131. [5] *Ibid.* cols. 132–3.

[6] *Ibid.* col. 135. Diomedes, Priscian and Nebrija are also cited here.

second *ama/amare*; *amato/amator*.[1] Perhaps he was originally attracted to Varro's system by its neatly symmetrical dichotomies, but his insistence on regarding every formal ending as a sign of tense alone forced him to squeeze into it every possible form, producing an asymmetrical and ungainly framework which contrasts oddly with the precision of his dichotomies elsewhere.

On the analogy of his definition of case as a 'specialis terminatio nominis', Ramus defines person as a 'specialis terminatio verbi',[2] a definition in marked contrast to those of the Ancients and his Humanist predecessors in terms of the person speaking, spoken to or spoken about. Here again, however, he implicitly admits the defects of his system by setting up a class of *verba infinita* which lack personal endings.

Seeking a formal dichotomy for the classification of the conjugations, Ramus finds it in the forms of the future indicative, and sets up two conjugations in -*bo* and two in -*am*. His division is thus largely the traditional one, but with a formal justification other than that of the infinitive endings. The infinitive, again illustrating Ramus' love of dichotomies, has two *species*, the one *infinita* in person only, the other *infinita* in person, form and tense. The first is the traditional infinitive or *infinitum perpetuum*, the second, the *participiale infinitum*, covering the gerunds and supines.[3] Since these latter receive the *species* (but not the reality) of case from the noun, and from the verb 'significationis vim, & adsignificationem temporis', Ramus also calls them *verba participialia*.[4] He is obviously motivated by his determination to define every word-class or subclass in terms of one or other of the two principal *categoremata* noun and verb, and to prove his point he does not hesitate to have recourse to semantic arguments alien to his system, with its declared aim of defining 'nulla significationis facta mentione, sed finium tantum'. Balancing the *verba participialia* in a neat dichotomy are the *nomina participialia* or participles, which can be regarded as *voces numeri cum genere et casu* and therefore nouns.

Inconsistently enough in view of the professed rigour of his exclusion of meaning as a criterion, Ramus quotes in support of his

---

[1] *Grammatica*, p. 49. Cf. O. Jespersen's remark, *The Philosophy of Grammar*, New York, 1965, p. 49, to the effect that both Latin imperative tenses really refer to the future. Note is taken of the distinctive formal endings of the passives, without however any semasiological explanation in terms of the passing of *actio* into an object, etc.

[2] *Grammatica*, p. 51.   [3] *Scholae*, col. 137.   [4] *Ibid.* cols. 141–4.

division of the word-classes Priscian's definition of the *pars orationis* as a 'vox indicans mentis conceptum'. In this way he justifies his treatment of noun and verb as principal classes, and the other parts either as classifiable with these two or as 'appendices' of them and *syncategoremata*. These latter are however formally defined as *voces sine numero*,[1] with subdivisions of *voces singulae* (the adverbs, a term which includes prepositions and interjections) and *voces coniunctae* (the conjunctions). As befits *syncategoremata*, the criterion here is one of syntactic dependence, without however any reference to *semantic* dependence, the adverb being defined as 'vox sine numero, quae voci alii adjungitur',[2] and the conjunction as linking clauses. Surprisingly, the traditional semantically determined *significationes* of the conjunction are given, neatly arranged in dichotomies and sub-dichotomies – an arrangement which does not preclude condemnation of Gaza and other Greek grammarians for attempting to split the adverb, which is *infinitum*, into *significationum genera* corresponding to the ten categories of Aristotle.[3]

In the *Scholae*, syntax is dismissed in a brief note only two columns in length. Ramus is interested in formal morphological markers rather than in elements of structure, and his neglect of syntax ('secunda pars grammaticae') is typical of his age. Despite a division into *syntaxis vocum numeri* and *syntaxis vocum sine numero*, his treatment of it in the *Grammatica*, under the headings *convenientia* and *rectio*, does not differ materially from that in other grammars of the period. In order to preserve the symmetry of his dichotomies, he attributes syntactic agreement to both adverb and conjunction. Otherwise he follows the usual course, with its employment of semantic criteria, its references to *adiectiva laudis aut vituperii* and *verba promittendi*, etc. That Ramus allowed such criteria to stand is perhaps a witness to his lack of interest in syntax.

Opinions of Ramus' grammatical achievement have been diverse. L. Kukenheim sees in him a 'très lointain précurseur des structuralistes'.[4] O. Funke, while recognizing his desire to free grammar from medieval dialectics and apply to it purely formal criteria,[5] sees him as

---

[1] The section devoted to them in the *Scholae* is very short, consisting only of four half-page columns.
[2] *Grammatica*, p. 74. Priscian's influence is perceptible in the further definition of the adverb as 'tanquam adjectivum nominum, verborum, adverbiorum etiam ipsorum'.
[3] *Scholae*, col. 178.
[4] *Esquisse historique de la linguistique française*, Leyden, 1962, p. 18.
[5] 'William Bullokars *Bref Grammar for English* (1586)', *Anglia*, LXII (1938), p. 117.

belonging to that 'sprachphilosophische Nebenströmung' which includes Scaliger's *De causis* and Sanctius' *Minerva*. He none the less contrasts Ramus' somewhat arid approach with Scaliger's 'psychological' one, seeing them as extreme examples of their respective methods.[1] For I. Poldauf, Ramus' criticism of the philosophical foundations of classical grammar makes him a forerunner of Descartes, and a villain from whose method it took several centuries for linguistics to 'extricate' itself.[2] Closer to the truth is V. Salmon's view that had it not been for the early reaction in favour of semasiological principles (Ramus' views were neither widely followed nor followed for any length of time), the descriptive method in linguistics might have arisen several centuries earlier than it did.[3] Certainly, one must retain as the primary Ramistic feature the preference for form over meaning as a criterion of definition. It is none the less true that Ramus is able to apply this criterion rather more strictly in the theoretical *Scholae* than in the practical teaching grammars. Even in applying it to Latin, which as a synthetic language is more amenable to it than the analytic English or French, he experiences difficulties in catering for formally unmarked forms. His chief quarrel with his predecessors concerns their strong tendency to define grammatical functions in terms of *signification* rather than of *consignification* by means of formal linguistic features, as evidenced by the primacy accorded by Priscian to *vis et significatio*. But he equally censures them for their failure to follow Aristotle, either neglecting him completely or, as in medieval grammar, presenting a garbled account of his doctrine. His dilemma lies in his uneasy attempt to reconcile Aristotelian logic with the claims of usage and a formally based system of linguistic analysis. While his formal approach was to a large extent ignored by his successors, except for a brief period and by a limited number of authors, his Aristotelian preoccupations must be regarded as reinforcing the general trend towards an ever-increasing identification of grammar and logic. For the present-day reader his formal method will however continue to strike a curiously modern note. It is an absorbing mental exercise to speculate on the direction that might have been taken, had his ideas been generally followed, by a sixteenth-century structuralism.

[1] 'Grammatica Anglicana von P. Gr[eaves]. (1594)', pp. xii, xiv.
[2] 'Problems of English Grammar', pp. 48–9.
[3] 'James Shirley', p. 296.

The break with tradition: Ramus

Ramus' ideas spread rapidly throughout Europe, though his influence was on logic, rhetoric and education rather than on grammatical studies.[1] Ramus' own application of his system to the French vernacular appeared, as we have seen, in 1562. His Latin grammar was published in London and Cambridge in 1585. The only major adoption of his formally based system for Latin was by the Spanish scholar Sanctius, whose *Minerva* (1587) will form the subject of the next section of this study. Apart from Sanctius, Ramus' influence on Latin grammars appears only in a handful of authors whose works show a mixture of Ramistic and traditional features: the Scot Alexander Hume's *Grammatica nova* (1612), Kaspar Schoppe's *Grammatica philosophica* (1628), and Thomas Hayne's *Grammatices Latinae compendium* (1640). Only works by English authors – Paul Greaves' *Grammatica anglicana* (1594), described in its subtitle as 'ad unicam P. Rami methodum concinnata', and Ben Jonson's *English Grammar* (1640) – follow Ramus in a thoroughgoing attempt to apply his formal criteria to a vernacular language. Hybrids showing a mixture of Ramistic and semantically based features are Hume's *Of the Orthographie and Congruitie of the Britan Tongue* (c. 1617),[2] Alexander Gil's *Logonomia Anglica* (1619), and Charles Butler's *English Grammar* (1633). Here one may note two things: Ramus' grammatical influence, apart from Sanctius, is almost exclusively confined to British authors, and this influence is delayed until well into the seventeenth century. In France, his formally based *Grammaire* found no echo, and his influence on educational thought ended with the Jesuit ascendancy. His influence on logic remained however deep-seated, Ramism being still very much alive in the universities as late as 1630. F. P. Graves remarks not without justice that in certain features of Ramistic thought there 'must to some extent be sought the spiritual ancestry of Descartes, [and] the Port-Royalists'.[3]

Opposed in Italy except at Bologna, Ramus' ideas met with equal hostility in Spain, apart from his follower Sanctius, who taught the liberal arts on Ramistic principles at the University of Salamanca. In the countries of northern Europe, on the other hand, Ramus owed a greater popularity than he perhaps otherwise might have gained to

[1] For a full account of Ramus' influence v. F. P. Graves, *Petrus Ramus*, pp. 209–21; W. S. Howell, *Logic and Rhetoric*, pp. 178–80, 187–93, 282; P. Rossi, *Francis Bacon*, pp. 41, 145–8, 175–6.
[2] This grammar did not appear in printed form until H. B. Wheatley's Early English Text Society edition of 1865.   [3] *Petrus Ramus*, p. 211.

his status as a Protestant martyr, a popularity which W. and M. Kneale[1] persist in regarding as 'unfortunate' for the countries concerned. Certainly, the area of his greatest influence was Protestant Germany, where almost every chair of philosophy eventually came to be occupied by a Ramist. The Melanchthonian logic in general use at Protestant universities was however based on Aristotle, and here as elsewhere in Europe Ramistic teaching became subject to attacks by Aristotelians. Religion came to the aid of the latter for the Lutherans supported Philip Melanchthon (himself a Lutheran) against Ramus on the grounds that Ramistic principles were an off-shoot of Calvinism. After bitter polemics, Ramistic teaching was by the early seventeenth century forbidden at a number of universities, and a compromise was sought in a combination of Scholastic logic, Melanchthonian Aristotelianism, and certain elements of Ramus' dialectic, a combination whose practitioners came to be known as Philippo-Ramists. The compromise was however an uneasy one, resulting in general in the promotion of Aristotelian principles rather than Ramistic ones.

Since Ramus' ideas had most success in Protestant areas, it is not surprising that they found fertile ground in Scotland and at Puritan Cambridge. In Scotland they were spread through the influence of the Regent, the Earl of Murray, who had been a pupil of Ramus, became established at the University of St Andrews, and were enthusiastically popularized by Roland MacIlmaine. The latter's publication in London in 1574 of both the earliest Latin version of Ramus' *Dialectica* to appear in England, and the earliest English translation of it,[2] ensured the influence of Ramus on English logic and rhetoric during the late sixteenth and the whole of the seventeenth century. W. S. Howell indeed goes so far as to attribute to these two works the establishment of trends resulting in 'almost a complete monopoly for Ramus' logical and rhetorical theory in England in the early part of that epoch and . . . a position of considerable weight throughout'.[3]

Though St Andrews was the first centre of Ramism in Britain, Cambridge was not long in following suit. By the early 1570s there

[1] *Development of Logic*, p. 302.
[2] *The Logike of . . . P. Ramus Martyr, newly translated . . . per M. R. Makylmenaeum Scotum*, London, 1574.
[3] *Logic and Rhetoric*, p. 187. Howell discounts the commonly cited influence of George Buchanan and Andrew Melville on the spread of Ramism in Scotland.

were indications that the Aristotelian supremacy in logic and rhetoric was beginning to lose ground. Ramus' logic was already being expounded by Laurence Chaderton (or Chatterton), and when it was attacked by the Scholastic logician Everard Digby it found a vigorous defender in William Temple. In 1580, Digby attempted to reassert the Aristotelian position by the publication of his *De duplici methodo libri duo, unicam Petri Rami methodum refutantes*. Under the pseudonym F. Mildapettus, Temple immediately retaliated with his *Admonitio de unica P. Rami methodo*,[1] defending Ramus' single method which had brought order to the confusion of the liberal arts. As Digby was probably Francis Bacon's tutor at Cambridge it may well be, as F. P. Graves suggests,[2] that this controversy was at the origin of Bacon's opposition to deductive systems. As for Oxford, though it was still the bastion of Aristotelianism in England, W. S. Howell[3] rightly rejects the view that no interest in Ramus' theories was shown there. Charles Butler, author of the *English Grammar* cited above, played an important role in the spread of Ramism into the schools, and the President of Corpus Christi College, John Rainolds, also helped in its diffusion. In general however Oxford remained hostile, in spite of a continued English interest in Ramus which is underlined by the poet Milton's publication, as late as 1672,[4] of an *Artis logicae plenior institutio* based on Ramus' method.

Most of the facts given in this brief summary are common to the standard works, dealing with various aspects of Ramus' thought on non-grammatical topics, which I have cited above. If I have repeated them here, it is in order to give some idea of the breadth and importance of Ramistic influence in the intellectual context of the times. Ramus resembles Scaliger in that he marks the transition between the medieval and the modern world.[5] According to R. R. Bolgar, he deserves to rank among the forerunners of Bacon and Galileo, his criticisms of the thought of his day being 'as essential to Bacon's logic of discovery and to Galileo's method of analysis and construction as manure is to a growing plant . . . an essential tributary in the stream that takes us to Locke and Newton'.[6] He remains however a

---

[1] An English version, *From Francis Mildapet of Navarre to Everard Digby of England: An Admonition that the Single Method of Peter Ramus be Retained and the Rest Rejected*, also appeared in 1580.

[2] *Petrus Ramus*, p. 212. [3] *Logic and Rhetoric*, pp. 189–93.

[4] This work was in fact composed forty years earlier.

[5] v. R. H. Robins, *Short History*, p. 102. [6] *The Classical Heritage*, p. 289.

forerunner, a reviser of the old order rather than an innovator, a typical man of the Renaissance who in reforming Aristotelian logic uses the tools of Aristotelian logic. His only real innovation, his formal grammatical system, having had but a short vogue, it is his work on methodology that is his important contribution to the thought of his time. Though W. and M. Kneale[1] regard his logical method as involving merely a 'specious rearrangement of the old [Aristotelian] material, which was no gain', Ramus' *Dialectique* has been called the most important philosophical work in French up to Descartes' *Discours de la méthode*.[2] Certainly, Ramus' ideas were to the forefront in the century-long debate on method which preceded Descartes' work, and may even have been one of the primary causes of that debate. But in attempting to apply his rigid method to linguistic analysis Ramus perhaps became prisoner of his own system, collating isolated facts without being able to impose upon them – since he had no real overall theory of language, or in Saussurian terms of *langue* as opposed to *parole* – an overriding principle other than that of Aristotelian methodology. For Bacon, Ramus' use of his single method and his forcing of everything into contrasting dichotomies could only have an injurious effect on science:

> ... for it was a kind of cloud that overshadowed knowledge for a while and blew over . . . For while these men press matters by the laws of their method, and when a thing does not aptly fall into these dichotomies, either pass it by or force it out of its natural shape, the effects of their proceeding is this, the kernels and grains of sciences leap out, and they are left with nothing in their grasps but the dry and barren husks.[3]

An intermediary between the medieval world and the new, Ramus was soon to be overtaken by more powerful, more modern minds, by men such as Bacon and Descartes. The *Discours de la méthode* spelled the end of his reign as a methodologist, and the reaction against Aristotle was to be carried much further than he had taken it. His interest for present-day readers lies in what men of his own day ignored, or tried but briefly and let fall, namely his formal approach to linguistic analysis. In this he was several centuries before his time.

[1] *Development of Logic*, p. 302.
[2] v. W. S. Howell, *Logic and Rhetoric*, p. 153.
[3] *De augmentis scientiarum*, in R. L. Ellis, J. Spedding, and D. D. Heath, *The Works of Francis Bacon*, London, 1887–92, I, 663.

SANCTIUS

The third great grammatical innovator of the sixteenth century, the Spaniard Francisco Sánchez de las Brozas, alias Franciscus Sanctius Brocensis, published in 1562 his *Verae brevesque grammatices Latinae institutiones*, a normative grammar which already embodies certain of his more distinctive contributions to grammatical theory. Reference is made in it to another work in progress, the celebrated *Minerva*[1] which finally appeared in 1587. It is this latter work which will be examined here as representing the definitive exposition of Sanctius' doctrine. Outspoken and independent, sometimes turbulent, Sanctius was an early exponent of the necessity of inculcating Latin by means of the vulgar tongue, and he was several times reprimanded for using this method during his tenure of his chair at the Collegium Trilingue in Salamanca. The first elements of his *Verae institutiones* are imparted in the vernacular, a procedure which he openly defends in his *Arte para en breve saber Latin* of 1576. The subtitle of the *Minerva* – *de causis linguae Latinae* – is a deliberate echo of Scaliger,[2] distinct traces of whose method are to be found in it. It also begins with a ritual bow in the direction of Nebrija and his already century-old castigation of the 'barbari' among medieval grammarians. Sanctius maintains that he brings nothing new to grammar – he had a reputation as a seeker after novelty to live down – but aims simply to restore to its due place that *antiquitas* which the said 'barbarity' had laid low.[3] He sees himself as the successor of Nebrija, who had not succeeded in extirpating all the 'roots' of Scholasticism, and whose work his own grammar is manifestly designed to supplant in the universities. In Spain much later than elsewhere, medieval conceptions continued to reign almost unchallenged.

Sanctius assumes that in the 'original' language[4] things received

---

[1] *Francisci Sanctii Brocensis . . . Minerva: seu de causis linguae Latinae*, Salamanca, 1587. M. Breva-Claramonte ('Sanctius' *Minerva* of 1562 and the Evolution of his Linguistic Theory', *Historiographia Linguistica*, II, 1 (1975), pp. 49–66) notes the existence of a hitherto unknown 1562 edition of the *Minerva*. It is however, as the author remarks, the 1587 edition that contains Sanctius' fully developed theory. This article came to my notice too late for any fuller reference to be made to the 1562 edition.

[2] v. *ibid.* lib. i, cap 1. (The first edition of the *Minerva* being rare, and succeeding editions variously paginated, reference is here made to book and chapter rather than to page.)

[3] *Ibid.* preface.

[4] Whichever it was ('quicunque ille fuit') – most grammarians assumed it to be Hebrew.

their names 'ab ipsa natura' but that later languages, on the contrary, each have their own individual 'nomenclaturae ratio'. Divergence in nomenclature between languages is caused by the fact that 'eiusdem rei diversae sunt causae', a view which recalls Scaliger's doctrines[1] and Sanctius' subtitle. C. García has devoted a long analysis, in his study of Sanctius,[2] to the question whether his view of language is Platonic or Aristotelian, naturalist or conventionalist. In support of the Platonic thesis, he cites the opinions of the contemporary Spanish philosopher Vives and of Sanctius' friend Fray Luis de León. Certainly, Sanctius' view of the origins of nomenclature is Platonic. Against this however must be placed the possible influence on his ideas of the Aristotelians Villapando, Sánchez el Escéptico and Fernando de Herrera, and the fact that Sanctius by no means excludes the view of names as 'velut instrumenta rerum et nota'.[3] There is nothing in Sanctius' theory, as García points out, to contradict the arbitrary nature of the linguistic sign. The sign is applied to things 'adhibito consilio', that is after the intervention of reason has assigned the necessary *causae*. The Platonic view appears to apply only to the *original* language. Sanctius is really perhaps neither a Platonist nor an Aristotelian in these matters, but a proponent of the role of reason, a rationalist, tempering the doctrine of the arbitrariness of the linguistic sign by his search for those *causae* which alone supply the key to the *rationes* of both words and things. His rationalistic approach is indicated by his belief that 'rerum omnium reddenda sit ratio',[4] but he sees language as not amenable solely to reason, but also to tradition and authority. Grammar is to be determined 'ratione primum, deinde testimoniis & usu', grammarians being *custodes* of the language, not *auctores*.

Sanctius' division of grammar is the Ramistic one into *etymologia*[5] and *constructio*. Like Scaliger and Ramus, he follows Aristotelian principles of classification. *Littera* being a part of *syllaba*, *syllaba* of *dictio* and *dictio* of *oratio*, it follows that none of them singly can be the subject of a separate division of grammar. He adds to the vague definition of grammar as an 'ars recte loquendi'[6] (equally found in

---

[1] Scaliger however held that names do not originate 'a rerum natura', but that the word is a 'nota rerum' arbitrarily imposed (*De causis*, cap. lxviii).

[2] *Contribución a la historia de los conceptos gramaticales: la aportación del Brocense*, Madrid, 1960.

[3] *Minerva*, i, 1.

[4] *Ibid.* i, 1.

[5] Sanctius does not in fact use this term.

[6] *Ibid.* i, 2.

Scaliger and Ramus) the more linguistic, syntactic requirement 'cuius finis est congruens oratio', and proceeds to divide *oratio* into *voces, seu dictiones* which are identical with *partes orationis*.[1] The *vox* is defined as 'qua unumquodque vocatur',[2] in a word-for-word repetition of Ramus' circular definition which I have not encountered elsewhere. The brief survey of previous systems of classification of the parts of speech also follows Ramus' *Scholae* closely in places, sometimes with almost exact correspondences,[3] and the structuralist view that the grammarian should be able to distinguish the word-classes 'etiam si sensum verborum non intelligat'[4] equally bears Ramus' and Scaliger's imprint.

Sanctius concludes that the parts of speech are three: the *nomen*, *verbum* and *particula* found in 'all oriental languages' and more particularly in Hebrew, with its noun, verb and *dictio consignificans*.[5] He assumes that Greek and Latin must have had the same three word-classes initially, citing in his support Augustine's three-part system 'ex Aristotelis sententia'. He then quotes Plato's division of *res* into *permanentes* and *fluentes* whose *notae* are noun and verb respectively (the medieval conception reintroduced by Scaliger) and repeats without acknowledgment Scaliger's view of preposition and adverb as *modi* 'per quem causarum ratio explicaretur'.[6] This Aristotelian three-word-class system leads him to count pronoun and participle with the noun, but to reject interjections as identical in all languages, therefore *naturales* and as such excluded by Aristotle's dictum that word-classes are established 'ex instituto, non naturā'.[7]

In Aristotelian manner, following Ramus and Scaliger, *figura* and *species* are dealt with as universal accidents common to all word-classes before the treatment of the individual parts of speech. In Ramistic fashion a preliminary chapter is also devoted to number,

---

[1] The medieval distinction between *vox*, *dictio* and *pars orationis* is thus lost.

[2] Appendix to the *Minerva*, f. 1ᵛ.

[3] García does not, set as he is on seeing Sanctius as the great Spanish precursor of modern linguistics, mention his considerable debt to Ramus. He has achieved the *tour de force* of writing a book on Sanctius without referring many of his major tenets to their undoubted source. Ramus is mentioned only in passing as part of the 'sporadic reactions' against Aristotelianism (*Contribución*, p. 38).

[4] *Minerva*, i, 2.

[5] Though Sanctius also makes reference to the three-word-class system of Arabic, it is doubtless illusory to look for Arab influence in his work. The roots of his system are Aristotelian.

[6] Cf. however *Minerva*, i, 1, where he cites Scaliger as his model 'in multis'.

[7] *Minerva*, i, 2.

with Ramus' classification of the word-classes into *voces numeri participes* (noun, verb, participle) and *voces numeri expertes* (preposition, adverb, conjunction).[1] Sanctius retains the traditional names for his subclasses, and it is not always clear whether he wants to set up three parts of speech or six. Those features distinguished 'a sola significatione' are expressly excluded from the province of the grammarian.[2] Plainly, Sanctius is much indebted to Ramus and Scaliger, especially the former. In such definitions as that of the noun as a 'vox particeps numeri casualis cum genere',[3] the closeness of the resemblance precludes any possibility of Sanctius' having arrived independently at the Ramistic system. This presumed plagiarism continues through such definitions as those of case ('specialis nominis differentia') and gender ('differentia nominis secundum sexum'). Both the definitions and the discussion that follows are clearly taken from Ramus' *Scholae*, but nowhere does Sanctius acknowledge these borrowings or similar ones in the other word-classes. In what follows the coincidence of doctrine with Ramus and Scaliger will not therefore be enlarged upon, but the emphasis will be on what is peculiar to Sanctius himself.

On the face of it, Sanctius perpetuates Ramus' distinction between the substantive as a *nomen generis simplicis*[4] and the adjective as a *nomen trium generum*. Where he differs however is in his opinion that the adjective does not in fact have gender, but *terminationes* or *personae* 'ad genus', i.e. gender-marking terminations referring not to the adjective itself, but to the substantive. As in Ramus' system, noun and pronoun are treated as members of the same word-class, but Sanctius plainly regards them as equal substitutes for each other, *Annibal* in 'Annibal peto pacem' being treated as a substitute for *ego*. It is by such arguments that he contrives to keep his three-word-class system intact. Equally, with all other nouns, his pronoun signifies *res ipsas*.[5] The verb he defines according to Ramistic principles, rejecting Aristotle's definition in terms of the consignification of time as touching the *effecta et adiuncta* of the word-class rather than its *causae*.[6] In the same way as gender is not an accident of adjectives,

---

[1] *Minerva*, appendix, f. 1ᵛ.

[2] *Ibid.* i, 3. One should note however that the appendix *De partibus orationis* is more prone to semasiological definition than the grammar itself. It seems to follow the earlier *Verae institutiones* rather than the *Minerva*.

[3] *Minerva*, appendix, f. 1ᵛ.

[4] 'Quod cum uno genere declinatur.'

[5] *Minerva*, i, 2.   [6] *Ibid.* i, 12.

so is person, defined as in Ramus in terms of morphological endings, not an accident of substantives. In the sentence *Petrus videt parietem* the verb has person, but its subject and object do not. If every substantive in the nominative case is in practice described as being in the third person, it is only by virtue of its syntactic relationship to the verb of which it is subject.[1] On this view of person it follows that the only true impersonal verbs are the infinitives, the customary impersonals containing person by ellipse and hence being personals. To think otherwise is to contradict 'totum Platonis, & Aristotelis dogma'.

Mood, as in Ramus, has no place in the verb, though Sanctius admits the existence of this category elsewhere, i.e. in the *casus sextus* ('tuo iussu feci') and in adverbs ('male currit'). Like Ramus, he tries to force the modal forms into a common temporal scheme, ignoring however the features Ramus incorporates from Varro's aspectual framework and contenting himself with the more usual Roman five-tense system. He thus has two present forms (*amo/amem*), two 'infecti' (*amabam/amarem*), two perfects and pluperfects and (counting the imperative as one) three futures. This gives, as he remarks, three natural tenses covered by as many as eleven formal *differentiae*. The second form in each set can however also be regarded as a future.[2] Voice is reduced to the two, active and passive, found in Scaliger. Every *motus* being either *actio* or *passio*, philosophy can find nothing between these two terms: 'quod in rerum natura non est, ne nomen quidem habebit'. This philosophical approach is a marked feature of the later books of the *Minerva*, and is in curious contrast to the formally conceived Ramistic approach to definition in book i. Sanctius rejects this approach when he castigates earlier grammarians for determining voice according to formal endings, as if the nature of the verb 'per terminationes, & accidentia, non per essentiam esset indicanda'. By this criterion of *essentia*, formally differing verbs like *afficio, prosequor* are counted 'activa naturā'.[3] Sanctius has thus moved full circle from the formal approach in book i and is advocating a purely semasiological approach. The application of such criteria leads him to regard intransitive verbs as *prima activa* 'more active' than verbs which can take an object and which, without

---

[1] This doctrine is the opposite of that of Priscian, who appears to follow Apollonius in regarding the third person of the verb as *infinita*, defined and delimited only by the addition of a pronoun subject attributing *certam personam* (H. Keil, *Grammatici Latini*, II, 577).
[2] *Minerva*, i, 13.   [3] *Ibid.* iii, 2.

that object, give only an 'imperfectum sensum'. The justification for this, Aristotle's 'Quae se ipsis contenta sunt, meliora sunt, quam quae egent aliis',[1] presents a strange contrast with the professed rejection in the first book of those semantic elements which are 'magis Philosophi quam Grammatici'. Doubt inevitably arises as to whether Sanctius understood the implications of the definitions he took over, perhaps mechanically, from Ramus. Certainly, in the books other than the first one he seems more concerned to make grammar conform to Aristotelian logic than to draw the linguistic conclusions of Ramus' structuralism. His logical preoccupations are perhaps most marked in his increasing tendency to prove his point by ellipse, a procedure which involves an appeal to meaning. 'Caesar est albus' being logically 'Caesar est albus Caesar', Scaliger can thus be rebuked for regarding the verb *sum* ('fundamentum, sive radix omnium verborum') as signifying *accidens* as well as *substantia*.[2]

The real interest of Sanctius' grammar lies in the syntax,[3] which is much longer than is customary in the sixteenth century, the only other exception being the extensive treatment in Linacre's *De structura*. It is curious that Scaliger, much of whose analysis is based on syntactic considerations, devotes only a few pages to syntax, and Ramus even less. In Sanctius' treatment certain original features are determined by idiosyncrasies in his handling of the word-classes. Having for instance excluded gender from the adjective, he is obliged to make it agree with its substantive in number and case only. Similarly, noun-subject and verb agree in number only, not in person. His view of the sentence is a logical one expressed in terms of Aristotelian philosophy: 'Ex nomine et verbo tanquam ex materia et forma constuitur oratio.'[4] This use of the terms *materia* and *forma* in the sense in which Scaliger uses them brings us to what is for modern readers the central interest of Sanctius' syntax, namely his abundant treatment of ellipse. Here, in an approach whose obvious forerunner is Linacre, certain linguistic structures in common use are regarded as abbreviations of underlying expanded structures, the subject *Annibal* e.g. in the sentence *Annibal peto pacem* being explained

---

[1] *Ibid.* iii, 3. [2] *Ibid.* iii, 5.

[3] The remaining word-classes are, following Ramus, words devoid of number (*voces expertes numeri*) defined syntactically.

[4] The logical terms *subiectum* and *praedicatum* have however still not displaced *suppositum* and *appositum*, which Sanctius, following medieval practice, still uses.

as an abbreviation of *Ens Annibal* or *Qui sum Annibal*.[1] The parallel with Linacre's *me authore* = *me enti authore* is obvious. In the same way, Sanctius analyses the phrase *longo post tempore* as an abbreviation of *longo tempore, post id tempus*.[2] Anyone who has read both the *Minerva* and the Port-Royal Grammar of 1660 cannot but be struck on the one hand by the parallel between Sanctius' expansions and the Port-Royalists' celebrated rewriting of *Dieu invisible a créé le monde visible*,[3] and on the other by the relevance of these abbreviations and expansions to N. Chomsky's theory of a 'deep structure' in language underlying and predetermining the abbreviated 'surface structure' of actual discourse.[4]

Chomsky himself was quick to note the parallel between his own analyses and the Port-Royal approach, and sought to give his theories a historical and philosophical dimension by pointing out the affinities of Port-Royal doctrine with certain notions in Descartes. His *Cartesian Linguistics*,[5] subtitled 'a chapter in the history of rational thought', showed however no awareness of developments in linguistic thought which predated the Port-Royal Grammar and Descartes by a century and more, and the book attracted considerable criticism for this reason.[6] One has the impression that Professor Chomsky read the vernacular *Grammaire générale et raisonnée* of 1660 without consulting the Port-Royal Latin Grammar – the *Nouvelle Méthode pour apprendre facilement la langue Latine* – of 1644, which had gone into eight editions by 1681. Had he consulted this latter work, he would have noted that Sanctius is there expressly named as the source of certain doctrines in the Port-Royal Grammar. His defence is that Sanctius was primarily concerned with textual explanation:

There is no doubt that in developing his concept of ellipsis as a fundamental property of language, Sanctius gave many linguistic examples that superficially are closely parallel to those that were used to develop the [Port-Royal] theory of deep and surface structure . . . It seems, however, that the concept of ellipsis is intended by Sanctius merely as a device for

---

[1] *Minerva*, ii, 2.   [2] *Ibid.* iii, 12.
[3] *Dieu qui est invisible a créé le monde qui est visible.*
[4] v. Chomsky's 'Goals of Linguistic Theory', *Current Issues in Linguistic Theory* (*Janua Linguarum*, Series minor, XXXVIII), London, The Hague, Paris, 1964, p. 9.
[5] New York, 1966.
[6] v. H. Aarsleff, 'The History of Linguistics and Professor Chomsky', *Language*, 46 (1970), pp. 570–85; R. Lakoff's review of C. Lancelot and A. Arnauld, *Grammaire générale et raisonnée*, ed. H. Brekle, Stuttgart-Bad Cannstatt, 1966, in *Language*, 45 (1969), pp. 343–64; V. Salmon's review of Chomsky's *Cartesian Linguistics* already cited.

the interpretation of texts. Thus, to determine the true meaning of an actual literary passage, one must very often, according to Sanctius, regard it as an elliptical variant of a more elaborate paraphrase. But . . . the clear intent of a philosophical grammar was to develop a psychological theory, not a technique of textual interpretation.[1]

One may here make the point that when as noted above Sanctius expands *longo post tempore* into *longo tempore, post id tempus*, he is primarily concerned with proving that prepositions without a case-marked word to govern do not, as the traditional view held, 'degenerate' into adverbs. In other words, he is at pains to make clear that underlying the seeming adverbial construction of the shorter phrase there is a longer prepositional one which he plainly regards as more consonant with a reasoned linguistic structure. Here, his interest is clearly linguistic rather than textual, and one must agree with V. Salmon that he was fully conscious of the psychological implications of his method.[2]

Chomsky's views on the Port-Royal Grammar's indebtedness to Descartes are a matter to which we shall return later. Suffice it for the moment to confirm that a number of the expansions proposed by Port-Royal in the *Nouvelle Méthode* for Latin and in more tentative form in the *Grammaire générale* do indeed have close parallels in Sanctius. The drawing of attention to elliptical constructions was of course no new thing in grammar. Ramus had pointed out several such constructions, and Linacre had treated the matter at some length. But the roots of all this lie even farther back, in medieval grammar, and depend on the notion – and it is precisely this notion that interests Chomsky, and explains his anxiety to link Port-Royal with Cartesian mentalism – that there are underlying concepts in the mind of which linguistic constructs are an abbreviation, and that the fundamental structure of language is revealed when the logical sequences left unexpressed in actual discourse are reconstituted.[3] Thomas of Erfurt's *Grammatica speculativa* recapitulates the

---

[1] *Language and Mind*, New York, 1968, pp. 15–16.

[2] Review of Chomsky, *Cartesian Linguistics*, p. 178. Sanctius gives as an example of an unexpanded phrase: 'Vel me monere hoc, vel percontari puta: Rectum est, ego ut faciam.' He expands it 'grammatice' as 'Vel tu puta me monere tibi hoc negotium, vel tu puta me a te hoc negotium percontari: Quia si hoc negotium, quod negotium abs te rogo, rectum negotium est, ideo te illud negotium rogo, ut ego idem negotium faciam.' This would seem to have little to do with the interpretation of texts. As he remarks, quoting Quintilian: 'Aliud est Latine, aliud Grammatice loqui.'

[3] Cf. Ramus' 'natural logic' in the mind.

argument step by step: Aristotle says that linguistic structures are symbols of mental concepts; it follows that the end of syntax is the expression of such concepts;[1] hence syntax must operate on two levels, 'secundum sensum' and 'secundum intellectum'. The first type occurs when all mental *constructibilia* of a syntactic group are expressed 'voce', that is to say by the actual formal elements of discourse: *ego lego*. The second occurs when one or more *constructibilia* are not expressed 'secundum vocem', but apprehended 'ab intellectu': *lego*. In other words, there is not an exact correspondence between discourse and the underlying *mentis conceptum*. Hence the constant search in medieval and Humanist grammar for expanded structures into which more succinct ones can be 'resolved'. The *Grammatica speculativa* itself resolves *lege* into *impero te legere*[2] thus laying bare the three mental concepts (four, if *ego* be added) underlying the imperative singular. Its doctrine that the mental concept of 'being' underlies all verbs[3] leads to medieval and Humanist 'resolutions' of the type *amat = est amans*,[4] where the underlying concepts of 'being' and 'loving' are as it were dissected out. One could multiply examples from Humanist grammar, with its common expansions of *curro* into *curro cursum*, of *triste* into *tristis res*, etc., and of the impersonal verb *pluit* into *Deus pluit*.

Sanctius is noteworthy rather for the extreme extension he gives to all this, than as its inventor. Previous Humanist grammarians quite commonly noted the discrepancy between surface and deep structure in the impersonal verb, and Sanctius says nothing new when he declares that the verb cannot signify anything without a subject.[5] From the *accusativus cognatae significationis* of other Humanist grammarians (*curro = curro cursum*) it is but a short step to his and Linacre's *nominativus cognatae significationis* (*curritur = cursus curritur* or *currere curritur; pluit = pluvia pluit*).[6] In resolutions such as *miseret me tui = misericordia tenet me tui*, he acknowledges the authority of

[1] Cap. xlv [Aristotle, *De interpretatione*, cap. 1.]: '*Ea quae sunt in voce, sunt notae passionum earum, quae sunt in anima* . . . ergo constructio . . . in Grammatica, est finaliter propter exprimendum mentis conceptum.'   [2] Cap. xxvii.
[3] Cap. xxvii: 'hoc verbum, *est*, in omni verbo includitur, tanquam radix omnium'. Cf. Peter of Spain's view (p. 47, note 2 above) of the verb *to be* as the root of all other verbs.
[4] Despauterius, e.g., makes this resolution.
[5] 'Verbum sine supposito nihil significat.' Scaliger had already stated that the impersonal verb necessarily contains a subject.
[6] The expansion *pluit = pluvia pluit* occurs in Linacre's *Rudimenta* of 1527.

Priscian, who proceeds in this fashion and in turn evokes the example of Apollonius. Certain of Sanctius' analyses are conceived in very similar terms to those of the Port-Royal Latin Grammar, as e.g. the explanation of the third person imperative *amet* as equal to *moneo ut amet, fac ut amet*, or *volo ut amet*. Even more striking is the parallel between certain elements in Sanctius and the *Grammaire générale*'s teaching on relative clauses: 'the relative can form part of the subject or attribute of . . . the main clause. For it never constitutes either the entire subject or the entire attribute: but one must add the word which the relative replaces in order to make it the entire subject, and some other word to make it the entire attribute.'[1]

The doctrine involved here is already implicit in Sanctius' 'Vidi hominem, *qui homo* disputat',[2] an obvious expansion of 'Vidi hominem qui disputat', and his 'hoc negotium, *quod negotium* abs te rogo' cited above.[3] There are a number of such instances in which, as R. Lakoff points out, 'the most interesting and explicit analyses in the *Nouvelle Méthode latine* and the *Grammaire générale et raisonnée* trace their lineage back to Sanctius'.[4]

This established, the point at issue is whether or not Sanctius was conscious of dealing with something akin to a 'deep' and 'surface' structure in language, whether, in Chomsky's terms, he was a proto-transformational grammarian. Certainly, he and Linacre are the first Humanist grammarians to put any real emphasis on sentence structure as opposed to morphology. Humanist grammar in general is word-based, but for Sanctius the end of grammar is syntax: 'Oratio sive syntaxis est finis grammaticae.' Further, with the example of Scaliger's *causae* before him, he assumes language to have an inherent *ratio*[5] which is amenable to investigation: 'unless you subject to thorough scrutiny the *causae* and *rationes* of what you are dealing with, you can have no true view of it. But a perverse idea has entered many minds . . . that there are no *causae* in the Latin grammar and speech, and no *ratio* to be sought out . . .'[6] By *sermo*, which I have

---

[1] C. Lancelot and A. Arnauld, *Grammaire générale et raisonnée*, Paris, 1660, p. 70 (my translation).   [2] *Minerva*, ii, 9.   [3] P. 104, note 2.

[4] v. review of Lancelot and Arnauld, *Grammaire générale et raisonnée*, p. 363.

[5] In her excellent review, R. Lakoff translates *ratio*, not I feel very happily, as *logic*. I see it rather as an informing and underlying mental structure, though I have preferred to leave both it and the term *causa* untranslated.

[6] *Minerva*, i, 1: 'nisi artis tuae, quam tractas, causas rationesque probe fueris perscrutatus, crede te alienis oculis videre. At invasit multos perversa quaedam opinio . . . in Grammatica et sermone Latino nullas esse causas, nullamque penitus inquirendam esse rationem . . .'

translated in the above passage by *speech*, Sanctius means discourse, utterance, everything that de Saussure would include under the term *parole*, whereas *ratio* (V. Salmon is surely right in this interpretation)[1] seems at times to represent for him a dynamic force *underlying* discourse. If we translate *sermo* by surface structure and *ratio* by deep structure, we see that the recognition of these two features is not specifically Port-Royalist or Cartesian. Any doubts as to Sanctius' assumption of a linguistic dichotomy of the Saussurean *langue/parole* type must in any case be dispelled by his remark that since all things in the universe exhibit the twin facets of *materia* (substance) and *forma* (accident), so also language must have this dual nature.[2] He thus perpetuates Scaliger's treatment of language as a substance, using the term *materia* to indicate phonetic structure, and *forma* to indicate semantic content.

Sanctius' discussion of ellipse is much more detailed than that in either of the Port-Royal grammars, and makes the important point that the notion of ellipse is a necessity in a theory of linguistic analysis – 'doctrinam supplendi esse valde necessariam'. Further, those elements to be supplied in an expansion of a given construction are those which are essential to *ratio*, those 'sine quibus Grammaticae ratio constare non potest'.[3] This discussion of ellipse makes, according to R. Lakoff, 'two important points that are transformational in nature':

One concept is the recovery of deletion: one needs to be able to tell from the surface structure what was present in the deep structure. Second is the concept of the division between an underlying abstract structure (simple syntax) and a superficial structure (figurative syntax) . . . There must be rules to bridge the gap between universal and logical language and specific, illogical languages.[4]

Sanctius seems to be aware of both these concepts, and there is no doubt in his mind as to which takes precedence, the *ratio* of the underlying linguistic system, or the *sermo* of discourse. The *ratio* of all things, including language, must first be made clear, and only afterwards should details of the actualization of this *ratio* (in the case

---

[1] v. Review of Chomsky, *Cartesian Linguistics*, p. 175.
[2] *Minerva*, i, 2: 'Praeterea quum res omnes constent ex materia et forma, oratio idem constabit.'
[3] *Ibid*. iv, 2.
[4] Review of *Grammaire générale et raisonnée*, p. 361.

of language, items of usage) be given.[1] Among twentieth-century linguists, V. Brøndal takes up again, in his discussion of the nature of the linguistic sign, precisely this 'opposition between the word as formal unit and articulated thought, between *vox* and *ratio*, between δεῖξις and λόγος'. He remarks that the question needs to be reconsidered in the light of the grammatical system as a whole, upon which it would clearly emerge that while the word is the linguistic unit on the morphological level, it is the 'link of articulated thought' (*chaînon de la pensée articulée*) that is the unit of syntax.[2] J. Lyons similarly notes the relationship between underlying semantic and surface syntactic structures:

It is not unlikely that a greater concentration of interest upon the theory of semantics will bring linguists back to the traditional view that the syntactic structure of languages is very highly determined by their semantic structure: more especially by the 'modes of signifying' of semantically-based grammatical categories.[3]

He adds however that any attempt to reintegrate such an approach into modern grammatical theory would have to meet the rigorous demands of twentieth-century structural linguistics.

Sanctius did not succeed in his aim to supplant Nebrija as the official grammarian of Spain. Virtually unheeded in his own country, he had more success outside its borders. Sanchez Barrado[4] places him among the great philosophers of language, while C. García sees him as the precursor of rationalism,[5] as in A. Tovar's words the originator of 'the whole era of rationalism, natural law and universal reason'.[6] García none the less notes with approval (though how inaccurately!) that in practice Sanctius ignores his rationalistic principles in his approach to grammar.[7] Those parts of Sanctius' work which are

[1] *Minerva*, i, 1: 'Non igitur dubium est, quin rerum omnium, etiam vocum, reddenda sit ratio . . . Reliquum est igitur ut omnium rerum ratio primum adhibeatur, tum deinde . . . accedant testimonia.' Cf. also, *loc. cit.*: 'Usus porro sine ratione non movetur . . . Nihil autem potest esse diuturnum . . . cui non subest ratio.'

[2] *Essais de linguistique générale*, Copenhagen, 1943, p. 117.

[3] *Introduction to Theoretical Linguistics*, Cambridge University Press, 1969, p. 481.

[4] 'Estudios sobre el Brocense', *Revista crítica Hispano-Americana*, V (1919), pp. 13–14.

[5] *Contribución*, p. 47. Similarly I. Poldauf, 'Problems of English Grammar', p. 48. Poldauf claims that in the works of Melanchthon, Scaliger and Sanctius 'Latin definitely ceases to be regarded as a means of logic.' Concerning Sanctius at any rate it is possible to entertain serious reservations as to the truth of this.

[6] 'Toda la era de la ilustración, el racionalismo, el derecho natural y la razón universal.' v. Tovar's introductory study to M. de la Pinta Llorente's *Procesos inquisitoriales contra Francisco Sánchez de las Brozas*, Madrid, 1941, pp. vii–viii.

[7] *Contribución*, p. 162.

most admired by García, with regret that they are subordinated to logical principles, are undeniably Ramistic.[1] His claim that there is no grammarian in the entire period comparable to Sanctius in originality[2] falls to the ground as soon as the extent of his debt to Scaliger (with whom it is true he often disagrees) and to Ramus is realized. In view of the fact that – his treatment of ellipse apart – Sanctius takes most of his ideas from Ramus and Scaliger and the rest from Aristotle, Tovar's and García's patriotism can only be regarded as impressive. Sanctius is in fact victim of a curious confusion. Having plagiarized Ramus' formal system, he tries to wed it to Aristotelian logic and Scaliger's preoccupation with the psychologically based *causae* of language. He gives the impression of a convinced exponent of a logical, rational basis to language who has muddled his argument by beginning with someone else's formal definitions based on the premise that the grammarian must ignore the underlying meaning of linguistic structures.

In view of what has been said above as to Sanctius' interest in *ratio* and the laying bare of a 'deep structure' based on it, it is difficult not to disagree also with I. Michael's evaluation of his work. Calling him with some justice 'the first modern grammarian', he ascribes to him an empirical approach of which he is far from being the exponent:

The renaissance grammarians were right in repudiating the excesses of a logical and *a priori* approach to grammar; they were right in returning to the actual behaviour of words. What they lacked (and it is the great merit of Sanctius that he realised this) was a robustly empirical outlook which would enable them to ask how best to describe the observed behaviour of words.[3]

It is true that Michael adds that Sanctius 'demands evidence, in the name not of logic but of reason'. But he entirely misses the point that Sanctius looks behind the 'observed behaviour of words' to the underlying logical structure. The detailed observation of discourse is certainly there in Sanctius, in nearly six hundred pages of assorted trivia. But hidden among the trivia, as R. Lakoff notes, are a number of very sophisticated insights into the nature of language and the

[1] Among contemporaries or near contemporaries of Sanctius García mentions only Nebrija, Scaliger and a few vernacular grammarians such as Villalón.

[2] *Contribución*, p. 165.

[3] *English Grammatical Categories and the Tradition to 1800*, Cambridge University Press, 1970, p. 34.

syntax of Latin.[1] Since however he has no real theory of *langue* in the Saussurean sense, his analyses take place at the level of discourse. Lost in a welter of actual usage, he is unable to extract from it a principle of linguistic codification. Without such a principle, the resources of Aristotelianism having been exhausted, linguistic studies had reached an impasse, to be broken through only when the Port-Royal grammarians began to seek the necessary metalanguage for linguistic analysis not in discourse itself, but in logic.[2] Sanctius' *Minerva* remains none the less a plea for the primacy of reason in grammar, for the seeking out and exemplification of the *ratio* underlying discourse, and it is this facet of his work, in view of the renewed interest shown of late in the Port-Royal *Grammaire générale et raisonnée*, that holds appeal for modern readers. In this regard Sanctius is further proof of the fact that much in grammatical theory formerly attributed to the seventeenth century, and more specifically to Port-Royal, is already present in sixteenth-century and even in medieval thought.

[1] Review of *Grammaire générale et raisonnée*, p. 357. With the added commentaries of Scioppius and Petrizonius, later editions of the *Minerva* run to some 1,000 pages.

[2] v. J.-C. Chevalier, *Histoire de la syntaxe: naissance de la notion de complément dans la grammaire française (1530–1750)*, Geneva, 1968, pp. 502–4. Chevalier sees the excesses of Hobbesian nominalism in the seventeenth century as the direct result of the type of linguistic analysis practised by Sanctius.

3. THE SEVENTEENTH CENTURY: WORDS VERSUS THINGS

THE REJECTION OF FORMALISM

Peter Ramus' legacy to grammatical studies was a formally based, 'structuralist' approach, that of Sanctius an insistence on the application of reason to grammar, on the underlying *ratio* of language exemplified by his investigation of ellipse. Both inherited from Scaliger the ordering of grammar within an Aristotelian logical framework and the Aristotelian three-word-class system.[1] In the early and mid-seventeenth century Aristotle's influence remains strong, and the tendency to see grammar as amenable to reason and logic results in an ever-growing bias toward semasiological definition at the expense of formal elements. The influence of Ramus' formal system is confined to the early decades of the century when, taking into account both Latin and vernacular grammars, there is an interval of twenty or thirty years during which an attempt is made to break with the old semantically based grammar and introduce a formalist approach. The attempt, largely confined apart from Ramus' own French grammar to Britain, is however doomed to failure, as the rationalistic seventeenth century confounds grammar and logic ever more closely and seeks the basis of language in reason rather than in details of structure. No grammarian of Latin seeks to repeat Ramus' essay at a grammar conceived almost wholly in formal terms, but a few works, which may be considered before passing on to the main currents of seventeenth-century grammar, show – in parallel with the contemporary mixed approach of Philippo-Ramistic logic – a mingling of Ramistic formal and traditional semasiological features. They are Alexander Hume's *Grammatica nova* and *Prima elementa grammaticae* of 1612, Kaspar Schoppe's *Grammatica philosophica* of 1628, and Thomas Hayne's *Grammatices Latinae compendium* of 1640. Paul Greaves' *Grammatica anglicana* (1594) and Ben Jonson's *English Grammar* (1640), which attempt to apply the full rigour of Ramus' method to

---

[1] Though Ramus sets up four word-classes, his scheme rests on the trio noun, verb and *syncategoremata*.

English, are outside the scope of this study, as are the formal/ semasiological hybrids represented by Hume's *Of the Orthographie and Congruitie of the Britan Tongue* (*c.* 1617),[1] Alexander Gil's *Logonomia Anglica* (1619) and Charles Butler's *English Grammar* (1633).

Hume's *Grammatica nova*, intended to replace Despauterius' grammar in the schools of Scotland, was in fact so prescribed by the Scots parliament, but its adoption was prevented by the bishops. An expanded version of his *Elementa*, it is rare among grammars of the period in giving a careful documentation of its author's reading. He claims to have given ten years' thought to the 'restoration of grammar', reading Valla, Sulpitius, Aldus Manutius, Melanchthon and above all Linacre, whom he names as his principal source. Finding none of these satisfactory at all points, and displeased by the 'obscurity' and 'barbarity' of Despauterius, he finally turned to Ramus, 'cuius methodus in multas apud nos penetraverat'.[2] Ramus enjoyed a greater following in Scotland than in England,[3] the Scots Regent having been his pupil, as was also G. Buchanan the translator into Latin of Linacre's *Rudimenta*.[4] His method being however too logical for Hume's taste – 'non ita grammaticam, ut logicam Ramus mihi visus est elaborasse' – he set out to write his own grammar, at first basing himself on received authorities (he mentions Varro and Priscian among others), but increasingly following his own bent. Schoppe (1576–1649), on the contrary, is almost wholly under the influence of Sanctius. A German who had studied at Heidelberg and Ingolstadt, he produced an 'improved' edition of Sanctius' *Minerva*, and from 1618 to 1630 lived in Milan, where he brought out his *Grammatica philosophica*.[5] Known as the *canis grammaticus* because of his sharp feuds with other scholars, he Italianized his name to Scioppio, further Latinized to Scioppius. As Sanctius' influence was perhaps greater in Italy than elsewhere, it is not surprising that Scioppius should have been affected by it. He must in fact have been among the

---

[1] This grammar remained unprinted until the Early English Text Society's edition of 1865.

[2] *Grammatica nova in usum juventutis Scoticae*, Edinburgh, 1612, preface (dated 1608).

[3] For a discussion of the spreading of Ramus' ideas in Europe v. F. P. Graves, *Petrus Ramus*, pp. 209–18.

[4] O. Funke, 'Grammatica Anglicana von P. Gr[eaves]. (1594)', states that it was Buchanan who introduced Ramistic doctrine into St Andrews, and that his pupil A. Melville (the *Melvinus* of Hume's preface?) made Ramus' work known in Glasgow at about the time it was beginning to penetrate into Cambridge.

[5] I have used the Amsterdam edition of 1659. Despite its title, Scioppius' work is not a 'philosophical' grammar.

first to be so influenced, for he was shown the copy of the *Minerva* which the then Spanish ambassador had brought with him to Rome.[1] He obviously however regarded himself as in some measure an innovator, for the flattering foreword to the 1659 edition of his work credits him with the suppression of grammatical monstrosities 'quae ne Sanctius quidem potuit olfacere'. Hayne, apart from the Ramistic content of his work, is slightly indebted to the Germans K. Finck and C. Helwig, whose Latin grammar of 1615[2] follows the 'philosophical' trend but with distinct Ramistic formal features.

Like their models, these three grammarians display an inability to define the *word* in structural terms, Scioppius retaining Sanctius' (i.e. Ramus') 'quo unumquodque vocatur', while Hume defines it as 'quae aliquid significat' or 'quae certam rem significat', thus taking over the traditional noun definition to do duty for the *vox*. Following Aristotelian principles, derivation and composition are regarded as accidents of the word, not of the individual parts of speech. Hayne then treats number and person as accidents of all four declinables, abandoning Ramus' use of person as a *specialis differentia* separating noun and verb. Hume's criterion in classifying the word-classes is however not number, but person. To Ramus' *vox numeri* and *sine numero* he opposes *vox personalis* ('quae personam notat') and *impersonalis*,[3] but his thoroughly mixed approach is indicated by his definition of person as a 'subsistentia rei voce notata',[4] a definition poles apart from Ramus' completely formal 'specialis terminatio verbi'.

Having substituted *person* for Ramus' number in defining the word-classes, Hume describes the noun, which in Ramistic fashion includes the pronoun, as 'vox unius personae, per Genera & Casus flexa', in contradistinction to the verb which is 'omnium personarum'. A consequence of the importance given, following Linacre, to person in Hume's system is his attempt to tie it in with case, which is defined as an 'affectio nominis ad societatem personarum variati'. His view of person is at first sight similar to that in Linacre's syntax, where it seems to be equivalent to morphological ending capable of congruence. Hume appears however to see case as the formal element in syntactic relations, with person as the semantic *vis* which is

---

[1] v. Port-Royal Latin Grammar, preface.
[2] *Grammatica Latina studio et opere Caspari Finckii et Christophori Helvici*, Giessen, 1615.
[3] *Elementa*, p. 2.
[4] Cf. Diomedes' 'persona est substantia rationalis' (H. Keil, *Grammatici Latini*, I, 334).

expressed by them. Illustrations of this are his view of the construction noun in nominative + noun in genitive (*Pamphilus Chremetis*) as the expression of *diversa persona* 'a re in rem transiens diversis casibus', and of the construction *suo patre* as the expression of *eadem persona* 'quae in una re subsistens uno casu effertur'.[1] In gender there is an attempt at the establishment of natural distinctions in the grouping of masculine and feminine as *verum genus* (corresponding to the *verus sexus* of the real world), and the introduction of a *fictum genus* (Ramus' term for the neuter) appropriate to *res sine sexu*. The attribution by the Latin language of masculine or feminine gender to *res sine sexu* is then termed *genus usurarium*.[2] There is here a mistaken identification of grammatical gender with sex and an attempt to force Latin grammar into a scheme more consonant with reason. Scioppius and Hayne similarly do not allow the gender system of their models to remain unchanged. In line with Sanctius' assertion that the adjective 'non habet genus, sed terminationes', Scioppius defines his noun-class as either showing *genus* or having a 'terminationem generi quadrantem'. But in order to stress the purely structural implications of gender marking in the adjective he is more careful in his definition of gender than Ramus and Sanctius. It is a *differentia nominis* not simply 'secundum sexum' but 'secundum sexus *notam*'.[3] In the substantive this *nota* is provided, as in Ramus and Sanctius, by the preceding *hic haec hoc* of the paradigms. In *hic felix*, however, *hic* belongs not to the adjective but to a following substantive understood by ellipse.[4] Hayne feels obliged to add to the formal gender-marking definition of adjective and substantive the medieval one in terms of syntactic dependence, but curiously transposed into terms of accidents. The substantive 'expresseth his *number* without any other words helpe', the adjective 'needeth an other word to express his *number and gender*'.[5] Scioppius, while repeating Sanctius' formal definition of adjective and substantive, brings in a semasiological element quite foreign to the Ramistic system with his remark that the substantive signifies *cosa*, *chose* or *Ding* in the vernaculars.[6]

The Ramistic predilection for dichotomies is reflected in Hume's careful setting out of declension. A primary division into *ennoma* ('quae certa forma flectitur') and *anoma* (the pronouns) is followed

---

[1] *Grammatica nova*, p. 21.
[3] *Grammatica philosophica*, p. 4 (my italics).
[4] *Ibid*. p. 84.
[6] *Grammatica philosophica*, p. 5.

[2] *Elementa*, p. 13.
[5] *Compendium*, pp. 5–6.

by a subdivision of the former into *analoga* and *paraloga*, of the *analoga* into *justa* ('quae justis syllabis perficitur') and *contracta*. Finally, the *declinatio justa* is divided into *parisyllaba* and *imparisyllaba*, and the former of these into *prima* (nouns in *-us*, *-a*) and *secunda* (nouns in *-er*).[1] After this scrupulous formal classification it is curious that Hume treats noun derivation, including comparison, in the semasiological terms of *mutatio significationis*.[2] Hayne similarly repeats the Roman grammarians' subclassifications of the noun into extra-linguistic semantic categories such as the *nomen patrium*. This refusal to accept Ramus' system unalloyed, with all its implications as to the exclusion of meaning as a criterion, is indicative of the general temper of the times. One has the impression that the Ramistic method was momentarily fashionable, but that elements of it were merely grafted onto a universally accepted semasiological system which grammarians were profoundly reluctant to change. They find in any case, as Ramus did, that the formal system is not uniformly applicable even to such a highly synthetic language as Latin. Hume for instance finds it necessary to divide his noun into *genuinum* ('quod per sua genera, & suos casus flectitur') and *adulterinum*, a term applied to those word-forms (e.g. infinitives) which, of themselves genderless and undeclined, can function grammatically as nouns.[3]

Hume's verb, true to his view of person as the chief criterion in determining the word-classes, is a 'vox omnium personarum per tempora, et modos variata'.[4] His semasiological bent does not allow him to follow Ramus in dismissing mood from the verbal system. The moods are however not named other than as *primus, secundus* and *tertius*,[5] and are differentiated formally by endings indicating person and number 'certis finibus'. Person and number are similarly indicated by the infinitive, but 'nullis finibus' by means of a preceding pronoun in an oblique case. Tense is defined in circular fashion as an 'affectio Verbi e differentiis temporis nota' (i.e. as an accident indicating time), mood as an 'affectio verbi ad pronunciandi usum accommodata'.[6] Tense is further oddly described as *praesens* or

---

[1] *Elementa*, pp. 15–17. [2] *Grammatica nova*, pp. 44–5.
[3] *Grammatica nova*, pp. 20, 51. This distinction seems to be peculiar to Hume.
[4] *Elementa*, p. 3. The model for Hume's scheme is no doubt Linacre, who counted person as an accident of all declinables, with case and gender as distinctive features of the noun, mood and tense of the verb.
[5] Indicative, subjunctive and imperative. [6] *Grammatica nova*, pp. 7–8.

absens, praesens referring to an action 'quae nunc est'. Hume has a Linacre-inspired division of the future into *absolvendum* ('scribam') and *absolutum* ('scripsero'), incorporating a Varronian completive/ incompletive aspectual feature. Varronian too is the division of preterite tenses into *infecta* and *confecta*, though Hume does not extend the term *infecta* to his present and first future. Voice is treated in solely formal terms. Ramistic formalism is however breached, as in the noun, by the introduction of semantic considerations. Formal distinctions are blurred by the introduction of the semasiological concept of the *vis verbi* to differentiate *nomina verbalia* and *participialia*. The former[1] do not retain the *vis* of the verb, resembling it in *significatio* but differing from it in *consignificatio*. The distinction is grammatically sound and true to Ramistic principles, but Ramus would not have explained it in terms of the *vis verbi*. A further semantic confusion is introduced by the notion of a *nomen activum* which equally with the transitive verb can effect the transition of *vis activa* from *persona agentis* to *persona patientis* (expressed by a 'passive genitive').[2] Scioppius too classifies certain categories, such as voice, 'ratione significati' (semasiologically) rather than 'ratione speciei' (formally).

Hume follows Linacre in extending his primary criterion of person to syntactic relations, a medieval trait which may have appealed to him because it provided him with a category applicable to both *etymologia* and *syntaxis*. He accordingly divides syntax into *personalis* (covering formal congruence and case government) and *impersonalis*. The *suppositum* being 'sui generis, casus, numeri, & personae', it is the *appositum* (which may be either verb or noun) that must be brought into congruence with it. A noun *appositum* does not agree with its *suppositum* in person, but only in gender, number and case. Person has however an important role to play in *rectio*, which is defined as affecting *voces* 'diversae personae unius in aliam transeuntis'.[3] Here the word *persona* seems to be used in the syntactic sense it has in the *Grammatica speculativa*, where structures such as *filius Socratis* are assigned to the *constructio transitiva personarum*. Hume appears however to extend this notion of syntactic person to the government of case by

---

[1] *Nomina* 'quae actionem significant'.

[2] *Grammatica nova*, pp. 63–4. Hume's adverb, in contrast, shows a marked absence of the usual plethora of *significationes*, being formally classified into *adverbia prima* and *derivata*.

[3] *Elementa*, p. 30.

the verb.[1] Interesting is his terminology in explaining *filius Socratis* as a subject governed by a preceding adjunct.[2] These terms are plainly taken from logic, and this is an early use in grammar of *subiectum* for the logical subject of an utterance, though Hume does not apply it to the subject of a verb. The *voces impersonales*, being *syncategoremata*, are sometimes required to be in congruence with the verb. A verb expressing *motus* or *quies* must be accompanied by an adverb expressing the same, and verbal tenses by an appropriate temporal adverb. These are of course semantic agreements, not formal ones. Hume is obviously motivated by the desire to make his syntactic categories universally applicable, what is appropriate to the *voces personales* having its neatly balancing counterpart in the *voces impersonales*. To achieve this end he does not hesitate to invent supposed semantic 'agreements' to balance the formally based ones. But his entire syntax is in fact semantically conceived in terms of the transition of the *vis* of one part of speech into another, rather than in formal and structural terms.

There is in these authors a confusion of semantic and formal categories. Typical of this confusion is Scioppius who, obviously a fervent admirer of Sanctius, seems to have parroted his formal Ramistic definitions without any real awareness of their implications. His *Grammatica philosophica* is a curious mixture of formal word-class definitions, Ramistic dichotomies, and semasiological treatment of most of the secondary points of grammar. Though not strictly speaking a 'philosophical' grammar, his work is thoroughly contemporary in its attempts to equate grammar and logic, in its straining of language to fit logical requirements and in its explanation of anomalies by means of ellipse.[3] In his grammar and those of Hume and Hayne there is a gesture towards formalism, no more.

[1] The *constructio transitiva actuum* of the *Grammatica speculativa* (caps. xlviii, li) excludes the notion of person, where there is signification 'per modum actus' (*lego librum, Socrates currit*), employing it only where there is signification 'per modum substantiae' (*Socrates albus, filius Socratis*). Cf. the ancient view of person as a 'substantia rationalis'.

[2] *Elementa*, pp. 28–31.

[3] L. Kukenheim, *Esquisse*, p. 24, is however mistaken in regarding Scioppius and his contemporaries as the *inventors* of such expansions as e.g. *vivo = vivo vitam*. They are present in grammars of much earlier date.

The three authors just considered do little more than clothe the Ramistic formal system with a semasiological framework. Hume particularly shows a semasiological bias in advance of that of his Humanist models. The general tone of the approach adopted by seventeenth-century grammarians is illustrated by John Danes' dismissal of the often-quoted 'Quanto eris melior Grammaticus, tanto peior Dialecticus',[1] reflecting the careful medieval separation of grammar and logic, as a '*Vox bove digna*, a speech as sottish as false.'[2] The general tendency in mid-seventeenth-century grammar is that of a flight from formally based definition in the direction of an ever more semantically based approach in which the grammarian needs to know his logic. Formally based grammar progressively disappears from about 1640 on, but it is interesting to note the lone survival of a purely formal grammar in Edward Leedes' *Graeco-Latinum Compendium* of 1693.[3] A Greek grammar written in Latin, and as such outside the scope of this study, it is none the less worth citing as a work in which virtually the only semasiological definition is that of the sentence (*oratio*) as a 'Dictionum compositio quae sensum perfectum declarat'. Such definitions as that of the preposition as a 'dictio indeclinabilis quae declinabilibus praeponitur', or of the article as a 'pars orationis casualis quae aliis praeponitur', are in the largely formal Greek tradition of definition initiated by Dionysius Thrax. It is interesting to find still extant, at the end of the seventeenth century, a formalism which owes nothing to Ramus but goes back via Greek grammatical tradition to Thrax and the first century B.C.[4] Apart from such lone eccentricities, however, the emphasis becomes increasingly semasiological as the century advances. The most important Latin grammarian, the Dutchman Gerard Johannes Vossius (1577–1649), whose vast *De arte grammatica*[5] appeared in 1635, is firmly in this tradition. One of the great polymaths of his age, he was appointed Professor of Eloquence at Leyden in 1622,

---

[1] Ascribed to Johannes Dullardus.

[2] *A Light to Lilie. Being an Easie Method for the Better Teaching and Learning of the Grounds of the Latine Tongue*, London, 1637, p. v.

[3] *Ad prima rudimenta Graecae linguae discenda Graeco-Latinum compendium*, London, 1693.

[4] The chief exception to the formal parallels with Thrax is in the Aristotelian time references in noun and verb definitions found also in Gaza's Greek grammar of 1495.

[5] *Gerardi Iohanni Vossii de arte grammatica libri septem*, Amsterdam, 1635. This work runs to over twelve hundred pages.

Professor of History at Amsterdam in 1631, was offered a chair of History at Cambridge, and became a Canon of Canterbury in 1629. His *De arte*, known from the 1662 edition onward as the *Aristarchus*, by which title Bishop Wilkins of Chester refers to it, was still being published in Germany two centuries after its first appearance. It became the standard grammar for Germany and Holland. Vossius also rewrote Lithocomus' Latin grammar, which had been in use in the Low Countries since 1575, a task he likens to the cleansing of the Augean stables.[1] Though the authors of the Port-Royal Latin Grammar[2] describe Vossius as having followed Sanctius and Scioppius 'presque en tout', often simply copying them, there is in fact a widespread Varronian influence in his work similar to that in the sixteenth-century Italian grammarian Corradus. Imitative though he may be, it is however Vossius who holds the stage in mid-century theory.[3]

In England the influence of Lily, sole grammarian permitted in the schools, continues to be strong, and examples of grammars based on him could be multiplied. Suffice it to name John Brinsley's *Posing of the Parts*,[4] Christofer Syms' *Introduction to the Latine Speach*,[5] John Danes' *Light to Lilie*, Charles Hoole's *Latine Grammar*,[6] and Edward Burles' *New English Grammar*.[7] The poet Milton's *Accedence Commenc't Grammar* of 1669 calls for no comment. He does not mention his source, saying his work 'will declare sufficiently to them who can discern', but it is obviously Lily. In Danes' work, by far the most frequent references to sources are those to Varro, Vossius and Scaliger, who together with Sanctius must be regarded as the major influences of the first half of the seventeenth century. These minor grammarians tend to be heavily derivative, Danes for example following Lily often word for word in his *Light to Lilie*,[8] and in his

---

[1] In the preface to the third edition of this revision, *Latina grammatica*, Leyden, 1631.

[2] C. Lancelot, A. Arnauld and P. Nicole, *Nouvelle Méthode pour apprendre facilement la langue Latine*, 8th ed., Paris, 1681, preface, pp. 4–5.

[3] Cf. John Danes, *Paralipomena orthographiae, etymologiae, prosodiae*, London, 1638/9, p. [xi]: 'Ecquis de Arte Grammatica post Vossium? Strenue quidem ille Atlas Grammaticum hoc coelum suffulcit.'

[4] *The Posing of the Parts: Or, A Most Plaine and Easie Way of Examining the Accidence and Grammar*, London (2nd ed.), 1615.

[5] *An Introduction to, or, the Art of Teaching, the Latine Speach*, Dublin, 1634.

[6] *The Latine Grammar Fitted for the Use of Schools*, London, 1651.

[7] *Grammatica Burlesa or a New English Grammar*, London, 1652. Despite its title, this work is a grammar of Latin.

[8] The foreword gives Melanchthon and Scaliger as sources, but Danes proposes to reproduce Lily's grammar almost unaltered.

Paralipomena leaning closely on Vossius and, beyond him, on Varro and Scaliger, though one suspects that his knowledge of Varro derives from Vossius and possibly Linacre. As for Hoole's work, it is in fact Lily's grammar with various formal features excluded and a superimposed Aristotelian framework in the ordering of the accidents. The lesser grammarians are overshadowed in England by Lily, and on the Continent by the giants Scaliger, Sanctius and Vossius. They are however sometimes indicative of a general trend, and among English minor grammarians of Latin the work of James Shirley is an interesting illustration of the movement away from the formal approach and toward the identification of grammar with logic. This process can be followed, as V. Salmon mentions in her article on Shirley,[1] in the successive versions of his *Via ad Latinam linguam complanata* (1649),[2] reissued in 1651 as the *Grammatica Anglo-Latina* and in 1656 as *The Rudiments of Grammar*. A close comparison indicates that the 1649 edition is much more formal in bent than the later ones. V. Salmon notes[3] that these successive versions well illustrate the contemporary confusion of three methods of classification: the morphological (formal), the structural (syntactic) and the semasiological (defining a relationship to the categories of reality). She rightly stresses the early roots of the first two methods, but seems to regard the third as a largely eighteenth-century trait toward which the seventeenth century is tending. It is one of the contentions of the present study that such features, long ascribed to the eighteenth century, are in fact of medieval and even earlier origin.

Typical of the growing rationalistic approach is the seventeenth-century discussion as to whether grammar is a science. Vossius[4] concludes that it is not, since its object, *oratio*, has no immovable and invariable *essentia* 'a qua certae fluant passiones de subjecto demonstrabiles'.[5] Science being 'rerum aeternarum', it follows that gram-

---

[1] 'James Shirley', p. 291.

[2] *Via ad Latinam linguam complanata: The Way made Plain to the Latine Tongue*, London, 1649.

[3] 'James Shirley', p. 289. In certain features Shirley's *Manuductio: or, A Leading of Children by the Hand through the Principles of Grammar* (2nd ed., London, 1660), a simple school grammar, represents a return to formal definition.

[4] The *De arte grammatica* consists of seven books: I. *De literis*; II. *De syllabis*; III–VI. *De vocum analogia, et anomalia*; VII. *De sermonis constructione*. The work is not consecutively paginated. Books I–II are paginated 1–313, III–IV 1–403, V–VI 1–248, and Book VII 1–272. Reference is accordingly made here to book and chapter headings, and to page numbers within the appropriate series, e.g. *De arte*, III, iii, 15.

[5] *De arte*, I, ii, 9.

mar, concerning itself with 'res contingentes' and 'notiones secundae', is not a science. Equally in the name of a rational approach, the ancient division of *grammatica exegetice* concerned with the interpretation of classical authors is rejected, the sole province of the grammarian being *grammatica methodice*. The contemporary preoccupation with universal grammar is reflected in the division of grammar into *naturalis*, treating categories believed to be common to all languages, and *artificialis*, dealing with those peculiar to a given language. Upon each of these divisions Vossius imposes the four parts *orthoepia, prosodia, analogia* and *syntaxis*, the traditional Humanist plan, but with the term *etymologia* replaced by *analogia*. The latter term stems from Vossius' belief that the whole of this part of grammar, the *particulae* excepted, is explicable in terms of analogy and anomaly.[1] The province of the *analogia* is 'vocabularum discrimina', the criteria employed being semantic ones. Shirley's initial definition of *etymology* as concerned with 'the proprieties of several words, especially in the difference of the Terminations',[2] finds increasingly less favour with grammarians as time goes on.

Priscian's formal definition of the *dictio* as a minimum unit of sentence structure is of course not acceptable to Vossius and his contemporaries, who prefer a definition in terms of signification. Vossius rejects it on the grounds that the *dictio* is in fact not a *pars minima*, being further divisible into syllables and letters. He is unable to perceive what A. Martinet calls the 'double articulation' of language,[3] by which letters (or in modern terms phonemes) are minimal parts on the phonological level (*partes minimae vocis*), and words (or rather morphemes) are minimal parts on the semantic level (*partes minimae orationis constructae*). He prefers the 'true definition' of the word (taken from Aristotle's *De interpretatione*), as that which has signification by itself, but does not contain parts separately capable of signification[4] – a definition on the level of lexical meaning that entirely ignores both compound words and grammatical function.

The classification of words similarly corresponds to the triple classification imposed by Aristotelian philosophy upon things in the real world. Just as *res naturales* differ in *forma, materia* and *accidens*, so

[1] *Ibid.* III, i, 2.
[2] *Via ad Latinam linguam complanata* (1649), p. 1.
[3] For an explanation of this term v. A. Martinet, *Éléments de linguistique générale*, Paris, 1960, pp. 17–19.
[4] *De arte*, III, i, 2.

do *voces* differ *formā* (in class),[1] *materiā* (from each other within the class boundaries) and *accidente* (individually in such matters as case). Priscian's conclusion that since the criterion for distinguishing them is 'uniuscuiusque proprietatis significatio' there can be neither more nor less than eight word-classes is not maintained. Noun and verb being isolated as principal classes on the logical Aristotelian grounds that 'ex his solis perfecta conficitur oratio', Vossius sees no reason why the remaining classes should not be defined in terms of these two. He therefore seems ready to assign the pronoun, in Ramistic fashion but not for Ramus' reasons, to the noun-class. The participle may be considered now a noun, now a verb, not for the traditional reason that it partakes of the nature of both, but on grounds arising out of the Aristotelian theory of predication. It is a noun if *subjectum* of its sentence and (since *Homo est valens* = *Homo valet*) a verb if *praedicatum*[2] – a logical standpoint from which grammatical considerations are excluded. The remaining classes being *consignificantia* of noun and verb, Vossius is left with a three-word-class system (for which no doubt he is indebted to Sanctius) of noun, verb and conjunction (Aristotle's σύνδεσμος).[3] In his anxiety to classify all parts of speech under one or other of these three headings, Vossius goes so far as to say that what are traditionally termed adverbs might equally well be called verbs (*utinam* venias = *opto ut* venias), adjectives (hoc *juste* agis = haec actio *justa* est), or even pronouns (*una* illic fuimus = *ego et alter* illic fuimus). This is Sanctius' doctrine of ellipse taken to extremes. It illustrates the common contemporary notion that the 'sense' of an utterance can be expressed grammatically in a number of different ways each equally valid, a notion necessary to the idea of a 'universal grammar' expressing concepts which each individual language expresses in its own way. It is also, in that the second phrase is in each case an expansion making more explicit the meaning only implied in the first, an example of an awareness of 'surface' and 'deep' structure. The procedure, growing out of Sanctius' use of ellipse, consists in replacing one structure by another, 'equivalent' in meaning but more amenable to logical explanation, containing

[1] Vossius prefers the term *classes* to the traditional *partes orationis*.
[2] *De arte*, III, i, 5. Vossius is the first grammarian noted by V. Salmon ('James Shirley' p. 293) to use the terms *subjectum* and *praedicatum* alongside the usual *suppositum* and *appositum*. Corradus had however already used, in his *De lingua Latina* of 1575, *subjectum* and *attributum* exclusively.
[3] *De arte*, III, i, 6. The *Latina grammatica* (p. 6) envisages the possibility of four classes: 'duas principes, duas [adverbum et coniunctio] his servientes'.

noun or pronoun subject, verb and words consignifying with them, and then explaining the grammar of the first structure in terms of that of the second.

The Aristotelian basis of much of the *De arte* is obvious. The 'perfecta cuiusque rei cognitio' consists for Vossius in the recognition of *essentia* and *accidentia*, the former being made known confusedly by the definition of a word-class, more distinctly by the various *species* into which that word-class is divided. Here, he is simply putting into a reasoned statement what was implicit in Roman and Humanist practice and explicit in the medieval system of *modi essentiales, accidentales* and *speciales*. Each word-class is considered under the three aspects applied by Aristotle to his ten categories of reality: *definitio, divisio* (into *species*), and *proprietates* (i.e. accidents).[1] In accordance with Aristotle's doctrine of the primacy of the general, derivation and composition, as accidents of all word-classes, are treated at the outset, as are number and person as accidents of all classes except the *particulae*. In dealing with number, the existence of formally plural but semantically singular words like *Athenae* leads to the conclusion that meaning, not form (*vocis inflexio*), must be the primary criterion. Person is not necessarily present in any word-class. All nouns are of the third person, but only when taking part in a syntactic structure. Standing alone they are, vocatives excepted,[2] devoid of person. The theory is based on the fact that the infinitive of the verb, which can function as a noun, has of itself neither person nor number. It follows that all other nouns must be of the same nature, and hence 'vel nullius, vel omnis personae'.[3] The remaining accidents of all word-classes except the *particulae* are *analogia* and *anomalia*. Vossius seems to be alone among grammarians of his own or the preceding century[4] in resurrecting the ancient analogy/anomaly controversy in order to apply it to grammatical accidents. Behind this is no doubt Varro, whose division into *genus foecundum* (declinables) and *genus sterile* (indeclinables), and classification of derived forms as voluntary (*Roma/Romanus*) and natural (*Roma/Romae*), are cited in support.

Vossius' approach to the definition of the noun is entirely semasiological, the period being in general characterized by the progres-

---

[1] *De arte*, III, vi, 24.
[2] The view that all vocatives are of the second person is traditional in Latin grammar.
[3] *De arte*, III, iv, 20.
[4] Apart from imitators such as the Englishmen Danes and Hoole.

sive abandonment of what formal criteria remain from the Roman/ Humanist mixed approach according to both formal and semantic considerations. Though formal elements intrude in discussions of accident, there is an increasing reluctance to use them in defining a word-class. Since the definition is regarded as conveying the *essentia* of a given part of speech, it is plain that formal differences are not regarded as essential. Among followers of Lily there is a tendency to eliminate without comment the formal elements of his definitions, as do Brinsley and Hoole in defining substantive and adjective. These elements appear to have been removed even from editions of the *Regia grammatica* itself, for Christofer Syms, who exceptionally attaches great importance to variation by 'termination' or by 'tipes and figures', of which he finds traces in Lily's grammar, censures the King's Printer for removing such formal indications as being 'impertinent superfluities', and leaving only a vestige of them in the treatment of the adjective.[1] Rejecting formal means of distinguishing noun from verb, Vossius falls back on the Aristotelian semantic criterion of the consignification of time, including it however as an element of definition in the verb only.[2] Dismissing Donatus' definition in terms of the signification of a *res* as equally applicable to the pronoun, he finally decides on the criterion of immediate signification (*nomen primo significat rem, pronomen secundario*) as best expressing the *essentia* of the noun. It is a 'vox ex instituto rem primo significans',[3] an immediate signification of reality.

On logical grounds Vossius makes the substantive/adjective distinction the primary dichotomy in the noun, with precedence over the division into proper and common. He is not the first grammarian to do this, but the reasons he invokes (Aristotle's division of τὸ ὄν – *quod est* – into 'quod per se subsistit' and 'quod in alio est ut accidens') is typical of his rational approach and represents an interesting return to medieval practice in the name of logic.[4] The formal definition of the adjective in terms of gender-marking is rejected, for *animans* e.g., though marking a possible three genders with a single termination, can also function as a substantive, 'per se subsistere in oratione'. Subdivisions such as this below the level of the word-class

---

[1] *Latine Speach*, pp. [12]–[13].
[2] In the *Latina grammatica* (p. 9) it appears in the noun definition also.
[3] *De arte*, III, iii, 15. The 'ex instituto' (by arbitrary convention) stems from Aristotle. It is not clear why Vossius does not extend it to the rest of the word-classes, which are equally *ex instituto*.   [4] *De arte*, III, vi, 24.

are to be decided not on formal grounds, but 'ab significatione, quae est forma essentialis, & quasi anima vocis'.[1]

In considering the *proprietates* of the noun, Vossius eliminates by logical argument all but three of the traditional ten accidents.[2] Donatus' *qualitas* is excluded on the grounds that it pertains to the noun's οὐσία (*essentia*) rather than to its *proprietates*, and *significatio* is superfluous since no word can be *essentialis* without at the same time signifying something.[3] The sole 'communes nominum affectiones' are *genus, casus* and *declinatio*, the latter being in Varronian fashion *directa* (noun cases) or *transversa* (*motio* and *comparatio* in the adjective). Gender is seen as strictly speaking a *discrimen sexus* applicable only according to natural criteria. If *animal* is neuter it is not as a result of such an application, but 'quia neutro modo construitur'. In *grammatical* terms, therefore, gender is not a *discrimen secundum sexum*, but a *secundum sexus nota* determined 'propter solam structuram'. On this view adjectives indicate gender only 'ex accidenti', and Vossius follows Sanctius in remarking that if adjectives were formally invariable the whole question of gender in Latin would be 'inanis ac supervacua'.[4] Grammatical gender is imposed not *a natura* but *ab instituto*, a distinction being made between the natural term *muliebre* and the grammatical term *femininum*. The primary division of gender is into *simplex* and *compositum*,[5] the *simplex* being further divided into *principale* (masculine and feminine, 'quod natura novit') and *minus principale* (neuter). The fact that Vossius reserves the term *principale* to those genders known in nature and calls its two animate subdivisions *virile* and *muliebre* would seem to indicate an attempt to set up a category of natural gender (*genus simplex*) as opposed to grammatical gender (*genus compositum*), reserved to those words, i.e. adjectives, that indicate two or three genders by formal variation.[6] Semantic and formal criteria (Vossius continually insists that *virile* and *masculinum, muliebre* and *femininum* are not overlapping terms) are to be kept rigorously apart. He accordingly sets up separate classes of 'communia significatione' and 'communia constructione', with the former of which he can include the *epicoena* as being 'communia

[1] *Latina grammatica*, p. 10.
[2] *Species, figura, persona, numerus, qualitas, significatio, comparatio, genus, casus, declinatio*. The first four of these Vossius excludes as common to more than one word-class.
[3] *De arte*, III, viii, 31.
[4] *Ibid.* III, ix, 33.
[5] I.e. natural and grammatical.
[6] *De arte*, III, ix, 35.

significatione, non structurā'.[1] Only adjectives are 'omnis generis', not by virtue of their own gender – 'proprie nullius sunt generis' – but 'ratione convenientiae cum substantivo'.[2] Thus does Vossius attempt to bring order into the chaos of the Roman and Humanist treatment of gender, with its conflicting formal and semantic criteria. In dealing with case however he is obliged to rely on purely formal considerations. He notes Priscian's rejection of a seventh case on the grounds that no formal difference justifies it. Were it permissible to 'mutare vim ablativi' to give birth to an extra case, it would be equally licit to 'mutare vim accusativi' etc. and set up new cases *ad infinitum*. Vossius concludes that there cannot be more cases than there are 'differentes terminationes, diversumque officium constituentes'.[3] Several *significations* may well be covered by one formal termination, but a fresh grammatical case cannot be set up for each new syntactic or semantic relation the mind of man can invent. Sanctius, Frischlin and Scioppius are therefore at fault in establishing an extra Greek case on non-formal grounds.

Rejecting traditional definitions in terms of noun substitution, Vossius defines the pronoun (in contrast to the noun signifying 'rem primo') as 'quod primario nomen respicit; secundario vero rem significat',[4] the Apollonian definition in terms of the indirect signification of reality given by Scaliger. Almost all pronouns are adjectives, therefore 'omnis generis', a reasoning which would seem to contradict his earlier statement that adjectives are 'proprie nullius generis'. *Ego, tu* and *sui* are however substantives signifying 'rem per se subsistentem'.[5] Here again, Vossius is perpetuating medieval doctrine, which posited for the pronoun both a *modus per se stantis* and a *modus adjacentis*.[6]

The essence of the verb lies for Vossius in the signification of *agere, pati* or *esse*,[7] not, be it noted, in the signification of *actio, passio* or *ens*, which are signified by nouns such as *calefactio*. The verb *consignifies* time ('adsignificat tempus sine casu') and *signifies* 'agere,

[1] *Ibid.* III, xv, 61 and xvii, 68–9. In the *Latina grammatica* (p. 13) Vossius clarifies this distinction. *Constructione communia* are those nouns (e.g. *parens*) which admit an adjective 'utriusque generis'. *Significatione communia* are those which apply to either sex (*homo, animal*) but admit adjectives of one gender only.

[2] *De arte*, III, xviii, 73 and xvii, 71.   [3] *Ibid.* III, xlv, 223.

[4] *Ibid.* III, iii, 15. The definition in the *Latina grammatica* is in more traditional terms.

[5] *Ibid.* VI, viii, 181.

[6] Cf. *Grammatica speculativa*, cap. xxii.

[7] With an added reference to *esse*, this is precisely Melanchthon's definition of over a century earlier (*Grammatica*, 1527 ed., f. 26ʳ).

pati, vel esse'.[1] Syms' *Latine Speach*[2] similarly holds the verb to be the 'kernel' of language since all discourse is of doing, suffering or being. But whereas Syms notes that what distinguishes the verb from the remaining word-classes is its possession of an individual set of 'terminations and adjuncts', Englished by Lily's 'signes and significations', Vossius and his imitators regard *meaning*, active or passive, as the key to its nature. Hoole's and Shirley's[3] definition of the verb in Vossius' terms as a 'pars orationis, quae esse aliquid, agereve aut pati significat' is in fact that of Lily minus the added 'modis et temporibus inflexa'. This seventeenth-century tendency to define the verb in terms of voice rather than of mood and tense and to exclude all formal criteria is however not new. Shirley's and Hoole's definition is, the reference to *esse* apart, that found in Melanchthon's *Grammatica* of 1527 – a striking illustration of the return beyond the abandoned Ramistic formalism back to earlier wholly semantic conceptions. What the seventeenth century has added is an insistence that the doing, suffering or being is that 'of a Substantive called the Nominative case',[4] underlining the verb's function as one of the two terms in a logical proposition. The state of thought on the matter at the end of the century is neatly summed up in A. Lane's definition: 'a word that signifies the Action, Passion, or Being of a thing, and may be conjugated in good Sense with a Substantive of the Nominative Case before it, and without a Nominative Case cannot make Sense . . .'[5] Since in all verbs a subject in the nominative case can be 'tacitly understood',[6] earlier grammarians' explanations of certain impersonal verbs by means of a 'nominativus cognatae significationis', as in Priscian's *me poenitat = poenitentia poenitat me*, can be rejected. The so-called impersonals, generally thought to lack a personal subject (and hence, says Vossius, *innominativa* rather than *impersonalia*), are in fact found to have one. In 'me miseret alterius', *me* acts as subject (not *naturā suā*, but as an element of the same value as a noun in the nominative) and *miseret alterius* as predicate. The ground on which 'surface structure' is explained has shifted to the logical one of whether it can be shown to contain both elements of a proposition.

[1] *De arte*, III, iii, 15. The *Latina grammatica* (p. 90) has only 'dictio variabilis, quae agere, pati vel esse significat'.

[2] p. [20].   [3] *Rudiments* (1656).

[4] W. Clare, *Via naturalis . . . or, the Natural Way to Learn the Latin Tongue*, London, 1688, p. 13.

[5] *A Rational and Speedy Method of Attaining to the Latin Tongue*, London, 1695, p. 11.

[6] *De arte*, V, i, 2.

Vossius sees the verb as 'triplicis significationis' (*agere, pati, esse*) but 'quadruplicis formae' (active, passive, neutral, deponent), implying a recognition that his tripartite semantic division does not square with the linguistic facts. He solves the problem by treating the *neutra* as *activa absoluta* whose action is not transient but immanent.[1] He notes that formally passive verbs can be used actively, and formally active verbs passively.[2] Similarly semantic are Burles' definitions of active and neutral verbs:

A *Verb Active* like a *Noun Adjective*, leaveth the mind unsatisfied, without the help of another word:

as, *amo* . . .

A *Verb Neuter* like a Noun Substantive satisfieth the understanding without the help of another word:

as, *pugno* . . .[3]

The definition of grammatical categories in terms of the 'unsatisfied mind' is hardly a linguistic procedure, but it is indicative of the general drift of the age.

Sanctius' contention that the verb has no moods is rejected, without any reference to its source in Ramus. Vossius recognizes however only the three moods indicative, imperative and subjunctive (*adiunctivus*). The others, optative, concessive, potential etc. are dismissed as corresponding to no formal differences in Latin.[4] The infinitive may *à la rigueur* be counted a mood but, following Scaliger, *potestate* not *actu*. Danes, who (more particularly in his *Paralipomena*) follows Vossius closely, defines mood as 'that which to the signification of a Verbe addeth the manner of signifying',[5] but rejects optative and potential as differing from the subjunctive *only* in 'manner of signifying' and not also in 'voice' (i.e. form), arguing that if semantic criteria alone are invoked there will be 'as many moods as there be affections of the mind'.[6] Moods are thus, as with Priscian, *inclinationes animi*, but they must be formally marked. This is in direct contrast to Scaliger, who excludes the formally marked infinitive on the grounds that 'nullam animi inclinationem ostendit'.[7] The term

---

[1] *Ibid.* V, ii, 6–8, an explanation in use in earlier grammars.

[2] Cf. Despauterius' classes of semantically determined *verba activa* and formally determined *verba activi generis*.

[3] *Grammatica Burlesa*, pp. 41–2.

[4] *De arte*, V, viii, 38–9. Cf. Roman practice, where Servius' *concessivus modus* e.g. is set up for the purely semasiological reason that 'altercationes interrumpit et tollit nobis contentionem' (H. Keil, *Grammatici Latini*, IV, 505).

[5] *Light*, p. 15. [6] *Ibid.* p. ix. [7] *De causis*, cap. cxiiii, p. 237.

'manner of signifying' is seen to have changed its meaning since medieval grammar, whose *modus significandi* represented a grammatical distinction, not merely the addition to a word-class of a semantic 'affection of the mind', a modification of lexical content. It is true that the *Grammatica speculativa* quotes Petrus Heliae's definition of mood as a 'varia animi inclinatio, varios eius affectus demonstrans', but it refutes any view that equates verbal mood with a mental *inclinatio* on the level of grammatical function.[1] In accordance with the general seventeenth-century trend, the consignification of grammatical features by formal markers is in general not merely ignored, but expressly denied by Vossius, on the grounds that accidents do not change a word's essential nature.[2]

The establishment of the 'essence' of a word-class (he uses both the Latin word *essentia* and the Greek term οὐσία) plays an important role in Vossius' system. If he finds the ancient definitions of the adverb at fault it is precisely because they misjudge its essence, which consists in an ability to modify not merely verbs but other word-classes as well. Nor can it be described in Melanchthonian terms as indicating the *circumstantiae* of the verb, i.e. more particularly time and place, for many adverbs signify *qualitas*. Vossius accordingly modifies the traditional definition as follows: 'Adverbium est vox, quae nomini, verbo, aut participio, additur ad circumstantiam, aut qualitatem eius significandam.'[3] The reference to *qualitas* is taken up by other grammarians, who find in the definition of the adverb as denoting 'the Manner or Quality of an Action'[4] a neat parallel to that of the adjective as denoting the manner or quality of a *thing*.

The Roman definition of the preposition as that which is preposed is similarly condemned by Vossius as not indicating the essence of the word-class, and as being equally appropriate to certain conjunctions. Scaliger's definition of it as signifying motion or rest is also unacceptable, as Scaliger himself saw, since he tried to make prepositions such as *ob* and *propter*, which signify a cause, fit into his system by ascribing to them an 'original' signification in terms of *motus* and *quies*. Vossius remarks that to satisfy Scaliger's definition *ob* and

[1] v. cap. xxviii. Cf. C. Thurot, *Extraits*, pp. 17, 179, for P. Heliae's doctrine of the verb, which adds little to Priscian.

[2] *De arte*, V, x, 54: 'Accidentia rei non mutant essentiam eius.'

[3] *Ibid.* III, ii, 15. This definition unites Melanchthon's view of the adverb as signifying *circumstantia* and Nebrija's view of it as signifying *alguna qualidad* in the verb.

[4] So Lane, *Rational and Speedy Method*, p. 22.

propter, even if one accepts that they denote a cause, must at the same time connote motion or rest, or cease to be prepositions.[1] In an attempt to meet all possible objections, he defines the preposition as a 'vox, qua nomen adiungitur verbo, ad causam, locum, tempus, coniunctionem aut privationem significandam'.[2] M. H. Jellinek notes[3] that he defines similarly to Melanchthon. This is true in so far as Melanchthon sees the preposition as exercising a linking function between noun and verb, but Vossius' further qualification is more explicit than Melanchthon's 'quod aliquam facti circunstantiam significat'[4] and goes back to Frischlin's division of prepositions into *temporales, causales, privativae, comitativae* and *locales*. Vossius gives an alternative definition of the preposition as a 'particula casum regens' or (to differentiate it from adverbs and interjections which do not of their own nature govern cases, but take part in constructions where a case-governing preposition is 'understood' by ellipse) 'naturā suā casum regens'.[5] The so-called inseparable prepositions are excluded as being *partes vocis*, therefore inapt, as Priscian saw, to be members of a word-class. Priscian had however allowed them the *vis* and *significatio* of prepositions, but Vossius notes that some of them (e.g. *re-* in *repono*) have the *vis* of adverbs,[6] and that prepositions, in composition or otherwise, are not infrequently the semantic equivalent of adverbs.[7] Other grammarians of the period take a similar view of the preposition as in effect an adverb governing a case,[8] a view which is in line with the traditional doctrine that prepositions not constructed with a case-inflected word 'degenerate' into adverbs. Lane accordingly defines them in a definition appropriate to the adverb as denoting 'some Circumstance of an Action' – perhaps ultimately going back to Melanchthon's 'aliquam *facti* circunstantiam'. No doubt Lane links the preposition with *action* in order to have it conform to his view of the 'particles' as *syncategoremata* of the verb, and therefore has it signify *circumstantiam actionis* rather than Linacre's[9] *circumstantiam rei*. His grammatical system is based on a dichotomy between *actio* and *res*, but he none the less attaches the preposition, like the adverb, to *actio*.

---

[1] *De arte*, VI, xxii, 227.
[2] *Ibid.* III, iii, 15.
[3] *Geschichte*, II, 96.
[4] *Grammatica* (1527 ed.), f. 41^r.
[5] *De arte*, VI, xii, 227.
[6] *Ibid.* VI, xxiv, 234. Once again, one notes the difficulties caused by the lack of a theory of the morpheme.
[7] *Ibid.* III, i, 6.
[8] So Lane, *Rational and Speedy Method*, p. 22.
[9] *Rudimenta*, p. 43.

Vossius' long syntax (272 pages) is concerned almost exclusively with case government and minutiae of usage.[1] Worthy of note however is his refusal to consider an *oratio* only as that which makes complete sense. It is any group of 'voces conjunctae', i.e. of words in a syntactic relationship.[2] On the whole, however, his approach is semasiological, in keeping with the general trend in seventeenth-century grammatical theory. By and large, he is still in the Humanist tradition, much indebted to Scaliger and Sanctius, and to the former and Ramus for the Aristotelian approach to the ordering of the subject matter. Ramistic also is his rejection of *grammatica exegetice*, which is the province of rhetoric rather than of grammar. What is new is his division of grammar, following the tenets of the 'universal' grammarians, into *natural* (common to all languages) and *artificial* (peculiar to a given language), and his insistence on anomalous structures being rewritten as structures semantically congruent with a logical proposition containing a subject and predicate. Though he has not himself written a universal grammar, much of his work is in the spirit of the 'philosophical' grammarians of the eighteenth and the latter part of the seventeenth centuries, notably his view that the (Aristotelian) classification of reality must have its counterpart in the divisions imposed on language. He stands in a continental European line of development that runs from Scaliger and Sanctius to the Port-Royal Grammar and the rationalism of Descartes. In England, grammarians were to undergo the influence of that other pole of seventeenth-century thought represented by Baconian sense-realism and the Sensualism whose chief exemplar is Locke. In the movement in favour of a universal language and grammar these twin currents, Rationalism and Sensualism, were both to be influential.

Vossius being the last great grammarian to stand at one and the same time in the Humanist tradition and in the movement initiated by Scaliger and Sanctius, he marks, though his grammar long continued to be dominant in conservative circles, the end of an epoch. On the one hand no more vast philological works on the scale of his *De arte* were to be produced. On the other certain elements in his work are prophetic of the orientation of grammatical theory in the

[1] The *Latina syntaxis*, Leyden, 1631, a companion volume to the *Latina grammatica*, similarly does not call for comment.
[2] *De arte*, VII, i, 1.

131

second half of the century. It will therefore be appropriate at this point to examine certain features of post-Humanist thought about language.

WORDS, NAMES AND THINGS

By 1600, the task Humanism had set itself was completed. Classical studies reigned in the schools, but the Humanists had finally been obliged to make a compromise with society and abandon many of their original aims.[1] Humanistic studies continued in the byways of philology and rhetoric, a rhetoric which thanks to Ramus now occupied itself almost exclusively with matters of style and delivery. The pretensions of the emergent administrative classes of the sixteenth century had required a high-flown rhetoric which reached extreme lengths in the use of 'ink-horn terms' and in the excesses of Lily's *Euphues*. Ramus' divorce of rhetoric from the other liberal arts in the name of the scientific limitation of the boundaries between subjects had encouraged the view of rhetoric as mere added ornamentation, as inessential to the core of a logical argument:

This general art of Speech is twofold, both Grammer and Rhetorick; but the difference is this, that Grammer carrieth the matter in a buget neither too big nor too little, like one of those Irishmen with Breeches without pockets. *Rhetorica* carrieth it in a fine bag full of laces, yet not altogether full, for there are more words than matter . . .[2]

In reaction against this verbosity, there developed a call for plainness, not least in sermons, for an end to the 'bastard kind of eloquence that is crept into the Pulpit, which consists in . . . flourishes, metaphors, and cadencies'.[3] Behind the opposition of *words* to *matter* in the passage from Alexander Richardson's *Logicians School-Master* (1657) quoted above there lies the growing seventeenth-century conviction that *words* no longer accurately reflect the reality of *things*. This view had been implicit in certain pronouncements of the preceding century. Erasmus for example had already laid down that knowledge was of two kinds, of things and of words, that of things being the more important, and Melanchthon had advised his pupils to read such authors as would increase their comprehension of things. As we have seen, the notion of the precise signification of a

[1] v. R. R. Bolgar, *The Classical Heritage*, pp. 365–6.
[2] Alexander Richardson, *The Logicians School-Master or, a Comment upon Ramus Logick*, London, 1657, p. 8.
[3] Joseph Glanvill, *An Essay Concerning Preaching*, London, 1678.

thing by a linguistic sign was already being lost sight of, except among grammarians still under the influence of Scholasticism, by the earlier part of the sixteenth century. Increasingly, as that century advanced, men were beginning to turn their attention to natural phenomena, to the world of *things*, and becoming impatient with a florid rhetoric that did not correspond to the presumed simplicity of the natural order. Hand in hand therefore with the loss of the notion of precise grammatical signification, there goes the simplistic notion that there ought to be an exact one-to-one correspondence between words and things. From this it is but a short step to a generalized distrust of words – particularly among the new men of science – as not giving a true picture of reality, or even as distorting truth. Paralleling the seventeenth-century quarrel between upholders of empirical enquiry and supporters of Humanist philological culture (the celebrated 'Battle of the Books'), is the opposition *words* versus *things*, an opposition assisted in good measure by the prestige of Francis Bacon.[1]

The seventeenth-century obsession with tangible phenomena is conditioned by the revolutionary changes in economic, social and intellectual attitudes that characterize that century. If in 1600 the English intellectual is, to cite P. Rossi,[2] half medieval, by 1660 he is half modern. At the forefront of the great changes taking place in these decades stands Bacon (1561–1626), whose 'life-giving power . . . penetrated the farthest nooks and crannies' of the period.[3] The sixteenth century had seen very little in the way of scientific progress. Great interest had been shown in astrology and alchemy, and, via Neo-Platonism, in the esoteric doctrines of the Cabbala, with a resultant tendency to explanation of the universe in terms of the naturalism of Telesio and Campanella, or in pantheistic terms. Bacon's age witnessed, in contrast, such far-reaching changes that it may be considered fundamentally different from all preceding ages. Copernican theory and the work of Kepler and Galileo in astronomy, the new geographical discoveries, the advances in scientific and political thought, all had played their part in extending both material

[1] v. L. Formigari, *Linguistica ed empirismo nel Seicento inglese*, Bari, 1970, pp. 70–1.

[2] *Francis Bacon*, p. x.

[3] v. R. F. Jones, 'Science and Language in England of the Mid-Seventeenth Century' (reprinted from *The Journal of English and Germanic Philology*, xxxi (1932)), in *The Seventeenth Century: Studies in the History of English Thought and Literature from Bacon to Pope*, Stanford University Press, 1951, p. 143.

and psychological boundaries, while the application of mathematics to natural phenomena had encouraged the idea that words ought to have the rigour of mathematical symbols. Bacon's self-appointed task was to forge an instrument of scientific thought commensurate with the altered face of things, to make the intellectual world coincide in extent with the newfound breadth of the material one. This task involved a complete break with the Aristotelian tradition which was already, as we have seen, under assault from various quarters, though it would be a mistake to assume that the new scientists were all violently anti-Aristotelian, or that by the middle of the century they were not free to oppose him at will.[1] Significant in this regard is the prefatory letter to Seth Ward's anonymously published *Vindiciae Academiarum* rejecting the view of the universities put forward by John Webster in his *Examination of Academies*:

He [Webster] supposes . . . that they are so tyed up to the Dictates of Aristotle, that whatsoever is taught either against or besides him by way of refutation or supply, they do by no meanes admit of . . . Which is notoriously false . . . there is not to be wished a more generall liberty in point of judgment or debate, then what is here allowed.[2]

It must none the less be remembered that the Scholastic method of instruction was still very much in vogue at the universities in the earlier part of the seventeenth century. Though Aristotle was no longer studied at second hand in medieval commentaries such as those of Peter Lombard, but in the new direct translations of his works, classical studies continued to have a Scholastic basis. Chairs of astronomy and geometry had been founded at Oxford in 1619, and a chair of natural philosophy in 1621, but the University's Aristotelian bias remained largely unaffected. In spite of the stimulus given to 'natural philosophy' by men like Seth Ward, Wren and Wilkins, who were founder members of the new Royal Society, V. H. H. Green[3] is no doubt right in holding that it would be 'injudicious' to suppose that their activity reflected a general reaction against Scholastic learning. In 1660, Aristotle and the Scholastic method were still dominant at Oxford. This meant the continuance of the bias towards the study of being, of *essentiae* and *causae*, of forms

[1] v. B. J. Shapiro, *John Wilkins 1614–1672: An Intellectual Biography*, University of California Press, Berkeley and Los Angeles, 1969, p. 105.
[2] *Vindiciae Academiarum Containing, Some Briefe Animadversions upon Mr. Websters Book, Stiled The Examination of Academies*, Oxford, 1654. The prefatory letter is signed *N.S.*
[3] *A History of Oxford University*, p. 67. v. also pp. 53, 55.

and qualities, towards making the truth of a given statement depend on whether or not it squared with an already accepted general axiom. Among the new men of science, however, the emphasis was no longer on *being* but on *becoming*,[1] and on the necessity of deriving the general axiom from a prior examination of sense data.

To Aristotle's theory of art as the imitation of nature Bacon opposed his theory of the 'congruity of natural and artificial phenomena'.[2] In accordance with the utilitarianism of the new Puritan bourgeoisie, who saw language as a means to an end, that end being the study of nature, such a theory demanded that language, too, exhibit a congruity with the external world. It involved an attack on Scholasticism, which represented for Bacon an empty verbosity which tried to make reality square with *a priori* reasoning, and whose practitioners he condemns in his enumeration of the contemporary 'distempers of learning': 'The second [distemper] . . . did chiefly reign amongst the schoolmen . . . their wits being shut up in the cells of a few authors (chiefly Aristotle their dictator) as their persons were shut up in the cells of monasteries and colleges . . .'[3] In the *Novum Organum* of 1620,[4] so entitled in obvious reference to Aristotle's *Organon*, Bacon sets forth, in opposition to the deductive method of Aristotelianism, his inductive method of discovering truth:

There are and can be only two ways of searching into and discovering truth. The one [the Aristotelian deductive method] flies from the senses and particulars to the most general axioms, and from these principles, the truth of which it takes for settled and immoveable, proceeds to judgment and the discovery of middle axioms. And this way is now in fashion.[5] The other [the Baconian inductive method] derives axioms from the senses and particulars, rising by a gradual and unbroken ascent, so that it arrives at the most general axioms last of all. This is the true way, but as yet untried.[6]

[1] v. B. Willey, *The Seventeenth Century Background: Studies in the Thought of the Age in Relation to Poetry and Religion*, London, 1934, p. 6.

[2] v. P. Rossi, *Francis Bacon*, p. 61.

[3] *Of the Advancement of Learning* (1605), in *The Philosophical Works of Francis Bacon, Reprinted from the Texts and Translations, with the Notes and Prefaces, of Ellis and Spedding*, ed. J. M. Robertson, London, 1905, p. 54.

[4] W. and M. Kneale, *The Development of Logic*, p. 309, call this work the 'first modern attempt to formulate a doctrine of scientific method'.

[5] M. De Wulf, *Medieval Philosophy*, p. 131, remarks however that there is already to be found among certain Scholastics, notably Duns Scotus, 'a keen analysis of the methods of induction, of the ways in which we may pass from the observation of *particular* cases to the law which governs all'.

[6] *Novum Organum* (aphorism xx), in J. M. Robertson (ed.), *The Philosophical Works of Francis Bacon*, p. 261.

This doctrine dealt the final blow, among scientists at any rate, to Aristotle's dogma of *universaliter primum*, the primacy of the general. It also established Bacon, with his emphasis on due observation of the 'senses and particulars', as what has been called 'the first sense realist'. The first axiom of his philosophy is that knowledge can only be attained by experience. Those things only are real which can be actually perceived, and B. Willey makes a valid criticism of Bacon, and indeed of our whole modern intellectual climate, when he states that the rejection of Scholasticism 'led to an undue elevation of empirical "truth", an attribution to it of a special privilege to represent "reality"'.[1] It also led to Bacon's rejection of Plato, whom he accused of allowing ideas to rule reality, and whom he regarded as ultimately responsible for the Scholastic reliance on verbal demonstrations. The Platonic 'forms', or abstract transcendental entities of matter, have obviously no place in a sense-based system such as Bacon's, and he rejects them along with Aristotle's ten categories. Bacon's treatment of knowledge as experience, his preoccupation with 'senses and particulars', clearly foreshadows the doctrines of Sensualism, which hold that experience is nothing more than sense perception.

This insistence that only *things* perceptible to the senses are real has important consequences for linguistic studies in that it affects the attitude to abstract ideas or 'universals'. Since these latter are not tangible to the senses, they come to be regarded as mere names or symbols, as *nominalia* rather than *realia*. The philosophy of experience is Nominalistic, standing in a direct line of enquiry stemming from the Scholastic Nominalists and William of Ockham. Such a philosophy is necessarily antagonistic to Aristotelian world-views.[2] One of its consequences, alongside the seventeenth century's preference for *things*, is what amounts to an obsession with *names*. The new primacy accorded to things and sense data, to concrete descriptions of reality, meant that Aristotle's ten categories no longer constituted a sufficient framework for the description of the new knowledge. In his projected reform of logic Bacon accordingly reverses the Aristotelian order by placing *dispositio* after *inventio*, holding like Ramus that material must first be amassed before a judgment can be made

[1] *The Seventeenth Century Background*, p. 23.
[2] v. K. Fischer, *Francis Bacon of Verulam: Realistic Philosophy and its Age*, translated from the German by J. Oxenford, London, 1857, pp. 410–12.

upon it. Though Bacon was a lively critic of Ramus, comparison of passages in their works reveals striking similarities, Bacon's division of logic under the four heads *invention, judgment, memory* and *tradition* being obviously Ramistic.[1] Of Ramus' celebrated three rules (of truth and certainty, of justice, and of wisdom) Bacon ignored the second, but adapted the first and third to his own particular uses. What is new, and full of significance for the intellectual trend of the period, is Bacon's insistence that the end of logic is 'a chaste, holy, and legal wedlock with things themselves'.[2] Bacon's basic quarrel with traditional philosophy is that it obscures the view of *things*, substituting verbal for real solutions. The new philosophy is however founded on doubt, on a Nominalist scepticism as to whether true knowledge can ever be attained. Renaissance culture, the heir to Scholastic Nominalism, had its roots in doubt and finally, faced with its inability to produce a valid explanation of the universe, terminated in scepticism. Montaigne (1533–92), whose *credo quia impossibile* reflects this scepticism, opposes to faith in human knowledge a faith in nature, which alone, apart from the self, is amenable to observation. This trust in nature, a forerunner of Rousseau's doctrines, is buttressed by the Neo-Platonic naturalistic cults of the Renaissance.

Bacon places the observation of nature on a scientific footing, but is still sceptical as to the possibility of any direct knowledge of things. On the one hand, man's mind of its very nature inevitably distorts the knowledge it receives from the senses; on the other, words themselves have no reliable correspondence to what they portray. In the *Advancement of Learning* Bacon discusses three 'profound kinds of fallacies' in the mind of man, illustrated by his celebrated 'idols' of the *tribe* (fallacies inherent in the human reason), of the *cave* (those peculiar to each individual), and of the *market-place* (those deriving from language and society).[3] These last idols are intrinsic to human existence. The only remedy against them, as against the other idols, is the 'formation of ideas and axioms by true induction',[4] and greater

---

[1] *Of the Advancement of Learning*, in J. M. Robertson (ed.), *The Philosophical Works of Francis Bacon*, p. 111.

[2] *Distributio operis*, in *The Works of Francis Bacon*, ed. J. Spedding, R. L. Ellis and D. D. Heath, I, 139.

[3] In the *Novum Organum* these groups have become four: of the tribe, of the cave, of the market-place, and of the theatre (these last deriving from the influence of philosophers).

[4] *Novum Organum* (aphorism xl), in J. M. Robertson (ed.), *The Philosophical Works of Francis Bacon*, p. 264.

care in definition. In the *Novum Organum,* among the 'Idols which beset men's minds' those which present one of the greatest obstacles to the clear perception of reality are these idols of the market-place: 'words are imposed according to the apprehension of the vulgar. And therefore the ill and unfit choice of words wonderfully obstructs the understanding . . . words . . . throw all into confusion, and lead men away into numberless empty controversies and idle fancies.'[1] Quite apart from Bacon's distrust of the 'apprehension of the vulgar', his desire for a clear view of *things* induces in him what R. F. Jones[2] describes as a certain antipathy to language:

let us consider the false appearances that are imposed upon us by words . . . [which] as a Tartar's bow, do shoot back upon the understanding of the wisest, and mightily entangle and pervert the judgment; so it is almost necessary in all controversies and disputations to imitate the wisdom of the Mathematicians, in setting down . . . the definitions of our words and terms . . .[3]

This is the first of the three 'distempers of learning', when men 'study words and not matter',[4] having 'withdrawn themselves too much from the contemplation of nature and the observations of experience, and . . . tumbled up and down in their own reason and conceits'.[5]

The seventeenth-century words/things dichotomy, whether rooted in Bacon's philosophy or not, is undeniably well attested in his works. A contributory cause of this dichotomy, according to V. Salmon,[6] may be the misinterpretation of the common rhetorical tag 'res et verba' – which the preceding century correctly understood as 'subject matter and words' – thus reinforcing the divorce between words and things that is all-pervading in seventeenth-century

---

[1] *Ibid.* (aphorism xliii), Robertson, p. 264.

[2] For a discussion of Bacon's attitude to language, v. Jones' article 'Science and language' cited above.

[3] *Of the Advancement of Learning,* in J. M. Robertson (ed.), *The Philosophical Works of Francis Bacon,* pp. 119–20.

[4] Cf. in the Latin translation (*De dignitate et augmentis scientiarum,* 1623) of the *Advancement of Learning:* 'Hic itaque cernere est primam literarum intemperiem, cum *verbis* studetur non *rebus*' (my italics).

[5] *Of the Advancement of Learning* (J. M. Robertson's edition), pp. 54, 59.

[6] *The Works of Francis Lodwick: A study of His Writings in the Intellectual Context of the Seventeenth Century,* London, 1972, pp. 81–2. v. also A. C. Howell, '*Res et verba*: words and things', *ELH A Journal of English Literary History,* 13 (1946), pp. 131–42. Howell discerns a seventeenth-century tendency to assume that '*words* should represent *things*, not metaphysical and abstract concepts', and finds the clearest expression of this tendency in the deliberations of the Royal Society.

thought. Within the context of this debate, an ancient controversy begins once again to assume importance, that is to say the nature versus convention (φύσις versus νόμος or θέσις) argument as to whether names have a natural correspondence to things, or are arbitrarily imposed by an agreed convention between speakers.[1] Aristotle, as we have seen, inclined to the latter view. The seventeenth century, increasingly distrustful of the idea of a natural correspondence between words and things, none the less tended to think that in the 'original language' (generally thought to be Hebrew) this natural affinity did in fact exist, but had unfortunately been obscured in later languages. Such speculation ties in with the Renaissance nature-philosophy stemming from Neo-Platonism, the Rosicrucians and the Cabbala, with a mystical belief in the 'language of nature' used by Adam in naming Creation. The 'original names' given to things by Adam must have had an exact correspondence with reality, since he, knowing the nature of every thing, therefore knew its correct name: 'Every thing in nature is distinct, and I apprehend them so with my Logick; and they being so, must needs have distinct names . . . *Adam* by seeing into the nature of every Creature, could see their names, though we cannot do it.'[2]

It is this hankering after a language which would exactly mirror phenomena that lies in large part behind the seventeenth-century search for an artificial language more precise than the natural ones. The spread of nature-philosophy and Cabbalistic notions in England was encouraged by certain passages in John Webster's *Academiarum examen* (1654), based on these doctrines and the teaching of the 'divinely-inspired Teutonick' Jakob Boehme: 'the mind receiveth but one single and simple image of every thing, which is expressed in all by the same motions of the spirits . . . but men not understanding these immediate sounds of the soul . . . have instituted, and imposed others, that do not altogether concord, and agree to the innate notions.'[3] This kind of reasoning was opposed by anti-Platonists such as Samuel Parker, who argued for the conventionalist viewpoint:

the use of Words is not to explaine the Natures of Things, but only to stand as marks and signes in their stead . . . it has been an ancient and

---

[1] v. R. H. Robins, *Short History*, pp. 17–19.
[2] A. Richardson, *The Logicians School-Master*, p. 13.
[3] p. 32. v. H. Aarsleff, 'Leibniz on Locke on language', *American Philosophical Quarterly*, 1 (1964), p. 180.

creditable Opinion of the *Platonists*, that Names have in them a natural resemblance and suitableness to things . . . But words . . . can have no likeness to anything but sounds . . . And I therefore conclude that the office of Definitions is not to explain the Natures of things, but to fix and circumscribe the signification of Words . . .[1]

The obsession with names has a profound influence on grammatical studies. Humanist authors had already blurred medieval grammatical distinctions by instituting the new equation *vox = dictio = pars orationis*, but had still held, by and large, to the cardinal grammatical truth that 'Grammatica est de signis rerum': *nomen significat rem*. It was left to the seventeenth century to operate the final transformation *vox = nomen = name*:

> when we look at, or consider a thing Grammatically, we first give it a *vox* that is a name . . . Some call it *dictio*, some *vocabulum*, but *vox* is best, because it names the thing from his special use . . . And that definition of *nomen*, of a thing that may be seen, felt, heard, or understood, is erroneous; for I can see, feel, or understand a thing, and yet name it not.[2]

The linguistic sign being no longer available to mediate between the mind and reality according to an arbitrary convention, A. Richardson, the author of the above passage, concludes that there must be a *natural* affinity between names and things. Slackness in grammatical definition is accompanied by an insistence that words ought to mirror nature. Sanctius had already foreshadowed this insistence, first by declaring himself ready to believe 'with Plato', at any rate as far as the 'original' language was concerned, that 'Nomina . . . & verba rerum naturam significare', and secondly by concluding that where there is no natural phenomenon there can be no corresponding name.[3] For the seventeenth century, the names Adam gave to creatures were the *real* names,[4] for he could 'view essences in themselves, and read forms without the comment of their respective properties'[5] – a power seventeenth-century philosophers longed to imitate. The knowledge of the 'real names' of things was thought in certain mystic circles to confer this power, hence the popularity of

---

[1] *A Free and Impartial Censure of The Platonick Philosophie*, Oxford, 1666, pp. 61–3.

[2] A. Richardson, *The Logicians School-Master*, pp. 19–20.

[3] *Minerva*, f. 6ʳ: 'quod in rerum natura non est, ne nomen quidem habebit'.

[4] Cf. Sanctius, *ibid. loc. cit.*: 'Omne enim quod vocavit Adam animae viventis ipsum est nomen eius.'

[5] From a sermon of 1662 by Robert South, v. *Sermons Preached on Several Occasions*, vol. I, Oxford, 1823, pp. 37–8.

the Cabbalistic doctrines in Europe after the expulsion of the Jews from Spain in 1492.[1] In spite however of strongly-held beliefs as to the natural affinity between name and thing, and the desire of the new science to link word and thing closer together by means of careful definition, the empiricists' preference for things over words is equalled only by the zeal with which linguists transform grammatical elements from symbols of reality to mere items of lexis, to names. Typical of this approach is Christofer Syms' definition of the noun: 'a name . . . given to . . . things, whereby they may be conceived in the mind of man, and by which one man may express his meaning to another touching those things which noun, name or word signifieth.'[2] *Noun, name* and *word* would in earlier grammatical theory have represented separate and distinct grammatical concepts. It should not be forgotten however that in England this trend was initiated by Colet, in Lily's grammar, over a century earlier.

The exemplar of this tendency to extreme Nominalism is the philosopher Thomas Hobbes, for whom words are names, and the parts of speech are names. Further, since Hobbes is a Sensualist, language for him originates in the giving of names to mental after-images of sensations, and generic ideas or 'universals' are nothing more than mere names, expedients for communication. *Word* and *name* thus become identical terms, for 'A name is a word taken at pleasure to serve for a mark, which may raise in our mind a thought like to some thought we had before.' Words in connected discourse are speech, 'of which every part is a *name*'. A proposition, in these terms, is simply 'a speech consisting of two names copulated, by which he that speaketh signifies he conceives the latter name to be the name of the same thing whereof the former is the name'.[3] In Hobbes' philosophical system as stated in the celebrated *Leviathan*, universals can have no real existence: 'nothing in the world [is] universal but names; for the things named are every one of them individual and singular'.[4] Elsewhere he underlines this:

The universality of *one name* to many things, hath been the cause that men think the *things* are themselves universal; and so seriously contend, that besides Peter and John...there is yet something else that we call

[1] v. H. Aarsleff, 'Leibniz on Locke', p. 180.
[2] *Latine Speach*, p. 42.
[3] *Elements of Philosophy: I. Concerning Body*, in *The English Works of Thomas Hobbes*, ed. W. Molesworth, vol. I, London, 1839, pp. 15, 16, 30.
[4] *Leviathan: I. Of Man*, in *ibid.* vol. III, London, 1839, p. 21.

man; viz. *man in general*, deceiving themselves, by taking the universal, or general appellation, for the thing it signifieth...It is plain therefore, that there is *nothing* universal but *names*...[1]

For Hobbes, as M. Oakeshott stresses in the preface to his edition of the *Leviathan*,[2] reasoning can never go beyond the world of names:

[It] gives us conclusions, not about the nature of things, but about the names of things. That is to say, by means of reason we discover only whether the connections we have established between names are in accordance with the arbitrary conventions we have established concerning their meanings.[3]

As Oakeshott notes, for Hobbes a true proposition is not an assertion about the real world. On the one hand, 'truth consisteth in the right ordering of names in our affirmations', hence the constant emphasis on definition in the *Leviathan*.[4] On the other, Hobbes shares the Nominalist scepticism as to the reliability of the evidence of the senses: '*whatsoever accidents* or qualities our senses make us think there be in the *world*, they be *not* there, but are *seeming* and *apparitions* only ... And this is the *great deception of sense*.'[5]

All this could only reinforce the doubts of seventeenth-century thinkers as to the possibility of getting at the truth by means of words. This scepticism has its roots in the Nominalist philosophy of the late Scholastic period, a philosophy which Hobbes did more than any other philosophical writer to hand on to modern times. The theories of the medieval Nominalists and of their protagonist William of Ockham[6] are a matter to which we shall return in a later chapter when discussing the movement for a 'universal' grammar. The Scholastic controversies between Realists (who believed in the reality of universals) and Nominalists were to some extent the ancestors of the rationalist versus empiricist arguments of the seventeenth century.[7] The Nominalists' teaching that we can have no knowledge of actual things, that there can be no reliable agreement between concept and thing, no knowledge of absolute truth, paved

---

[1] *Human Nature: Or the Fundamental Elements of Policy*, in *ibid.* vol. IV, 1840, p. 22.

[2] *Leviathan or the Matter, Forme and Power of a Commonwealth Ecclesiastical and Civil*, ed. M. Oakeshott, Blackwell, Oxford [1946], p. xxiv.

[3] *Thomae Hobbes Malmesburiensis Opera philosophica quae Latine scripsit*, ed. W. Molesworth, vol. V, London, 1845, pp. 257–8.

[4] *Leviathan: I. Of Man*, in W. Molesworth, *The English Works*, III, 21.

[5] *Human Nature: or the Fundamental Elements of Policy*, in *ibid.* IV, 8.

[6] Ockham lectured at Oxford between 1317 and 1319. W. and M. Kneale, *The Development of Logic*, p. 313, note that he was still being studied there in 1675.

[7] v. V. Salmon's review of N. Chomsky's *Cartesian Linguistics*, p. 176.

the way for modern scepticism and an intellectual climate in which modern scientific enquiry could begin. Since they held that only through the senses can we have some kind of knowledge – and here again they are followed by Hobbes – they can also be regarded as the forerunners of the English philosophical doctrine of Sensualism. The meeting of these two trends in Hobbes produced an extreme Nominalism allied to an extreme materialism. On the one hand the universe 'is corporeal, that is to say, body . . . and that which is not body is no part of the universe',[1] i.e. only the material is real. On the other hand, we can have direct contact only with the world of names. In Hobbes' philosophy, *word* and *thing* achieve their extreme separation.

One of the great seventeenth-century debates centred on the question whether all knowledge comes to us through the senses, or whether on the contrary certain kinds of knowledge are natural to the mind, obtained from innate mental concepts present in each individual from birth. The relevance of this to linguistic studies is apparent. The Saussurean *langue/parole* dichotomy, the Chomskyan theory of deep and surface structure, both depend on the existence of mental concepts preceding the facts of discourse, as does the Port-Royal supposition that language is primarily based on the operations of the mind. The great protagonists of these two views are the philosophers Locke and Descartes, representing respectively the sensualist-empiricist and the rationalist currents in seventeenth-century thought. The mentalist theories of Descartes have relevance more particularly to the Port-Royal Grammar, and will be considered when that grammar is discussed. The theories of the opposing Sensualist school were to have a profound effect on educational method, and equally left their mark on grammatical studies. An *Essay* on education published *c.* 1670 by the pedagogue Mark Lewis is indicative of the trend: 'Whilst we instruct Children, according to the Law of Nature, we must proceed by Sense . . . The use of the outward Senses is, to be *mediums,* to let in Notions to the inward.'[2] He proceeds to demonstrate 'how most things in Grammar may be brought down to the Sense of Seeing'. His actual examples are naïve and without much value,[3] but his emphasis on learning

[1] *Leviathan*, chap. xvi.
[2] *An Essay to Facilitate the Education of Youth, by Bringing down the Rudiments of Grammar to the Sense of Seeing,* London [1670].
[3] For example, it is 'obvious to Sense' which English words take an article.

through the senses no doubt indicates a fashionable trend, which reinforced the contemporary tendency to think in terms of *things* and the *modes of things*.

A movement towards a more realistic application of classical learning had already taken form in the work of Montaigne in France and Mulcaster in England. Let the pupil be well furnished with things, said Montaigne, and words would follow. His accent on a practical programme of studies anticipates in some of its features the 'sense realism' of Bacon and the Moravian scholar Comenius, and may even have had a direct influence on their thought. But like so much else, this 'sense realism' was not an invention of the sixteenth and seventeenth centuries, but had its roots in medieval thought, which in turn based itself on Aristotle. Thomas Aquinas followed the Aristotelian doctrine that the mind, before receiving impressions from outside itself, is as it were a clean slate, a *tabula rasa*.[1] Whatever ideas are in the mind have arrived there via the senses: *Nihil est in intellectu quod non prius in sensu*. What is known directly via these sense impressions – *id quod cognoscitur* – is the thing itself, the object in the outside world. Thomists never doubted the possibility of the mind's attaining to knowledge of extra-mental phenomena.[2] But they recognized that there was a problem when one came to consider the extent of the correspondence between reality and our mental representation of it, and above all the validity of abstract ideas, of 'universals' such as the concept *man* (the species). They held that the correspondence between these abstractions and individual realities, though inadequate, gave on the whole a dependable picture of reality,[3] that *Universale est formaliter in intellectu, fundamentaliter in rebus*.[4] Thus they steered a middle path between a naïve realism positing an exact one-to-one correspondence between concepts and things, and an extreme idealism claiming that we can have knowledge only of our own mental states and their subjective modification of reality. For Thomists, truth is the correspondence between reality and the mind – *veritas est adaequatio rei et intellectus*[5] – and we can see how neatly this is balanced by the *grammatica est de signis rerum* of medieval grammar. The correspon-

---

[1] *Summa Theologica*, I^a, q. 79, art. 2.
[2] v. M. De Wulf, *Medieval Philosophy*, p. 20.   [3] v. *ibid*. pp. 38–40.
[4] De Wulf, *ibid*. p. 41, renders this as 'the whatness to which our mind gives the form of universality has a foundation in the extra-mental world'.
[5] v. *ibid*. p. 45.

dence between reality and the mind ties in with the correspondence between reality and the linguistic sign. The intellect *can* know the real world, and the abstract concepts or universals which it forms have real validity, for 'the intellect abstracts from the individual the universal which is contained in it'.[1] The Nominalists, as we have seen, denied the validity of universals and indeed the possibility of ever attaining to absolute truth. This Ockhamist, Nominalist trend is very much present in seventeenth-century thought, finding its extreme statement in the philosophy of Hobbes, and it explains on the one hand that century's obsession with names, and on the other the empiricists' impatience with existing languages which could never in the nature of things give an exact picture of reality, their search for a quasi-mathematical symbolism which would bring them closer to things, contact with which constitutes the only path to true knowledge.

Both of these trends, the preoccupation with things and the tendency towards nomenclature, meet in the Moravian scholar Jan Amos Komensky or Comenius (1592–1671). Caught up in the religious conflicts of the Reformation, Comenius was particularly interested in the abolition of the ambiguities of language, cause of disputes which otherwise might have been avoided. In his *Via lucis* (1642), whose modest aim was 'the improvement of all human affairs, in all persons and everywhere',[2] he suggested that confusion of thought might be avoided by means of an artificial language in which the number of names exactly equalled the number of objects denoted, and in which each name precisely defined the characteristics of the object to which it referred. Comenius' major preoccupation was the relation of words to things, the arrangement of vocabulary in conceptual classes. The necessary prerequisite to knowledge was the scrupulous classification of reality. This idea does not originate with Comenius, for English grammarians were already in the habit of arranging Latin vocabulary in conceptual classes to facilitate learning,[3] and in Italy in the preceding century Jacopo Publicio,

[1] E. Gilson, *The Philosophy of St Thomas Aquinas* (translation by E. Bullough of the 3rd ed. of *Le Thomisme*), Cambridge, 1924, p. 9.

[2] *Via lucis . . . rationabilis disquisitio, quibus modis . . . sapientia per omnes omnium hominum mentes . . . spargi possit*, 1668 ed., Amsterdam, p. 6 of dedicatory preface. An English edition, *The Way of Light*, also appeared in 1642.

[3] v. V. Salmon, 'Language-Planning in Seventeenth-Century England; Its Context and Aims', *In Memory of J. R. Firth* (ed. C. E. Bazell, J. C. Catford, M. A. K. Halliday and R. H. Robins), London, 1966, p. 381.

Cosimo Rosselli and others, mingling elements from rhetorical tradition and Lullism,[1] had introduced the idea of the encycyclopaedic 'tree of knowledge'. In his *Porta linguarum reserata* (1631),[2] an introduction to the study of Latin, Comenius had already utilized several thousand Latin words for the most familiar objects and ideas. It is however in his *Orbis sensualium pictus* ('The World of Sense Objects Pictured') of 1658 that Comenius fully applies the principles of sense realism. Widely influential for two centuries, this work appeared in an English translation by Charles Hoole which proved to be one of the most popular aids to the teaching of Latin vocabulary ever published. In the preface to his facsimile edition of this text,[3] J. E. Sadler calls it an attempt to frame 'a true anatomy of the universe'. Comenius' approach cannot be better illustrated than by a few quotations from his works:

> If thou askest, whats to bee learned? Have for answer, To know the difference of things, and to bee able to give its name unto every thing. Is there nothing more? Truly nothing at all. Hee hath laid the grounds and foundation of all learning, that hath thoroughly learned the nomenclature or surname of things.[4]

Accordingly, the *Vestibulum linguae Latinae*,[5] in setting out 'the Nomenclature of things', treats them under the headings *Divisio rerum, Modi rerum, Motus rerum* (consisting of *duratio, actio* and *passio*), *Circumstantiae rerum*, etc. The seventeenth-century scientists' tendency to group all natural phenomena under the headings *matter* and *motion* led to an attempt to impose the same terms on language, thus bringing it into the desired correspondence with nature. The belief grew up that words ought to describe *things* and the *motions of things*, to be *signa rerum et motuum*. Grammarians in turn defined nouns, adjectives and adverbs in terms of the denotation of things, qualities of things, or the manners or circumstances of things, and verbs purely in terms of being, action or the suffering of an action.[6] The reemployment in grammar of the medieval doctrine on adjective and

---

[1] For the doctrines of Raymond Lull v. below, p. 148.

[2] This work, also published under the title *Janua linguarum*, appeared in a bilingual English–Latin edition as *The Gate of Tongues*.

[3] Oxford, 1968.

[4] *Porta linguarum ... sive seminarium linguarum et scientiarum omnium/ The Gate of Tongues ... Or else A Seminarie or Seed-plot of all Tongues and Sciences*, London, 1631, p. 1.

[5] I have used here an English–Latin edition, *Vestibulum linguae Latinae rerum & linguarum fundamenta exhibens*, London, 1656.

[6] Cf. A. Lane, *Rational and Speedy Method*, p. 11, where the verb is defined as 'a word that signifies the Action, Passion, or Being of a thing'.

substantive, reinforcing and modifying the Ancients' view of the adjective as indicating the *qualitas* of the noun (cf. Charles Hoole's substantive indicating 'quid sit' and adjective 'quale sit'),[1] leads to the increasingly current notion of the substantive as signifying *rem in concreto*, the adjective *rem in abstracto*,[2] adjective and abstract noun being placed on the same semantic footing as indications of *qualitas*. Shirley's version of this doctrine in the *Via ad Latinam linguam* – substantives 'the names of *Things* declare', adjectives 'what *kinde* of things they are' – sets the tone for grammars in English for a long time to come.

The importance of things and the names of things for education is emphasized in the foreword to the *Orbis sensualium pictus* in Hoole's edition, the title-page of which recalls that 'Nihil est in intellectu, quod non prius in sensu', and which is prefaced by the words 'Adam gave names to all Cattell . . .':

The ground of this business is that sensual objects be rightly presented to the senses . . . we can neither act nor speak wisely, unlesse we first rightly understand all the things . . . It is a little book . . . yet a brief of the whole world . . . full of Pictures, Nomenclatures, and Descriptions of things . . . [to the end] that scarcrows may be taken away out of wisdomes Gardens.[3]

Comenius' *Ars Ornatoria*, published in London in 1664, consists of a *Grammatica elegans* or rhetoric teaching 'eleganter loquendi ars', an *Eruditionis scholasticae atrium* or compendium of things, and a grammar. This latter, as might be expected, reflects the doctrine set forth in the other works. The noun is defined as a word denoting a thing (*vox rem denotans*), the adjective or *adnomen* as a word denoting some manner of a thing (*aliquem rei modum*), and the pronoun as denoting a thing in the absence of a noun. The adverb denotes a manner (of being, action or suffering of an action), the preposition a circumstance, and the verb, in customary seventeenth-century terms, *esse*, *actio* or *passio*, these being 'motus rerum'. Apart from these definitions in terms of *things*, the approach is purely semasiological: the word is a *sonus aliquid significans*, the exclamation expresses *animi sensum*, and the sentence is described in logical terms as questioning, affirming or denying something about something.[4] Interesting in

---

[1] *Grammatica Latina*, p. 21.   [2] Thus in John Danes' grammars.

[3] *Joh. Amos Commenius's Visible World: Or, A Picture and Nomenclature of all the Chief Things that are in the World*, London, 1659.

[4] *Johannis Comenii Ars ornatoria, sive Grammatica elegans, et eruditionis scholasticae atrium, rerum & linguarum ornamenta exhibens: Cui insuper accessit grammatica ejusdem janualis*, London, 1664. The definition of the sentence here given may be compared with that in the Port-Royal Grammar.

reflecting Comenius' preoccupation with *things* and in illustrating a trend in the grammatical theory of the period, his grammar is otherwise of little value. We have seen that A. Lane's grammar, *A Rational and Speedy Method of Attaining to the Latin Tongue* (1695), is similarly based on a *thing/action* dichotomy. By the end of the century the classification of the parts of speech is no longer based on the Humanist system, or on Aristotle via Sanctius, but on the 'philosophical' premise that everything that exists being a *thing* or the *manner of a thing*, an *action* or the *manner of an action*, grammar ought to reflect this division. Lane's four word-classes, corresponding to this quadripartite classification of phenomena, are accordingly substantive, adjective, verb and particle. His verb however indicates the action of a *thing*, and here he differs from the more mentalistic tradition of the Port-Royal grammarians, whose verb indicates, at two removes from reality, 'l'action de notre esprit'. The Port-Royal dichotomy is not between the manner and the action of a *thing*, but between the object and the manner of our *thoughts*, the verb being simply a mode of the latter.

Comenius lived in a world torn by religious strife, a world in which traditional knowledge no longer offered peace to the soul and the often disturbing new knowledge had yet to be assimilated. He sought to make the universe intelligible by labelling it, by marshalling its objects under conceptual heads. He could not but feel sympathy with the labours of the newly formed Royal Society, 'Torch Bearers of this Enlightened Age now bringing real philosophy to a happy birth'.[1] By 'real philosophy', of course, he means the natural sciences, based on experiment and the observation of phenomena. The first priority for this study is a collection of facts – the logicians' *inventio* – and it is this collection that Comenius sets out to provide, calling in his didactic works for the examination of Matter (vocabulary) before Form (grammar). In the history of ideas he is a connecting link between the Baconian 'sense realism' of the seventeenth century and the thirteenth-century Catalan scholar Raymond Lull. The latter, in an attempt to confound Mohammedan teaching and further the spread of Christianity, invented a system of grouped fundamental concepts that came to be known as the *Ars Magna*. Comenius' arranging of phenomena under conceptual heads – a *pansophia*, as he called it – is a continuance of this tradition. In his

---

[1] Preface to the *Via lucis*.

emphasis on *things* and his insistence on the obtaining of knowledge through the senses he is however distinctly Baconian, and must be regarded as Bacon's pupil.

If I have discussed Comenius at some length it is because he illustrates, as does no other writer of the period, at once the seventeenth century's tendency to *nomenclature* and its predilection for *things*. Among those who most directly felt his influence was the philosopher John Locke (1632–1704). He too holds that knowledge comes to the mind via the senses, that the mind is a *tabula rasa* upon which ideas are impressed by 'sensation' and 'reflection'. Concerned as it is with epistemology, his *Essay concerning Humane Understanding* became a kind of text-book for the Royal Society. Though published in 1690, it had taken him twenty years to write, and thus may be taken to reflect ideas current two decades before and associate him with that distrust of words which is one of the hallmarks of the early Royal Society[1] and a constant theme in Bacon. The latter had been concerned, particularly in his *Novum Organum*, with the question how 'invention', the discovery of subject matter, is attained empirically by means of experience. Locke, who stems from Bacon, seeks to solve the problem of how the mind arrives at experience. He is commonly regarded as the great adversary of the notion that the mind contains certain 'innate ideas' which are not obtained from sense experience – a question to which we shall return when discussing the importance of this notion for Port-Royal grammatical theory. His *Essay* sets out to give an 'Account of the Ways, whereby our Understandings come to attain those Notions of Things we have'.[2] Predictably, given the general trend of seventeenth-century thought, he concludes that there is no reliable correspondence between words and things: 'Because *Men* would not be thought to talk *barely* of their own Imaginations, but of Things as really they are; therefore they *often suppose their Words to stand also for the reality of Things.*'[3] It is true that for Locke most of our ideas come from the external world via sense experience – 'The Senses at first let in particular *Idea's*, and furnish the yet empty Cabinet' – and these ideas 'are lodged in the Memory, and Names got to them'.[4] The great majority of our ideas, those such as *yellow, heat, soft*, come from this source, which Locke calls

[1] v. V. Salmon, *The Works of Francis Lodwick*, p. 79.
[2] *An Essay concerning Humane Understanding*, London, 1690, Bk I, p. 1.
[3] *Ibid.* Bk III, chap. ii. [4] *Ibid.* I, 8.

sensation. A second kind of ideas however (though these too are ultimately furnished by experience), of the type *perception*, *thinking*, *willing*, come from our observation of our own mental processes, from 'the Perception of the *Operations of our own Minds* within us'.[1] Ideas from this source, which Locke calls *reflection*, could not be obtained from things external to the mind. Here he makes a departure from the simple *Nihil in intellectu quod non prius in sensu*. His reference to the 'Operations of our own Minds within us' recalls the Port-Royal doctrine of the three 'opérations de notre esprit' – *concevoir, juger, raisonner* – a doctrine of which he had first-hand knowledge during his stay in France between 1675 and 1679, when he read both the Port-Royal Grammar and the Port-Royal Logic. This incipient mentalistic tendency in Locke is reinforced by his view that words are 'signs of internal Conceptions',[2] marks standing for ideas within the mind: 'Words in their primary and immediate Signification, stand for nothing, but the *Ideas* in the *Mind* . . . those *Ideas* are collected from the *Things*, which they are supposed to represent'.[3] Words are not signs of immediate reality, but of concepts in the mind, which are themselves as it were intermediate signs between reality and word. Behind this theory there lies of course a long ancient and medieval tradition, from Priscian's description of the *pars orationis* as a 'mentis conceptum' down to the Scholastic definition of *orationes* as 'notae passionum earum, quae sunt in anima'. Locke's 'signs of internal Conceptions' are an exact rendering of the *Grammatica speculativa*'s 'signa conceptus mentis'.[4]

Locke realizes however that it is beyond human capacity to form a distinct and separate idea of every thing that the senses present to us, so that 'every particular Thing should have a distinct peculiar Name'.[5] Hence the need for abstractions or universals, a problem he tries to circumvent by distinguishing between the *real essences* (things in themselves) and the *nominal essences* of substances. Here again the Nominalist scepticism as to the possibility of abstractions having any reliable correspondence with reality appears, for even if 'the *real Essences* of Substances were discoverable . . . [we cannot] reasonably think, that the *ranking of things under general Names, was regulated by* those internal real Constitutions, or anything else but *their obvious*

---

[1] *Ibid.* II, 37.
[2] *Ibid.* III, 185.
[3] *Ibid.* III, 187.
[4] Cap. xlv.
[5] *Essay*, III, 189.

appearances.[1] In making this distinction between the *real* and the *nominal* essence of a substance, Locke makes clear that only the latter can be known: 'Between the Nominal Essence, and the Name, there is so *near* a *Connexion*, that the Name of any sort of Things cannot be attributed to any particular Being, but what has this Essence, whereby it answers that abstract Idea, whereof that Name is the Sign.'[2] The *nominal essence* constitutes the link between *name* and *thing*. Though Locke avoids the excesses of Hobbesian Nominalism, claiming that real knowledge *can* be had when 'there is a conformity between our ideas and the reality of things', it is plain that he regards this conformity as in general far from exact. Bacon had already expressed his profound scepticism as to the possibility of ever obtaining a true picture of the world from the senses: 'For it is a false assertion that the sense of man is the measure of things . . . the human understanding is like a false mirror, which . . . distorts and discolours the nature of things by mingling its own nature with it.'[3] In the final analysis, Locke too weakens the tie binding *words* and *things*.

The distrust of words is paralleled, as the seventeenth century advances, by a growing doubt as to the validity of grammar teaching. This is in part, as far as England is concerned, a protest against the long reign of Lily's Latin Grammar, the *Regia grammatica*, which alone was prescribed for use in the schools. John Brinsley's *Ludus literarius* of 1612 still recommends the 'continuall use of the bookes of construing of Lillies rules',[4] and writers of grammars are still careful, up to about 1660, to claim to be supporting Lily rather than superseding him.[5] After that date, however, the revolt against his grammar reached such proportions that in 1664 the Convocation of Canterbury proposed that a new *Regia grammatica* be drawn up, but the matter was not pursued. Similarly, a bill of 1675 in the House of Lords aimed at ousting Lily did not get beyond a first reading. Renaissance grammar was word-based, and this continued use of

[1] *Ibid.* III, chap. vi. For Bacon, too, words representing general conceptions represent unreal notions.
[2] *Ibid.* III, 195.
[3] *Novum Organum* (aphorism xli), in *The Philosophical Works of Francis Bacon*, ed. J. M. Robertson, p. 264. Cf. B. Willey's remark, *The Seventeenth Century Background*, pp. 27–8: 'Little meaning could have been attached, in the seventeenth century . . . to the theory that the mind is in some sense constitutive of reality, even a "fact" being in part a thing made, an act of the mind.'
[4] *Ludus literarius: Or, The Grammar Schoole*, London, 1612, p. 23.
[5] v. F. Watson, *The English Grammar Schools to 1660*, p. 278.

Lily's grammar to the exclusion of all others nearly a hundred years after Sanctius had begun to put more emphasis on the phrase as the grammatical unit, could only reinforce the notion of nouns, adjectives, verbs, etc. as units in their own right, existing apart from grammatical function. Outside England, Comenius noted in his *Didactica magna* (1632) that beginners were 'stupefied' by the mass of rules, exceptions to the rules, and exceptions to the exceptions they were required to learn. His doubts are echoed by Charles Hoole, translator into English of Comenius' *Orbis pictus* and writer of books on the teaching of Latin:

We generally . . . do teach children, as we do Parrats, to speak they know not what . . . [and] teaching little ones by Grammar only at the first, do pusle their imaginations with abstractive terms . . . which, till they be somewhat acquainted with things, and the words belonging to them . . . they cannot apprehend what they mean.[1]

One could multiply references to seventeenth-century opponents of grammar teaching, and even of grammar itself, whether it be the Baconian John Webster who would substitute for grammar 'symbolic, hieroglyphical, and emblematic ways of writing'[2] and teach children Latin without any reference to grammar at all, or Dr Joseph Webbe, who insists that a language should be learned from phrases, not from a word-by-word grammatical study.[3] An early exponent of the direct method in language teaching is the anonymous *Examen of the Way of Teaching the Latin Tongue* (1669),[4] which typically notes that traditional teaching methods have 'needlessly engag'd us to preferre the knowledge of *Words* to that of *Things*'.[5] Citing the case of a four-year-old French boy who had achieved a certain notoriety on account of his ability to converse in fluent Latin with his tutors, the author contrasts the ease of the direct method with the abstruse difficulties involved in the inculcation of the categories of grammar:

What concerns the *Ideas* of the different parts of discours, we must grant, that they cannot be understood, unless you make . . . the distinction of

---

[1] Foreword to Hoole's translation of the *Orbis pictus*.
[2] *Academiarum examen*, p. 24.
[3] *An Appeale to Truth . . . About the Best and Most Expedient Course in Languages*, London, 1622. v. V. Salmon, 'Joseph Webbe: Some Seventeenth-Century Views on Language-Teaching and the Nature of Meaning', *Bibliothèque d'Humanisme et Renaissance*, XXIII (1961), pp. 324–40.
[4] *An Examen of the Way of Teaching the Latin Tongue to Little Children, by Use Alone*, London, 1669. This is a translation of a French work (*Examen de la manière d'enseigner le Latin aux enfans*) published the previous year.   [5] *Ibid*. p. 16.

Substance, Accident, Place, Time, Action, Passion, and of all the Relations, thence resulting: which comprehends that part of the *Metaphysics*, we call *Categories* or *Predicaments*; which we know to be very abstract, they being only invented to facilitate the Mentall distinction of many things, which we commonly see confus'd in Nature.[1]

This author's complaint, that the amount of time spent on the acquisition of Latin by traditional methods is ludicrously disproportionate to the results obtained, may be taken as typical of many.

Grammar, having followed the general tendency towards nomenclature and having discarded the medieval insistence that words are signs of things, falls into the same disrepute as words themselves. All these trends in seventeenth-century views on language – the preference for things over words, the tendency to suppose that a given 'sense' can be rendered by various more or less reliable verbal combinations, the desire for a language which would mirror phenomena more closely, giving a one-to-one correspondence between sign and concept akin to that provided by mathematical symbols – all these elements, added to growing distrust of the grammar taught in the schools, converge in the latter part of the century in the movement for an artificial language and a universal grammar.

[1] *Ibid.* pp. 67–8.

4. UNIVERSAL GRAMMAR

The quest for a universal grammar applicable to all languages, so typical a product of the late seventeenth-century mind, is in fact present in linguistic theory of a much earlier date. The idea had already been mentioned in passing by Aristotle: 'As writing, so is speech not the same for all races of men. But the mental affections themselves, of which these words are primarily signs, are the same for the whole of mankind.'[1] Among the grammarians of antiquity the question of 'language universals' was hardly touched upon, but the Aristotelian line of thought is found in the thirteenth-century scholar Robert Kilwardby's doctrine that grammar is not about conformity of speech with the rules of given individual languages, but about conformity of structure with rules abstracted from a number of such languages,[2] a statement which may be set beside Roger Bacon's view of grammar as identical in *substance* in all languages, but varying from one to another in *accident*.[3] The medieval Scholastics supposed their *grammaticae speculativae*, based as they were on the metaphysical structure of reality, to be of universal application. Pre-structuralist universal grammar must of necessity repose on non-formal criteria, and medieval grammarians take these criteria from Aristotle's philosophy, using notions of substance and accident, flux and permanence, the ability or inability (determined semantically) of an element of structure to stand alone, etc. If it be true that 'the ways in which a culture mentally dissects nature are returned in the linguistic categories of that culture's language',[4] it is equally true that they are returned in any metalanguage that is applied to linguistic

[1] *De interpretatione*, 1, in H. P. Cooke, *Aristotle: The Organon*, p. 115. Cf. W. and M. Kneale, *The Development of Logic*, p. 45: '[Aristotle] implies that it is the *thoughts* to which the predicates "true" and "false" primarily belong, apparently on the ground that while the *spoken words* are different for different peoples, the *thoughts* . . . are the same for all alike.' (My italics.)

[2] Cited in C. Thurot, *Extraits*, p. 127.

[3] *Greek Grammar*, ed. E. Nolan and S. A. Hirsch, Cambridge, 1902, p. 27: 'Grammatica una et eadem est secundum substantiam in omnibus linguis, licet accidentaliter varietur.'

[4] R. G. Godfrey, 'Late Medieval Linguistic Meta-Theory and Chomsky's Syntactic Structures', *Word*, 21:2 (1965), p. 254.

analysis.[1] The particular type of universal grammar in vogue is inevitably a reflection of the philosophical or logical system underlying it. Though this system varies from age to age or from one practitioner to another, at least the major grammatical categories, noun and verb, are in all universal grammar systems established according to non-formal criteria.[2] Classifications in formal terms, however, are in the nature of things largely limited to individual languages,[3] hence present-day descriptive linguists' insistence on formal techniques has been paralleled by a profound reluctance, until quite recently, to concede validity to universal grammar. Contrariwise, there would seem to be little doubt that the semasiological bent of seventeenth-century grammarians, their increasing reluctance to define in formal terms, paved the way for the vogue of universal grammar in their own and the eighteenth centuries. Quite apart from this fashion for semantically based description, however, the importance of Scaliger and Sanctius as forerunners of the universal grammarians can scarcely be exaggerated. With their emphasis on *causae*, on a reasoned explanation of language, an underlying *ratio* to linguistic structure – and above all Sanctius' implicit recognition of a 'surface' and a 'deep' structure in his treatment of ellipse[4] – they prepared the ground for later scholars who found in logic the supporting metalanguage they required for their systems.

As early as 1605, Bacon's *Advancement of Learning* posits two kinds of grammar, 'the one popular, which is for the speedy and perfect attaining of languages . . . the other philosophical, examining the power and nature of words as they are the footsteps and prints of reason . . .'.[5] This is expanded in the *De augmentis* of 1623, where Bacon refers to *grammatica literaria* and a proposed *grammatica*

---

[1] Noting that a theory of a particular language depends on a meta-theory, R. G. Godfrey (*ibid.* p. 253) finds that Thomas of Erfurt 'relies heavily on the terminist logic of his time . . . in a way that parallels pretty closely the reliance of Chomsky on modern symbolic logic and mathematics'.

[2] Cf. C. F. Hockett, 'The Problem of Universals in Language', *Universals of Language* (ed. J. H. Greenberg), M.I.T. Press, Cambridge (Mass.), 1963, p. 18: 'A major form-class distinction reminiscent of "noun" versus "verb" is universal, though not always at the same size-level.'

[3] But as R. H. Robins notes, 'Noun and verb in universal grammar', *Language*, 28 (1952), p. 294, the word-classes other than noun and verb can often be defined at least in part in terms of their syntactic relationship with these two classes.

[4] Linacre's very detailed treatment more than sixty years before Sanctius should not however be overlooked. Sanctius' relative importance lies in the fact that it was he, rather than Linacre, who directly influenced Port-Royal theory.

[5] *The Philosophical Works of Francis Bacon*, ed. J. M. Robertson, p. 122.

philosophica, which latter 'should diligently inquire, not the analogy of words with one another, but the analogy between words and things, or reason',[1] for, he adds once more, 'words are the footsteps of reason'. The noblest kind of grammar would be that which handled 'the various properties' of languages. Bacon's philosophical grammar does not however have much to do with logic, but seems to be regarded as a means to the sociological and psychological study of different peoples. Further details would have been welcome, but Bacon gives a mere mention to the subject. His suggestions none the less find an echo in 1659 in Bassett Jones' *Herm'aelogium*, an attempt, in itself of no great interest, to classify words according as they denote being, motion or quality. Significant of a trend is Jones' subtitling of his work 'an Essay at the rationality of the art of speaking'. He claims to have been inspired to his labours by Bacon's remarks on grammar and by his desire to have the mind 'practice her own power upon the nature of things', and though he makes the customary claim to be only supplementing Lily's work, he dismisses it as 'compos'd on the meer score of Authority', stating a preference for *rational* over *authoritative* grammar. His standpoint, a year before the publication of the Port-Royal *Grammaire générale et raisonnée*, is that of a universal grammarian: '... the Nations, differing in vocality ... do nevertheless in point of Syntaxe agree as one; therefore also manifesting the product of words to be more from nature, as of Sentences from Reason ...'[2] It is clear that for Jones it is the *underlying reasoned structure* that is the same in all languages. The parallel between the passage quoted above and certain remarks by the twentieth-century linguist V. Brøndal is very striking, for Brøndal makes precisely the same distinction between 'systems with fixed terms, that is to say words and forms which vary from age to age and from nation to nation', and a universal syntactic faculty: 'the movements of thought which put those terms into operation, namely the propositional function, the faculty of sentence-formation, which always and everywhere remains identical, universal and permanent, because it is inherent in permanent and universal human thought.'[3]

[1] *Ibid.* p. 523. As the original Latin has it, philosophical grammar would treat 'analogiam inter verba & res sive rationem'.

[2] *Herm'aelogium; or, an Essay At the Rationality of the Art of Speaking: As a Supplement to Lillie's Grammar, Philosophically, Mythologically, & Emblematically*, London, 1659, preface. v. also V. Salmon, review of N. Chomsky, *Cartesian Linguistics*, p. 172.

[3] *Essais de linguistique générale*, p. 14 (my translation).

Jones' approach is interesting as an illustration of the trend of thought in the mid-seventeenth century. The first self-consciously universal grammars appear however much earlier in the century in such works as Christopher Helwig's *Libri didactici*, a treatment of four classical languages prefaced by a 'universal grammar'.[1] Helwig was at first a co-worker with the German vernacular grammarian Ratke (Ratichius) in the educational reforms associated with Köthen, where a universal grammar in German (the *Köthener Sprachlehr*) was brought out in 1619.[2] Though published in the same year, Helwig's work is in fact earlier than the *Sprachlehr*,[3] and he had already cooperated with Kaspar Finck in the production of a Latin grammar[4] closely based on Scaliger, with a distinct bias towards a universal, philosophical approach. The great exemplar of the philosophical grammars with universal pretensions is however that of the Italian Tommaso Campanella, which appeared in 1638.[5] In a similar tradition is the *Grammatica audax* (1654) of the Spanish bishop Caramuel y Lobkowitz whose work, like that of Campanella, represents in many respects a return to Scholasticism and to medieval views on universal grammar. A second strand in the seventeenth-century renewal of interest in language universals lies in the work of the language-planners, foremost among whom are George Dalgarno and Bishop Wilkins of Chester, who stem from the British empirical tradition initiated by Bacon. On the Continent, where rationalism had a stronger hold, universal grammar is further represented by the epoch-making *Grammaire générale et raisonnée* of Port-Royal, long ascribed to purely Cartesian sources but whose true antecedents, as I shall attempt to show, are Scaliger and Sanctius and, to some extent, Campanella and Caramuel. In what follows, I propose to deal first

---

[1] C. Helvicus, *Libri didactici, Grammaticae universalis, Latinae, Graecae, Hebraicae, Chaldicae*, Giessen, 1619. Having posed his principles in the *Grammatica universalis*, Helwig wrote a very simple Latin grammar consisting largely of a description of formal elements. Both were translated into German, appearing respectively as *Sprachkünste* and *Lateinische Sprachkünste* (Giessen, 1619).

[2] An example of the continued interest of German vernacular grammarians in universal grammar is J. G. Schottel's *Teutsche Sprachkunst* of 1641, in which (V. Salmon, *Francis Lodwick*, p. 122) 'the structure of language is viewed as a permanent and transcendental entity, established by God and nature, not deducible from usage, but requiring to be sought out by the grammarian'.

[3] v. M. H. Jellinek, *Geschichte*, I, 91.

[4] *Grammatica Latina*, 2nd ed., Giessen, 1615. M. H. Jellinek, *Geschichte*, II, 3, mentions only this second edition.

[5] *Philosophiae rationalis partes quinque, Videlicet: grammatica, dialectica, rhetorica, poetica, historiographia*, Paris, 1638.

of all with these last two authors and the language-planners, and then, in a separate chapter, to examine the sources of Port-Royal theory.

The Port-Royal Grammar has come into renewed prominence of recent years as a result of N. Chomsky's attempt to find historical parallels for his transformational theories. A new orientation of scholarly endeavour has reawakened a long-dormant interest in language universals, in the premise that 'in the deeper levels of linguistic structure languages will be found to share aspects of form that are a common possession realized differently at the surface in different languages'.[1] Already in 1965, R. Godfrey notes a remarkable increase in interest in mentalistic linguistics, prompted by the belief that 'taxonomic or empiricist methodology has failed to explain the real facts of language'.[2] Prior to this latest wave of interest, attempts had indeed already been made at various times in the present century, by members of European schools of linguistics, to reinstate some form of general grammar. Attention may be drawn more particularly to L. Hjelmslev,[3] who opposed to the *états concrets* of each given language the *état abstrait* common to all, and to V. Brøndal,[4] who suggested the four Aristotelian categories of substance, quantity, quality and relation as a basis for classification. Of more cogent interest as an indication of contemporary trends is the conference on Universals of Language held at New York in 1961, which attracted contributions from several eminent linguists. J. H. Greenberg's introduction to the proceedings of this conference notes that an enormous amount of empirical data having been amassed by descriptive techniques, the time would seem ripe for 'generalizing efforts on a wide scale' as linguistic science's own particular contribution to a general science of human behaviour.[5] There seems indeed to have been a wide measure of agreement at this conference as to the direction linguistics should take in the immediate future, 'shifting its concern from the uniquely differen-

[1] R. H. Robins, *Short History*, p. 126.

[2] 'Late Medieval Linguistic Meta-Theory', p. 251. Godfrey adds that 'Phonology now seems much less important, much less revealing of the true nature of language, than does syntax and the formal characterization of the sentence, since it is within this area that the creativity of language is primarily manifested.'

[3] *Principes de grammaire générale*, Copenhagen, 1928.

[4] *Les parties du discours*, Copenhagen, 1948. v. R. H. Robins, 'Noun and verb in universal grammar', *Language*, 28 (1952), p. 293.

[5] *Universals of Language*, ed. J. H. Greenberg, M.I.T. Press, Cambridge, Mass., 1963, p. ix.

tial to the broadly general'[1] and 'passing from the bare study of variegated languages . . . to become a thoroughly universal science of language'.[2] Among conference participants only R. Jacobson made any reference to pre-twentieth-century endeavours:

For centuries this field has been a no-man's land, and only a few philosophical contributions – from the medieval treatises on *grammatica speculativa*, through John Amos Comenius' *Glottologia* and the rationalist essays of the 17th and 18th centuries, to Husserl's[3] and Marty's[4] phenomenological meditations, and finally to the modern works in symbolic logic – have ventured to lay the foundations of a universal grammar.[5]

In common with other participants he is far from recommending a return to traditional mentalistic linguistics, and emphasizes the 'strictly relational character' of those language universals, that 'inventory of simple relations common to all tongues of the world', which present-day methodology is so well equipped to establish. Only these relations can form the basis of an 'adequate universal model', previous endeavours to define interlingual variants in 'absolute metrical terms' being doomed to failure.[6] What is however of particular interest for the present study is Jacobson's insistence that present-day linguists are by no means justified in 'ignoring or underrating' the work of previous centuries in universal grammar, a knowledge of which he regards as an antidote to 'the dangerous fallacies with which the so-called creeping empiricism is too often menaced'.[7] With these words in mind, we may proceed to an examination of the seventeenth century's contribution to the centuries-old debate on language universals.

[1] C. E. Osgood, 'Language Universals and Psycholinguistics', *ibid.* (ed. J. H. Greenberg), p. 236.

[2] R. Jacobson, 'Implications of Language Universals for Linguistics', *ibid.* (ed. J. H. Greenberg), pp. 217–18. One may note also the later conference on 'Universals in Linguistic Theory' held at the University of Texas in April 1967, which similarly noted that 'a profound change has occurred in linguistic thinking in the last decade', and that it no longer makes sense to describe a language 'in terms of its own structure alone' (E. Bach and R. T. Harms, eds., *Universals in Linguistic Theory*, New York, 1968, preface, p. vi).

[3] E. Husserl, *Logische Untersuchungen*, Halle, 1913 (2nd ed.).

[4] A. Marty, *Untersuchungen zur Grundlegung der allgemeinen Grammatik und Sprachphilosophie*, Halle, 1908.

[5] *Universals of Language*, ed. J. H. Greenberg, p. 218.

[6] *Ibid.* p. 209.   [7] *Ibid.* p. 218.

CAMPANELLA (and Finck–Helwig *passim*)

Tommaso Campanella (1568–1639) is yet another of those figures who stand between two worlds, a link between the old Aristotelian and Platonic philosophies reintroduced by the Humanists, and the new Baconian empiricism. In this he is fully representative of his times. A Dominican educated in the Scholastic tradition, his avowed aim was the reconstruction of Scholastic philosophy, but he was also attracted by Bernardino Telesio's anti-Aristotelian nature philosophy, and was accused by the Inquisition of magical practices and irreligion. In many ways a man of the Middle Ages – he hankered after a return to the medieval unity of Church and State – in other respects he anticipates Locke and Descartes. Both Aristotelianism and Platonism have an important place in his work, yet it would perhaps not be exaggerating to describe him as a precursor of Bacon, both in his system of classification of the sciences and in his positing of an empirical naturalism.[1] The Italian nature philosophy itself constitutes a link between the medieval and the modern world, looking back to Antiquity and the Age of Faith, but, in its emphasis on nature, looking forward to the new age of scientific enquiry. Campanella achieved a synthesis of Telesian naturalism, Platonism and Thomism, resting on principles which give cause to regard him as the precursor not only of Bacon but, more particularly, of Descartes. Holding the Aristotelian doctrine of the obtaining of knowledge through the senses, he has none the less a Baconian insistence that knowledge of nature should be sought not in Aristotle, but in the natural phenomena themselves. Knowledge is obtained from experience of external and internal facts, the former consisting in sense-perceptions, the latter in reflection, in the consideration of the certainty of one's own existence.[2] The parallels with Locke's derivation of our ideas from *sensation* and *reflection* ('the Perception of the Operations of our own Minds within us') and with Descartes' 'Cogito, ergo sum', are striking.[3] Campanella's Platonism, on the other hand, leads him to set up a science of *being*, whence the importance of the notion of *essentia* (a term he prefers to Aristotle's

---

[1] If not a precursor of Bacon, Campanella must undeniably have been acquainted with his work.

[2] v. K. Fischer, *Descartes*, pp. 113–14.

[3] V. Salmon, in her review of N. Chomsky's *Cartesian Linguistics*, gives facts and dates to prove that Campanella could not have been influenced by Descartes.

substantia) in his grammatical system, which reposes on a dichotomy between *being* and *action*. It is also perhaps behind his belief that all natural objects are endowed with sense, a belief that stems either from Renaissance pantheism and nature philosophy or directly from Plato's theory of the world-soul, and is already present in his first philosophical work of 1591 in which he speaks of the 'sensus rerum'. In view of this Platonic trend in his thought, it is not surprising to find that he holds to the theory of an original natural affinity between words and things, an affinity which later languages have obscured.[1] In common with other scholars of his age, Campanella was anxious to restore this original affinity in order to get rid of ambiguity and confusion. Descartes had suggested that precise conceptual classifications (such as those of Comenius) might serve in the forming of a universal language, an idea which was taken up by a group of French philosophers and scientists in the 1630s. Campanella in turn suggested that a 'philosophical' language might be set up in which names would be imposed 'ex rerum natura et proprietatibus',[2] in accordance with the contemporary notion that words could and ought to be made to correspond with nature. *Things* must first be known – no Nominalist, Campanella is convinced of the certainty of knowledge – then *names* given. It follows that the imposing of names is the function not of the grammarian, but of the philosopher: 'prius enim oportet res scire; ac deinde nomina rebus scitis imponere; grammaticus enim conservat, enucleat, non invenit, nec imponit'.

Campanella's *Philosophiae rationalis partes quinque* offers a philosophical treatment of the five branches of knowledge: grammar, dialectics, rhetoric, poetics and historiography. Contrary to Vossius, it defines grammar as a science, an 'ars instrumentalis Politiae humanae' whose end is the rational indication of the perceptions of the mind, and which is natural to man as a *homo politicus*, but artificial in its ordering of individual *voces* and *orationes*.[3] Grammar is divided into *civilis* and *philosophica*, which corresponds to the ancient division into *exegetice* and *methodice*, the *grammatica civilis* being not a *scientia* but resting on the authority of the best authors. Campanella places the grammar of Scioppius in this category. *Grammatica*

---

[1] *Realis philosophiae epilogisticae partes quatuor*, Frankfurt, 1623, p. 160.

[2] *Philosophiae rationalis partes quinque: Prima pars (Grammatica)*, p. 152. (In succeeding footnotes this work will be referred to as *Grammatica*.) v. V. Salmon, *Francis Lodwick*, pp. 25, 78, 88.

[3] *Grammatica*, pp. 1–2. An *ars instrumentalis* is an *ars* that has a definite end.

philosophica, on the contrary, is based on reason. It is a method of investigation of the apprehension by the intellect of things as they are found in Nature, noting *essentias, actus*, and *habitudines*. Its method is that of the *Grammatica speculativa*[1] and Thomas Aquinas, proceeding 'ex rei natura', a method wrongly condemned by the common run of grammarians[2] whose systems are 'ex autoribus', not 'ex rebus', and who base their normative approach on the literature of antiquity rather than on the signification of phenomena. It considers 'voces propter res', not 'res propter voces', and its concern is not 'aetas linguae' (i.e. the 'best' period of a language as reflected in literature) but 'rationalitas'.[3] The twelfth-century rejection of the literary school of Orleans by the dialecticians of Paris has here its counterpart five hundred years later. Beneath Campanella's philosophical approach there lies a return to medievalism.

The view of the word taken by the philosophical grammarians is in fact the medieval one, and is in marked contrast to the vague lexicographical approach of the general run of seventeenth-century grammarians. Finck–Helwig go out of their way to emphasize the function of the word as a linguistic sign, quoting Petrus Hispanus' definition of the *vox significativa* as a 'signum aptum natum ad aliquid repraesentandum intellectui per auditum', and its parallel in Scaliger's *dictio* which is a 'nota unius speciei, quae est in animo'. The medieval equation *dictio = vox significativa* reappears in their work, where 'dictio ultra vocem importat significatum' – an anticipation of much that is of importance in twentieth-century linguistics. This view of the word as an indissoluble association of the two facets mental concept and phonetic form[4] lies behind F. de Saussure's well-known schematization in which these facets, rendered respectively as *signifié* and *signifiant*, together make up the linguistic sign.[5] A similar 'dualist' approach to referential definitions of meaning has been adopted by several modern linguists. It lies for instance behind C. K. Ogden and I. A. Richards' 'triangle of reference' with its three terms symbol, thought and referent and its positing of 'causal relations' between thought and symbol,[6] a scheme which J. Lyons

---

[1] Of 'Scotus', as Campanella has it.
[2] 'Grammatici vulgares.'   [3] *Grammatica*, p. 6.
[4] Vague definitions of the word such as Ramus' and Sanctius' 'quo unumquodque vocatur' entirely lose sight of this double nature of the linguistic sign.
[5] v. *Cours de linguistique générale* (5th ed.), Paris, 1955, pp. 99, 158.
[6] *The Meaning of Meaning*, New York (no date, first published 1923), pp. 10–12.

has called 'little more than a reformation of the scholastic *vox significat mediantibus conceptibus*'.[1] Lyons himself rejects, as a stumbling-block to operational adequacy, any theory which defines meaning in terms of a relation between signifier and thing signified,[2] while J. R. Firth's 'context of situation' approach to semantics equally has no room for the 'dualist' thesis.[3] S. Ullmann however defines meaning as a 'reciprocal relation between name and sense, which enables them to call up one another', where *name = signifiant* and *sense = signifié* (mental content),[4] thus accepting de Saussure's premises, but noting that such definitions need expanding in order on the one hand to avoid an 'atomistic view of language, in which each word would be regarded as an isolated and self-contained unit', and on the other to provide for 'multiple meaning'.[5] This latter requirement leaves the way open for modifications such as that proposed by V. Brøndal, who suggests a kind of double sign which would provide both for the lexical 'kernal' (*noyau*) of the word and its grammatical behaviour as a part of speech (*classe*), every word necessarily presenting these two aspects.[6] This would represent a return to the medieval insistence on a *modus signandi*, conferring a lexical meaning on a word, being always accompanied by a *modus significandi* giving it an added grammatical status as a part of speech, an insistence to which Lyons concedes 'a certain validity'.[7] Lyons' quotation of a Russian example in which a 'grammatical meaning' is 'superimposed' upon the 'lexical meaning' of a word, and the conclusion he draws, are of interest for any attempt to link earlier grammatical theory with trends in present-day linguistics:

To this extent, the traditional theory of the 'modes of signifying is correct: it must be reformulated, of course, within a more satisfactory theory of syntactic structure...In the present state of syntactic theory, the distinction between grammatical and lexical items is somewhat indeterminate.[8]

[1] *Structural Semantics: An Analysis of Part of the Vocabulary of Plato*, Blackwell, Oxford, 1963, pp. 1–2.   [2] v. *ibid*. p. 1.
[3] v. 'General Linguistics and Descriptive Grammar', *Papers in Linguistics 1934–1951*, Oxford, 1957, p. 227: 'My own approach to meaning in linguistics has always been independent of such dualisms as mind and body, language and thought, word and idea, *signifiant et signifié*, expression and content. These dichotomies are a quite unnecessary nuisance, and in my opinion should be dropped.'
[4] *The Principles of Semantics*, 2nd ed., Glasgow and Blackwell, Oxford, 1957, pp. 70, 69.
[5] *Semantics: An Introduction to the Science of Meaning*, Blackwell, Oxford, 1962, pp. 62–3.
[6] *Essais de linguistique générale*, p. 118.
[7] *Introduction to Theoretical Linguistics*, p. 436.   [8] *Ibid*. pp. 437–8.

Against this one may set U. Weinreich's view that there is 'no special kind of meaning such as "grammatical meaning"', but 'merely special signs which have the grammatical (not semantic!) property of obligatoriness'. Weinreich sees this position as the sole tenable one, since it is the only one which guarantees the separate autonomy of semantic and grammatical criteria.[1] R. Jacobson, on the other hand, regards 'the consistent distinction between grammatical and lexical meanings' as a *conditio sine qua non* of 'new high-level generalizations' in grammar.[2]

Besides foreshadowing present-day 'dualist' theories of the linguistic sign,[3] Finck–Helwig already show certain features which it has been customary to regard as 'Cartesian' or as a specifically Port-Royal contribution to grammatical theory. They see the linguistic sign not as a direct indication of reality (cf. Roman grammar's, *nomen significat rem*), but as communicating 'animi nostri sensus et conceptus'. The ideas we have of things are introduced into the mind by the senses as *imagines rerum* or *notiones*, of which words are signs.[4] This approach – which is obviously that of Scaliger – both incorporates medieval and seventeenth-century doctrine concerning the obtaining of knowledge through the senses, and anticipates the Port-Royal view of words as indications of mental concepts. 'Quid est aliud pars orationis, quam mentis conceptum?' Priscian had asked, and neither he nor the Schoolmen would have quarrelled with Campanella's definition of the word as a 'sonus...naturalibus instrumentis formatus, ad significandum aliquid simplex mente conceptum'.[5] Priscian's false analogy[6] between *elementa mundi* and linguistic segments is however also continued, Campanella seeing the

---

[1] 'On the Semantic Structure of Language', *Universals of Language* (ed. J. H. Greenberg), p. 135.

[2] 'Implications of Language Universals for Linguistics', *ibid.* (ed. J. H. Greenberg), p. 214. Cf. p. 217: 'An intralingual classification of words which would at last tie together the problems of lexicology and grammar is an essential prerequisite to the cross-language investigation of lexical uniformities.'

[3] Helwig's 'Vox est nota conceptus mentis separata...Eius Materiale, est sonus articulatus. Formale, significatio' (*Libri didactici*, p. 14) corresponds precisely to de Saussure's view.

[4] *Grammatica Latina*, p. 4: 'rerum notiones a rebus in mentem primum per sensus sine medio humano profectae sunt...Sicut igitur imagines rerum sunt notiones intellectui, ita voces sunt illarum notiones'.

[5] *Grammatica*, p. 13. The word *simplex* is intended to exclude the interjection, which declares *passiones et affectiones* 'complexe per modum orationis, non per modum vocabuli', and is an element of syntax.

[6] Cf. R. H. Robins, *Short History*, p. 23.

literae, corresponding to *corpuscula* in the world of things, as remote causes of the *vocabula.* But in the last analysis Campanella's view of word function is the medieval one. To the *Grammatica speculativa*'s doctrine of the mind as apprehending the *modi essendi* (the properties of things) which are then seen as *modi intelligendi passivi* (the mind's concept of those properties),[1] there corresponds in close parallel Campanella's view of the mind as apprehending *res simplices,* which are then manifested in *vocabula* in such a way that the *ratio conceptus* is expressed.[2] It is these 'res conceptae, uti sunt in natura' which are then joined together in *oratio,* which signifies 'complexiones rerum conceptarum'.[3]

Though it is the *vox significativa* that is the province of the grammarian, Finck–Helwig are clear that it is not lexical meaning or nomenclature that concerns him, but those *grammatical* meanings consignified by formal devices: 'ita, ut non versetur in ipsis significationibus, verum in proprietatibus significationum, quales sunt in Nomine & Verbo flexiones, in illo [sc. in nomine] etiam Genera, comparationes, casus, in hoc [sc. in verbo] tempora & persona'.[4] The debt to Ramus is obvious. What marks Helwig's approach as being in the same medieval tradition as Campanella's is his view of formal variation as indicating 'varios significandi modos',[5] paralleling Campanella's view of word inflection as functioning 'ad variationem modi significandi'.[6] The doctrine is precisely that of Ramus, but Ramus had deliberately chosen not to express it in medieval terms. More important however, in both Helwig and Campanella, is the logical distinction which makes of noun and verb (in Campanella also the participle) primary word-classes, and of all the rest semantically dependent *syncategoremata.*[7] The two primary classes are distinguished by Campanella on the basis of the signification of *essentia* and *actus.* His definition of the noun as a 'vocabulum, pars Orationis declinabilis . . . significans essentiam cuiusque rei ex impositione'[8] is thus seen to be ultimately the medieval one in terms of signification *per modum entis.*[9] The use of the word *significans* marks off the noun (as

---

[1] Cap. iv.   [2] *Grammatica,* p. 14.   [3] *Ibid.* p. 15.

[4] *Grammatica Latina,* p. 4, with acknowledgments to Ramus' *Scholae.*

[5] *Libri didactici,* p. 1.   [6] *Grammatica,* p. 17.

[7] Helwig thus has a three-word-class system of *Nomen, Verbum,* and *Advocabulum.*

[8] 'Significans ex impositione' is a rendering of Aristotle's (*De interpretatione,* cap. 2) σημαντικὴ κατὰ συνθήκην.

[9] More particularly as the *Grammatica speculativa* describes this mode as 'rei inhaerens, ex hoc quod habet essentiam'. Helwig's definition (*Libri didactici,* p. 2) of the noun as 'quo aliquid nominatur' is by contrast in the vague style of the majority of seventeenth-century grammarians.

also the verb and participle) from those word-classes which merely *consignify* something concerning an essence or an act. In Helwig this definition in terms of the signification of *essentia* is reserved to the substantive. His definition of the latter as 'quod essentiam significat' and of the adjective as 'quod essentiam talem significat'[1] are the usual seventeenth-century definitions in terms of *substantia* and *qualitas* put into terms of the signification of essence. This view of the substantive as signifying essence is taken from Scaliger, whose preference for the term *essentiale* rather than *substantivum* is quoted by Finck–Helwig.[2]

Campanella sets up a semasiologically determined series of ten *modi* in which the noun signifies essence. Some signify 'essentiam puram', others (e.g. *humanum*) 'essentiam ut adiunctam alteri essentia'. Yet others signify essence as it concerns an act: 'essentiam actionis' (*lectio*), 'essentiam patientis' (*factura*), 'essentiam instrumenti actus' (*auditorium*), 'essentiam ordinatam ad actum' (participial nouns), etc. The semasiological *species* of Roman grammar are replaced by a new set (some members of which are semantically identical with those they replace) with meanings described in terms of the signification of essence. The comparatives figure here, not for reasons of formal ending, but because they signify 'essentiae comparationem'.[3] Unlike Helwig, who attaches a Ramistic importance to formally marked accidents, Campanella regards formal endings as no more than 'respectus additos essentiis'.[4] He subdivides the noun-class according to the six criteria *essentia* (substantive/adjective), *quantitas* (common/proper), *numerus*, *ordo* (primary/derivative), *sexus* and *formatio* (simple/compound).[5] Substantive and adjective are defined in medieval fashion as signifying 'per modum subsistentis per se' and 'per modum adiacentis alteri'.[6] The seventeenth-century tendency to bracket the abstract noun with the adjective on the grounds that both signify *qualitas* is not followed.[7] Though Campanella is well aware that on the level of lexical meaning *albedo*

---

[1] *Libri didactici*, p. 4.

[2] *Grammatica Latina*, p. 40. This grammar usually repeats Melanchthon's and Scaliger's (sometimes also Ramus') definitions of the word-classes.

[3] *Grammatica*, p. 19.   [4] *Ibid.* p. 20.

[5] Drawing an analogy with the real world, which also has forms *simplices* and *compositae*.

[6] *Grammatica*, p. 21.

[7] Cf. Finck–Helwig's '*Ex Qualitate* nomen est vel Substantivum, vel Adjectivum'. They point out however that the logical categories concrete and abstract are not always exactly paralleled in grammar (*Grammatica Latina*, pp. 39–40).

does not signify a 'res subsistens in se', he classifies it as a substantive because on the level of grammatical function it signifies '*per modum subsistentis*'. In the face of much seventeenth-century opinion to the contrary he reasserts the medieval view: 'Grammaticus respicit modum significandi, non rem significatam.' Equally, however, he rejects the formal approach of Ramus and his school as being 'non a natura Nominum, sed a signo adiacente'.[1] He notes that not every adjective is logically an accident, *rationalis* e.g. being counted by the logicians (and, one may add, by the medieval *Grammatica speculativa*)[2] as a substantive on the grounds that it is identical in signification with *homo*. Campanella however insists that, since grammar regards only their *modus significandi*, such words are *grammatically* adjectives.[3] The medieval grammarians would no doubt have retorted that such words do indeed have a *modus significandi*,[4] but not the *modus* 'inhaerentis alteri secundum esse' reserved to adjectives. Campanella solves the dilemma by setting up two classes of adjective, the one (*rationalis, humanus*) 'substantiale', and adjectival in *vox* (i.e. form) only, the other (*doctus, albus*) 'accidentale', and adjectival in both *vox* and *res*.

Word derivation is regarded not as a formal matter, but as involving the establishment of semasiological categories having their origin in the *fons* constituted by the essences of things, an explanation based on the etymology of *derivare*. On this view, since essences are signified by nouns all verbs must be noun derivatives. Where exceptionally a noun is derived from a verb it is not *secundum naturam*, but the verb in question must itself be assumed to be derived from an essence even if the said essence has no nominal counterpart in the language.[5] All derived forms are accordingly distributed among semasiological categories signifying essence, or act as related to essence, *amator* signifying 'essentiam cum virtute ad actum', *amor* 'ipsum actum, ut essentia et quidditas[6] est', *indolentia* 'essentiam plenam actu', etc. Campanella must be aware that it is form that is behind the recognition of these words as derivatives, but he none the

---

[1] *Grammatica*, p. 22.
[2] Cap. x.   [3] *Grammatica*, p. 48.
[4] The *Grammatica speculativa*, since they signify 'substantiam, quae secundum esse alteri non inhaeret', regards them as forming with other substantives, as in *animal rationale*, a construction 'incongrua de se, tamen per appositionem admissiva'. (Cap. x.)
[5] *Grammatica*, p. 25.
[6] *Quidditas*, the 'whatness' of a thing, its essence (coined no doubt on the analogy of *qualitas*), is a term dear to medieval logic.

less defines them in wholly semantic terms[1] (*servile* e.g. is used 'cum pertinet aliquid ad esse dicimus'), forgetting his much-stressed dictum that 'Grammaticus respicit modum significandi, non rem significatam.' In the division of the noun *a sexu* he similarly defines according to *res significata*[2] ('Masculinum est quod masculum in sexu rerum significat') but notes that genders are 'designated' by the preceding *hic haec hoc* in the Latin paradigms and by the article in the vernaculars. He seems to be of the opinion that grammar ought ideally to follow natural gender and the *sexus* distributed to natural phenomena by the Pythagoreans, remarks that grammatical usage 'non semper naturae correspondet', and praises in this respect the English language's way of expressing 'per certas voces certos sexus'.[3] It is true that case is defined formally as a 'mutatio nominis in fine', but Campanella goes on to define the nominative as the 'rei nominatio' *par excellence*, and the *casus obliquus* in similar semasiological fashion as that which, having named a thing, additionally 'ad aliquid circa rem spectat'. He does however deplore the use of a single formal ending to indicate more than one case relation, and notes that the function performed by case in the classical languages is performed in the vernaculars by the 'article'.[4]

Campanella's grammar of the noun is thus seen to be based on the signification of *essentia*, a conception differing from the medieval one only in the terms in which it is expressed. But in addition to the *substantia* and *qualitas* of Roman grammar, his noun signifies *quantitas, forma, actus, actio, passio, relatio* (all regarded as essences) and even *non-ens* (e.g. the noun *nihil*), whose essence can be given at least 'in intellectu'.[5] In this system, the remaining word-classes are similarly to be defined in terms of the signification or consignification of *essentia*. The pronoun however, following Scaliger's doctrine of indirect signification,[6] consignifies not 'essentiam immediate' but 'personam essentiae' or 'essentiam ut personatam', that is to say the 'individualitates & particularitates' of an essence. It is accordingly a 'vocabulum declinabile consignificans personas, vel personalia essentiarum'.[7] It still has its Priscianic function as a substitute for the

---

[1] *Grammatica*, pp. 26–7.
[2] In marked contrast to Helwig's Ramistic definition of gender as a 'differentia Nominis juxta sexum'.
[3] *Grammatica*, pp. 28–30.   [4] *Ibid.* pp. 34–5.
[5] *Ibid.* pp. 18–19.
[6] Cf. Scaliger's and Vossius' definition of the noun as 'rem *primo* significans'.
[7] *Grammatica*, p. 37.

proper noun, though this aspect is omitted from the definition as not touching the essential nature of pronouns which is to represent 'essentiarum existentias' or, more specifically, to indicate 'existentiam primo' but 'essentiam secundario'. If one compares Scaliger's view of the pronoun as signifying 'nomen primo, rem secundario', and bears in mind that in Campanella's system it is not *res* but *essentia* that is signified by the noun, it follows that for the latter grammarian it is *essentia* that is indirectly indicated by the pronoun. Once again, he has taken an existing grammatical doctrine and dressed it up in philosophical terms. His pronoun cannot however signify without a noun, either expressed or implied, hence the employment in the definition of *consignificans* rather than *significans*.[1] But since it is none the less regarded as a substitute for the proper noun, it follows that the latter must also, as its semantic equivalent, denote *essentia personata*. On the level of connotation, however, it 'pronominalizes'. The name *Petrus* being equivalent to *hic homo filius Ionae*, it must equally with the pronoun signify *existentia*, but 'secundario' or 'in obliquo', its main role as a noun being to signify *essentia* 'primo' or 'in recto'. Herein lies its difference from the pronoun, which indicates *existentia* 'in recto', *essentia* only 'in obliquo'.[2] By these philosophical arguments Campanella meets the contentions of those who, like Ramus and Sanctius, hold that there is no definition of the pronoun that is not equally applicable to the noun.

Person is for Campanella 'quod per se aliquod particularizatum & distinctum ab aliis, & indivisum in se, sonat'. Hence, far from indicating Priscian's *substantiam meram* (i.e. *sine qualitate*) or, as medieval grammar rephrases it, signifying *per modum indeterminatae apprehensionis*, the pronoun *particularizes* substance, represents it as *personata*. 'In suis causis' (a phrase reminiscent of Scaliger) all things have *essentia pura*, the concept *homo* e.g. existing as a pure essence in the mind of God. The human mind however can perceive this concept only in the particular form *hic homo*, investing it with *persona* in order to bring it 'ad existentiam'. It is in this sense that the pronoun may be said to signify *existentiam primo* and to consignify person. It does not signify *subsistentia*, which is proper only to substances and can be signified only by the noun, but *existentia*, a property of all things which

---

[1] This is the opposite of the Ancients' view that the noun *consignifies* person while the pronoun *signifies* it. Cf. Alvarus' late-sixteenth-century *De institutione grammatica*, which also has this reversal. [2] *Grammatica*, p. 39.

however only manifests itself 'in persona alicuius, vel in individuo aliquo corpore', not *per se*. Here the pronoun rejoins the adjective, which is concerned with *existentia*, not *subsistentia*, the pronominal adjectives (termed by Campanella *personalia*) having a personalizing function *vis-à-vis* the noun: *filius* signifies essence, *filius meus* the same essence 'personata'.[1] The noun indicates something as *subsisting*, the pronoun simply as *existing*. To do this the pronoun attributes person, Campanella's definition thus approaching the Roman one in terms of the signification of 'personas finitas', but supplying it with a philosophical justification.

The subdivision of the pronoun takes place, like that of the noun, according to the six criteria *essentia, quantitas, numerus, ordo, sexus* and *formatio*. These are preceded by a primary distinction *a personis*, the signifying of persons being the *proprium essentiale* of the pronoun. The division *ab essentia* is again that into substantive and adjective, defined in medieval terms as signifying *existentia* or *persona* 'quasi per se existentem' or merely 'adiacentem'.[2] *Hic, iste, ille* and *ipse* are counted, contrary to custom, as *substantiva*. Their marking of gender *per voces tres* is not retained as a criterion classing them as adjectives, for it is the *modus significandi*, not the *accidentalitas vocabulorum*, that is grammatically the deciding factor. Similarly, in the construction *equus meus* it is not formal agreement that indicates the presence of an adjective, but the fact that a certain 'esse meum' or 'meitas' is adjoined (*adiacet*) to the concept expressed by *equus*. Even standing alone, *quidam* and *omnis* are adjectives, because the concept to which they are adjoined (e.g. *homo*) is 'understood'. Since they cannot signify *per se*, they were wrongly termed substantives by the Ancients. Campanella follows here the logicians, who refused to give these words the status of *termini significativi*, calling them *consignificativi* or *syncategorematici*. In *quidam lapis* the word *quidam* does not indicate the essence of the stone, but 'lapis deductus ad existentiam aliquam'. It is for comparable reasons that the pronoun is held to substitute for the proper noun only and not for the common noun, for what can *omnis homo* mean other than every individual man, *Petrus, Ioannes, Franciscus*, etc.?[3]

In the discussion of number Campanella shows a sudden solicitude for form in his suggestion that the plurals of *ego* and *tu* ought more

---

[1] *Ibid.* pp. 37–8. [2] *Ibid.* p. 40.
[3] *Ibid.* pp. 40–1.

aptly to be *egones* and *tunes*. The traditional subclasses of *demonstrativa, possessiva, gentilia* and *relativa* are retained, but the distinction between demonstratives and relatives is made on the basis of sense perception. Since no *essentia* can be indicated 'in sensu' except in so far as it is 'deducta ad existentiam' (i.e. 'personata'), the demonstratives 'serviunt sensatis demonstrationibus personarum, vel essentiarum personatarum'. The relatives, on the contrary, 'non ostendunt ad sensum, sed quasi ad memoriam'.[1] Again, a traditional classification is kept but supplied with a philosophical justification, in this case the medieval and seventeenth-century empiricist doctrine of the obtaining of knowledge through the senses.

The verb signifies, in contradistinction to the noun, not *essentia* but *actus*. Since the *actus* is however an *actus essentiae*, Campanella's view may be thought to be ultimately identical with the medieval one of the verb as signifying *per modum esse*.[2] At first sight his definition seems to be the customary seventeenth-century one in terms of the signification of *actio, passio* or *esse*: 'est vocabulum declinabile, significans ex impositione, rerum actum, sive essendi, sive existendi, sive operandi, sive agendi, sive patiendi'.[3] Campanella's verb does not however signify an *actio* (which the noun is also able to do) but an *actus actionis*. First, it can signify an *actus essendi* ('homo est animal'), when the verb *sum* performs its copulative function of joining together 'notiones, non res'.[4] In addition to its use as a copula, the verb substantive[5] signifies being as 'ipsam essentiam ut est essentia'. This non-copulative use (as in 'Petrus est') is catered for by the reference to 'actus existendi', where an *actus existentialis* rather than *essentialis* is signified. 'Actus operandi' refers to intransitive verbs, an *operatio* differing from an *actio* in being unable to pass into an object. The features indicated by the words 'agendi' and

---

[1] *Ibid.* p. 46.

[2] More particularly as the *Grammatica speculativa* (cap. viii) describes the *modus esse* as 'rei inhaerens ex hoc quod habet fieri'. Interesting for its relevance to the medieval approach is E. Sapir's treatment of the referents of noun and verb as respectively 'existents and occurrents' (*Totality*, LSA Language Monographs 6, 1930, p. 1; *Selected Writings*, Berkeley and Los Angeles, 1949, p. 123). R. Jacobson points out ('Implications of Language Universals for Linguistics', *Universals of Language* (ed. J. H. Greenberg), p. 209), that this instance of 'simple relations among grammatical universals' is 'correlated but never merges with the likewise universal difference of two syntactic functions – subject and predicate'.

[3] *Grammatica*, p. 50.   [4] *Ibid.* p. 51.

[5] Every act being either *substantialis* or *accidentalis*, the medieval distinction between *verba substantiva* and *adiectiva* is retained.

'patiendi', though catered for in the definition of the verb, are for Campanella properly speaking not the province of grammar but of 'metaphysics',[1] therefore presumably on the lexical level of *res significatae* rather than the grammatical level of the *modi significandi*. The indication of *actio* or *passio* does not, any more than the possession of mood and tense, constitute the essence of the verb.[2] Its true nature lies in the indication of an 'actum fluentem ab essentia',[3] a view which coincides with Scaliger's and medieval grammar's doctrine that it indicates *res fluentes* in contrast to the *res permanentes* signified by the noun. A further argument against counting signification with tense as the *proprium* of the verb lies in the absence of tense in the *verbum substantiale*, and in the lack of formal markers of tense in the Chinese verb.[4] In any case, Campanella's system excludes such formal markers from the essence of a word-class,[5] admitting them only (and then grudgingly) as criteria for the division into sub-classes.

In the verb these criteria are *essentia* (governing voice distinctions), *persona, numerus, tempus, ordo* and *formatio*. Campanella notes that the traditional voice distinctions are neither consistently *secundum rem* nor consistently *secundum vocem*,[6] and distinguishes *secundum rem* only (i.e. semasiologically) the five classes *essentiale* ('sum'), *existentiale* ('existo'), *operativum* (intransitives), *activum* (transitives), and *passivum*.[7] Since each of these 'proceeds' from the one immediately preceding it in this list, all are ultimately reducible, as in Scaliger's system, to *being*.[8] Though Campanella defines the verb as *declinabile* and uses the terms *casus* and *declinatio* to describe its formal variations, it is but rarely, as in the division of impersonal verbs into active and passive *secundum vocem*, that he uses formal criteria to make a grammatical distinction. Where he can draw a philosophical parallel

---

[1] *Grammatica*, p. 51.

[2] But cf. *ibid.* p. 57: 'Proprium est verborum in temporibus significare.' Against this however one may further cite the 'significare actum rerum est verbo essentiale' of p. 52.

[3] Cf. Finck–Helwig's approval of Scaliger's doctrine that both *actio* and *passio* are reducible to *esse* (*Grammatica Latina*, p. 160).

[4] *Grammatica*, p. 52.

[5] Cf., as an indication of the acceptance of Ramus' views in some quarters, Finck–Helwig's view (in discussing mood) that 'Grammaticum non tantum Metaphysice & Physice contemplari adsignificationes vocum, sed imprimis Grammatice, id est, respiciendo *terminationem*.' (*Grammatica Latina*, p. 172).

[6] *Sequor*, e.g., is active *secundum rem* but passive *secundum vocem*.

[7] *Grammatica*, pp. 52–3.

[8] Cf. *ibid.* p. 76, where Campanella remarks that, *curro* being resolvable into *ego sum currens*, 'omnis actus resolvitur in essentiam'.

he does so, as when he makes the three moods indicative, imperative and optative correspond to the three *primalitates Metaphysici*. Although mood is broadly defined as 'cuiusque rei qualitas', only these three philosophically acceptable *primalitates* are given the status of *facultates* of the verb around which the tenses can be organized. Subjunctive and infinitive have a subordinate status as 'aliae rationes' of tense, used as *appendices* to other verbs.[1]

The participle is a declinable part of speech signifying 'essentiam simul cum suo actu, vel actum cum essentia, cuius est actus'.[2] This is not, as Campanella is quick to point out, the same thing as the traditional definition in terms of accidents, in which the participle receives case and gender from the noun, tense and *significatio* (i.e. voice) from the verb, number and *figura* from both. Campanella's participle must by definition take its *significatio* from both noun and verb. If it took it only from the verb it would be able to signify *actus*, but not *essentia cum actu*.[3] Only by taking it from both verb and noun can it signify both *actus* and *res*. It is not however its *ratio propria* to 'participate' in the nature of both noun and verb. Only on the level of grammatical function, in its *modus significandi*, is its double character manifested.[4] Where there is no such grammatical function, as in the *nomina participialia*, Campanella still however classifies on the basis of the signification of *actus* and *essentia*.[5] Two of these nouns indicate 'potentiam ad actum' (*amabile, amativum*), two signify 'essentiam cum actu praesenti' (*amans, amatum*), and two 'essentiam cum actu futuro' (*amaturum, amandum*).[6]

Following Campanella's guiding principle, the *syncategoremata* also are defined in terms of *essentia*, specifically as expressing *circumstantiae* of essences or as linking them.[7] The preposition (or *adnomen*, as Campanella prefers to call it) is seen as adhering to the noun in the same way as the adverb is attached to the verb. Their syntactic

[1] *Ibid.* pp. 58–60.
[2] *Ibid.* p. 70. This seems to imply the same standpoint as the *Grammatica speculativa*'s definition (cap. xxvi) of the participle as signifying 'per modum indistantis a substantia'.
[3] In his syntax Priscian notes that the participle signifies 'et substantiam [Campanella's *essentiam*] ipsius qui agit vel patitur, et actum vel passionem'.
[4] *Grammatica*, p. 71.
[5] Since the *nomina participialia* signify 'essentiam cum suo actu essendi, vel existendi, etc.', they seem not to differ in definition from the participle itself.
[6] *Grammatica*, p. 26.
[7] Cf. Helwig's third part of speech, the *advocabulum*, divided into *circumstantivum*, *continuativum* and *affectivum* (i.e. adverb, preposition and interjection).

functions are therefore similar,[1] the adverb being that which 'verbo adhaeret significanti actum',[2] the preposition that which 'nomini adhaeret significanti essentiam'.[3] The semantic function of the preposition is to consignify *respectus et circunstantias*, a function which recalls Melanchthon's view of this word-class as linking the verb to a noun which signifies 'aliquam facti circunstantiam'.[4] Campanella's definition accordingly describes it as 'indeclinabile, consignificans rerum seu essentiarum cum suis actibus respectus & circunstantias'.[5] The stipulation 'cum suis actibus' may have its counterpart in Melanchthon's bringing of the verb into the prepositional relationship, especially in view of Campanella's insistence on this relation taking place 'per actum essendi & existendi & agendi', etc.[6] The preposition performs in most respects for the noun those functions performed by the adverb for the verb, exception made of the indication of *qualitas, quantitas* and other 'praedicamentalia', which are indicated by the adverb for the verb, by the adjective for the noun substantive. There is much minute logical classification of the type that describes *a, ex* as indicating 'respectum principii ad terminum, qua principii', *ad, in* as indicating 'respectum principii ad terminum qua terminum', etc.[7]

Whereas the preposition consignifies the *respectus* and *circumstantiae* of *essentia* (and hence for all practical purposes of the noun), the adverb consignifies those of *actus* and in addition indicates certain *praedicamentalia* of quality, quantity, time, place, etc. It is a 'vocabulum indeclinabile consignificans circunstantias praedicamentales, & affectiones, modificationesque actus'.[8] Those things which are said to 'circunstare' the signification of the verb have to do not with *essentia*, but with *existentia*. The conjunction must similarly be defined in terms of *essentia* and *actus*. It consignifies *copula essentiarum*, but in order to keep it distinct from the prepositions, some of which also signify

---

[1] The seventeenth century found it increasingly unnecessary to make a clear-cut distinction between adverb and preposition. Cf. Helwig's view of them as differing in semantic dependence on noun and verb, the preposition being semantically 'incomplete' (*Libri didactici*, pp. 8–9). Campanella has not used medieval sources here, but has gone back to erroneous Ancient sources.

[2] *Grammatica*, p. 78.   [3] *Ibid.* p. 74.

[4] *Grammatica* (1527 ed.), f. 41ʳ.   [5] *Grammatica*, p. 74.

[6] *Ibid.* p. 75. But cf. also Thomas of Erfurt's definition (*Grammatica speculativa*, cap. xl) of the preposition as 'significans per modum adjacentis alteri casuali, ipsum . . . ad actum reducens' (i.e. governing a case-marked word and *relating it to an action*).

[7] *Ibid.* pp. 75–7.

[8] *Ibid.* p. 78. Again, there is an evident link with Melanchthon.

coniunctio as a *respectus*, Campanella specifies that the *essentiae* thus conjoined be 'inter se relatae ad unum actum'. In 'Petrus cum Ioanne' *cum* merely indicates a *relatio societatis*, whereas in 'Petrus et Ioannes sunt homines' *et* conjoins the two nouns *in actu essendi*. The conjunction is therefore somewhat cumbersomely defined as follows: 'est vocabulum indeclinabile consignificans copulam essentiarum, inter se relatarum ad unum actum; aut rerum & simul actuum earum inter se, & propterea in oratione coniungit caeteras partes orationis & sententias.'[1]

Since any utterance involves the declaration of *aliquis actus* concerning *aliquis essentia*, Campanella's syntax is conceived in the same philosophical terms as his *etymologia*. The essences are in themselves *impermistae*, free of any order imposed by conjunction or disjunction. Such an order can only be established 'per proprios actus, dum altera [essentia] in alteram extenditur', by a 'rerum coniunctio et disiunctio per actum' which gives rise to grammatical construction, whose variety reflects the multiplicity of such acts.[2] Just as the *etymologia* was largely conceived in terms of *essentia*, so the syntax is seen in terms of *actus*. As the *partes orationis* are the same in number as the *genera vocabulorum*[3] based on *essentia*, so the rules of *constructio* (a term reserved to case government) are equal in number to the possible *genera actuum*. To the seven orders of verbs (expressing *actus essendi*, *existendi*, *operandi*, etc.) there accordingly correspond seven rules of government.[4] The rules of concord are those traditionally found in Latin grammars, restated in terms of Campanella's philosophical system and declared to be proper to all languages. The agreement of a verb with its nominative subject is that between *actus* and *id, cuius est actus*.[5] Similarly the concord of adjective and substantive is that between *accidens* and *id, cuius est accidens*. It is easy to see why, having reduced language to a logical correspondence with universally valid philosophical properties of phenomena, Campanella and the universal grammarians assumed that the grammatical categories corresponding to these properties would be equally valid

---

[1] *Ibid.* pp. 83–4. Priscian is alone among the Roman grammarians in retaining this double function of syntactic linking and consignification. His word-for-word translation describes the conjunction as 'coniunctiva aliarum partium orationis, quibus consignificat' (H. Keil, *Grammatici Latini*, III, 93). The other Roman grammarians retain only the linking function, as does the *Grammatica speculativa*, though the influence of logic leads some medieval grammarians to refuse meaning to the conjunction or to attribute to it only an *imperfecta significatio* (v. J. J. Baebler, *Beiträge*, p. 80).

[2] *Grammatica*, p. 99.   [3] *Ibid.* p. 15.   [4] *Ibid.* p. 100.   [5] *Ibid.* p. 95.

for all languages. Their mistake lay in assuming a close logical correspondence between the categories of philosophy and those of language, in supposing that the world view of Greco-Latin philosophy would inevitably be mirrored in the same way by each individual idiom.

The rules of case government are those common to the great majority of Latin grammars, but with added explanations in terms of Campanella's philosophical approach. The customary simple statement to the effect that the substantive verb requires a nominative both before and after it (*Homo est animal*) is buttressed by the explanation that 'praedicatum substantiale non sequitur ad actum essendi, sed continetur in illo'.[1] Sentences of the type *Homo est albus* are justified in terms of the predication of an *actus accidentalis* 'per modum essendi', *albus* being predicated of *homo* not as being the same but as being 'quasi ens idem', the same in person but not in substance. In a similar way, those *verba accidentalia* which are constructed with both a preceding and a following nominative (*Petrus manet moestus*) are held to connote *actus non essentiales* 'per modum essentialem'.[2] The treatment of these two questions alone is a sufficient indication of how close, even at this late date, Campanella remains in cast of mind to the Schoolmen. The logical approach to the remaining aspects of verbal syntax is no less intricate. If the verb *esse* is used to denote possession (*liber hic est Petri*) it is because it connotes the verb *habere*, these two verbs being explained in terms of each other 'per commutationem significationis': *esse homo = habere humanitatem = esse rationalis*.[3] The treatment of verbs expressing *actus existendi* involves the establishment of various *modi existendi*: 'ad in subiecto' (*albedo est in pariete*), 'ad in causa' (*omnia sunt in Deo*), 'ad in effectu' (*Deus est in mundo*), etc. These fine distinctions have nothing whatever to do with grammar, the grammatical construction involved being the same in every one of them.

Of more interest, in view of its implications for Port-Royal theory, is his definition of discourse (*oratio*) in medieval fashion as an arrangement of words whose purpose is the expression of complex notions in the mind:[4]

first we conceive simple things in our minds, then make them manifest by an appropriate arrangement of words, in such a way that the *ratio* of the

---

[1] *Ibid.* p. 100.   [2] *Ibid.* p. 101.   [3] *Ibid.* pp. 101–2.
[4] *Ibid.* p. 15: 'Oratio est vocabulorum complexio, ordinata ad manifestandum quidquid animo complexe concipitur.'

concept is expressed. Then we join together the concepts of things as they are in nature, and make an utterance.[1]

This leads to a distinction between words taken singly as signs of things, and their syntactic arrangement as a connected series of concepts: *Vocabula ergo significant res: oratio complexiones rerum conceptarum.* There is obvious relevance here to Bassett Jones' view, already cited,[2] which takes 'the product of words to be more from nature, as of Sentences from Reason',[3] and to Bishop Wilkins' treatment of the proposition as a periphrastic arrangement of 'things and notions of a more simple nature'.[4] Of more importance is the status of Campanella's view of syntax as a precursor of Port-Royal doctrine. Since the Port-Royal *Logic* treats 'judgment' and 'proposition' as equivalent terms, its definition of judgment as that action of the mind by which, in making an affirmation, we 'join together various ideas', is seen to have an affinity, if not indeed an affiliation, to Campanella's approach. Equally of interest, given its relevance to the 'deep' and 'surface' structure question, is his expansion of *volo* (as a reply to the question *vis panem?*) into *ego volo panem*, where 'una dictio non facit orationem, nisi subauditis pluribus dictionibus', *ego* and *panem* being contained 'virtute' in *volo*.

In spite of Campanella's insistence that *res significatae* are not the province of the grammarian, he is truly of his age in his employment of fine semantic distinctions taken from logic. One wonders what compelling urge to minute classification of the universe leads him to make a distinction, for example, between the phrases *oculus in capite* (expressing 'existentiam ad in toto') and *pisces in mare* (expressing 'existentiam ad in cognato'),[5] a procedure which consists in listing the categories of reality rather than demonstrating the categories appropriate to linguistic description. His approach *secundum rem* rather than *secundum vocem* has led him to catalogue the qualities and relations of *res* rather than those of grammar. Using the categories of Scholastic, i.e. ultimately of Greco-Roman philosophy, he inevitably arrives at the world-view reflected by them and believes it to be universally valid. Scholastic philosophy is based on the *quidditas*, the 'whatness' of things, that is to say on their *essence*. It makes a

---

[1] *Ibid.* p. 15: 'prius concipimus animo res simplices, deinde vocabulis manifestamus ore concinnatis, ita ut rationem conceptus exprimant. Deinde coniungimus res conceptas, uti sunt in natura, et facimus orationem.'

[2] Above, p. 156.
[3] *Herm'aelogium* (1659), preface.
[4] v. below, p. 198.
[5] *Grammatica*, p. 103.

distinction however between *essence* and *existence*, for without *existence* (the determination or *actus primus* of any being) an *essence* remains merely potential. An act or actuality (*actus*) is 'any present degree of reality', whereas *potentia* is 'the aptitude or capacity of reaching that stage of reality'.[1] These various elements, *essentia, existentia, actus* and *potentia*, constitute as it were the framework of Campanella's grammar, the metalanguage on which his system is based. In his *Medieval Philosophy Illustrated from the System of Thomas Aquinas*, M. De Wulf notes that the relation of act and potentiality is found (a) between accident and substance, (b) between form and matter, (c) between existence and essence, and gives the following scheme of the various elements involved:[2]

$$
\text{essence } (\textit{essentia}) \begin{cases} \text{substance} \begin{cases} \text{prime matter} \\ \text{substantial form} \end{cases} \\ \\ \text{accidents} \begin{cases} \text{quantity, action,} \\ \text{quality, time,} \\ \text{space, relation} \end{cases} \end{cases}
$$

existence (*esse*)

Campanella's grammatical system is quite obviously clothed in the categories of Scholastic philosophy. As a Dominican he was well versed in Thomism and medieval grammatical theory, and though his preoccupation with *things* and the necessity for grammar to be congruent with them, and his reliance on the doctrine of sense-perception, are recognizably seventeenth-century traits, their source is medieval thought rather than Baconian empiricism. It is significant that he begins his grammar with a condemnation of those who facilely reject the medieval approach 'ex rei natura', with its attempt to make the facts of language square with the metaphysical structure of reality. His method, though bearing the rationalistic impress of the age – he calls reason 'rex sermonum'[3] – is still curiously close to that of the *Grammatica speculativa*. Rather than a new departure, his work is a restatement of grammar in the terms of Scholastic philosophy.

The writing of Campanella's grammar took place against the background of a general European reaction against Ramus and Calvinism and in favour of Scholastic logic. At Oxford, a Scholastic type of teaching was being carried on in the 1630s, encouraged no

[1] M. De Wulf, *Medieval Philosophy*, p. 78.   [2] *Ibid*. p. 79, note 1.
[3] *Grammatica*, p. 26.

doubt by the conservative tendencies of Archbishop Laud, installed as Chancellor in 1630, whose aim was to bring the University back to religious orthodoxy. There was undoubtedly a renewed interest in Aristotle and in Scholastic philosophy, though, as V. H. H. Green remarks, it is not easy to deduce from it anything more than 'a certain conservatism of attitude which would evidently lend support to the maintenance of the *status quo* in Church and state'.[1] A number of logics were published in England at this time – the most important of them by 1620[2] – with the aim of restoring Scholasticism while preserving certain Ramistic elements, though there as elsewhere that kind of 'Philippo-Ramist' compromise worked less to the advantage of Ramus than to that of Melanchthonian Aristotelianism and Scholastic logic. In 1673, for instance, Obadiah Walker's prescriptions for the education of the young still include an example of how 'fancy descants upon, and menageth' Aristotle's ten predicaments, which he claims, seventy years after Bacon's *Advancement of Learning*, to be of value for 'invention'.[3]

CARAMUEL

In Spain, where Humanism was late in penetrating, another philosopher in the Scholastic tradition, the Cistercian bishop Juan Caramuel y Lobkowitz (1606–82), had some interesting things to say in his *Grammatica audax* (1654),[4] consisting of the three parts *methodica, metrica,* and *critica*. The *grammatica metrica* (the Humanists' *prosodia*) has to do with syllables, while the *grammatica critica* has in fact little connection with grammar, dealing rather with logic, physics, and Scholastic and moral theology. The interesting section for the student of universal grammar is the *grammatica methodica*, which claims to treat grammatical questions 'philosophically' and is described as 'ab omnibus linguis praescindens'.[5] Caramuel states that as far as he knows only 'Scotus',[6] Scaliger and Campanella have produced what he calls *grammaticae speculativae*. He has obviously had access to the work of the two latter grammarians, to whom he

---

[1] *A History of Oxford University*, p. 60.
[2] e.g. Samuel Smith's *Aditus ad logicam* (1613). v. W. S. Howell, *Logic and Rhetoric*, p. 285.
[3] *Of Education, Especially of Young Gentlemen*, Oxford, 1673, pp. 138–9.
[4] *Caramuelis praecursor logicus, Complectens grammaticem audacem, cuius partes sunt tres, methodica, metrica, critica*, Frankfurt, 1654.
[5] *Ibid.* title-page.   [6] i.e. Thomas of Erfurt.

prefers 'Scotus' as containing less to displease him. Speculative grammar he defines as that which pertains to no particular region or people, but whose 'meditationes abstractissimae' provide laws appropriate to all languages.[1] The Scholastic bias of his grammar is apparent. He distinguishes in medieval fashion between *materia* (phonetic form) and *forma* (meaning), emphasizing that while every word is *materialiter* a *vox* or arrangement of potentially meaningful sounds, every such arrangement is not a *dictio* or word. The *dictio* is a *vox significans*.[2] Like Campanella he seems to hold that names should be imposed by the philosopher, and praises whatever *Nomenclator* decreed that all Chinese words should be monosyllables. Presumably he thinks that in Chinese there is a one-to-one correspondence between words and things, for he quotes in support the well-known Scholastic tag 'Non sunt multiplicanda entia absque necessitate.'[3] In this he is at one with the artificial language-planners of the seventeenth century, whose aim was to cut out the synonyms and redundancies of natural language.

In dealing with the linguistic sign he sees the 'material' elements of the word as 'transubstantiated' into meaning, which is treated in Scholastic theological terms as a *transsubstantiatio moralis*.[4] This is an extreme statement of the Saussurean type of doctrine, which involves in a mentalist form what R. H. Robins calls 'a dualist referential relation between the word, or sign, and its meaning', a doctrine which many present-day linguists have rejected in favour of contextual theories of meaning such as that of J. R. Firth.[5] Such excursions into theology apart, Caramuel's conception of the sign is that of the 'Doctor Africanus' (St Augustine): 'Signum est . . . quod praeter speciem quam ingerit sensibus facit aliud in nostram notitiam devenire.'[6] Thomistic Scholastics believed that the mind is not simply a reflection of external reality, but that knowledge is a product of two factors, the object which is perceived and the mind which does the perceiving. The sensation received from an object acts in concert with a creative power in the mind, the *intellectus agens*, which operates upon sense data, so that the obtaining of knowledge has

---

[1] *Grammatica audax*, p. 3.   [2] *Ibid.* p. 4.
[3] Ascribed to Ockham, and known as 'Ockham's razor'.
[4] *Grammatica audax*, p. 4.
[5] R. H. Robins, 'Some Considerations on the Status of Grammar in Linguistics', p. 94. Robins notes (p. 95) that Bloomfield's theory of meaning is contextual in type, though 'the context is restricted to items that would pass muster in behavioural terms'.
[6] *Grammatica audax*, p. 5.

both a passive aspect (the *species impressa* or sense impression) and an active one (the *species expressa* or reaction of the mind to that impression). As M. De Wulf puts it:

We directly attain to reality . . . [but] the impression received, is discovered only as the result of reasoning . . . We perceive directly reality itself, and not our subjective modification of it. We perceive it thanks to a close collaboration between sense and intellect.[1]

Caramuel resembles Campanella in being not a sceptical Nominalist but a Realist, holding that the linguistic sign gives us certain knowledge of phenomena. He poses the question whether words give us direct knowledge of things themselves, or whether that knowledge comes to us indirectly through the medium of mental concepts.[2] Does the word 'homo' signify *a man* directly? Or does it signify the concept directly and the actual phenomenon *man* indirectly? He notes Aristotle's teaching that things are signified by concepts and concepts in turn by words, but he none the less regards concept and word as 'aequipollentia signa, res immediate significantia', signs equivalent in value giving a direct signification of reality.[3] One may compare Locke's interposition, between name and reality, of 'nominal essences', of which names are the signs, and his belief that real knowledge is attained only when 'there is conformity between our ideas and the reality of things'. For Caramuel reality, concept and word are congruent.

The sign can be *natural* or *artificial*, the natural sign signifying a thing independently of human agreement or consensus, the artificial one depending on arbitrary convention.[4] It is difficult to know what Caramuel means by this distinction, reminiscent of the old nature versus convention controversy, unless it is the same as that made by Campanella between the perceptions of the mind as natural to man, and the artificial ordering of *voces* in individual languages, or by Vossius between *grammatica naturalis*, dealing with what is common to all languages, and *artificialis*, dealing with what is peculiar to a given language. Caramuel classes *voces*, however, as 'signa naturalia', a striking parallel with Bassett Jones' already quoted dictum that the nations differ in 'vocality' but agree in 'syntax', thereby showing 'the product of words to be more from nature, as of Sentences from

---

[1] *Medieval Philosophy*, pp. 42, 43, 45. v. also pp. 20–1, 24–5.
[2] 'An voces significent immediate res ipsas, an mediate?'
[3] *Grammatica audax*, p. 9.   [4] *Ibid.* p. 5.

Reason'.[1] It may well be that Caramuel classes the 'artificial' *orationes* with what is called *verbum mentis* (internal discourse, the *ratio* or reasoned system of language), and the 'natural' *voces* with the *verbum oris* (external discourse, speech). Certainly he seems to make this Saussurean *langue/parole* type of distinction.[2]

The chapter entitled *De modo significandi* does not cover matter the medieval grammarians would have included under this heading, but contains much Scholastic logic and in parts reads like a treatise on rhetoric. It also discusses theological questions such as why, when in God there is neither first nor last, we conceive of the Father as prior to the Son and of both as prior to the Holy Spirit. Throughout Caramuel's grammar there is, side by side with linguistic insights, a great deal of logical and metaphysical speculation of this order. Much of the grammatical material similarly does not call for comment, being either of Humanist origin or a reintroduction of medieval concepts. Both strands of thought are present, for instance, in his definition of the noun as a 'vox significationis per se stantis; habens numerum cum genere & casu, sine variatione temporis et personae'.[3] More pertinent to later grammatical theory is his division of nouns into *abstracta* and *concreta* (hitherto terms of logic). The concrete nouns are further divided into *substantiva* and *adiectiva*, and the adjectives into thirteen classes obviously based on Aristotle's ten categories, giving the following scheme:[4]

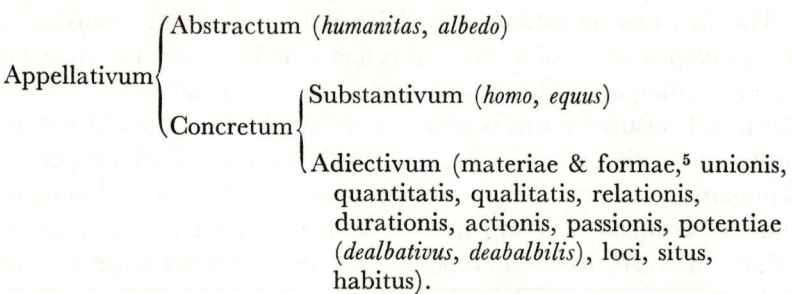

Appellativum
- Abstractum (*humanitas, albedo*)
- Concretum
  - Substantivum (*homo, equus*)
  - Adiectivum (materiae & formae,[5] unionis, quantitatis, qualitatis, relationis, durationis, actionis, passionis, potentiae (*dealbativus, deabalbilis*), loci, situs, habitus).

Balancing the dichotomy in the concrete noun, Caramuel retains the medieval distinction between verbs substantive and adjective,

---

[1] *Herm'aelogium* (1659), preface. One may note that for the *Grammatica speculativa* (cap. xlv) it is 'voces significativae in prolatione', i.e. the sentence or *oratio*, that express a reasoned sequence :'expressio mentis conceptus compositi, est finis constructionis'.

[2] v. V. Salmon's review of N. Chomsky, *Cartesian Linguistics*, p. 174.

[3] *Grammatica audax*, p. 20.   [4] *Ibid.* p. 21.

[5] i.e. Aristotle's *substance* and *accident*.

defining the verb substantive as the *judicativa copula* joining two nouns ('called in logic subject and predicate'), as in *Petrus est legens*. Quoting Aristotelian sources in support,[1] he defines the verb adjective as equivalent to copula plus predicate: *legit = est legens*.[2] This view of the copula goes back of course to Abelard, who rejected Aristotle's opinion that the consignification of time is what distinguishes verb from noun, preferring as the peculiar characteristic of the verb its ability to join together the two parts of a logical proposition.[3] But expansions of the type *legit = est legens* were already to be found in medieval grammar and in Despauterius and Vossius, and apart from the term *judicativa copula*, recalling the Port-Royal view of the proposition as a 'judgment',[4] Caramuel adds here nothing new. More interesting, as an anticipation of Port-Royal doctrine, is his equating of the present participle with relative pronoun plus verb: *amans = qui amat*. His explicit statement that these two structures are identical in meaning – 'idem est dicere' – shows a conscious awareness of 'deep' and 'surface' structure. This awareness is however demonstrable in the pages of Priscian, whose treatment of the participle, which must have been common knowledge among Renaissance grammarians, shows close parallels with Caramuel's approach. For Priscian participles exist to compensate for defects in the verb which lacks case.[5] As the pronoun is a noun substitute, so is the participle a verb substitute, *Homo loquebatur et eum audivi* being replaceable by *Hominem loquentem audivi*. Conversely, where no participle exists in Latin (which e.g. has no equivalent of the Greek past participle active), the verb, linked with the 'infinitivum nomen substantivum' *qui*, takes its place.[6] The participle may thus in turn be regarded as a substitute for the structure *qui* plus verb. The Port-Royal restatement of *canis currens* as *canis qui currit*[7] thus goes via Caramuel right back to Priscian. In using such expansions, Caramuel seems to regard grammar as a matter of congruence with logical propositions, and indeed his book contains an

[1] In the *De interpretatione*, 12, Aristotle remarks *passim* that a verb such as 'walks' may be replaced by 'is walking'.

[2] *Grammatica audax*, p. 31.

[3] v. W. and M. Kneale, *The Development of Logic*, pp. 206–7.

[4] A. Arnauld and P. Nicole, *La Logique ou l'art de penser: Contenant . . . plusieurs observations nouvelles propres à former le jugement*, Paris, 1662, pp. 134–5: 'jugement s'appelle aussi *proposition* . . . cet action de nostre esprit est marquée dans le discours par le verbe *est* . . .'

[5] H. Keil, *Grammatici Latini*, II, 553: 'quod deest verbis, id est casus, compleant coniuncta nominibus'.

[6] *Ibid.* II, 565.   [7] *Grammaire générale*, p. 69.

opening statement to the effect that *grammatica speculativa* (i.e. universal grammar) is an introduction to logic.[1] The growing seventeenth-century tendency to regard grammar as the handmaid of logic is reflected in A. Richardson's *Logicians School-Master* of 1657: 'wheresoever there is Grammer, there is also Logick; where there is Logick, there is not alwayes Grammer . . . [which is] the carrier of Logick betwixt men . . .'[2] Richardson concludes that 'Speech is a garment to cloath our reason', in other words, that the 'deep' structure of *ratio* can be clothed in diverse 'surface' structures yet remain the same: 'Logick doth act and bring the thing to my understanding & afterwards Speech is the carrier of it.' The *langue/parole* dichotomy is here clearly stated, and is the foundation of universal grammar, of the doctrine that 'all the languages in the world are but as so many idioms of the same Grammer, and not divers Grammers'.[3]

THE LANGUAGE-PLANNERS

The search for a universal grammar valid for all languages is closely bound up with the seventeenth-century universal language movement. The distrust of grammar as taught in the schools is paralleled by a feeling that Latin is no longer appropriate as the *lingua franca* of scientific thought. On the one hand it abounds in exceptions and redundancies. On the other it takes longer to acquire than can be justified by the results, taking up time which could be spent on other studies. John Robotham's preface to his bilingual sixth edition of Comenius' *Janua linguarum* (1643) puts the case succinctly:

No marvell if it be so long before wee can reach the *pith* of the matter, when so much time is mis-spent in the *bark* of words: yea when the onely study of the *Latin* tongue draines up above a quarter of a competent age: and if so large a space be wasted in the *imitation* of a meer *verbalist*; how many ages will be requisite to the *perfection* of a *realist*?

The seventeenth century was desperately eager to reach 'the pith of the matter', and this desire to arrive more quickly at the heart of things, allied to growing competition from the vernaculars, meant that Latin was no longer first choice as a language for learned dis-

---

[1] Cf. V. Salmon's quotation (p. 176 of her review of N. Chomsky's *Cartesian Linguistics*) from Alsted's *Encyclopedia*, Herborn, 1630: 'The special function of general grammar lies in this – to harmonize grammatical concepts or entities with concepts or entities of logic.'
[2] Pp. 8, 15.   [3] *The Logicians School-Master*, pp. 1, 5.

course. Conscious of its shortcomings in this respect, Leibniz (1646–1716) had advocated the construction of a kind of basic Latin, but he abandoned that idea, turning instead to the possibility of an artificially constructed scientific language, a *lingua philosophica* or *characteristica universalis*, though he never got to the point of drawing up detailed plans. I do not intend to retrace in detail here the history of the universal language movement, which has already been treated at greater length and more competently than would be either possible or appropriate in this study. The reader is referred to the works mentioned in the note below,[1] which have been indispensable for the short sketch which follows. It would be superfluous to emphasize the parallels between universal grammarians and projectors of universal languages, for their aims spring from the same roots in seventeenth-century thought. Both are concerned with what Bacon calls, in his suggestions for a philosophical grammar, 'the analogy between words and things', and with purging given languages and their grammars of ambiguities and redundancies. Certain features of e.g. Caramuel's grammar recall the language-planners' prescription that words should indicate more closely the properties of things, while the language-planners themselves sometimes append a universal grammar to their projects.

As with 'philosophical' grammar so also with universal language, some of the early indications of the direction of thought are to be found in Bacon, who, noting Aristotle's doctrine that 'words are images of cogitations', suggests that non-verbal symbols – 'whatsoever is capable of sufficient differences, and those perceptible by the sense' – might equally well be used to express mental concepts. His distrust of *words*, allied to his desire to come as close as possible to *things*, are both no doubt behind his reference to the 'Characters Real, which express neither letters nor words in gross, but Things or Notions' used by the Chinese.[2] In the *Advancement of Learning* these

---

[1] B. De Mott, 'The Sources and Development of John Wilkins' Philosophical Language', *The Journal of English and Germanic Philology*, LVII (1958), pp. 1–13; O. Funke, 'On the Sources of John Wilkins' Philosophical Language (1668)', *English Studies*, 40 (1959), pp. 208–14 and 'Zum Weltsprachen-problem in England im 17 Jahrhundert', *Anglistische Forschungen*, 69 (1929), pp. i–v, 1–163; and the already cited R. F. Jones, 'Science and Language in England of the Mid-Seventeenth Century'; V. Salmon, *The Works of Francis Lodwick*, and 'Language-Planning in Seventeenth-Century England'; B. J. Shapiro, *John Wilkins*. (J. Knowlson's *Universal Language Schemes in England and France 1600–1800*, Toronto Univ. Press, 1975, came to hand too late to be consulted.)

[2] *Of the Advancement of Learning*, in J. M. Robertson (ed.), *The Philosophical Works of Francis Bacon*, p. 121.

non-verbal signs or *notes* represent mental concepts, are 'notes of cogitations', but in the later *De augmentis* they have become simply 'notes of things',[1] consonant with Bacon's theory that phenomena can be reduced to a limited number of elements or 'simple natures' each capable of being represented by a non-verbal symbol. The *notes* have an obvious affinity with the theory of emblems developed in Bacon's essay on the art of memory,[2] described by P. Rossi in the following terms:

> Bacon defined the 'emblem' as an image that has a certain analogy to the place and thus stimulates the memory, providing the means of recalling what is to be found. The emblem's function was therefore to lead intellectual concepts onto a sensory level where memory is more easily impressed.[3]

There is a parallel here with Hobbes' definition of the name or word as 'a mark, which may raise in our mind a thought like to some thought we had before', and Bacon's catalogue of 'simple natures' each with its corresponding quasi-mathematical symbol is matched in aridity by Hobbes' view that 'REASON is nothing but *reckoning*, that is adding and subtracting'.[4] Thinking for Hobbes is the manipulation of signs which have a one-to-one correspondence with their referents, and in this regard his view of logic as a *Computatio* is revealing. He is an illustration of how much the contemporary universal language movement owed to the development of mathematics, leading to a belief that verbal language could be replaced by the clarity of a system in which each phenomenon in the universe would have its corresponding symbol unambiguously denoting its nature and properties. It is this belief that is behind Seth Ward's suggestion that 'Symboles might be found for every *thing* and *notion*'.[5] The same idea is repeated in Leibniz' *De arte combinatoria* (1666),[6] with its notion of a *calculus ratiocinator*, a quasi-mechanical operation whose inspiration comes from Raymond Lull's *Ars magna* and Hobbes' *Computatio sive logica*, and which Leibniz sees as one of the tools of a Baconian-type logic of discovery (*logica inventiva*).[7] The

---

[1] v. P. Rossi, *Bacon*, p. 167.

[2] *De augmentis*, in *The Works of Francis Bacon* (ed. R. L. Ellis, J. Spedding and D. D. Heath), I, 649.   [3] *Bacon*, p. 168.

[4] *Leviathan*, in *The English Works of Thomas Hobbes* (ed. W. Molesworth), III, 30.

[5] *Vindiciae academiarum*, p. 21.

[6] Contained in C. J. Gerhardt (ed.), *Die philosophischen Schriften von Gottfried Wilhelm Leibniz*, vol. 4, Berlin, 1880.

[7] v. W. and M Kneale, *The Development of Logic*, pp. 325–6.

belief in the possibility of an exact correspondence between sign and referent rests of course on a mistaken view of language,[1] though Hobbes is in any case unable to subscribe to the classifications of phenomena under conceptual headings that are at the basis of universal language projects, since for him as a Nominalist they are classifications not of *things*, but of *words*.[2]

Much of this insistence on clarity and exact definition was a reaction against the vague mysticism of the Neo-Platonists. The Platonic strain[3] was of great importance in English Humanism, manifesting itself first in Colet, Erasmus, More and Elyot in the early sixteenth century, and later, in the middle of the seventeenth, in the Cambridge Platonists, who were united against Hobbes' materialism, to which they opposed Plato and Descartes and elements whose roots were in Italian nature philosophy and the teachings of Telesio. Their belief in a natural affinity between language and phenomena was at the opposite pole to Hobbes' austere mathematical approach. The Hobbesian point of view, and indeed part of the ethos of the universal language movement, is well expressed in Samuel Parker's *Free and Impartial Censure of the Platonick Philosophie*:[4]

the use of Words is not to explaine the Natures of Things, but only to stand as signes in their stead, as Arithmetical figures are only notes of Numbers; and therefore Names are as unable to explaine abstracted Natures, as figures are to solve *Arithmetical Problems* . . . [Words] being Notes of things, unless their significations be settled, their meaning must needs be Equivocal and uncertain; that is, unless it be determined of what things such particular Names are signs, no man shall be able to signifie his Thoughts to another, because he will use uncertain signs.

In early studies of the seventeenth-century universal language movement in England, the importance of Bacon and Hobbes as sources was emphasized at the expense of other contributions.[5] More

---

[1] Cf. R. H. Robins, 'Grammar, Meaning, and the Study of Language', *The Canadian Journal of Linguistics*, 9:2 (1964), p. 103: 'Reference is not the same thing as linguistic meaning, nor can one properly demand a referent for every meaningful component of a sentence. Reference, i.e. attachment to some discrete component of the world of experience . . . is only one . . . of many semantic functions.'

[2] v. *De Corpore*, I, ii, in *Opera Latina* (ed. W. Molesworth), I, 22–5; *English Works* (ed. W. Molesworth), I, 25–8.

[3] For a discussion of Platonic doctrine, v. the introduction to *Plato: Apology, Crito, Phaedo, Symposium, Republic*, ed. L. R. Loomis, New York, 1942.

[4] Pp. 61, 63.

[5] e.g. O. Funke, 'Weltsprachenproblem', and R. F. Jones, 'Science and Language in England'. Funke's study deals largely with the phonetic approach of the English language-planners.

recently it has been objected that not only did Bacon not have in mind a 'philosophical language' of the type later produced by Bishop Wilkins but merely a 'universal character', but also his distrust of words did not permit him to envisage the possibility of a reliable correspondence between word and referent.[1] Such however was the prestige of even a minor suggestion when made by him, that language-planners in England almost automatically cited his name in support of their projects. But it was not only in Britain that an interest in artificial languages was developing, though elsewhere it was chiefly indebted to that other great strand in seventeenth-century thought, the mentalistic rationalism of Descartes, and in France owed much to the indefatigable Father Mersenne. The latter was active in the intellectual salons of Paris, the position of that city as the centre of European thought in the middle of the century being in large part a result of his cosmopolitan contacts. He appears to have been the first European scholar to suggest the setting up of an artificial language,[2] with the aim of course of rendering scientific discussion more clear and concise. Research in this direction was stimulated by Descartes' letter of November 1629 to Mersenne, proposing a language in which words would have an analogy to things. A number of scholars took up the idea, which involved not only a classification of concepts, but also the fashioning of an instrument of scientific thought. The conclusions of a group of amateur scientists in Paris on the subject, published in 1636,[3] were known in England by 1640. On the one hand Descartes' contribution to mathematics no doubt played an important role, while on the other interest was focused on the systematic classification of concepts.

As was inevitable in view of his concern with such classifications, Comenius, who seems to have been influenced by Mersenne, also took up the idea of a universal language in his *Via lucis*. In common with his contemporaries, Comenius' primary aim is the abolition of ambiguity, the establishment of a 'universal antidote to confusion of thought':

a language which shall be (1) Rational . . . (2) Analogical, containing no anomaly in any matter: (3) Harmonious, bringing no discrepancies

---

[1] v. V. Salmon, 'Language-Planning', p. 385.

[2] In his *Harmonie universelle*, not published until 1636. v. V. Salmon, 'Language-Planning', p. 388.

[3] v. *Recueil général des questions traitées ès conférences du Bureau d'Adresse*, Lyons, 1966, ii, 154–5.

between things and the concepts of things . . . everything in our new language must be adapted to the exact and perfect representation of things.[1]

Behind the attempts by Comenius and others to list the 'concepts of things' there lies, as mentioned above, the *Ars magna* of the thirteenth-century scholar Raymond Lull, a system of fundamental concepts and proposed symbolic expressions of them. Lull's particular brand of algebraic logic is linked with Renaissance encyclopaedism as a source of the seventeenth-century notion that all complex ideas can be expressed by combinations of signs. Relevant here is Leibniz' *De arte combinatoria*, which is based on the premise that composite ideas can be reduced to a kind of alphabet of simpler ones (cf. Bacon's 'simple natures'), out of which a language mirroring the complexities of the universe might be constructed by combination. L. Formigari goes so far as to see Lull as the distant ancestor of all the universal language projects.[2] Comenius' *pansophia*, in the line of thought initiated by Lull, represented an attempt to range phenomena in ordered gradations, in a 'ladder of being' which must have its counterpart in language. The 'chain of being' idea current in the seventeenth century presupposed an ontological correspondence between the order of the universe and the order of the mind. This idea is rooted in Neo-Platonic doctrine, according to which the divine powers are unfolded in the cosmos in a series of gradations, decreasing in perfection as they move from the divine source into the forms of the world of sense. He who penetrates the secrets of nature penetrates also those of the Divine, hence seventeenth-century interest in the Jewish Cabbala, which claimed to have received those secrets in primitive times, and in the anti-Aristotelian nature philosophy of Telesio. Out of this desire to penetrate the secrets of nature grew, in addition to the demand that there should be a one-to-one correspondence between word and thing, the notion that a word should be more than a mere symbol, and should indicate the nature and essential properties of the thing symbolized. It is no accident that Campanella's interest in Telesian nature philosophy should be accompanied by his concern with the *essentiae* of Scholasticism. The task of expressing these essences was assigned by some scholars to the phonetic elements of words, each individual sound

---

[1] *Via lucis*, pp. 186, 191.

[2] *Linguistica*, p. 127. Formigari calls Lull the 'precedente remoto' of these projects.

corresponding to a particular property in the world of things. Caramuel's grammar contains a scheme for the verb 'to be' in which *a* represents essence, *e* existence, *y* eternity, and so on, giving for 'I am' the series of verbal forms *sam, sem, sym*, etc.[1] All these elements, the ordered gradation of concepts, the one-to-one correspondence, the expression by sounds of essential characteristics in the referents, are present in Comenius' *pansophia*, which for Formigari[2] constitutes the inspiration for Seth Ward's idea of a universal language and, through him, for Bishop Wilkins' celebrated *Essay Towards a Real Character and a Philosophical Language* (1668).

B. De Mott claims that in the late 1630s Comenius was 'the best known European proponent of a new language', holding that it was his visit to England in 1641 and the publication in English of his *Via lucis* in the following year that awakened Englishmen's interest in universal language projects. Certainly, Comenius' opinions were followed by the Silesian educationist Cyprian Kinner, and there is evidence to show that Samuel Hartlib, an enthusiast for a 'real character' whose circle was in touch with Mersenne, introduced Kinner's ideas to British language-planners around 1650.[3] Whereas De Mott holds that the English linguists' 'notion of a language of things . . . was in significant measure a contagion transmitted from abroad',[4] V. Salmon disagrees with this estimate, seeming to regard the universal language movement in England as, apart from certain Cartesian sources, largely *sui generis*.[5] Whatever the truth of the matter, it is established that the English Royal Society, founded in 1662, had an important role to play in the movement for a universal language. Apart from its interest in the promoting of a plain style, several of its members, notably John Wallis, had concerned themselves with the 'perfection' of the English vernacular, and the suggestion had even been made that an Academy, analogous to the *Académie française* of 1635, be founded with this end in view. As time went by, though the members of the Royal Society never ceased to proclaim their indebtedness to him, it became evident that any even

---

[1] *Grammatica audax*, pp. 31–2.   [2] *Linguistica*, p. 135.

[3] B. De Mott, 'The Sources and Development of John Wilkins' Philosophical Language', pp. 4, 5, 8.

[4] *Ibid.* p. 11.

[5] As V. Salmon notes ('Language-Planning', p. 384), there are factors such as the English interest in non-phonetic shorthand to be taken into account when attributing sources. For her discounting of Comenius' influence on the British language-planners v. pp. 372–80 of her article.

partially successful attempt to establish a universal language would have to be based on conceptual classification rather than simply on a 'real character' as envisaged by Bacon. The last scholars of any standing to produce a system not based on a classification of concepts were Cave Beck (1657) and Athanasius Kircher (1663).[1] Beck's preface echoes the aims of the Royal Society language-planners, claiming that a *universal character*, 'if happily contrived, so as to avoid all Equivocal words, Anomalous variations, and superfluous Synonomas (with which all Languages are encumbred . . .) would much advantage mankind'.[2] Under the impulse given to rational enquiry by the newly founded Society and the nucleus of scientists meeting at Oxford from which it grew, several of its members undertook a study of the questions raised by Bacon and Descartes, notably George Dalgarno and John Wilkins, whose *Ars signorum* (1661) and *Essay Towards a Real Character and a Philosophical Language* (1668) have similarities in approach, and Francis Lodwick.[3] The universal language movement concerns the present study only in so far as its aims are similar to, or constitute the impetus to, those of universal grammar. These three authors are of interest in that, in spite of Hooke's assertion that grammar was no concern of the Royal Society,[4] they append to their projects attempts at 'philosophical' grammars, thus providing material for the student of grammatical theory.

Lodwick has the distinction of having produced the two earliest attempts at a universal language. His *Common Writing* (1647) aims strictly speaking at the production not of an artificial language but of a form of writing 'common to all Languages' and 'legible and intelligible, in all Languages whatsoever'. To this end, however, he deems it necessary to preface his orthographical treatise with a universal grammar. In his second book, *The Ground-Work . . . For the Framing of a New Perfect Language* (1652), Lodwick attempted to

[1] v. V. Salmon, *Francis Lodwick*, p. 22.

[2] *The Universal Character, By which all the Nations in the World may Understand One Anothers Conceptions*, London, 1657.

[3] The work *A Common Writing: Whereby Two, Although not Understanding One the Others Language . . . May Communicate Their Minds One to Another*, dated 1647 and signed *F. L. W.* with the comment that 'this work commeth not from a Scholar, but a mechanick', is by the Fleming Lodwick (or Lodowyck), who was elected to the Royal Society in 1681. For biographical details v. E. J. Dobson, *English Pronunciation 1500–1700*, 2nd ed., pp. 272–3, and V. Salmon, *Francis Lodwick*.

[4] v. M. M. C. McIntosh, 'The Phonetic and Linguistic Theory of the Royal Society School, from Wallis to Cooper', unpublished Oxford University B.Litt. thesis, p. 20.

frame an artificial language appropriate for science, repeating the view of Campanella and Caramuel that the imposition of names is the province of the 'philosopher', together with the current notions that the order of nature should be reflected in language and that names ought somehow to indicate the essential properties of the things named:

The proper names of things to give them signification is the work, we suppose, of a sound Philosopher, who from the knowledge of things and their order in nature, should give them names accordingly, describing that in them by their name, by which in the naming they may be known.[1]

In a somewhat clumsy attempt to make language congruent with natural phenomena, he classifies all other 'words of speech' under the three heads *action, quality, help,* corresponding to the traditional verbs, adjectives and adverbs. The interest of the inadequate grammar appended to the *Ground-Work,* which uses Lily's *signs* to distinguish moods (defined as 'the manner of expression') and cases, is chiefly lexical. Minor points arising from the grammatical section of *A Common Writing* will be treated below in analysing the contribution to grammatical theory of Dalgarno and Wilkins.

George Dalgarno, an Oxford schoolmaster and a Scot, benefited from the assistance of Oxford scientists – John Wilkins, Seth Ward, John Wallis and others – all future members of the Royal Society, and all professionally interested in Dalgarno's attempt to provide a 'gateway' to the sciences. He shared their yearning for a language, appropriate to scientific discourse, which would (in the words of the claim he makes for his own *universal character*) promote 'a great deale of clearnesse to the acts of the understanding, in Gramaticall, Logicall, and Metaphysicall Criticismes'. In accordance with the general trend among later language-planners, his *Ars signorum* (1661) is based on a system of conceptual classification of 'simple notions' into seventeen abstract classes, such as *ens, substantia* and *corpus,* subdivided in Aristotelian fashion into *species* and *differentiae.* The foundation of such classifications as Dalgarno's is in fact Aristotle's ten predicaments, eked out with categories from Scholastic philosophy. Claiming to catalogue reality as a preliminary to the apportioning of symbols to each class of things, these scholars take as their

[1] *The Ground-Work or Foundation Laid, (or so intended) For the Framing of a New Perfect Language: And an Universall or Common Writing. And Presented to the Consideration of the Learned, By a Well-Willer to Learning,* 1652, p. 10. For a complete list of Lodwick's works, and reproductions of *A Common Writing* and *The Ground-Work,* v. V. Salmon, *Francis Lodwick.*

starting-point the Aristotelian classification, and then seek properties in phenomena to correspond to it. As the universal grammarians take the categories of Latin and Greek to be appropriate to all languages, so do the language-planners fit reality into the framework of Greek and Scholastic philosophy. Dalgarno's classification, it goes without saying, is intended to result in a more thorough knowledge of *things*, in 'penitiorem et interiorem rerum cognitionem'.[1] His utilitarian goals are illustrated by the fact that, as V. Salmon has shown,[2] he originally set out to improve an existing system of 'brachigraphy' or shorthand. Within England perhaps British pragmatism, as much as intellectual currents originating in the Descartes–Mersenne circle, was responsible for the interest shown in the universal language movement. For the student of grammatical theory, the incidental points Dalgarno makes about language are however more interesting than his suggestions for a 'universal character'. In so far as they concern themselves with grammar in addition to conceptual classification and symbolization, the framers of artificial languages are influenced by the theories of the 'philosophical' and universal grammarians. Nowhere is this more striking than in the primacy given to logic. At the outset of his work Dalgarno warns against any attempt to 'separate the inseparable', to divorce grammar and logic[3] which, differing only as does the sign from that which is signified, are merely complementary facets of the same science.[4] It is interesting to set beside this the views on the relationship between grammar and logic expressed by a participant in the 1961 conference on Language Universals already referred to:

The investigation of discourse in its logical aspects is not a fashionable pursuit, but it seems to be one of the most important frontiers of linguistics for the decades ahead . . . [But] the study of the 'logical' aspects of discourse, as part of semantics, must remain autonomous of the grammatical analysis so that their interrelation may be meaningfully compared . . . But if these cautions are observed, the investigation is legitimate and promising. *For logic is congenial to language.*[5]

[1] *Ars signorum, vulgo character universalis et lingua philosophica*, London, 1661, p. 33.
[2] 'The Evolution of Dalgarno's Ars Signorum' *Studies in Language and Literature in Honour of Margaret Schlauch*, Warsaw, 1966, pp. 353–4. This article gives a full treatment of the question of Dalgarno's indebtedness to an anonymous shorthand system.
[3] *Ars signorum*, p. 7: 'Cave . . . ne inter judicandum, non separanda separes, id est, partem Logicam et Grammaticam'.
[4] *Ibid.* p. 18: 'omnino eorum [sc. signorum et signatorum] eadem debet esse scientia'.
[5] U. Weinreich, 'On the Semantic Structure of Language', *Universals of Language* (ed. J. H. Greenberg), p. 119 (my italics).

The last sentence in this passage could well have been written by one of the seventeenth-century universal grammarians themselves.

The most important of the language-planners is John Wilkins, Warden of Wadham College, Oxford, a member of the Oxford circle of scientists who constituted the nucleus of the future Royal Society, and ultimately Bishop of Chester. The Royal Society was of course Baconian in outlook, representing the chief contemporary embodiment of Bacon's principles, and there can be no doubt of the high regard in which Bacon was held by Wilkins. The latter's indebtedness to Bacon hardly needs arguing, though attempts have been made to show that seventeenth-century English scientists were by no means as solely committed to empiricism and experimentation as has been supposed. B. J. Shapiro for instance claims the influence of Descartes to have been at least equal to that of Bacon, seeing Baconian empiricism in the pure state as largely confined to non-scientists. The Society's frequent encomiums to Bacon she attributes to the latter's standing as a 'persuasive symbol' behind which scientific activity was almost obliged to range itself.[1] As to the immediate sources of Wilkins' celebrated *Essay*, opinions vary, B. De Mott finding evidence in the papers of Samuel Hartlib for an influence by Comenius and his Silesian follower Cyprian Kinner,[2] while O. Funke doubts this, preferring Dalgarno as Wilkins' source, a belief in which he is encouraged by a statement in a letter from John Wallis to the first president of the Royal Society, pointing out the importance for Wilkins of Dalgarno's work.[3] B. J. Shapiro similarly discounts Comenius' influence, tracing Wilkins' project back to the one described by Seth Ward, Professor of Astronomy at Oxford, in his *Vindiciae academiarum* of 1654, which provides support for Shapiro's positing of a Cartesian influence on Wilkins: '... all Discourses being resolved into sentences, those into words, words signifying either simple notions or being resolvable into simple notions, it is manifest, that ... all the sorts of simple notions [can] be found out, and have Symboles assigned to them ...'[4] For V. Salmon it is Lodwick and Dalgarno who stand behind Wilkins' *Essay*, the former having

---

[1] *John Wilkins*, p. 205.

[2] B. De Mott, 'The Sources and Development of John Wilkins' Philosophical Language', p. 1.

[3] O. Funke, 'On the Sources of John Wilkins' Philosophical Language (1668)', pp. 208–9.

[4] v. B. J. Shapiro, *John Wilkins*, p. 209.

assisted Wilkins, who had been engaged on his project since at least 1657, by lending him his unpublished work, and Dalgarno being on record as having felt that Wilkins was indebted to his own researches.[1] Though Wilkins makes no acknowledgment to either Lodwick or Dalgarno in his preface, it would seem that his work was to at least some extent undertaken jointly by various Fellows of the Royal Society. An important indication is of course given, as far as the grammatical section of the *Essay* is concerned, by Wilkins' own citation of his sources:

[Natural grammar] hath been treated of but by few, which makes our learned *Verulam* [i.e. Bacon] put it among his *Desiderata*; I do not know any more that have purposely written of it, but *Scotus* in his *Grammatica Speculativa*, and *Caramuel* in his *Grammatica Audax*, and *Campanella* in his *Grammatica Philosophica*. (As for *Schioppius* his Grammar, of this title, that doth wholly concern the Latin tongue;) Besides which, something hath been occasionally spoken of it, by *Scaliger* in his book *de causis linguae latinae*; and by *Vossius* in his *Aristarchus*.[2]

The works of 'Scotus' (i.e. Thomas of Erfurt) had been reprinted in Paris in 1605 and, edited by the Englishman Wadding, at Leyden in 1639,[3] so there is no doubt that the *Grammatica speculativa* was known to English linguists in the seventeenth century. Campanella's writings were also known in England soon after publication. It is however surprising that Wilkins should list Vossius' *Aristarchus sive de arte grammatica* but not Sanctius' *Minerva*, to which Vossius is deeply indebted, and which had been edited in 1654 by Scioppius whose own grammar Wilkins mentions.

In any case, Wilkins obviously regards the authors he cites simply as forerunners, and his own work as breaking new ground. He begins by dividing grammar into 'natural and general' and 'instituted and particular', divisions which obviously correspond to Vossius' *grammatica naturalis* and *artificialis*, and Campanella's *philosophica* and *civilis*: '*Natural* Grammar, (which may likewise be stiled Philosophical, Rational, and Universal) should contain all such Grounds and Rules, as do naturally and necessarily belong to the Philosophy of letters and speech in the *General*.'[4] 'Instituted and particular' grammar is defined, following Scaliger, as a *scientia loquendi ex usu*.

---

[1] v. *Francis Lodwick*, pp. 30–1.
[2] *An Essay Towards a Real Character and a Philosophical Language*, London, 1668, p. 297.
[3] v. V. Salmon, review of N. Chomsky, *Cartesian Linguistics*, p. 169.
[4] *Essay*, p. 297.

'Natural' grammar is established by 'abstracting from those many unnecessary rules belonging to instituted Language', a task which Wilkins found 'of no small difficulty, considering the little help' to be had from the predecessors he cites,[1] who 'did not sufficiently abstract their rules according to Nature'.[2] For him as for other seventeenth-century thinkers, 'instituted' language was largely responsible for the confusion of thought concerning natural phenomena which had been kept in being by the old philosophies. Hence his thoroughly contemporary interest in conceptual classification and symbolism, which would lead to a better 'knowledge of things' and contribute to the settling of religious disputes by 'unmasking wild errors, that shelter themselves under the disguise of affected phrases'. His first task, accordingly, was the 'regular enumeration and description of such things and notions, as are to be known, and to which names are to be assigned'.[3] As with learning in general, so with grammar, a necessary preliminary to knowledge is the cataloguing and conceptual classification of the world of things. This procedure recalls Comenius' *Orbis pictus*, and whether Wilkins underwent the direct influence of Comenius or not, it is undeniable that such concepts formed part of the common intellectual patrimony of the times.

Wilkins' classificatory framework, in contrast to the astonishing modernity of much that he has to say on phonetics, grammar and semantics elsewhere in his *Essay*, is Aristotelian, depending on the predicamental classes of substance and accident and on the devising of symbols denoting genus and species. It is here that modern attempts to establish Language Universals decisively part company with the seventeenth-century approach:

> Such attempts should not be identified with earlier approaches based on categories formulated *a priori* from supposed necessary categories of thought derived from normative logic . . . the standard synchronic and diachronic procedures . . . form the indispensable bases for arriving at generalizations about language.[4]

Wilkins' system of classification arises neither from an empirical analysis of language nor from a close observation of nature, but from a ready-made philosophical categorization which things are made to

---

[1] *Ibid.* prefatory epistle to the reader.

[2] *Ibid.* pp. 297–8. Wilkins thinks his own work 'less erroneous in this respect than the rest'.

[3] *Ibid.* p. 297.

[4] J. H. Greenberg (ed.), *Universals of Language*, editor's introduction, p. ix.

fit. The ambiguity of Aristotle's ten categories was in any case such that writers on logic have been led to wonder whether he was 'classifying symbols or what they symbolize, words or, in a very wide sense, things'.[1] The question is important, being relevant both to the widespread Nominalism of seventeenth-century language theory, and to that century's preference for things over words, its search for terms that would have an exact correspondence to the things signified. Wilkins' forty conceptual classes, including thirty-four *genera* grouped according to the predicaments of substance, quantity, quality, action and relation, with each *genus* further subdivided into *differences* and *species*, were already, at the time he applied them, thought not to correspond to the actual divisions found in nature.[2] By 1700 Thomas Baker, author of *Reflections upon Learning*, finds Wilkins' scheme only 'plausible at a distance'. He accepts that, the office of language being not to express words but things, 'we must first be agreed about the nature of things, before we can fix Marks and Characters to represent them'. Where he is sceptical is as to the possibility of such an agreement, given the system of conceptual classification in fashion with certain language-planners:

> ... when Bishop Wilkins first undertook this design *Substance and Accidents* were a receiv'd Division ... but were he to begin now and would suit his design to the Philosophy in vogue, he must draw a new Scheme and instead of *Accidents* take in Modes, which are very different from Accidents both in Nature and Number.[3]

An alternative method to the Aristotelian one, again based on logical concepts, was in fact in use in language-planning circles, deriving from the idea that each thing in the world has its corresponding 'simple notion' expressible by a single word.[4] This idea, which has perhaps its origin in Bacon's doctrine of 'simple natures', is at the basis of Leibniz' *De arte combinatoria* and of Seth Ward's statement, quoted above, that words either signify simple notions or are 'resolvable' into them. The concept of a 'simple notion' in a one-to-one relationship with its corresponding symbol was obviously an attractive one, though it led the language-planners into what

---

[1] W. and M. Kneale, *The Development of Logic*, pp. 25, 27, 29. These authors conclude that Aristotle is concerned with 'the classification of things signified by terms'.

[2] They had been criticized, e.g., by Comenius.

[3] *Reflections upon Learning, Wherein is Shewn the Insufficiency Thereof, in its Several Particulars*, 2nd ed., London, 1700, pp. 17–18. (1st ed., Cambridge, 1699.)

[4] V. Salmon, *Francis Lodwick*, p. 108, traces this doctrine to N. De-Lawne's *The Elements of Logick* (1624), translated from the French of Pierre du Moulin.

R. H. Robins[1] has called an 'atomization of meaning' comparable to that in the work of certain present-day generative grammarians. Dalgarno's table of simple notions stems from this approach, as does Wilkins' note that his own tables contain only 'things and notions . . . of a more simple nature', more complex notions having to be expressed periphrastically.[2] Translated to a grammatical level, this doctrine, in which an item of linguistic structure contains and is analysable into a number of 'notions of a more simple nature', would seem to have affinities with Sanctius' and Vossius' use of ellipse. It is thus no surprise to find that Wilkins views grammar as a 'necessary help' for combining the 'simple notions into Complex Propositions and Discourses'.[3]

The treatment of the seventeenth-century language-planners given here has necessarily been perfunctory, and what it owes to the authors listed at the outset will be obvious. Universal grammar cannot however, at any rate in its English manifestations, be discussed apart from the universal language movement with which it shares so many reciprocal influences. It remains to consider the specifically grammatical contribution of Lodwick and Dalgarno and, above all, Wilkins. Despite his list of sources, it would not seem that the last-named took anything of moment from Caramuel's grammar.[4] The overriding influence, as I shall endeavour to show, is that of Campanella. Wilkins' division of grammar[5] into *etymology, syntax* and methods of notation by 'marks and sounds' does not differ, apart from the omission of prosody, from the customary Humanist one. His *etymology* concerns itself with two things: the 'formal' (in the Aristotelian, that is to say semasiological, sense) differences between words, and the 'accidental changes' of inflection and composition. On the 'formal' level, there is an initial division into *integrals*, capable of semantic independence, and *particles* not thus capable, i.e.

---

[1] *Short History*, p. 116. (Robins cites D. W. Bolinger, 'The atomization of meaning', *Language*, 41 (1965), pp. 555–73.) Cf. F. de Saussure (*Cours de linguistique générale*, 5th ed., p. 97), who refutes the view of language as 'une nomenclature, c'est-à-dire une liste de termes correspondant à autant de choses. Cette conception . . . laisse supposer que le lien qui unit un nom à une chose est une opération toute simple, ce qui est loin d'être vrai.'

[2] *Essay*, p. 295. Cf. Locke, *Essay*, pp. 45–6: 'When the Understanding is once stored with these simple *Ideas*, it has the power to repeat, compare, and unite them . . . and so can make at Pleasure new complex *Ideas*.'

[3] *Essay*, p. 297.

[4] One may note however that in his division of nouns into *concrete* and *abstract* he is preceded by Caramuel.

[5] The grammar occupies pp. 297–384 of the *Essay*.

the division into *partes principales* and *syncategoremata* found in Sanctius and Vossius and in other universal grammars of the period. Whereas however this results in a three-word-class system of noun, verb and *consignificantia* in the works of Sanctius, Vossius and Campanella, in Wilkins' *Essay* we have a two-class system in which the verb does not have separate status. The definition of integrals, with its emphasis on the signification of *essentia* and *actio*, recalls Campanella:

By *Integrals* or Principal words, I mean such as signifie some entire thing or notion: whether the *Ens* or Thing it self, or the *Essence* of a thing, as *Nouns Neuters*, whether concrete or abstract; or the Doing or Suffering of a thing as Nouns *Active* or *Passive*; or the manner and affection of it, as *Derived Adverbs*.[1]

This reflects the seventeenth-century tendency to regard the universe as consisting of things and actions, and the modes of those things and actions. Where Wilkins differs from the usual grammatical approach is in his view of the noun as able to signify *res*, *actio* or *passio*, these last two having traditionally been regarded as the province of the verb. Melanchthon had defined the noun as signifying 'rem, non actionem' in contrast to the verb's 'agere aut pati',[2] a distinction devoid of grammatical sense, but equally untrue on the level of lexical signification at which it operates. Vossius had already drawn attention to the fact that a noun such as *calefactio* signifies an action, and attempted to find a way out of the dilemma by having the noun signify *actio*, *passio* or *ens*, and the verb *agere*, *pati* or *esse*. He lacked however the grammatical tools to make this distinction, which is plainly that which medieval grammar expressed as signification *per modum entis, qui est modus permanentis* (the noun) and *per modum esse, qui est modus fluxus* (the verb).[3] On the level of lexical meaning, on which he too is operating, Wilkins rightly sees no reason to make a distinction between noun and verb. Dalgarno has similarly only one primary word-class, the noun, of which all other classes are *flexiones* or *casus*. Given the overriding importance of 'being' (*ens*) in his system, the verb is no more than a 'case or inflection' of the noun.[4]

The minor grammatical status accorded to the verb by Wilkins may originate in Campanella's doctrine that all verbs are derivatives of *essentia*, any act being ultimately an *actus essentiae*. More important

---

[1] *Essay*, p. 298. [2] v. p. 38 above.
[3] *Grammatica speculativa*, cap. viii. [4] *Ars signorum*, p. 62.

than the role of the verb is that of the copula, which, though included among the consignifying *particles*, is 'essential in every compleat sentence'. The remaining particles, including the pronoun defined as a substitute for an integral, and the interjection as a substitute for a sentence or a 'complex part' thereof,[1] are by contrast inessential. In a similar dichotomy, prepositions are treated as particles constructing word with word, and non-derivative adverbs (the derived ones are counted as integrals) and conjunctions as particles constructing sentence with sentence. Finally, certain particles are regarded as 'declarative of some accident', the *article* indicating an accident of an integral, *mood* an accident of the copula, and *tense* an accident of either. Here Wilkins commits the common seventeenth-century error of ignoring grammatical consignification. Tense cannot be a *grammatical* accident of integrals (i.e. nouns and certain adverbs), since it is only *signified* by some and not, as in the verb, *consignified* by all. Wilkins' use of accidents is reminiscent of Lodwick's 'distinctionall additions' employed as adjuncts to a system of *radixes* whose meanings are presumably common to all languages. Lodwick's overall division of the word-classes differs however from Wilkins' in being based solely on *actio*, with a dichotomy between verbal *radixes* signifying action and non-verbal ones not signifying action, the latter divisible on the one hand into noun and pronoun, on the other into the four traditional indeclinables.[2]

In defining nouns Wilkins remains within the semasiological tradition initiated by Colet, describing them as 'those instituted words which men do agree upon for the appellations of things'.[3] Once again the aim of seventeenth-century grammar, confirmed by Dalgarno, is seen to be nomenclature according to logical principles: 'The grammarian ought to impose names according to logical concepts and rules deduced from the nature of things themselves.'[4] In defining substantive and adjective Wilkins none the less follows

---

[1] *Essay*, p. 298. Cf. Vossius' description of the interjection as a 'dictio per se sententiam perficiens'. E. Vorlat, 'Progress in English Grammar 1585–1735' (University of Louvain doctoral thesis, 1963), ii, 192, quotes Wilkins' 'As Nouns are notes or signs of *things*, so Pronouns are of Nouns', but gives no indication of having realized that he is simply echoing Vossius and Scaliger. She similarly regards Wilkins as the originator of the traditional view of the interjection as a sentence substitute.

[2] *A Common Writing*, p. 1.

[3] Cf. Vossius' '*ex instituto* . . . *rem* significans' and Campanella's 'significans essentiam *cuiusque rei ex impositione*'.

[4] *Ars signorum*, p. 18. ('Grammaticus secundum Ideas & Regulas Logicas a Rerum ipsarum natura . . . petitas, Nomina . . . imponere debet.')

Campanella in reintroducing the medieval notion of signification 'per modum subsistentis per se' and 'per modum adjacentis alteri',[1] together however with the typical seventeenth-century qualification that the substantive is 'every Noun which in conjunction with a Verb makes a compleat sentence'.[2] All 'radical' (i.e. non-derivative) words in a language ought ideally to be substantives, but owing to the defective nature of extant languages certain notions which logically should be expressed by substantives are expressed by adjectives or by 'an Aggregate of words'. They are all however to be considered as in reality 'simple Substantives'. These substantives are of three kinds, according as they signify a *thing*, an *action* or *passion*, or a *person* seen as agent or recipient of action. The parallel with Campanella's nouns signifying 'essentiam puram', 'essentiam actionis' and 'essentiam patientis' is obvious. Starting with basic substantives such as *lux* and *calor* ('substantives of the *Thing*') Wilkins can derive from them *illuminatio* and *calefactio* ('substantives of the *Action*'), τὸ *illuminari* and τὸ *calefieri* ('substantives of the *Passion*'), *illuminator* and *calefactor* ('substantives of the *Person* agent') and *illuminatus* and *calefactus* ('substantives of the *Person* patient').[3] Those substantives which signify neither action nor passion are 'nouns neuter'. The substantives active and passive are intended to cover 'the same notion' as the Latin and Greek infinitives, and Wilkins seems to make no real grammatical distinction between his substantives of the *thing*, his substantives 'capable of an Action',[4] and the actives and passives 'commonly called verbs' that can be formed from the latter. This derivation is justified by the argument (again obviously from Campanella) that whatever has an *essence* must also have an *act*.[5] Ideally therefore, every substantive in a language ought to have its corresponding verb.[6] The philosophical hair-splitting involved is well illustrated by the following paragraph.

[1] E. Vorlat, 'Progress', II, 52, notes this approach without any indication that it is not Wilkins' own invention.   [2] *Essay*, pp. 298–9.

[3] *Ibid.* p. 299. Substantives of *action* and *person* can themselves at times be radicals from which are derived other types of substantive. *Magistratus* e.g. is a 'radical of the person' from which is derived the 'substantive of action' *gubernatio*. Then, using Latin as his model, Wilkins has to invent a corresponding 'substantive of the thing' active (*gubernans res*) or passive (*gubernata res*).

[4] Cf. Campanella's subclass (e.g. *amator*) of nouns signifying 'essentiam *cum virtute ad actum*'.

[5] Campanella argues that every *actus* is an *actus essentiae*.

[6] Cf. Campanella's assumption that every verb is derived from an essence, even if that essence is not represented in the language by any noun.

As for such things which have not of their own any proper Act of *Doing*, they are not capable of the derivation of Active and Passive, *ob defectum materiae*; as in the words Stone, Mettle, *&c.* But the Verbs belonging to such Radicals can be only Neuter, denoting the Act of Being or becoming; unless when they are compounded with the Transcendental mark [one of Wilkins' orthographical devices] of Causatio, which will adde to them a Transitive sense, as Petrifie, Metallifie, *&c.*[1]

With a slight variation from Campanella's system in terms of the signification of *essentia*, Dalgarno sees the reality language seeks to convey as an *ens* or *res* divisible not into substance and accident but into concrete and abstract, simple and compound, complete and incomplete.[2] It is interesting to note however that he refuses to regard the word *lapis* as signifying a substance to the complete exclusion of accident ('est enim conceptus *accidentis* non minus essentialis lapidi, quam substantiae'[3]), thus refuting the widespread seventeenth-century view of the substantive as indicating *substantia*, the adjective *qualitas* (i.e. accident). To the term *substantia* he prefers *concretum*, and classifies his *entia concreta* into *corporea*, *spiritualia* and *composita* (i.e. *homines*). Such divisions, like that of his *concreta materialia* into *mathematica*, *physica*, *artefacta*, etc., have more to do with philosophy than with grammar and are the equivalent, on a more philosophical level, of the Ancients' plethora of semantic subdivisions of the noun. A parallel use of the logicians' terms *abstractum* and *concretum* is presented by Wilkins' division of substantives into concrete (signifying 'the *Ens* or thing it self') and abstract (signifying 'the Essence of things'). This is however none other than the usual contemporary division into substantives signifying *res ipsa* and other substantives signifying, together with adjectives, *qualitas*.[4] The abstracts may, like the concretes, be neuter, active or passive: neuters denoting 'the naked Essence of a thing'[5] (*deity*), actives 'a proclivity to Action'

[1] *Essay*, p. 300.

[2] The substance/accident dichotomy is then applied to the *ens incompletum* alone. Alternatively, the *ens* can be triply classified into *substantia, accidens* and *compositum*.

[3] *Ars signorum*, p. 37.

[4] E. Vorlat, 'Progress', 1, 102, rendering this as 'the entity itself and the qualities, considered by themselves, are expressed by a substantive, but when referring to a *thing* the qualities are denoted by an adjective', seems to think this common seventeenth-century view original to Wilkins.

[5] Here one may note first the confining of the signification of *ens* to the concrete noun, whereas for the *Grammatica speculativa* every noun necessarily signifies *per modum entis*; and secondly the restriction of the signification of *essentia* to the abstract noun, whereas for the *Grammatica speculativa* (cap. viii) the *modus entis* inheres in *all* things by virtue of their possession of *essentia* ('ex hoc quod habent essentiam'). Wilkins' dichotomy also runs counter to Campanella's definition of *all* nouns as signifying 'essentiam cuiusque rei'.

(*amorousness*), passives 'a capacity or fitness for receiving . . . an action' (*amiableness*).[1] The view of abstract substantives as denoting 'a proclivity or capacity'[2] coincides with that of Campanella. That the adjective (which may similarly be concrete or abstract, each in turn active, passive or neuter)[3] is bracketed with *qualitas* is shown by its description as the name given to the 'adjunct natures' of things:

the notion of them consisting in this, that they signifie, the subject or thing to which they are ascribed, to have in it something belonging to the nature or quality of those Adjectives, which are predicated of it, or limited by it.[4]

Wilkins' complete system of substantive and adjective is as follows:

Concrete substantives

Neuter: *calor* or τὸ *calere*
Active: *calefactio*
Passive: τὸ *calefieri*

Abstract substantives

Neuter: *caloritas*
Active: *calefactivitas*
Passive: *calefactibilitas*

Concrete adjectives

Neuter: *calidus*
Active: *calefaciens*
Passive: *calefactus*

Abstract adjectives

Neuter: *caloritativus*
Active: *calefactivus*
Passive: *calefactibilis*.[5]

The closeness of the parallel with Campanella may be brought out by juxtaposing his and Wilkins' descriptions of certain adjectives.

[1] *Essay*, p. 302.
[2] *Ibid.* p. 299.
[3] The *adiectiva concreta activa* and *passiva* are the participles of traditional grammar.
[4] *Essay*, p. 302. Cf. Priscian: 'adiectiva . . . aliis appellativis . . . adici solent ad manifestandam eorum qualitatem' (H. Keil, *Grammatici Latini*, II, 58). E. Vorlat, 'Progress' *loc. cit.*, *supra*, appears to think this approach an original philosophical discovery of Wilkins.
[5] To the adjectives there corresponds a set of adverbs in each series.

Wilkins	Campanella
Concrete active (*calefaciens*)	Participial noun signifying 'essentiam cum *actu* praesenti' (*amans*)
Abstract neuter (abstracts representing 'a proclivity or capacity') (*caloritativus*)	Participial noun with 'potentiam ad actum' (*amativus*)
Abstract active (*calefactivus*)	Noun signifying '*essentiam* cum possibilitate *activa*' (*calefactivus*)
Abstract passive (*calefactibilis*)	Noun signifying '*essentiam* cum possibilitate *passiva*' (*calefactibilis*)[1]

or of certain substantives:

Wilkins	Campanella
Abstract neuters denoting the 'naked Essence' of a thing	A class of nouns signifying 'essentiam puram' (*amor*)
'Substantives of the Action'	Nouns signifying 'essentiam actionis'
'Substantives of the Passion'	Nouns signifying 'essentiam patientis'

These correspondences would seem to be more than fortuitous, and indicate the extent to which Wilkins has based himself on Campanella.

The urge to minute semantic classification of the noun is a trait common to Roman, Humanist and seventeenth-century grammar. Increasingly, as time goes on, it is not even remotely connected with corresponding differences in form. Wilkins' derivation of *gubernatio* from *magistratus* is on the level of lexical meaning alone, though it has its correspondence in the orthographical devices he uses to distinguish a 'substantive of action' from a 'radical of the person'. Lodwick's classification of the noun (*drinker* = 'actor', *drunkard* = 'inclination', *drink-house* = 'the place accustomary to the action', etc.[2]) seems equally eccentric until it is realized that his six classes correspond to six formal terminations found in Dutch and Latin, and will each have its 'distinctionall marke' in his system of writing. His

---

[1] Cf. Campanella's *Grammatica*, pp. 19, 26.
[2] *A Common Writing*, pp. 8–9. To fill gaps in his system as applied to English, Lodwick suggests the coining of such words as *laughard*.

remaining classifications do not however have even this justification. It is difficult to take seriously his treatment of *Peter, man* and *horse* as 'permanent' nouns and *murderer* as a 'temporary' one, or his division of the former three into 'more proper' (*Peter*) and 'less proper'.[1] His system of 'posed signs' indicative of case, corresponding to the 'signs' *of, to* and *from* in English, is obviously indebted to Lily. Behind his method lies a clumsy mingling of Latin (as in the positing of 'Patriall, Gentile, and Patronimical names') and English (as in the proposed formally invariable adjectives).[2]

In treating the verb Wilkins claims that it 'ought to have no distinct place amongst Integrals in a Philosophical Grammar', being in reality the copula plus an adjective: *caleo = sum calidus, calefacio = sum caleficiens, calefio = sum calefactus.*[3] In his article on Wilkins' sources O. Funke wonders whether this analysis is original to Wilkins, or taken from one of his forerunners.[4] The immediate precedents would appear to be Campanella, Caramuel's definition of the verb substantive as a *judicativa copula* joining two nouns in a logical proposition, as in *Petrus est legens* (the verb adjective being equivalent to copula + predicate)[5] and Scaliger's remark that in *Caesar est clemens* the word *est* is a 'nota coniunctionis' by means of which clemency is predicated of Caesar.[6] The verb substantive had for a long time, of course, been regarded as the root and foundation of all other verbs,[7] expansions of the type *legit = est legens* being common in medieval grammar,[8] and in Humanist works such as those of Despauterius. Wilkins, noting the sequence verb-substantive plus present-participial-adjective = verb-adjective, takes the logical further step of using past-participial and non-participial adjectives as the second component.[9] This type of expansion is prominent in Dalgarno's work, which analyses the surface structure *amamus* into four distinct

---

[1] *Ibid.* pp. 7–9.

[2] The verb similarly is to 'remaine without distinction in respect of person or number' simply because such distinctions have been reduced in the English verb.

[3] *Essay*, p. 303.

[4] 'On the Sources of John Wilkins' Philosophical Language (1668)', p. 213. It may be noted that Leibniz' proposed artificial language would treat verbs as equal to *esse* + adjective, and substantives as equal to *ens* + *res* + adjective. (v. L. Couturat, *La Logique de Leibniz d'après des documents inédits*, Paris, 1901, p. 70.)

[5] *Grammatica audax*, p. 31.

[6] *De causis*, cap. cx, p. 220.

[7] Scaliger: 'fundamentum, sive radix omnium verborum'. Thus also Peter of Spain in the mid-thirteenth century, v. p. 47, note 2 above.

[8] v. J. P. Mullally, *The Summulae Logicales of Peter of Spain*, p. xc.

[9] Cf. also the Port-Royal Grammar's analysis *rubet = is red*.

parts: subject pronoun, present tense, copula, and present participle, in which the copula itself is devoid of tense. Though the verb is a derivative of *ens*, the copula is not, but constitutes 'aliquid distinctum a Notione *Entis*'. It is the *pars formalis* of the proposition, a 'Signum actus Mentis *Judicativi*', a definition which both recalls that of Caramuel, and constitutes an independent statement of the Port-Royal position that the verb (i.e. copula plus adjective) indicates 'un jugement de notre âme'.[1] Tense is extrinsic to this function of affirmation, which makes of the copula the 'pars Essentialis & maxime Principalis propositionis'.[2] In the resolution of *amamus* into *nos* + present tense + *sumus amantes* the copula, bearing no tense, can in fact be replaced by the expression of affirmation *ita*, again parallel-ing the Port-Royal view that 'la signification commune à tous les Verbes . . . est celle de l'affirmation'.[3] Similarly with Wilkins the copula, 'essential and perpetual' in every sentence, 'serves for the uniting of the Subject and Predicate in every Proposition'. He regards subject and predicate, 'as the Logicians do', as respectively everything that precedes and everything that follows the copula.[4]

Wilkins defines the *particles* (of which the copula is one) as 'less principal words, which may be said to consignifie, serving to circum-stantiate and modifie those Integral words, with which they are joyned'.[5] They are either *grammatical*, serving to 'circumstantiate' the primary sense of an *integral* by means of inflection, abbreviation, etc., or *transcendental*, varying the primary sense by 'trope', etc. Here again, Wilkins' definitions have their roots in those of traditional grammarians, his description of the preposition recalling both the linking function ascribed to it by Melanchthon, and Campanella's view of it as consignifying *respectus et circunstantias*: '[Its] proper office it is to joyn Integral with Integral on the same side of the *Copula*; signifying some respect of *Cause*, *Place*, *Time*, or other circumstance . . .'[6] He shows the typical late seventeenth-century tendency to regard prepositions and adverbs as forming basically one and the same word-class, for his preposition in compounds 'modifies the Act after the same manner as Adverbs do'.[7] Those adverbs which are not

---

[1] The Port-Royal Grammar appeared in 1660. Dalgarno's work was published in 1661, but had been in preparation for some time before that. Caramuel's similar definition dates however from 1654.

[2] *Ars signorum*, pp. 63–5. [3] *Grammaire générale et raisonnée*, p. 115.

[4] *Essay*, p. 304. [5] *Ibid.* p. 304.

[6] *Ibid.* p. 309. Wilkins' acquaintance with Campanella's work is shown by his citing of the term *adnomen* for the preposition. [7] *Ibid.* p. 312.

derived from *integrals* (and hence themselves *integrals*) are either pronominal derivatives, modes of the verb, or conjunctions.

The articles, the moods and the tenses are regarded as particles, but as *servile* particles in contrast to the 'more Absolute' ones already treated, and as serving to express more fully certain accidents. The description of the article is taken from English practice, with a division into enunciative (*a, an*) and demonstrative (*the*), the latter giving 'a peculiar Emphasis to its Substantive'.[1] Moods are primary (indicative and imperative) and secondary, the latter being used in 'modal propositions' whose being, doing or suffering is considered 'not *simply by it self*, but *gradually in its causes* from which it proceeds either *Contingently* or *Necessarily*'.[2] Contingent propositions are those Englished by *can, could, may, might, will, would,* necessary ones those involving *must, ought, shall, should* – an explanation which may be thought to owe something to Lily's system of 'signs'. Mood is the province of the copula, but tense concerns both the copula and the *integrals,* Wilkins holding that tense should be 'according to the true Philosophy of Speech' a feature of substantives as well as of verbs.[3] It is however the copula, not the verb itself, that is regarded as inflected for mood and tense. Exceptions are propositions such as *homo est animal, Deus vivit,* in which the copula is simply a link expressing an 'indefinite time' unmarked in extant languages but for which a philosophical grammar ought ideally to provide some mark of distinction.[4]

In dealing with the 'accidental difference' of words, Wilkins notes that the rules of inflection of the classical languages are not suited to the vulgar tongues, the explanation of whose analytical procedures 'ought to be founded upon the Philosophy of speech and such *Natural* grounds, as do necessarily belong to Language' rather than treated in terms of case, 'which is not so essential and natural to Substantives, as to be provided for in the word it self, by varying the Terminations of it'. He takes the Port-Royal view of case as an abbreviation of a prepositional phrase, as 'nothing else but that obliquity in the sence of a Substantive, which is caused and signified by some Preposition annexed to it'.[5]

---

[1] *Ibid.* p. 315.   [2] *Ibid.* p. 316.

[3] Thus, to a Latin 'present' substantive *amatio* there ought ideally to correspond a perfect and future *amavitio* and *amaturitio.*

[4] *Essay,* p. 353.

[5] *Ibid.* p. 352.

Though Wilkins sets out to produce a grammar (or rather a universal system of writing capable of transcribing the concepts of general grammar) applicable to all languages, he obviously assumes that such languages will conform in structure to the model of Latin. Though he points out ways in which Latin falls short of what an ideal philosophically based language should be, his system is modelled on that language. He takes the categories he finds ready to hand in it, applies to them doctrines from the grammatical works of his predecessors, expressed in philosophical terms culled in part from Campanella, and assumes the whole to have universal validity. Perhaps sufficient parallels have been drawn here to prove that Wilkins' major source, in the grammatical section of the *Essay*, is Campanella. The latter, in turn, relies heavily on the *Grammatica speculativa* and Scholastic philosophy, so that Wilkins, for all his apparent modernity, is ultimately indebted to that philosophy and to medieval grammar.

The first thoroughgoing attempt by an Englishman at a universal grammar after Wilkins is A. Lane's *Rational and Speedy Method* of 1695. Its predecessor by a few years, W. Clare's *Via naturalis*, is a less important work ostensibly in reaction against Lily. It uses the latter's system of *signs*, and its definition of the noun as 'the name of a thing' is that of Colet, but the *signs* are treated as adjuncts to *integral words* (i.e. nouns and verbs), a term Clare has taken either from Wilkins or from C. Cooper's *Grammatica linguae Anglicanae* of 1685. By the end of the century, even a minor grammarian such as Lane divides grammar into two parts, the first purporting to give 'such Precepts as are common to all Languages', the second the rules peculiar to Latin. Indicative of the general trend is his claim that his work will inculcate 'the Art of Reasoning'. Though Lane claims that words enter into syntactical relationships 'of their own Nature', the touchstone is logic, a readiness to expand surface structures into more logical ones held to be semantically equivalent, as in the resolution in Wilkins' manner of verbs into copula plus adjective (*albeo = sum albus*), the treatment of the adverb as an abbreviation of a prepositional phrase, or Lane's inability to conceive of the word *amicus* without the addition of *vir* 'understood'.

In England, as has been shown, the production of universal grammars is very much bound up with the universal language movement and its presupposition of a correspondence between the ontological order of nature and the linguistic order. Universal language, and hence universal grammar, are supposed to reflect the world of things – Campanella's insistence on proceeding 'ex rei natura' is noteworthy in this respect – through the mediation of a framework of concepts giving a replica of the framework of things. The image they give of phenomena is therefore dependent, as in Wilkins' use of Aristotle's categories and his reliance on Campanella's Scholasticism, on the philosophical system of classification in vogue. Aiming to come closer to things, these authors are prone to the very subjectivism which the seventeenth century so passionately sought to avoid.

The great grammatical event of the second half of the century, from our modern standpoint, is however the publication in 1660 of the *Grammaire générale et raisonnée* of Port-Royal, which is commonly bracketed not with Baconian empiricism but with the second of the twin pillars of seventeenth-century thought, the mentalism of Descartes. This grammar, whose full influence, though immense, was delayed until the following century, will in view of its importance form the subject of the final chapter of this study. Enough has been said already to put the reader on his guard against the not unusual estimate of the Port-Royal authors as the inventors of general grammar and indeed of grammatical concepts which were common-places of medieval and Humanist doctrine. Such grandiose claims as that the Port-Royal grammar or Descartes was the first to approach 'the problem of changing the orientation of linguistics from "natural history" to "natural philosophy"' [1] are seen to have little substance when the contributions of Caramuel and Campanella are taken into account. In the final analysis the opposition between general and special grammar, far from owing its genesis to Descartes,[2] is a legacy of medieval thought of which linguists such as Wilkins were fully aware.

[1] N. Chomsky, *Cartesian Linguistics*, p. 59.
[2] Descartes possibly formulated his 'method' around 1620. v. V. Salmon, review of *Cartesian Linguistics*, p. 174.

5. PORT-ROYAL

The heirs to the grammatical approach of Scaliger and Sanctius, and to the 'philosophical' grammars of Campanella and Caramuel, were the linguists, logicians and theologians of the Port-Royal community near Paris, whose celebrated *Grammaire générale et raisonnée* appeared in 1660. The 'Messieurs de Port-Royal' were Jansenists, followers of the austere doctrines – including predestination and the impossibility of complete atonement for sin – promulgated by Cornelius Jansen (1585–1638), bishop of Ypres. These doctrines grew up at a time when the Catholic Church was exposed to danger on two fronts, from the growing power of Protestantism, and from Jesuit opposition to traditional Catholic tenets contained in the theology of St Augustine. The Jansenists saw their aim as in part the revival of Augustinianism, an aim which made them bedfellows with Protestants on this particular point, and involved them in fierce polemics against the Jesuits. Their most famous representative was Pascal, whose *Pensées* and *Lettres provinciales* spread the Jansenist cause in seventeenth-century France. It was however in the teaching of Descartes that they found the philosophical bases for their thought. Though his system contained elements of which they could not approve – his rationalistic outlook was not compatible with the doctrine of revealed truth – as Augustinians the dualistic mind/body opposition in his work had a certain appeal for them. Antoine Arnauld in particular, co-author with Claude Lancelot of the *Grammaire générale*, was an admirer of Descartes, to whom he wrote in June 1648 that he had 'read with admiration and approved almost entirely of' his metaphysical writings.[1] Arnauld's collaborator on the Port-Royal *Logic*, P. Nicole, was however much less convinced of the value of Cartesianism, and one should bear in mind with H. Aarsleff that it would 'seem potentially dangerous to ignore the fact that the Port-Royalists had significant disagreements with

---

[1] v. F. Cadet, *Port-Royal Education*, transl. from the French (*L'Education à Port-Royal*, Paris, 1887) by A. D. Jones, London, 1898, p. 27.

Descartes'.[1] None the less, the educational practice of their schools, the famous *Petites Ecoles de Port-Royal*, was based on Cartesianism,[2] on pedagogical reform and opposition to the methods used by the Jesuits and the universities. Though various dates have been given for the foundation of these schools,[3] they were probably not functioning to any real extent before 1646. In contrast to prevailing methods of education, they aimed at the development of reasoning powers rather than memory, and had a practical bent consonant with the austere goals of Jansenism. By 1661 however, the *Petites Ecoles* had been closed by royal command,[4] and a general directive of 1670 to all Jesuit houses to combat the philosophy of Descartes was followed shortly afterwards by a parliamentary petition from the University of Paris seeking a ban on its teaching. This did not prevent the Port-Royalists from continuing their polemics or from publishing works on language and education, but their schools remained closed.

THE PORT-ROYAL LATIN GRAMMAR

The textbooks used in the schools were largely the work of Antoine Arnauld and Claude Lancelot, the latter's *Nouvelle Méthode pour apprendre facilement et en peu de temps la langue latine*, a frankly pedagogical work, appearing in 1644. Unlike the Jesuits and other contemporary educators, the Port-Royalists approached the teaching of Latin through the vernacular, inculcating first of all what was immediately accessible to their pupils. In England at this time there was a parallel movement in favour of an approach to Latin via the native tongue. In accordance with this principle Lancelot's grammar, intended to replace the long-established Despauterius in the schools, was drawn up in French.[5] That the aim was primarily pedagogical is evident from Lancelot's remark in the preface that he proposes to deviate as little as possible from what is customary in

---

[1] 'The History of Linguistics and Professor Chomsky', p. 573.

[2] v. J. W. Adamson, *Pioneers of Modern Education 1600–1700 (Contributions to the History of Education III)*, Cambridge University Press, 1905, p. 260.

[3] R. H. Robins, *Short History*, p. 123, following Cadet, gives the date 1637; F. P. Graves, *A History of Education*, gives 1643.

[4] R. Donzé, *La Grammaire générale et raisonnée de Port-Royal*, Berne, 1967, p. 12, gives the date of closure as 12 March 1660.

[5] The author of the *Examen de la manière d'enseigner le latin aux enfans* (1668), an early proponent of the direct method, similarly advocates that explanatory matter be given in French. (v. p. 21 of the English translation, *An Examen of the Way of Teaching the Latin Tongue*, already cited.)

instructing children in Latin. The first edition of the work is accordingly a straightforward teaching grammar, rejecting superfluous minutiae as inappropriate to practical pedagogy, claiming to achieve in six months what Despauterius would take three years to accomplish, and praising Ramus' teaching maxim 'Few rules and much practice.' Apart from this practical bias, it does not differ appreciably from the average Humanist teaching manual, and could be passed over without comment were it not that the third edition of 1654 contains revisions which change in very important respects the whole orientation of the syntactic section of the work. Between 1644 and this third edition there had occurred an event of capital importance for Lancelot's understanding of sentence construction – he had had access to Sanctius' *Minerva*.[1] The preface to the third and succeeding editions of the *Nouvelle Méthode* informs the reader that Lancelot made a deliberate effort to document himself on the contribution made by his predecessors to the 'art' of grammar. Sanctius is singled out for special praise, his *Minerva*, described as rare and difficult to obtain, having been read 'with the greatest possible care, and with a satisfaction to which I cannot give adequate expression'.[2] What specifically impresses Lancelot in Sanctius' work is his approach to syntax, a study – conspicuously absent in Scaliger's *De causis* – to which he brings 'insights incomparably more penetrating than those of his predecessors'.[3] His appeal consists in his having reduced syntax to 'first principles', in his abstraction from the tangle of usage of generally applicable laws. The whole art of grammar, according to these principles, consists in demonstrating that the 'figurative construction' of discourse, containing elements which are 'understood without being expressed',[4] is reducible to the 'essential construction' of the underlying linguistic system. He who would excel in the art of grammar has but to follow this method: 'de rappeler cette construction figurée aux loix de la simple, & de

[1] The difference between the two editions were first pointed out by G. Sahlin, *César Chesneau du Marsais et son rôle dans l'évolution de la grammaire générale*, p. 13.

[2] *Nouvelle Méthode pour apprendre facilement et en peu de temps la langue latine*, 5th ed., Paris, 1656, p. 8: 'avec tout le soin qu'il me fut possible, & tout ensemble avec une satisfaction que je ne puis assez exprimer'. (In the titles of, and in quotations from, the Port-Royal grammars and logic, accents are inserted where modern practice requires them, and *u* and *i* are where necessary replaced by *v* and *j*. Otherwise the authors' original spelling is retained).

[3] *Ibid.* p. 8. Sanctius is described as having treated construction 'avec une lumière qui passe sans comparaison tous ceux qui l'ont devancé'.

[4] 'sous-entenduës sans estre marquées'.

faire voir que ces expressions . . . subsistent néantmoins sur les principes de la construction ordinaire & essentielle de la Langue . . .'[1] It is the method followed by Sanctius and his imitators Scioppius and Vossius, and it is to these three authors that Lancelot explicitly declares his indebtedness.[2] The silence concerning Ramus, apart from the reference to his maxim 'Peu de préceptes et beaucoup d'usage', is eloquent, though one may note that in the preface to the Port-Royal Greek Grammar[3] Sanctius is referred to as his 'disciple'. No less significant, in face of the readily acknowledged – and quite patent – debt to Sanctius and his followers, is the absence of any reference to Descartes or to Cartesian philosophy. The affiliation of the *Nouvelle Méthode* is a purely linguistic one.

When we come to examine the application to actual examples of Latin structure of the principles mentioned in the preface, what Lancelot owes to treatments of ellipse in Sanctius and Vossius becomes readily apparent.[4] As the section entitled *Remarques sur les figures de construction* makes clear in discussing ellipse, 'things which do not appear in the sentence must sometimes be understood'.[5] The ideal sentence underlying the elliptical construction ·is however identical with a logical proposition containing subject, verb and attribute, a view which necessitates the expansion of e.g. *Urbs Athenae* to *Urbs quae est Athenae*. The doctrine that no verb lacks a nominative subject either expressed or understood leads similarly to expansions of the type *vivitur = vita vivitur*, or *pluit = Deus pluit*, already familiar to readers of Linacre's *De structura*.[6] Linacre's treatment of *Cicero erat brevis staturae* as an abbreviation of *Cicero erat homo brevis staturae* is similarly paralleled by Lancelot's expansion of *homo est juvenis* into *homo est juvenis homo*. Neuter adjectives standing alone require an expansion of the type *triste = triste negotium*, the word supplied here being 'un mot d'aussi grande étendue dans sa signification que celuy de *res*'.[7] There is of course nothing new in all

---

[1] *Nouvelle Méthode* (1656), p. 9.

[2] *Ibid.* p. 10: '. . . j'ay allié ensemble ces trois Auteurs . . . tirant de chacun d'eux ce qui m'a paru de plus clair & de plus solide . . .'

[3] *Nouvelle Méthode pour apprendre facilement la langue grecque*, Paris, 1655.

[4] For a thorough discussion of Lancelot's debt to Sanctius v. R. Lakoff's review, already cited, of H. Brekle's edition of the *Grammaire générale et raisonnée*.

[5] *Nouvelle Méthode* (1656), p. 576: 'on doit quelquefois sous-entendre ce qui ne se trouve point du tout dans l'oraison . . .'

[6] Cf. Linacre's *sedetur = sessio sedetur*, and *pluit = Deus pluit* or *pluvia pluit*.

[7] Sanctius' plentiful use of the word *negotium* in various expansions has already been noted.

this. In discussing comparison with *quam*, the fourteenth-century Modistic grammarian Siger de Courtrai had treated *Achilles est fortior quam Eneas* as an abbreviation of *Achilles est fortior quam Eneas est*.[1] Apart from Linacre's numerous examples, Despauterius had already resolved *triste* into *tristis res*, such Humanist resolutions as *amat = est amans* had been common since medieval times, and Sanctius had expanded *Caesar est albus* into *Caesar est albus Caesar*. Yet even further back in time, before the Humanists and the medieval grammarians, antecedents for this type of abstract grammar can be found in the Ancients. Sanctius' explanation of *Annibal* in *Annibal peto pacem* as equivalent to *Ens Annibal* or *Qui sum Annibal* is nothing more than an application of Priscian's *Filius Pelei = (Ens) qui est filius Pelei*, an example which Sanctius himself quotes.[2] Lancelot's doctrine that the impersonal verb regularly cumulates in one word 'an entire proposition' consisting of subject, affirmation and attribute, with expansions such as *poenitet me = poenitentia poenitet me*, or *pluit = Deus pluit*, had equally been common since Priscian. His resolutions of imperatives (*sis = fac ut sis*) and of concessive and potential clauses similarly go back to Sanctius, as does his view of the relative pronoun as standing between two cases of its antecedent, his *Est pater quem amo = Est pater quem patrem amo* being obviously based on Sanctius' *Vidi hominem, qui homo disputat*.[3]

The operations specified here by Lancelot are ultimately traceable to that traditional section of grammar – the *grammatica exegetice* – whose business was to explain seeming obscurities in classical authors (on this point Chomsky's view of Sanctius is not completely astray), and which is the forerunner of a division of syntax into 'regular', and 'irregular' or 'figurative', the latter treating the figures of construction such as zeugma. Scioppius' *Grammatica philosophica* of 1628 has such a division into *Syntaxis regularis*, and *Syntaxis irregularis* or *figurata*.[4] The fact that Port-Royal education no longer practised Ramus' rigid separation of the three arts rhetoric, grammar and

---

[1] G. Wallerand (ed.), *Les Œuvres de Siger de Courtrai. Les Philosophes belges, VIII*, Louvain, 1913, p. 99: 'credo tamen nominativum magis regi a *verbo subintellecto* quam a comparativo' (my italics).

[2] v. V. Salmon, review of N. Chomsky, *Cartesian Linguistics*, p. 178. As an example of the Port-Royal dependence on Sanctius, one may note their view (*Grammaire générale*, 2nd ed., 1664), identical with his, that only the infinitive is properly speaking an impersonal verb.

[3] For further discussion of parallels between Sanctius' and Lancelot's treatment of ellipse, v. above, pp. 103–6.

[4] Cf. the *constructio justa* and *constructio figurata* of Linacre's *De structura* (1524).

logic – and indeed condemned it out of hand – enabled Lancelot at the same time to make use of the 'figurative construction' of rhetoric, and to supply his expansions with a logical justification. What is new is his insistence that the task of the grammarian consists precisely in the rewriting of these figurative constructions in accordance with the 'ordinary and essential construction' of the language.[1] He is obviously fully aware that the workings of ellipse produce a 'surface structure' which can be restated in terms of the 'deep structure' of the ideal sentence. He even attempts to explain the phenomenon, pointing out that the impersonal verb is limited to the third person not through any defect in itself, but through 'un défaut de la chose qui luy puisse estre appliquée', thus bringing in an extra-linguistic criterion. Further, in traditional expansions such as *poenitet me = poenitentia poenitet me*, the proposed 'deep structure' did not stray far in form from the 'surface' one. In resolutions such as *poenitet me = poena habet me*, or *libet mihi = libido est mihi*,[2] Lancelot proposes however new formal structures which on the one hand are seen as exact semantic equivalents of the 'surface' structure, and on the other are logical propositions containing subject, affirmation and attribute. But even this is derivative, for behind Lancelot's analyses there lie Linacre's *Enallage*[3] and Vossius' insistence on rewriting certain structures as semantically equivalent propositions containing an explicitly stated subject and predicate: *hoc juste agis = haec actio justa est; una illic fuimus = ego et alter illic fuimus.*

One can easily see however what it was in all this that attracted Chomsky, though he appears to have restricted himself to the much sketchier treatment given in the *Grammaire générale et raisonnée*, whose treatment of ellipse he obviously regards as a specifically Cartesian procedure:

Cartesian linguistics characteristically assumes that language has two aspects . . . an inner and an outer aspect . . . we can distinguish the 'deep structure' of a sentence from its 'surface structure'. The former is the underlying abstract structure that determines its semantic interpretation; the latter, the superficial organization of units which determines the phonetic interpretation . . . a second fundamental conclusion of Cartesian

---

[1] The *Grammaire générale* (p. 145) regards the 'ordre naturel' of syntax (Linacre's *constructio justa*) as 'conforme à l'expression naturelle de nos pensées'. Of crucial importance here is the authors' reference (p. 147) to the *Nouvelle Méthode*, 'où on en a parlé assez amplement'.
[2] These resolutions appear in the second (1664) edition of the *Grammaire générale*.
[3] v. above, p. 54.

linguistics . . . [is] that deep and surface structures need not be identical. This point is brought out with particular clarity in the Port-Royal *Grammar*, in which *a Cartesian approach to language is developed, for the first time* . . .[1]

To this there are three cogent objections: (1) the point is brought out with considerably less clarity in the *Grammaire générale* than it is in the *Nouvelle Méthode latine*; (2) in any case it is not specifically Cartesian; and (3) this approach to language, whether one describes it as Cartesian or not, is not 'developed for the first time' by the grammarians of Port-Royal.[2] It is a great pity that the absorbing interest of the parallels Chomsky draws between this type of linguistic procedure and the techniques of modern transformational grammar has been largely obscured by the furore aroused by his misreading of linguistic history, and by his attribution to Cartesian philosophy of concepts which had been common currency among grammarians and logicians for centuries. The parallels are however of great interest, since for Chomsky it is precisely this 'deep'/'surface' structure dichotomy that lies at the heart of transformational grammar:

The generative grammar of a language should, ideally, contain a central *syntactic component* and two *interpretive components*, a *phonological component* and a *semantic component* . . . the syntactic component must provide for each sentence . . . a semantically interpretable *deep structure* and a phonetically interpretable *surface structure* . . .[3]

Chomsky notes that investigation of the semantic component of a transformational grammar is quite recent, and that 'It is in the system of underlying structures that are mapped onto the actual given string by transformational rules that the semantically significant categories and functions are represented.'[4] Considerations such as these lead him to turn away from the reigning school of American empirical descriptive linguistics, which operates only at the level of spoken utterance or discourse, and to lean toward the Saussurian

[1] *Cartesian Linguistics*, pp. 32–3 (my italics).

[2] Cf. L. G. Kelly, *Twenty-five Centuries of Language Teaching*, Rowley, Mass., 1969, p. 352: 'Most of the development work in general grammar was done by the scholars of Port-Royal. They took over the phrase from Alsted [*Encyclopaedia Universalis*, 1630], who invented the concept in 1606.' Alsted may have invented the term, but he certainly did not invent the concept of general grammar. Kelly is in fact aware of this, for he later (p. 354) quotes R. Bacon's 'the substance of grammar is one and the same in all languages, even if there are occasional variations'.

[3] 'Goals of Linguistic Theory', pp. 9–10.

[4] *Ibid.* p. 15.

concept of a mental system of *langue* underlying the facts of discourse or *parole*: 'The generative grammar internalized by someone who has acquired a language defines what in Saussurian terms we may call *langue* . . . The classical Saussurian assumption of the logical priority of the study of langue (. . .) seems quite inescapable.'[1] Chomsky's concept of *langue* differs however in important respects from that of de Saussure, which he regards as merely a 'systematic inventory of items'. He proposes in its place a 'Humboldtian conception of underlying competence as a system of generative processes', which will treat sentence formation as the province of *langue* rather than *parole*, and which will find place for that 'rule-governed creativity' which Chomsky posits as the principle governing the speaker-hearer's ability to form or recognize sentences which he has never heard before.[2]

Though it would be a vain search to look for the technical procedures of modern generative grammar in the *Nouvelle Méthode*, there would seem to be little doubt that this work, with no discoverable debt to Descartes, already makes assumptions that are identical with those a generative grammarian must make. R. Lakoff, though dismissing Chomsky's Cartesian claims, comes to the conclusion that the Port-Royalists were 'in some sense' generative grammarians:

I am drawn to this view by . . . their belief in an underlying universal logical level of language, related in some fashion to the particular, non-logical languages that we speak. This concept, however, depends on a deeper one: the intuitive belief that . . . language in its underlying form need not be the same as it looks on the surface, or that the figurative construction may be far removed from the deeper, or simple, construction.[3]

This intuitive belief would appear to be amply demonstrated by the discussion of ellipse in the *Nouvelle Méthode*, and to this extent the parallels Chomsky draws between Port-Royal theory and modern transformational practice are well founded, and indeed the *Nouvelle Méthode* provides more convincing justification for them than does the *Grammaire générale*. The complementary belief in an 'underlying universal logical level' of language is given support by Lancelot's

---

[1] *Ibid.* pp. 10–11.

[2] *Ibid.* p. 23, and *Aspects of the Theory of Syntax*, M.I.T. Press, Cambridge, Mass., 1965, p. 4. Cf. R. H. Robins, *Short History*, p. 174: 'Humboldt's theory of language lays stress on the creative linguistic ability inherent in every speaker's brain or mind. A language is to be identified with the living capability by which speakers produce and understand utterances, not with the observed products of speaking and writing . . .'

[3] Review of Brekle's edition of *Grammaire générale et raisonnée*, p. 344.

statement that the 'sure and established rules' he offers will stand the student in good stead in the learning of languages other than Latin. His assumption of a common logical basis to all languages is illustrated by his treatment of case government as equivalent to the structure preposition plus noun, and by his repetition of Sanctius' view that comparison may be expressed in all languages by a construction containing a 'particle', both of these syntactic explanations depending on the supposition of an underlying logical structure common to Latin and the vernacular languages. It is the observation of this common structure, rather than the learning by rote of items on the level of discourse, that is proposed to the student. The parallels between the two levels do not occur in a haphazard way but, as R. Lakoff notes, are 'constrained by universal facts about language'.[1] The employment of ellipse is accordingly restricted in the eighth edition (1681), which stipulates that a word cannot be held to be *sous-entendu* except in completing a construction known to exist in the usage of the language, and rejects on these grounds certain of Sanctius' expansions (e.g. *pugnandum est = pugnandum est* τὸ *pugnare*) which had been admitted to earlier editions.[2]

The interest of the *Nouvelle Méthode* is syntactic. The Humanists apart from Linacre had neglected this part of grammar, either devoting little space to it, or simply repeating notions already treated in the morphology, together with the 'three concords'[3] and endless semasiologically based minutiae of case government. One understands why J.-C. Chevalier regards the Port-Royal authors as the founders of modern syntax.[4] He is no doubt led to this view by the emphasis which these authors put on the sentence as the grammatical unit, on its coincidence with the logical proposition containing subject, affirmation and attribute. But enough has by now been said in this study to call attention to what this emphasis owes to the Port-Royalists' predecessors – the *Grammatica speculativa*'s view of syntax as the expression of mental concepts;[5] its realization that discourse

---

[1] *Ibid.* p. 353.

[2] Similarly *Grammaire générale*, pp. 123–4.

[3] Agreement of the adjective with its substantive, of the subject with its verb, and of the relative with its antecedent.

[4] *Histoire de la syntaxe*, p. 493.

[5] Cf. R. G. Godfrey, 'Late Medieval Linguistic Meta-Theory and Chomsky's Syntactic Structures', *Word*, 21:2 (1965), p. 255: 'Construction [for Thomas of Erfurt] is a deliberate, overt act of the human mind in which meaning forms (*constructibilia*) are united in order to express a composite mental concept.'

and *verbum mentis* do not always coincide; the medieval doctrine that the concept of 'being' underlies all verbs, leading to the analysis of the verb as consisting of affirmation plus attribute; Scaliger's and Sanctius' concept of a *ratio* underlying discourse and the latter's illustration of this point by his treatment of ellipse; Vossius' application to grammar of the Aristotelian theory of predication; Caramuel's view of the verb substantive as a *judicativa copula* joining a logical subject and predicate – without all these predecessors the grammars of Port-Royal could never have been written. In the demonstration of the relationship between 'deep' and 'surface' structure – and that is where the interest of the *Nouvelle Méthode* lies – Lancelot's immediate source is not any remarks of Descartes, but Sanctius. And behind Sanctius there is an impressive body of medieval and Renaissance precedent.

THE 'GRAMMAIRE GÉNÉRALE ET RAISONNÉE'

Any kind of justificatory theory, Cartesian or otherwise, is notably absent from the *Nouvelle Méthode*. Intended as a simple pedagogical grammar, it went into some twelve editions by 1698, and was still appearing in English versions as late as 1816. It was however completely eclipsed by the appearance, in 1660, of the celebrated *Grammaire générale et raisonnée*, written by Lancelot in collaboration with Antoine Arnauld. In view of the importance of this work for eighteenth-century grammatical theory, it is curious that its historical antecedents have never been thoroughly investigated. The preface to the Scolar Press facsimile edition[1] notes for instance that the 'extent to which it may justly be credited with originality has never been clearly stated', the possible importance of e.g. Campanella as a precursor of Port-Royal theory remaining still to be determined. It remarks however that 'Lancelot was undoubtedly the leading figure in the movement towards a new theory of grammar', a statement which must be weighed against Lancelot's insistence, in the preface to the *Nouvelle Méthode*, that he himself brings nothing new to grammatical theory, but owes all to his predecessors Sanctius, Scioppius and Vossius. Certainly, in the collaboration between Arnauld and Lancelot, it is the latter who must be considered the linguist. As R. Donzé points out,[2] it is he who brings to the

---

[1] Menston, England, 1967.   [2] *La Grammaire générale et raisonnée de Port-Royal*, p. 15.

collaboration a knowledge of the Latin grammatical tradition, whereas Arnauld's contribution was in the field of Cartesian logic. It is Arnauld's share in the work, allied to the almost simultaneous publication of the Port-Royal Logic (1662), which is responsible in Donzé's view for the widespread but erroneous view of the *Grammaire générale* as a completely new departure in grammatical theory based on Cartesian principles. To judge the Port-Royal Grammar in these terms is to ignore Lancelot's contribution, which is based on a centuries-old tradition.[1] Apart however from naming Scaliger, Sanctius, Scioppius (whose work, misled by its title, he regards as a 'philosophical' grammar), Vossius and Campanella, Donzé does not give further details, but proposes in the absence of detailed research on Lancelot's precursors to treat Port-Royal doctrine as 'un système clos'.[2]

The *Grammaire générale* makes two important claims: to be a general or universal grammar enunciating principles applicable to all languages, and to be based on reason. In part it represents a reaction against the preoccupation of contemporary vernacular grammar, as exemplified by Claude Vaugelas' *Remarques sur la langue française* (1647), with details of style and usage. The prevailing concern with such rhetorical matters was clearly anathema to Jansenist views, which included a puritanical rejection of style, and the Port-Royalists engaged in vigorous polemics with Vaugelas' supporters, notably Father P. Bouhours.[3] The ultimate basis of Vaugelas' approach, with its minutely detailed enquiry into preferred usage, was *le sens commun*. The preoccupation of his school with the niceties

---

[1] *Ibid.* p. 7: 'La publication presque contemporaine de la *Logique* . . . contribua à accréditer dans le public l'idée d'une doctrine grammaticale d'inspiration cartésienne, tirée tout achevée d'une conception nouvelle des rapports de la langue et de la pensée. Cette opinion . . . fait trop peu de cas du concours de Claude Lancelot . . . [qui] connaissait en effet fort bien une tradition grammaticale plusieurs fois séculaire.' H. E. Brekle, in the introduction to his critical edition of the Port-Royal Grammar (*Grammaire générale et raisonnée* . . . *Tome I: Nouvelle impression en facsimilé de la troisième édition de 1676*, Stuttgart-Bad Cannstatt, 1966), seems to follow the Abbé Fromant (*Supplément à la Grammaire générale*, 1766) in regarding Arnauld's contribution as the more important one. He concedes however (p. xv) that a final judgment must await a detailed comparison of the *Grammaire générale* and Lancelot's *Nouvelles Méthodes* for Latin and the vernaculars.

[2] *Ibid.* foreword, where he notes that 'l'étude des origines doctrinales de cet ouvrage serait du plus haut intérêt'. His own contribution to this study, limited as it is by his stated terms of reference, does not go beyond the remark (p. 26) that 'la grammaire spéculative et cartésienne ont pu agir conjointement sur Port-Royal'.

[3] For an account of the Jansenists' quarrel with Bouhours, v. T. Rosset, 'Le P. Bouhours critique de la langue des écrivains jansénistes', *Annales de l'Université de Grenoble*, XX, no. 1 (1908).

of *parole*, in the absence of any theory of an underlying system of *langue*, meant that they based their analyses solely on discourse,[1] an approach which, enclosing the linguist within the empirical details of a given language, leads ultimately, as Hjelmslev maintains, to linguistic nihilism. Their tendency toward the rigorous fixing of grammatical usage led them to apply to each individual item of usage a single immutable sense. Language must be precise and utilitarian, one meaning or function being assigned to one linguistic form. It was this belief that language could be *fixed* (or *ascertained*, as the corresponding English movement put it) that lay behind the linguistic practice of the *Académie française*, traditional guardian of the 'purity' of the French language. It also meant that all philosophical speculation, all attempt to provide a coherent grammatical *theory*, was banned from vernacular grammar-books for over a generation. Viewed against this background, the *Grammaire générale* represents a return to grammatical theory and to a more philosophical approach, an attempt to set the claims of reason above those of authority. It accepts that in a living tongue the best usage must be followed, even when it runs counter to analogy, but insists that usage can never be employed in a systematic undermining of analogy, for otherwise – and here the Port-Royal authors rejoin a major preoccupation of their times – the vernacular will remain uncertain, 'ne pourra jamais se fixer'.[2]

Despite the fact that it is written in French, the *Grammaire générale* is not however a grammar of the vernacular. Its concern is general grammar rather than the usages peculiar to given languages, but its inclusion in this study for that reason alone would equally involve the inclusion of vernacular general grammars such as the German *Köthener Sprachlehr* of 1619, or J. G. Schottel's *Teutsche Sprachkunst* of 1641. The reason it is considered here is because of the special relationship it bears to Lancelot's *Nouvelle Méthode latine*. The latter's convincing illustration of a 'deep' and a 'surface' structure in language, its numerous analyses that authorize us to consider Lancelot as at least in some sort a proto-transformational grammarian, contrast strangely with the sketchiness, the half-developed ideas, in the *Grammaire générale*. If however one treats the *Nouvelle*

---

[1] T. Rosset, 'Le P. Bouhours continuateur de Vaugelas', *ibid*. XX, 2 (1908), p. 217, notes that 'l'erreur des grammairiens et de Bouhours . . . a été de vouloir déterminer par des règles un emploi de formes qui dépend seulement de l'intention de l'écrivain'.

[2] *Grammaire générale*, p. 82.

Méthode as the exemplification of the theory – as R. Lakoff has suggested[1] – and the *Grammaire générale* and the Port-Royal Logic as explanatory manuals providing its justification, everything falls into place. Lancelot and Arnauld could assume that their readers were already familiar with the Latin Grammar,[2] and it is precisely its analyses that enable them to introduce elements of Cartesian philosophy into the *Grammaire générale* by way of explanation. Chomsky, assuming that the analyses were *inspired* by Cartesianism, got the whole thing wrong way round. But even in the case of the more theoretical *Grammaire générale*, it is possible to exaggerate the importance of the Cartesian element, to believe with L. Kukenheim that with this work 'le cartésianisme fait son entrée en grammaire; l'idée de "raison" tend à supplanter celle d'usage, dont l'utilité et la practicabilité sont mises en doute'.[3] This is no doubt true within the immediate context of vernacular grammar, but taken against the background of the history of linguistics it is completely false. Behind the Port-Royal approach to grammar there lies not only Campanella's *Grammatica philosophica* (1638), which had already dethroned the 'tyrant' usage and proclaimed reason 'Rex sermonum', but also a long medieval tradition. If, then, I consider the *Grammaire générale* here, it is not in order to give an exhaustive account of it, but to define its place within the Latin grammatical tradition already considered. As a direct result of the failure to situate it in its historical context, few grammatical works have been more subject to misconceptions. Even those who have seen that its theory reposes to a notable extent on medieval linguistic analyses have not realized that in certain important respects it distorts medieval doctrine and sets off at a new tangent.

As has been already noted, the *Grammaire générale* is not a grammar of the vernacular. It aims to provide a basis of theory appropriate to the description of any language, to explain 'les fondemens de l'art de parler', to give 'les raisons de ce qui est commun à toutes les langues', and to 'faire par science, ce que les autres font seulement par coustume'.[4] This approach started a veritable vogue for

---

[1] *Review of Grammaire générale*, p. 347. Lakoff regards the *Grammaire générale* as 'unintelligible' by itself. Her article gives a long and persuasive analysis of the question.

[2] Cf. R. Donzé's contention (*La Grammaire générale et raisonnée de Port-Royal*, p. 34) that the *Grammaire générale* 's'adresse visiblement à un lecteur . . . [qui a] une première connaissance des langues classiques'.

[3] *Esquisse*, p. 28.

[4] *Grammaire générale*, title page and p. 3.

general grammar, but though the influence of Port-Royal theory on European grammarians was immense, it was neither direct nor undelayed. It had no appreciable effect in England before the publication of Brightland's grammar in 1711, nor in Germany until late in the eighteenth century, and by the time its influence began to be felt it was no longer being presented in its original form. Before the early part of the eighteenth century, general grammar in England took its direction from Wilkins and the empirical tradition. Though the grammars of Wilkins and his fellow language-planners do of course contain a rationalist element, it is in France that rationalism develops as an important cultural force with serious implications for general grammar. Since however the *Grammaire générale* has so often been taken to be the source of major currents in eighteenth-century theory, perhaps one may be forgiven for underlining once more that general grammar is the invention neither of the Port-Royal authors nor of Cartesian philosophy. Beyond Campanella and Caramuel, it has its roots in medieval theory, as C. Thurot long ago pointed out: 'in the twelfth century, in which the principles of [Aristotle's] Second Analytics were strictly applied, grammar could not have been considered a science, if it had not been the same for all men . . .'[1]

Grammatical analyses of particular languages can of course be made without reference to meaning, once it is established that the elements being classified represent, for a native informant, meaningful discourse. A traditional system of universal grammar however presupposes by its very nature some kind of appeal to meaning, a semantic basis to classification, which in turn involves the making of certain basic assumptions concerning the parts of grammar:

> . . . if meaningfulness is to be made the main distinguishing criterion of grammar and grammatical structuring, as against phonology and phonological structuring, certain consequences are implied and must be taken into account. One would seem to be committed to at least the two following propositions: (1) The morpheme, or minimal grammatical element, is . . . a semantic element, and (2) Semantic values or meanings must . . . be attributed to grammatical categories.[2]

In making these points, R. H. Robins recalls Hjelmslev's dictum that 'every formal grammatical category has a semantic content',

---

[1] *Extraits*, pp. 126–7 (my translation).
[2] R. H. Robins, 'Some Considerations on the Status of Grammar in Linguistics', p. 93.

but rejects the basis in general psychological characteristics that Hjelmslev presupposes, and indeed any appeal to 'common mentality', to 'the inadequate theory of language as the outward manifestation of "inner" mental operations', as the basis for a belief in language universals.[1] It is here that the Cartesian bias of the *Grammaire générale* becomes relevant. The authors seem to suggest that language is primarily the representation of concepts in the mind, and only secondarily of external phenomena. The former are 'the objects of our thoughts',[2] and it is the mental concepts themselves which constitute the object of language, which thus becomes the mould in which thought is expressed, and hence amenable to logic. Words being signs for signifying thoughts – 'One cannot understand properly the various kinds of meaning that are enclosed in words, unless one has first well understood what goes on in our thoughts', says the *Grammaire générale*[3] – it follows that the end of language is to make known 'the operations of the mind', to serve in Leibniz' words as their 'best mirror'.[4]

This 'virtual identification of linguistic and mental processes'[5] is central to the 'Cartesian linguistics' discussed by Chomsky, who characterizes the *Grammaire générale* as developing for the first time a Cartesian approach to language. From Chomsky's definition of grammar as 'a device that (in particular) specifies the infinite set of well-formed sentences',[6] and his dismissal as marginal of any language theory that does not take into account the creative principle that enables a speaker to produce 'a new sentence of his language on the appropriate occasion',[7] it follows that, besides finding interest in any grammatical analysis in terms of deep and surface structure, he is also attracted by any kind of mental mechanism capable of generating this infinite set of sentences. He therefore

---

[1] 'Noun and Verb in Universal Grammar', *Language*, 28 (1952), p. 292. Cf. L. Bloomfield's distinction (*Language*, p. 166) between *lexical form* and *grammatical form*, and his treatment of the 'smallest meaningful units of grammatical form' or *tagmemes* on a different footing from the *morphemes* or 'smallest meaningful units' on the lexical level.

[2] *Grammaire générale*, p. 30.   [3] p. 27 (my translation).

[4] Leibniz calls words 'le meilleur miroir de l'esprit humain'. On this view, language no longer mirrors the universe.

[5] N. Chomsky, *Cartesian Linguistics*, p. 29.

[6] 'Goals of Linguistic Theory', p. 9. Cf. P. Kiparsky, 'Linguistic Universals and Linguistic Change', *Universals in Linguistic Theory* (ed. E. Bach and R. T. Harms), p. 171: 'For many features of universal grammar there is justification enough in the fact that without them it would simply not be possible to write grammars that account for the sentences of a language.'

[7] 'Goals of Linguistic Theory', pp. 7–8.

assumes, as underlying support to Robins' 'common possession realized differently at the surface in different languages', precisely that 'common mentality' that is condemned by Robins and, it goes without saying, by all schools of empirical linguists. His new-found enthusiasm for universal grammar now becomes comprehensible, for only its mentalistic approach can accommodate the 'creative aspect of language use' and thus provide 'a full account of the speaker-hearer's competence':[1] 'The central doctrine of Cartesian linguistics is that the general features of grammatical structure are common to all languages and reflect certain fundamental properties of the mind . . .'[2] These 'fundamental properties of the mind' are vital to his thesis, for it is they that assure the functioning of the 'rule-governed creativity', the 'system of generative processes', which enable the speaker–hearer to produce or recognize an infinite number of sentences based on a finite number of underlying ideal types.[3] The assumption of a common mentality here implied he regards as 'characteristically' Cartesian.[4] He notes, it is true, that apart from its supposed Cartesian origins Port-Royal linguistic theory can be traced back to Scholastic and Renaissance sources, and more particularly to Sanctius,[5] but against this must be set the fact that he looks upon the Cartesian origins of the *Grammaire générale* as a 'commonplace'.[6] This last assumption needs, I think, no comment. Cartesianism is not the source of the specifically linguistic ideas in the Port-Royal Grammar. Nor is it the *ultimate* source of those psychological and philosophical ideas that attract Chomsky. The supposition that there is an internal mental discourse underlying the external discourse of speech had already been made for centuries, and is not more characteristic of Cartesianism than it is of certain other schools of thought. The fact remains that it is from certain facets of Cartesian thought that Chomsky draws seeming support for his theories as to the 'creative aspect' of language:

[Descartes] arrived at the conclusion that man has unique abilities that cannot be accounted for on purely mechanistic grounds . . . ability to

---

[1] *Aspects of the Theory of Syntax*, p. 6. As is well known, Chomsky expresses the *langue/parole* dichotomy in terms of *competence/performance*, though the analogy is not a close one.

[2] *Cartesian Linguistics*, p. 59.

[3] Cf. E. Bach, 'Nouns and Noun Phrases', *Universals in Linguistic Theory* (ed. E. Bach and R. T. Harms), p. 91: '. . . I intend to suggest that the deep structures of sentences in different languages are identical; that is, I am subscribing to the idea of a universal set of base rules'.

[4] *Cartesian Linguistics*, note 63.   [5] *Ibid.* note 67.   [6] *Ibid.* note 3.

form new statements which express new thoughts . . . a species-specific capacity . . . undetermined by any fixed association of utterances to external stimuli or physiological states.[1]

He finds further support for these anti-mechanistic assumptions in G. de Cordemoy's *Discours physique de la parole* (1966), basing his thesis of the creative aspect of language use on two major premises: that 'linguistic and mental processes are virtually identical', and that whatever mental faculty it is that predetermines the creation of 'new statements which express new thoughts' is 'species-specific', i.e. reposes on an innate structure of the mind. Chomsky finds support for both these premises in Descartes and his forerunner Lord Herbert of Cherbury, and opposes to them the philosophy of Locke, whom he seems to regard as an arch-behaviourist.

We have already seen that it was a tenet of seventeenth-century thought that there is, or should be, a correspondence between language and natural phenomena. Medieval philosophy had already posited a natural affinity between the mind and things, holding that the mind is by its nature prediposed to arrive at the truth, defined by Thomists as an *adaequatio rei et intellectus*, a conformity of things with the understanding. In the Renaissance period this idea of an affinity between the mind and nature persisted in Telesian nature philosophy and in Neo-Platonic and Cabbalistic doctrine as part of a cosmology in which every element was a reflection of its counterpart. From this it was but a short step to the belief that the mind mirrors nature, and that if it is thought to be reflecting clearly, it can be assumed to be purveying the truth. Lord Herbert of Cherbury's *De veritate* (1624)[2] makes precisely this assumption, holding that truth must ensue if the faculties of the mind are 'brought into harmony with their objects', and that the entire doctrine of truth can be reduced to 'facultatum conformatio'.[3] Herbert's approach to the investigation of truth strikes a curiously Cartesian note, though he is yet another of those figures who stand at the cross-roads of thought, illustrating both Cartesian traits and a mingling of Scholastic, Neo-Platonic and even Stoic elements. It is curious how, in spite of severe condemnation, Scholastic doctrine persists in the seventeenth century. Descartes' philosophy is not without its Scholastic element,

---

[1] *Ibid.* pp. 3–5.

[2] *De veritate prout distinguitur a revelatione, a verisimili, a possibili, et a falso*, [London?], 1624.

[3] M. H. Carré (ed.), *De Veritate by Edward, Lord Herbert of Cherbury Translated with an Introduction*, University of Bristol, 1937, pp. 28, 17.

and one recalls Leibniz' discovery of the 'gold concealed in the Scholastic midden'.[1] In one sense Herbert's is a medieval mind. In another his ideas anticipate Cartesian rationalism and 'look beyond the whole course of English empiricism, by which for nearly two centuries they were submerged'.[2] Descartes received a copy of the *De veritate* from Mersenne in 1639, and its doctrine that when the mind is in harmony with natural phenomena it perceives the truth was to find fruition in Descartes' belief that whatever appears clearly and distinctly is true.

As with the empiricists so also with Descartes, whose philosophical system is rooted in scepticism, in the need to reject as false everything concerning which the least doubt can be entertained. Descartes concludes in his *Discours de la Méthode* (1637) that the only thing of which he can be entirely sure, apart from the existence of God, is that he is 'a substance the whole essence or nature of which is to think'.[3] The only phenomena of which he is certain are thus his own thoughts, mental concepts or 'ideas', some of which are clearer, and hence more likely to convey the truth, than others:

> . . . in regard to the ideas of corporeal objects . . . I find that there is very little in them which I perceive clearly and distinctly. Magnitude or extension in length, breadth, or depth, I do so perceive, to which we may also add substance, duration and number . . . [But] the ideas which I have of cold and heat are . . . far from clear and distinct . . .[4]

It is precisely those ideas that are conveyed according to empiricists by the direct medium of sense impressions, of which Descartes is least sure. The consequences for modern thought are far-reaching:

> The feeling that whatever can be clearly and distinctly conceived is 'true' means that the very structure of things is assumed to conform with the laws of the human mind . . . Cartesian thought reinforced the growing disposition to accept the scientific world-picture as the only 'true' one. The criterion of truth which it set up . . . [was that] the only real properties of objects were the mathematical properties . . .[5]

[1] '. . . aurum latere in stercore illo scholastico'.
[2] M. H. Carré (ed.), *De Veritate*, pp. 65–6.
[3] *Discourse on the Method of Rightly Conducting the Reason and Seeking for Truth in the Sciences*, transl. E. S. Haldane and G. R. T. Ross, in *Great Books of the Western World* (ed. R. M. Hutchins), 31, Chicago, 1952, p. 51.
[4] *Meditations on the First Philosophy* (*Meditation* III), transl. E. S. Haldane and G. R. T. Ross, in *ibid.* (ed. R. M. Hutchins), p. 85.
[5] B. Willey, *The Seventeenth Century Background*, p. 87.

The importance of the 'superior' truth of mathematical symbols for universal language systems and for Hobbesian logic has already been noted. If the structure of things conforms with mathematically precise laws of the human mind, linguists will be tempted, once having assumed this conformity, to confine their analyses to the workings of the mind without reference to external reality. When this happens, the doctrine *Grammatica est de signis rerum* is restated as *Grammatica est de conceptibus*.

Given the importance of mental operations for Cartesian philosophy, it is no accident that the Port-Royal Logic (1662), which has been described as one of the most popular textbooks of all time,[1] should be subtitled *l'art de penser*.[2] This work, the manual of Cartesianism, the logic which Descartes could have written but did not, is the application of principles contained in Descartes' *Discours de la méthode*. Descartes condemned the traditional Aristotelian logics which presupposed a body of knowledge rather than being instruments of discovery, putting the emphasis on arrangement rather than invention. 'The end of study', he said, 'should be to direct the mind towards the enunciation of sound and correct judgments on all matters that come before it.'[3] In addition to being an *art de penser*, the Port-Royal Logic therefore also promises in its subtitle 'several new observations suitable for training the judgment', and declares that the true office of reason is to indicate the right ordering of things. It defines its subject-matter as 'those reflections which men have made concerning the principal operations of the mind', namely concept formation, judgment, reasoning, and the arrangement of things in due order.[4] The last operation may be termed *method*, a reminder of the extent to which contemporary philosophy and educational theory concerned themselves with methodology. As an illustration of this one need only recall the various Port-Royal Latin, Greek and vernacular grammars, each claiming to teach by a *Nouvelle Méthode*.

These four parts of the Port-Royal *Logic* bring to mind the Scholastic logicians' *inventio* and *dispositio*, and the Ramistic–Baconian treatment of logic under the four heads *invention, judgment,*

---

[1] v. W. S. Howell, *Logic and Rhetoric*, p. 343. There were eight London editions between 1664 and 1700.

[2] A. Arnauld and P. Nicole, *La Logique ou l'art de penser: Contenant . . . plusieurs observations nouvelles propres à former le jugement*, Paris, 1662.

[3] *Rules for the Direction of the Mind*, transl. E. S. Haldane and G. E. T. Ross, in R. M. Hutchins (ed.), *Great Books of the Western World*, p. 1.

[4] *Logique*, p. 27: 'concevoir, juger, raisonner, and ordonner'.

memory and *tradition*. The Port-Royal authors were however in reaction against Scholasticism and Ramistic logic, ridiculing the attempt to prescribe strict boundaries for the sciences,[1] and the resemblances are purely superficial. The mental operation of judging, treated in Part II of the Logic, deals with the joining together of mental concepts and with affirmations and denials concerning those concepts, i.e. with logical propositions. Part IV, dealing with the mental operation of disposition, has to do with the ordering of ideas and judgments. The end of true logic is the forming of the judgment, and if Aristotle's ten categories – though admitted to the Logic – do not meet with wholehearted approval, it is because they contribute little to that formation, leading men to prefer verbal formularies to a precise knowledge of things: '. . . most human errors . . . [are the result of] false judgments from which wrong conclusions are drawn. Those who up to now have treated logic have been little inclined to seek remedies to this, which is the chief subject of those new reflections which will be found throughout this book.'[2] The authors leave us in no doubt as to the source of these reflections. Some they admit to have taken from 'a celebrated Philosopher of this century' (i.e. Descartes), and yet others from an unpublished work by Pascal entitled *De l'esprit géometrique*. The result of their approach is that though the Logic answers to Descartes' require-ments in being a theory of enquiry rather than a theory of com-munication,[3] it inaugurates what W. and M. Kneale call the bad fashion of confusing logic with epistemology.[4] Its concern is know-ledge conveyed by mental concepts, and the making of judgments or propositions about that knowledge. The whole of the first part con-sists of 'reflections on ideas, or on the first operation of the mind, which is called conception', that is to say a consideration of the mind's workings in the formation of ideas and the attaching of words to them. The *Grammaire générale* in turn takes these 'opérations de nostre esprit' as its basis, and it too sees the first of these operations as the formation of mental concepts. There is thus a close parallelism between the *Logique* and the *Grammaire*, the former being a logic containing grammatical material, the latter a grammar based on

---

[1] v. the *Premier discours* prefacing the Logic. W. S. Howell remarks (*Logic and Rhetoric*, p. 342) that Ramus' revisions now seem little more than 'a scholasticism with certain redundancies eliminated . . . certain reorganizations effected'.

[2] *Logique* (4th ed., 1675), p. 15 (my translation).

[3] v. W. S. Howell, *Logic and Rhetoric*, p. 347.   [4] *The Development of Logic*, p. 316.

logical principles. Even more than in the case of Ramus' logic and grammar they should be read together, the one completing the other. For both, the 'operations of the mind' and the existence of mental concepts or ideas are basic.

Chomsky remarks that the notion *idea* in Cartesian thought is 'crucial but difficult', and takes the use of the term as representing 'essentially, an object of thought' as most consistent with Descartes' general usage. But he seems to regard the virtual identification of linguistic and mental processes as peculiar to Descartes and his school and at the opposite pole to anything Locke ever said. As a corrective, one has only to consider the Nominalistic rationalism of the following excerpts from Locke's *Essay*:

> The use . . . of Words, is to be sensible Marks of *Ideas*; and the *Ideas* they stand for, are their proper and immediate Signification. Words in their primary and immediate Signification, stand for nothing, but the *Ideas* in the Mind of him that uses them . . . [Words] are names of *Ideas* in the Mind . . .[1]

Locke, just as much as Descartes, is a mentalist, and as a source for the 'creative aspect of language use' he would have served Chomsky's turn just as well. Where he differs from Descartes is on the *origin* of ideas. Chomsky insists, as a basis for his theory, on positing *innate* mental forms pre-determining the act of linguistic creation, whereas Locke, as is well known, was the antagonist *par excellence* of belief in such forms. That only these *innate* forms provide for Chomsky a sufficient basis for creative language use is made quite clear in his *Cartesian Linguistics*:

> The study of the universal conditions that prescribe the form of any human language is 'grammaire générale'. Such universal conditions are not learned; rather, they provide the organizing principles that make language learning possible . . . By attributing such principles to the mind, *as an innate property*, it becomes possible to account for . . . the fact that a speaker of a language knows a great deal that he has not learned.[2]

Present-day universal grammarians are not inevitably mentalists, as witness J. Lyons' remark that linguistic science has already gone a long way towards developing 'a metalanguage adequate for the description of all languages in categories that are not "mentalist"'.[3] Several speakers at the 1961 conference on Language Universals

---

[1] Pp. 185, 228.
[2] P. 59 (my italics).　　　　　[3] *Structural Semantics*, p. 3.

held in New York, quoting Bloomfield's celebrated 'The only useful generalizations about language are inductive generalizations'[1] in support, went out of their way to stress that universals can be set up without any appeal to a mentalistic thesis. J. H. Greenberg lists no less than forty-five 'implicational universals' established by empirical observation, with such statements, tentatively advanced as universally valid, as that 'languages with dominant VSO order are always prepositional', or 'languages with dominant order VSO have the adjective after the noun'.[2] C. H. Hockett's contribution to the conference takes a similar approach, noting that every language has deictic elements, first and second person singular pronouns, or 'elements [*markers*] that denote nothing but make a difference in the composite forms in which they occur'. This approach leaves aside all question of grammatical meaning, and indeed Hockett vigorously castigates any such mentalist approach: 'The assumption that such elements must denote something . . . has generated much bad mentalist philosophizing, populating the universe with abstract entities or the human mind with concepts, both of which are as useless as the luminiferous ether.'[3] It was left to R. Jakobson to make a wry reference to 'the whimsical prejudice against "semantics-oriented definitions", which, strange as it seems, may have filtered even into our Conference on Language Universals',[4] and to U. Weinreich to reject definitions of linguistic meaning in terms of 'use in the language' or 'the transitional probabilities between words', in order that semantics might free itself from 'a misguided positivism insensitive to the specificities of language'.[5]

Since however universal grammar of the type posited by Chomsky seeks to discover, underlying the 'surface' structure of individual languages, a 'deep' structure common to all, it is obvious that it must assume the pre-existence of mental concepts, the same in all men, of which the formal items of given languages constitute the actualization. Any attempts to prove that mental concepts or predispositions,

[1] *Language*, p. 20.
[2] 'Some Universals of Grammar with Particular Reference to the Order of Meaning Elements', *Universals of Language* (ed. J. H. Greenberg), pp. 62, 67.
[3] 'The Problem of Universals in Language', *ibid.* (ed. J. H. Greenberg), pp. 16, 17.
[4] 'Implications of Language Universals for Linguistics', *ibid.* (ed. J. H. Greenberg), p. 214.
[5] 'On the Semantic Structure of Language', *ibid.* (ed. J. H. Greenberg), p. 153. Weinreich adds that 'Bloomfield's neurological "reductionism" . . . misses the properly linguistic, "autonomous" structuring of man-made semantic systems.'

or at any rate some of them, are already present in the mind from birth, identical in every human being, is likely to have considerable interest for such a theory. In linking his own approach with certain features of the *Grammaire générale* and with Cartesian thought, Chomsky was anxious to prove that behind the creative mechanisms of generative grammar there lie inborn principles in the mind, common to all speakers, which predetermine the patterns those mechanisms will follow. In *Aspects of the Theory of Syntax* he contrasts the empiricist view of language acquisition, based on sense experience and induction, with that of Cartesian rationalism. Empiricism assumes a preliminary analysis of experience provided by 'peripheral processing mechanisms', the obtaining of knowledge being the result of the application of inductive techniques to the experience thus acquired. The Rationalist approach by contrast, according to Chomsky, holds that there are already present in the mind 'innate ideas and principles', which upon 'appropriate stimulation' determine the form the acquired knowledge will take.[1] Such a viewpoint is of course anathema to most present-day descriptive linguists, whose discovery processes are based on inductive, empirical methods, eschewing any mentalistic approach. For those however who consider Chomsky's suggestions worth pursuing, they raise three questions: (1) Is there any evidence in linguistic history that this concept of *innate* ideas was ever applied to grammatical theory? (2) Is it so applied by the *Grammaire générale*? and (3) Is it, as Chomsky implies, a necessary condition of universal grammar? To none of these questions does an affirmative answer seem possible. Chomsky's point of departure is various indications by Descartes, in particular this passage from his *Notes Directed Against a Certain Programme* (1647):

No ideas of things . . . are presented to us by the senses . . . in our ideas there is nothing which was not innate in the mind . . . except only those circumstances which point to experience – the fact, for instance, that we judge this or that idea, which we now have present to our thought, is to be referred to a certain extraneous thing, not that these extraneous things transmitted the ideas themselves to our minds through the organs of sense, but because they transmitted something which gave the mind occasion to form these ideas, by means of an innate faculty.[2]

---

[1] *Aspects of the Theory of Syntax*, pp. 47–8.

[2] Cited in *Cartesian Linguistics*, p. 67, from E. S. Haldane and G. T. Ross's translation in *The Philosophical Works of Descartes*, vol. i, New York, 1955.

Since this Cartesian doctrine determines Chomsky's attitude to the Port-Royal Grammar and to universal grammar in general, and since his interpretation of Descartes and of 'Cartesian linguistics' has exposed him to some severe criticism from various quarters, it will be appropriate to consider here some of the issues involved.

To some extent, as R. H. Robins suggests,[1] the Sensualist–Rationalist quarrel on this point is a matter of terminology rather than of basic difference, certain features of Locke's doctrine for instance providing parallels to the Rationalist thesis that the 'operations of the mind' are not directly due to sense experience. The debate really turns on the question of whether these operations are determined by an *innate* faculty. Apart from that particular question the two approaches, Sensualist and Rationalist, are united in medieval Thomistic philosophy, a source from which each separately flows. Thomistic epistemology was of course based on the ultimately Aristotelian doctrine of the obtaining of knowledge through the senses, on the dictum *Nihil est in intellectu quod non prius in sensu*, and the medieval debate centred on the correspondence between sense perceptions and the external world. For Thomists, the mind *must* derive its ideas from external phenomena via the senses, for left to itself it would be a blank sheet, a *tabula rasa*.[2] These two terms however, the passive receptive mind and the external objects indicated by sense impressions, are by themselves powerless to produce knowledge. For this a particular faculty of the mind is brought into play, 'an active virtue which renders the intelligible, contained potentially in sensible reality, actually intelligible'.[3] This creative power in the mind is called the active intellect, the *intellectus agens*. While Nominalists doubted whether this cooperation between sense perception and active intellect could in fact ever give us true knowledge of the universe, the Thomistic Realists held that the mind is by its very nature disposed to attain reality – *in cujus natura est ut rebus conformatur*.[4] This predisposition to the obtaining of sure knowledge was not however based on the Platonic doctrine of ideas as realities

---

[1] *Short History*, p. 112.

[2] Thomas Aquinas, *Summa Theologica*, I^a, q. 79, art. 2.

[3] E. Gilson, *The Philosophy of St Thomas Aquinas*, p. 191. v. also M. De Wulf, *Medieval Philosophy*, pp. 24–5. Cf. Scaliger's description (*De causis*, cap. lxvi) of the genesis of the word *horse*: 'Equi speciem ab equo eductam intellectus agens in intellectum possibilem impressit.'

[4] Thomas Aquinas, *De veritate*, q. 1, art. 9.

subsisting in the nature of things. E. Gilson expresses this doctrine as follows:

According to Plato, the human soul possesses a natural and innate knowledge of all things . . . everyone possesses the knowledge of things even before acquiring knowledge; and this amounts to asserting that the soul knows all . . . by innate species, naturally possessed by it.[1]

Though Thomism too speaks of species in the soul, it is clear that it does not mean by them *innate* species. 'Far from possessing innate knowledge, [the soul] is rather at first in potency in respect to all intelligibles',[2] and the *intellectus agens* abstracts from things themselves the intelligible species which it needs in order to attain to knowledge. For the Schoolmen this process has a passive aspect, the *species impressae* imprinted on the mind by sense perception, and an active one, the *species expressae* resulting from the intervention of the active intellect. It is interesting to note that the germs of knowledge are in the intellect itself, as preexistent *scientiarum semina* or *prima intelligibilium principia*, but these are not innate, but rather 'the first intelligibles which our intellect can reach in starting from sensible experience', known *per species a sensibilibus abstractas*.[3] This is ultimately based on Aristotle's doctrine that the soul achieves knowledge of things by receiving their forms or *species* into itself, which leads in turn to the notion of *natural signs* in the soul which, following indications in Aristotle's *De interpretatione*, were thought to be to some extent copies of external phenomena. These natural signs, which thanks to the influence of the Arab philosopher Avicenna (979–1037) came to be referred to in medieval epistemology as *intentiones*, could be combined into *propositiones mentales* which formed a veritable grammar of the soul.[4] Here we have yet another indication that medieval thought had established the dichotomy *verbum mentis* (internal discourse) and *verbum oris* (external discourse) centuries before Port-Royal's preoccupation with 'the operations of our minds' or any talk of 'deep' and 'surface' structure. William of Ockham defines the natural signs as those out of which the *propositio mentalis* is composed, in contrast to the *propositio vocalis* made up of formal phonetic elements. He calls the natural sign an *intentio*

---

[1] *Philosophy of St Thomas Aquinias*, p. 197.
[2] *Ibid.* p. 201.
[3] *Ibid.* p. 202.
[4] v. W. and M. Kneale, *The Development of Logic*, p. 228 and C. Prantl, *Geschichte der Logik im Abendlande*, IV, 109.

or *conceptus animae*.[1] It is this long medieval tradition that lies behind Scaliger's definition of the word as a 'nota unius speciei, quae est in animo'.

If carried to its extreme conclusions, naïve Realism, which requires an absolute one-to-one correspondence between reality and thought, leads to a view in which the consciousness contains a mirror-image of the external world. Its opposite, Idealism, the logical outcome of Nominalist theory, results in the attitude that we can only know 'the operations of our minds', our own subjective states. The great merit of Thomistic doctrine is that it steers a middle way between these extremes, requiring the intervention of a third factor, the *intellectus agens*, and holding that by its application the mind attains, not to a mere reflection of reality, but to an apprehension of it. In Gilson's words, it achieved a 'middle term between sensualism and Platonism . . . innate intellect without innate principles'.[2] In the seventeenth century however, certain authors are obviously assuming that these innate principles do in fact exist. The earliest of these is Lord Herbert of Cherbury, whose *De veritate*, first published in 1624, has been mentioned above. His acknowledged source is Stoic philosophy via Cicero.[3] He repeats the medieval view that there are certain 'principles or notions implanted in the mind', but although these *Common Notions* are 'stimulated' – again as in medieval doctrine – by objects perceived by the senses, 'no one, however wild his views, imagines that they are conveyed by objects themselves'.[4] These *notions* are something that we 'bring to objects from ourselves', and the question raises itself whether Herbert does not mean by them something analogous to the *intellectus agens* or the *prima intelligibilium principia* of Thomistic philosophy. He insists however that they are 'imprinted on the soul by the dictates of Nature itself' (cf. the 'natural signs in the soul' of medieval thought), and must be deemed to be not so much the outcome of experience as principles without which we should have no experience at all.[5] The Neo-Platonism in much of Herbert's work is evident, as in his assertion that the intellectual faculties can penetrate and influence

---

[1] *Summa totius logicae*, i. 12, cited by W. and M. Kneale, *Development of Logic*, p. 266.

[2] *Philosophy of Thomas Aquinas*, p. 203, note 27.

[3] v. *De veritate*, ed. M. H. Carré, p. 42, note 2.

[4] *Ibid.* p. 126. Cf. Leibniz, *Nouveaux essais sur l'entendement humain* (ed. E. Boutroux, Paris, 1886), p. 120: 'l'âme contient originairement les principes de plusieurs notions et doctrines, que les objets externes réveillent seulement dans les occasions'.

[5] *De veritate* (ed. Carré), pp. 132, 133.

the realm of sense perception, but the faculties of sense can never understand the domain of the intellect.[1] His cardinal tenet – 'I assert that the same faculties have been imprinted on the soul of every normal person'[2] – is of course grist to Chomsky's mill, and he culls from it and from his reading of Descartes the premise on which his claims for Cartesian theory are based:

That the principles of language and natural logic are known unconsciously and that they are in large measure a precondition for language acquisition rather than a matter of 'institution' or 'training' is the general presupposition of Cartesian linguistics.[3]

Chomsky need not however have confined himself to Descartes and Herbert, for in addition to Ramus' assumption of a 'natural logic' of the mind, we have Comenius' expansion of the theory of innate ideas:

. . . all men have innate Principles of three kinds, matching the necessities of all kinds of action, [namely] knowing, willing, and achieving. In every man there are innate Norms of knowledge, which are called *Common Notions*, and the Stimuli of Desire, which we name *Common Instincts*; and the organs for doing everything, which it may be permissible to call *Common Faculties* . . . Hitherto philosophers have spoken only of *Common Notions*.[4]

This positing of cognitive instincts on the same level as the affective and conative ones is just the kind of thing Chomsky is seeking. It is precisely because Comenius finds it 'evident that all men are necessarily united in these roots of Human General Intelligence' that he is able to frame his *pansophia*, a 'single and comprehensive scheme of Human Omni-Science'.

The topic of innate ideas, though expressed in terms of *common notions*, was thus already being aired before and contemporaneously with the publication of Descartes' writings, and indeed there are striking parallels between his treatment of Common Notions or Axioms[5] and Herbert's approach. But for Descartes not all ideas are innate, some being 'adventitious', and yet others seeming to be

[1] *Ibid.* pp. 30–1.
[2] *Ibid.* pp. 78–9.
[3] *Cartesian Linguistics*, p. 63, v. also *Aspects of the Theory of Syntax*, p. 49.
[4] *Via lucis*, p. 6 (my italics). The MS of this work was circulated in England during Comenius' visit of 1641–42.
[5] Cf. Descartes' *Principia philosophiae*, xlix, where he refers to 'veritas quaedam aeterna, quae in mente nostra sedem habet, vocaturque communis notio, sive axioma'.

'formed (or invented) by myself'. Moreover, in reply to criticism he appears to have modified his stance:

I never wrote or concluded that the mind required innate ideas which were in some sort different from its faculty of thinking; but when I observed the existence in me of certain thoughts which proceeded, not from extraneous objects . . . but solely from the faculty of thinking which is within me, then that I might distinguish [them] . . . from other thoughts ADVENTITIOUS or FACTITIOUS, I termed them INNATE. In the same sense we may say that in some families generosity is innate, in others certain diseases like gout or gravel . . . because they are born with a certain disposition or propensity for contracting them.[1]

The fact remains that there are for Descartes ideas, innate or not, which proceed, in contradiction of Scholastic philosophy, 'solely from the faculty of thinking that is in me'. H. Aarsleff notes[2] that these 'dispositions or propensities' appear to be insufficient for Chomsky who requires, in order to buttress his theory of language acquisition, the full postulate of innateness, a 'deep structure' of concepts already existent in the mind rather than a mere predisposition to acquire them.

It should be noted that even an out-and-out Sensualist such as Hobbes equally believes in the existence of mental concepts. Where he differs from Descartes and Herbert is in being unable to accept any origin for them other than sense perception. Though names are 'signs of our conceptions' and manifestly not 'signs of the things themselves',[3] it none the less remains true that 'there is no conception in a man's mind, which hath not at first . . . been begotten upon the organs of sense'.[4] All concepts are explained on a sensual basis, memory for instance being nothing other than an 'after-image on the retina, on a par with imagination, which is simply 'decaying sense'.[5] Hobbes' acquaintance with the Mersenne circle during his third visit to the continent in 1634–37 hardly seems to have influenced his ideas on this matter. In the work of Locke we find however a modification of the extreme Sensualist position which may well owe something to his years in France between 1675 and 1679, when he read the Port-Royal Grammar and Logic and no doubt acquainted himself more closely with the theories of Descartes.

---

[1] *Notes Directed Against a Certain Programme*, in *The Philosophical Works of Descartes*, transl. E. S. Haldane and G. R. T. Ross, vol. I, Cambridge, 1967, p. 442.

[2] 'The History of Linguistics and Professor Chomsky', p. 582.

[3] *Elements of Philosophy: I. Concerning Body*, in *English Works* (ed. W. Molesworth), I, 17.

[4] *Leviathan* (Part I, *Of Man*), in *ibid*. III, 1.   [5] *Ibid*. III, 5–6.

Locke is none the less firmly of the opinion that there are no innate principles in the mind, no 'primary Notions . . . Characters, as it were stamped upon the Mind of Man, which the Soul receives in its very first Being'. He believes, on the contrary, that 'Men, by the use of their natural Faculties, may attain to all the Knowledge they have, without the help of any innate Impressions'.[1] He seems to sell the pass however with his admission that the mind, though technically a *tabula rasa*, brings 'natural Faculties' (analogous to the medieval *intellectus agens*?) to bear on sense impressions in order to attain knowledge: '. . . this ready Assent of the Mind to some Truths, depends not either on native Inscription [i.e. innate ideas] nor the *Use of Reason*; but on a Faculty of the Mind, quite distinct from both of them . . .'[2] Locke is rooted in Bacon, that is to say he derives all knowledge from experience, from observation. But observation is of two kinds, that of 'external, sensible Objects', which Locke calls Sensation, and that of the mind's own 'internal Operations', which he calls Reflection. The latter, which equally with Sensation is based on experience, furnishes the understanding with a 'sett of *Ideas*, which could not be had from things without', such as *perception, reasoning, willing* and 'all the different actings of our own Minds'. Here Locke's theory rejoins Descartes' 'thoughts which proceed solely from the faculty of thinking which is within me', yet as a Sensualist he cannot bring himself to divorce these ideas completely from his sense-based system. Their source, 'though it be not Sense . . . yet it is very like it, and might properly enough be call'd internal Sense.'[3] H. Aarsleff points out that Locke never assumed that 'reason and its manifestation in reflection were not innate', but held on the contrary that 'Man is by nature [i.e. innately] rational.'[4] What Locke has in mind seems to be more or less that 'innate intellect without innate principles' which was posited by Thomism. The real point of interest is however Locke's admission, in common with Descartes and the Port-Royalists, of 'operations of our minds within'.

As Locke defended the Baconian, so did Leibniz defend the Cartesian thesis, though his influence came too late to have any marked effect on seventeenth-century theory, and his Locke-inspired *Nouveaux essais sur l'entendement humain*, written by 1704, were

[1] *Essay*, Bk I, chap. ii, p. 4.   [2] *Ibid*. Bk I, chap. ii, p. 7.
[3] *Ibid*. Bk II, pp. 37–8.
[4] 'The History of Linguistics and Professor Chomsky', p. 576 (Aarsleff's brackets).

not published until 1765. It would therefore be inappropriate to devote much space to him, were it not that here again Chomsky has used the type of argument advanced by Leibniz in an attempt to prove his point:

> . . . empiricist speculation has characteristically assumed that only the procedures and mechanisms for the acquisition of knowledge constitute an innate property of the mind . . . On the other hand, rationalist speculation has assumed that *the general form of a system of knowledge is fixed in advance as a disposition of the mind*, and the function of experience is to cause this general schematic structure to be realized and more fully differentiated.[1]

No one illustrates better than Leibniz, with his celebrated simile of the statue of Hercules, what Chomsky has in mind in the phrase italicized above. For him the innate dispositions of the mind are as it were veins in a block of marble, so arranged that the stone is 'predetermined' for the production of one particular statue – of, say, Hercules – rather than another. It is in this sense that he conceives ideas to be 'innate to us, as inclinations, dispositions, habits or natural virtualities'.[2] One may note that although in his *Posterior Analytics* Aristotle rejected innate ideas, his ἕξεις or dispositions of the soul with a *potentiality* for knowledge come none the less close to Leibniz' view, though the latter thought of his approach as Platonic and of Locke's as Aristotelian.[3]

Whether the various authors cited above accept or reject the doctrine of innate ideas, they all have in common a mentalistic belief in the presence in the mind of concepts whose existence precedes that of the words found to express them. In this matter the Port-Royal Grammar and Logic are indeed 'Cartesian', though as we have seen much of Descartes' doctrine of ideas is not uniquely his. The Logic defines mental conception as 'simply the view we have of the things that present themselves to our minds'.[4] Concepts, if clearly perceived, convey the truth, whereas the words which express them cannot be relied upon. Empiricism and Rationalism alike end up in a distrust of words. Since we hardly ever perceive a concept so clearly that we can separate it from the words that clothe it, Descartes condemns Scholasticism's faith in verbal formularies and – it is an old seventeenth-century complaint – regrets that men pay more

---

[1] *Aspects of the Theory of Syntax*, pp. 51–2 (my italics).
[2] *Nouveaux essais sur l'entendement humain*, ed. E. Boutroux, p. 125.
[3] *Ibid.* pp. 118–19.
[4] 1662 ed. p. 27 (my translation).

attention to *words* than to *things*. Neither words nor things enjoy the confidence of the authors of the Logic. The only matters in which they place complete faith are the conception one has of one's own self as 'une chose qui pense', and the consciousness of the workings of one's own thoughts. Knowledge of the external world comes solely through the mediation of the ideas in the mind.[1] As for the view that knowledge is obtained via the senses, the authors do not hesitate to call it *très absurde* and contrary to both religion and true philosophy. Their definition of the *idea* quite plainly stems from that given in Descartes' *Meditations*: 'Of my thoughts some are . . . images of the things, and to these alone is the title "idea" properly applied . . . But other thoughts possess other forms as well . . . and of the thoughts of this kind some are called volitions or affections, and others judgments'.[2] An *idea* then, for the Port-Royal Logic, is 'everything that is in our minds, when we can say with truth that we have a conception of a thing'.[3] This is none other than the *adaequatio rei et intellectus* of the Thomists. When the mind is focused clearly on its object, the resulting concept must correspond to reality: *conceptus significat rem*. Thus, when the *Grammaire générale* sets up its broad dichotomy between 'the objects of our thoughts' and 'the manner in which they are signified', it is no longer making the typical seventeenth-century distinction between *things* and the *modes* of those things, but is replacing it by one between *concepts* and the manner in which the thought process organizes those concepts. If I have spent some time in considering the contemporary preoccupation with *ideas in the mind*, it is not solely because Chomsky has interested himself in the question, but because the Port-Royal Grammar is a grammar not of words, but of concepts.

This emphasis placed on concepts has led some linguists to regard the *Grammaire générale* as reintroducing the medieval doctrine of the linguistic sign.[4] J.-C. Chevalier, noting that the central problem turns upon the nature of the sign, sees the Port-Royalists as approaching this problem 'by taking up once more the medieval concep-

---

[1] *Ibid.* p. 31: '. . . nous ne pouvons avoir aucune connoissance de ce qui est hors de nous que par l'entremise des idées qui sont en nous . . .'

[2] *Meditations on the First Philosophy* (*Meditation* III), transl. E. S. Haldane and G. R. T. Ross, in R. M. Hutchins (ed.), *Great Books of the Western World*, pp. 82–3.

[3] 1662 ed. p. 35 (my translation).

[4] cf. *Grammaire générale*, p. 27: 'Ainsi l'on peut définir les mots, des sons distincts & articulez dont les hommes ont fait des signes pour signifier leurs pensées'.

tion'.[1] Before him, L. Kukenheim had assumed a continuity of tradition with the *Grammatica speculativa*, seeing the Port-Royal Grammar as a link between medieval and modern (Saussurean) theories of the sign:

> The indisputable merit of these speculations is that they foreshadow some very modern problems in which the Scholastic formula 'vox significat mediantibus conceptibus' once again makes its appearance . . . Thus Scholasticism, via Descartes and Port-Royal, links up with the most modern linguistics.[2]

One may recall at this point that medieval grammarians saw signification as a process involving three terms: the external object, the mediatory concept, and the word with its twin facets of meaning and phonetic form. It is neither the phonetic form or *vox* as such, nor the concept as such, that are the province of the grammarian, but the *signum* made up of both: *Grammatica est de signis rerum*.[3] With its 'virtual identification of linguistic and mental processes' the *Grammaire générale*, in this matter the heir to a long seventeenth-century process of semasiologically-orientated development and at the opposite pole to Ramus, seems to lose sight altogether of the *vox* or formal component of the word.[4] Whereas Ramus and present-day descriptive linguists ban from their analyses all reference to the semantic component of the linguistic sign, the *Grammaire générale* finally, taking seventeenth-century trends to their logical conclusion, lets fall the formal element. *Vox significat mediantibus conceptibus* – the formally determined word signifies the thing by means of intermediary concepts – has been replaced by *Vox significat conceptum*, that is to say, in a system where *vox* and *conceptus* are in practice interchangeable terms, *Conceptus significat*. This is not a naïve criticism of the *Grammaire générale*, which as a mentalistically-based universal grammar is obliged to operate on the level of concepts. It is simply to point out how mistaken are those who regard Port-Royal doctrine as a return to the medieval conception of the linguistic sign.

There is however a further, and more trenchant difference between Port-Royalist and medieval theories of signification. The *Grammatica speculativa*, in a doctrine stemming from Aristotle, sees each part of speech as consisting of *dictio* plus *consignificatio*, of a

---

[1] *Histoire de la syntaxe*, p. 496.   [2] *Esquisse*, pp. 15–16 (my translation).
[3] *Grammatica speculativa*, cap. vi.
[4] True, the *Grammaire générale* has a preliminary section dealing with letters and sounds, but these formal elements are not integrated into its doctrine of the linguistic sign.

lexical element (*ratio consignificandi*) and a consignified grammatical element (*ratio consignificandi* or *modus significandi activus*). This *modus significandi activus*, consignifying a grammatical function, is not identical with Port-Royal's *manière de signifier*. The medieval linguistic sign, at word-class level, contains both a *significatio* and a *consignificatio*, catering for the word both as an item of lexis and as an active element in a syntactic structure. Modern semantics, in an approach which leads to an 'atomization' of meaning, has tended to concentrate on the former with an almost complete neglect of the latter:

> The most important works on semantics, such as Ullmann (1951)[1] ... are on the whole preoccupied with the one semiotic process of naming, i.e. with the use of designators in theoretical isolation; they pay relatively little attention to the combinatory semiotics of connected discourse.[2]

That is to say, as far as grammar is concerned, these works simply perpetuate the seventeenth-century interest in nomenclature. In accordance with this tradition the sign as envisaged by Saussurean linguistics – not without justice does Chomsky regard this approach as resulting in a mere 'systematic inventory of items'[3] – while appropriate to the *word*, does not take into account the *word-class* consignifying grammatical function. More in line with medieval concepts is Hjelmslev's conclusion, in discussing universal grammar, that every formal grammatical category has a semantic content. In his *Principes de grammaire générale* (1928)[4] he suggests a modification of de Saussure's diagram in which the sign would still include the two facets *signifié* and *signifiant*, but the latter would contain both an *image phonique* and an *image grammaticale*. An important medieval distinction, revived in Hjelmslev's treatment,[5] could thus easily be restored.[6]

---

[1] *The Principles of Semantics.*

[2] U. Weinreich, 'On the Semantic Structure of Language', *Universals of Language* (ed. J. H. Greenberg), p. 115.

[3] One may note here R. Godfrey's view ('Late Medieval Linguistic Meta-Theory and Chomsky's Syntactic Structures', *Word*, 21:2 (1965), pp. 255–6) that Thomas of Erfurt's description of the linguistic process 'agrees essentially with that of Saussure and, I believe, with the underlying theoretical basis that is more or less assumed by Chomsky'. De Saussure himself was at some pains to point out that his system did not constitute a 'nomenclature' (v. note 1 on p. 198 above).

[4] Pp. 115–16.

[5] v. also pp. 223–4 above.

[6] v. de Saussure's *Cours de linguistique générale* (5th ed.), p. 99. This proposed modification, besides its obvious debt to Hjelmslev, is the result of conversations with Dr John Gallup of Laval University, to whose wide knowledge of medieval philosophy and linguistics I have been more than once indebted.

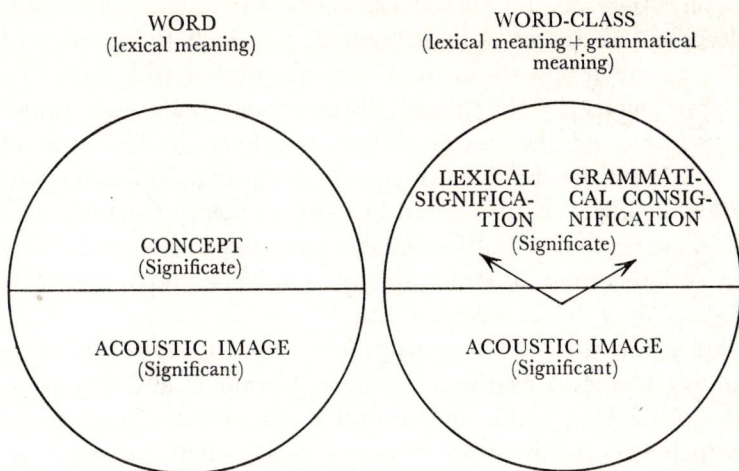

WORD
(lexical meaning)

WORD-CLASS
(lexical meaning + grammatical meaning)

CONCEPT
(Significate)

ACOUSTIC IMAGE
(Significant)

LEXICAL SIGNIFICA-TION
GRAMMATI-CAL CONSIG-NIFICATION
(Significate)

ACOUSTIC IMAGE
(Significant)

'Aliud est significare, aliud consignificare', as medieval grammarians do not tire of repeating. Here again the Port-Royal Grammar cannot be regarded as a continuation of medieval theory.

On a still more fundamental level, there is a further serious discrepancy between the medieval and the Port-Royal views of the process by which the mind apprehends phenomena and signifies them by means of language. The Modistic grammarians' point of departure, outside the mind and the linguistic system, lies in the *modi essendi*, the manner of being of things in the universe, the way they present themselves to the observer. These *modi essendi* are the remote causes of the actual embodiment of the linguistic process, with only a seeming parallel in the *objets de nos pensées* of the Port-Royal system. Medieval thinkers were however well aware that language does not directly mirror the universe, that the *modi signandi* and *modi significandi* are not the direct translation into linguistic terms of the *modi essendi*. What is actually conveyed by language is the mind's recreation of the universe it perceives, and it is here that the medieval tripartite system parts company with the bipartite one of the *Grammaire générale*. Between the existence of objects in the real world and their linguistic signification the *Grammatica speculativa* places an intermediate step, the mind's apprehension of those objects by means of the *modi intelligendi*. For the Port-Royal Grammar language has but one source, 'les objets de nos pensées', all else being 'manière de signifier'. The intermediate stage represented by the *modi intelligendi* – the *intellectus agens* or active intellect of Thomistic philosophy – is absent from its system, in which the mind simply observes its own operations. It is however precisely this element (cf. Locke's 'faculty of the mind' distinct from both any supposed innate ideas and the use of reason) which might have provided Chomsky with the creative principle he is seeking. Both behaviouristic Bloomfieldian linguistics and Port-Royal theory must necessarily remain barren and unfruitful without some recognition of the mind's intervention both in the structuring of its universe and in the creation and shaping of the linguistic system.

Here again then the Port-Royalists cannot be regarded as perpetuating medieval tradition. Scaliger, Caramuel and Campanella were still working within that tradition. The *Grammaire générale*, far from being a link between medieval and modern conceptions of language, represents a decisive break with the past. Nor can its ordering of the word-classes be categorized as wholly representing a return to Aristotelian conceptions.[1] Following the Port-Royal Logic, it sets out from the premise that – setting aside disposition, which is a procedure of logic – there are three 'operations of the mind': the forming of concepts, the action of the mind in judging, and the use of reason. Using these mental operations as the basis for the ordering of the word-classes, the authors make a binary distinction which differs from the Aristotelian dichotomy of semantically independent noun and verb and semantically dependent *syncategoremata*. On the one side they range those word-classes which result from the first operation and signify 'the objects of our thoughts'; on the other those classes which depend on the second operation and signify 'the form and manner of our thoughts'.[2] The former are noun, article, pronoun, participle, preposition and adverb; the latter verb, conjunction, and interjection. Both the substance of things and the manner in which they present themselves to us are 'objects of our thoughts'. Following medieval and much Humanist practice, substances 'subsist by themselves' and are signified by nouns substantive. The Aristotelian basis of this is obvious,[3] and recalls the Port-Royal

[1] I. Poldauf, for instance ('Problems of English Grammar', p. 162), appears to think that the Port-Royal Grammar follows Aristotle in this matter.

[2] *Grammaire générale*, p. 30. For a penetrating criticism of the criteria underlying the Port-Royal dichotomy v. R. Donzé, *La Grammaire générale et raisonnée de Port-Royal*, pp. 62–5.

[3] G. Sahlin (*César Chesneau du Marsais*, p. 159) speaks of 'la notion cartésienne de substance' and seems to think it an original discovery of Descartes.

Logic's refusal to 'generally condemn' Aristotle, while at the same time remarking that his 'constraint' cannot much longer be endured.[1] In practice, the authors are in fact by no means ready to jettison Aristotle completely, for as a contemporary English writer noted, much of their logic 'must be own'd to be borrowed from *Aristotle*, only by cloathing old *Terms*, under new Ideas'.[2] The philosophical distinction between substance and accident underlying the 'first origin' of substantives and adjectives is however judged to be insufficient, and the authors add to it the medieval syntactic criterion which distinguishes substantives as able to 'subsist by themselves in discourse', and adjectives as those words whose *manière de signifier* consists in their being 'joined to other nouns in discourse'.[3] Here the *Grammaire générale* is simply following medieval precedent, and an impressive amount of Humanist and seventeenth-century practice. Apart from medieval examples, the definition of substantive and adjective in the philosophical terms of the signification of substance and accident had appeared as early as 1481 in Nebrija's *Introductiones Latinae*, and had been perpetuated by Melanchthon and Scaliger. The syntactic criterion alone appears in Linacre and Colet, while the combined philosophical and syntactic definition is to be found in both Campanella and Vossius, the latter specifically invoking Aristotle's authority for it.[4] The procedure is seen to be far from being original to the Port-Royal authors, and the difficulties they experience in its application are precisely those already encountered by the *Grammatica speculativa*. The syntactic criteria imply that a noun whose lexical signification is that of an accident should none the less be classified as a substantive if its *manière de signifier*, that is to say its grammatical behaviour, is that of a substantive. Conversely, words whose lexical meaning indicates a substance should notwithstanding be classed as adjectives if they are

---

[1] 1675 ed., p. 37.   [2] T. Baker, *Reflections upon Learning* (2nd ed., 1700), p. 51.
[3] *Grammaire générale*, pp. 30–1.
[4] The syntactic criteria repose of course in the final analysis on the philosophical ones, the medieval syntactic *modus per se stantis* being a *modus determinati secundum essentiam*, while the *modus adjacentis* is a *modus inhaerentis alteri secundum esse*. In his interesting article on parallels between the *Grammaire générale* and modern linguistic theory ('Die Bedeutung der *Grammaire générale et raisonnée* – bekannt als Grammatik von Port-Royal – für die heutige Sprachwissenschaft', *Indogermanische Forschungen*, 72 (1967), pp. 6–7), H. E. Brekle notes that Lancelot transfers the substance–accident philosophical category to the syntactic level, without however noting medieval precedent. On p. 21 he similarly points out that the *Grammaire générale* has important methodological parallels with modern linguistic theory, but does not raise the question of what it owes to previous tradition.

syntactically dependent. In medieval grammar, difficulties arose with words like *rationalis*, which though signifying substance appear in syntactic congruence with other substantives,[1] and over those words such as *rex*, originally adjectival in meaning, which behave grammatically as substantives. Here may also be included those words (*filius*, etc.) which ancient tradition counted as adjectival on the grounds that they imply a dependent relationship.[2] These difficulties originate in the lack of a clear distinction between semantic and formal criteria, and between lexical and grammatical meaning, the *Grammatica speculativa* classing *rationalis* as a substantive simply because it regards it as identical in meaning with *homo*.

In an attempt to resolve these problems, the *Grammaire générale* has recourse to the medieval distinction between denotation and connotation. The word *rouge* clearly denotes redness, but connotes imprecisely ('confusément') *what it is* that is red. It cannot therefore stand alone, for *what it is* that is red cannot be clearly known without the addition of a substantive either expressed or understood. When this vague connotation is removed from the adjective it becomes a substantive, *rouge* becoming *rougeur*. Conversely, if the 'connotation ou signification confuse d'une chose' be added to substantives they become adjectives, *homme* becoming *humain*. If the adjective *humain* is in its turn deprived of connotation, the result is the substantive *humanité*. Since the authors' concern is those mental concepts deemed to underlie the grammars of all individual languages, they pay no attention to accompanying changes in form. The notion of connotation leads to the attribution of two significations to the adjective: 'the one distinct, which is that of the form [i.e. accident]; the other imprecise, which is that of the subject [i.e. the philosophical subject in which the accident inheres]'. The 'subject' however, though imprecise, is signified directly (*in recto*), while the 'form', though distinct, is signified indirectly (*in obliquo*). The adjective *blanc* accordingly signifies its subject (that which has whiteness) directly but imprecisely, whereas it signifies whiteness itself indirectly but just as clearly as does the substantive *blancheur*.[3] By

---

[1] *Grammatica speculativa*, cap. x: 'congrue substantivis adjunguntur'.

[2] *Grammaire générale*, pp. 31–3. J. Lyons, *Structural Semantics*, p. 72, gives the name 'converse terms' to pairs such as *pater/filius* each term of which implies the other. For medieval thinkers, if *filius* connotes *pater*, equally *pater* connotes *filius*. To Thomas Aquinas' 'dominus consignificat servum' and 'servus consignificat dominum' (*De potentia*, Q. 9, art. 4, objection 13) one may compare Scaliger's 'Servus significat possessionem, & consignificat substantiam' (*De causis*, p. 259).   [3] *Grammaire générale*, pp. 31–2.

philosophical arguments such as these the *Grammaire générale* arrives at that typically seventeenth-century bracketing of adjective with abstract substantive which has its roots far back in ancient definitions of the noun in terms of *substantia* and *qualitas*.[1]

The most immediate grammatical source of the Port-Royal doctrine that the adjective signifies the accident but connotes the substance of its substantive is Scaliger: 'Adiectiva enim *significant accidens*, et modum quo inhaeret substantiae: quare aliqua ratione *ipsam connotant substantiam*.'[2] The theory of connotation – used also in Nebrija's *Introductiones Latinae* of 1481 – had however long been a theme of logic, and is found in William of Ockham's treatment of *termini connotativi* or concepts whose meaning is susceptible to an analysis of the type *white = that which has whiteness*, or *Socrates is white* = the two propositions *Socrates is* and *whiteness inheres in Socrates*.[3] The exact parallel in logic to the Port-Royal theory is found in Ockham's *Quodlibeta*: 'The connotative noun properly signifies one thing primarily and another secondarily, one thing directly and another indirectly . . . An example is this concept white . . . It signifies its subject directly, and whiteness indirectly.'[4] It follows that the Port-Royal Logic is doing nothing new when it calls adjectives *termes connotatifs*. Even in applying these logical procedures to grammar the authors are by no means the first in the field. Apart from the early example of Nebrija, Scaliger had applied the notion of connotation to the adjective, and Campanella's treatment of the pronoun involves the logical concepts of signification *in recto* and *in obliquo*. The theory is less clearly set out in the *Grammaire générale* than in the Logic, whose linguistic analyses are not infrequently bolder and more striking than the relatively hesitant treatment in the Grammar. Regarding accident as a 'manner or mode' which modifies a thing, the Logic defines adjectives as follows: 'Those nouns which signify things as modified, marking primarily and directly the thing though more imprecisely; and indirectly the mode though more distinctly, are called adjectives or connotatives . . .'[5] Substantives such as *chaleur* and *justice*, on the other hand, 'signify primarily and directly the modes'. The analysis by

---

[1] v. above, pp. 37–8.
[2] *De causis*, cap. xcvii (my italics).
[3] v. C. Prantl, *Geschichte der Logik im Abendlande*, III, p. 386.
[4] V, Quaestio xxv (my translation).
[5] *Logique* (1675 ed.), p. 55 (my translation).

which the Logic explains the genesis of the abstract noun is worth quoting in full:

It must be noted that since the mind is accustomed to knowing most things as modified, because it hardly knows them other than through those accidents or qualities which strike the senses, it often divides the substance . . . into two ideas, of which it regards one as [philosophical] subject and the other as mode . . . Thus man is often considered to be the subject of humanity, *habens humanitatem*, and consequently as a thing modified.

And then that essential attribute which is the thing itself is treated as a mode, because it is conceived as being in a subject.[1]

It may be noted in passing that the idea that *homo* = *habens humanitatem* is precisely that of Campanella, who similarly treats the matter in terms of connotation, but on the basis that *esse* connotes *habere*: *esse homo* = *habere humanitatem*. It is analyses like this that permit the *Grammaire générale* to form its semantic equations *rouge* minus the connotation of the subject = *rougeur*, and *homme* plus the connotation of the subject = *humain*. Its cursory indications need to be completed not only by the *Nouvelle Méthode latine*, but also by reference to the Logic. The problem of those words (*roi, philosophe, soldat*) adjectival in meaning but grammatically substantives remains however intact, and the authors treat them as adjectives signifying accident and referring to a subject in which that accident inheres.[2] Their theory of adjective and substantive contributes little that cannot be found in earlier grammatical theory. The medieval treatment of substantive and adjective as categories partially congruent with the philosophical notions of substance and accident, the widespread seventeenth-century placing of adjective and abstract noun on the same footing as significations of *qualitas*, the idea of the adjective's connotation of substance – all of these are established points of doctrine. In the face of all this, it is impossible to agree with those who see the Port-Royal authors as brilliant originators, with for example I. Poldauf's view that, having rediscovered certain syntactic criteria via Aristotelian notions of substance and accident, they 'gave here the first, but

[1] *Ibid.* p. 55 (my translation).

[2] *Grammaire générale*, p. 33. Cf. R. Donzé's view (*La Grammaire générale et raisonnée de Port-Royal*, p. 67) of the Port-Royal theory of the noun as 'une belle illustration des erreurs auxquelles l'analyse conceptuelle conduit le grammairien'. Campanella (*Grammatica*, p. 21) sets up two classes of adjective, 'alterum substantiale, solaque voce adiectivum, ut *Rationale*, et *humanum* . . . Aliud accidentale, voce et re Adiectivum'.

decisive, impulse to the grammatical theorists'.[1] All they did, to repeat Thomas Baker's words, was to 'clothe old terms, under new ideas'. So many details of the *Grammaire générale* have been seized upon by linguistic historians as being original to Port-Royal theory, or as representing a completely new departure. Thus M. H. Jellinek[2] ascribes to it the merit of first perceiving that gender agreement is merely a formal syntactic device to 'rendre le discours moins confus'.[3] This idea goes back however to Sanctius' remark that adjectives are genderless,[4] having formal *terminationes ad genera* solely in order to facilitate syntactic congruence. Most commentators on the *Grammaire générale* (1) have not read the *Nouvelle Méthode latine* with its admitted debt to Sanctius and (2) have not read Sanctius.

The Port-Royal authors' treatment of case as expressible by a *particule* plus a noun belongs more especially to the consideration of vernacular grammar, as does their treatment of the article. Their approach to case underlines however their preoccupation with mental concepts common to all languages which are variously actualized in the 'surface structure' of individual languages. Of similar interest as an illustration of deep and surface structure is the function attributed to the relative pronoun of joining one proposition with another. By previous grammarians the word *quod* linking two clauses had been variously held to be relative pronoun, conjunction, or adverb. The *Grammaire générale* defines it as a relative 'stripped of its pronominal usage and retaining only its other usage of uniting the proposition in which it stands to another one'.[5] Thus is introduced the theory of the subordinate clause or *proposition incidente*, which can 'form part of the subject or attribute of another proposition, which may be called the principal one'.[6] It is in this discussion that it becomes particularly obvious that the *Grammaire générale* presupposes in its readers a knowledge of the Port-Royal Latin grammar. The view of the relative as linking two propositions around a single noun only makes complete sense if the illustration in that grammar –

[1] 'Problems of English Grammar', p. 162.

[2] *Geschichte*, ii, 186.

[3] *Grammaire générale*, p. 49.

[4] 'Nullius generis.' But behind Sanctius' treatment there lies Thomas of Erfurt's statement (*Grammatica speculativa*, cap. xvi) that adjectives 'genus non habent ex proprietate suae rei subiectae, sed ex proprietate rei substantivi nominis'.

[5] *Grammaire générale*, pp. 72–3.

[6] *Ibid.* p. 69. J.-C. Chevalier, *Syntaxe*, p. 503, is mistaken in thinking that this analysis first appears in the 1664 edition.

Est pater quem patrem amo - is borne in mind.[1] It is important, as R. Lakoff points out, that the exact details of the 'deep structure' be established: 'If one cannot assume that the antecedent is logically present, at some level of the grammar, both in the main clause and in the relative clause, it will be impossible to establish the second claim, that the relative clause serves as a connection between a main and a subordinate proposition.'[2] The authors' celebrated example *Dieu invisible a créé le monde visible*, containing the three underlying judgments (1) *Dieu est invisible*, (2) *il a créé le monde*, and (3) *le monde est visible*, where the second is the main clause and the other two are subordinate clauses or 'propositions incidentes', can be rewritten as the deep structure *Dieu qui est invisible a créé le monde qui est visible*.[3] The authors remark that the subordinate clauses are represented 'in our minds, without being expressed by words', a statement which Chomsky naturally seizes upon. But without a further expansion of the type proposed in the Latin grammar – *Dieu, lequel Dieu est invisible, a créé le monde, lequel monde est visible* – a link in the exposition is missing. The *Grammaire générale* presupposes a reading of the *Nouvelle Méthode*. Understood in this way, the relative plays an important role in the reconstruction of elliptic phrases, with *urbs Roma* rewritten as *urbs quae est Roma*, or *canis currens* restated as *canis qui currit*.[4] Here again however, the Port-Royalists are not innovating, but merely repeating resolutions of the type *amans = qui amat* equally present in the pages of Caramuel. The concept of abbreviation is of course a cardinal one for universal grammar, as in the authors' treatment of case-marked words as abbreviated prepositional phrases, but there too they are simply formalizing a doctrine implicit in existing vernacular theory.

Since the *Grammaire générale* sees the adverb also as the surface structure abbreviation of a prepositional phrase in the deep structure, it is treated after the preposition, and both, being manifestations of the 'first operation of the mind', are discussed before the verb which is a feature of the 'second operation'. Adverbs and prepositions, which function on the level of concept formation, signify like the

---

[1] The illustration in the *Nouvelle Méthode* rests in turn on Sanctius' *Vidi hominem, qui homo disputat.*

[2] Review of the *Grammaire générale*, p. 351.

[3] *Grammaire générale*, pp. 68–9.

[4] *Ibid.* p. 69. For an interesting discussion of an awareness of deep as opposed to surface structure in the *Grammaire générale* v. H. E. Brekle, 'Die Bedeutung der *Grammaire générale* ... für die heutige Sprachwissenschaft', pp. 4–6, 11–12.

noun 'the objects of our thoughts'. Conjunctions, interjections and verbs, operating on the level of judgment, signify 'the form and manner of our thoughts'. Scaliger's distinction between noun and verb signifying *things* and adverb and conjunction signifying *modes of things*[1] thus becomes, on the mentalistic level of the *Grammaire générale*, a distinction between word-classes signifying *objects of thought* (i.e. mental concepts) and those signifying *modes of thought*. In the Port-Royal dichotomy the oppositions are however differently arranged, with the verb among those classes that signify modes.

Having considered those word-classes that signify 'the objects of our thoughts', the *Grammaire générale* turns to those that signify 'the manner of our thoughts'. Its treatment of the verb has obvious parallels with Aristotle, as when it states that language is used not merely to signify mental concepts but almost always in the form of a judgment concerning those concepts, an affirmation modelled on a logical proposition. *La terre est ronde* is a judgment containing two terms: a subject about which an affirmation is made, and an attribute constituting that affirmation. Linking these two terms – and here the authors have an obvious debt to Campanella – is the verb substantive, the copula.[2] Affirmation being the principal 'manner of our thoughts', the verb is defined in Aristotelian terms as 'a word whose chief use is to signify affirmation'.[3] Here we may note that though Ancient grammar did not view the proposition in terms of an affirmation, or of a logical utterance containing subject and predicate, Priscian distinguished 'secundum dialecticos' two primary parts of speech, noun and verb, for the logical reason that they are capable by themselves of making complete sense, and followed Aristotle in terming the remaining word-classes *syncategoremata* or *consignificantia*.[4] The Port-Royal Grammar has sometimes been thought to be the first to reintroduce the Aristotelian notion of the verb as predicating something about a subject, G. Sahlin for instance regarding this notion as almost completely forgotten by contemporary scholars.[5] It is however already present in Scaliger's view of the verb as signifying something added to the meaning of the noun,[6]

---

[1] *De causis*, cap. lxxv.

[2] *Grammaire générale*, pp. 28–9.

[3] *Ibid.* p. 90. Cf. Aristotle, *De interpretatione*, cap. 3: ἔστιν ἀεὶ τῶν καθ᾽ ἑτέρου λεγομένων σημεῖον.

[4] H. Keil, *Grammatici Latini*, II, 54.

[5] *César Chesneau du Marsais*, p. 297.

[6] *De causis*, cap. clxii: 'aliquid, quod significato nominis adjiciatur'.

and above all in his treatment of the copula as a 'nota coniunctionis' predicating a quality of the subject.[1] The Port-Royal verb – on the same grammatical footing as the conjunction – is similarly the essential link binding together the two terms of the proposition, a view which again is implicit in Caramuel's definition of the verb substantive as a *judicativa copula* joining the logical subject and predicate.

In the early editions of the *Nouvelle Méthode latine* it is possible to follow the evolution of Lancelot's thought concerning the verb. At first he simply repeated Vossius' definition in terms of the signification of being, acting, or undergoing an action, setting up the divisions active and passive on the grounds that *omnis motus aut actio aut passio est*, and noting Scaliger's treatment of the verb substantive as the root and foundation of all other verbs. In the eighth edition of 1681 however, Lancelot having in the meantime undergone the influence of the logician Arnauld, the notion of the signification of *actio* and *passio* (equally rejected by Scaliger)[2] is dismissed as being just as appropriate to certain nouns. Campanella's and Scaliger's Modistic view of the verb as signifying an *actum fluentem* or *res fluentes* is also not retained. It would be difficult to state with absolute certainty that the Port-Royal authors underwent the influence of Campanella, but it is not without interest that Lancelot's reason for rejecting the signification of *actio* and *passio* as the verb's essential function is precisely that which Campanella gives. The change in Lancelot's thought on the matter is illustrated by an important passage inserted into the 1681 edition:

The reasoning of these authors [Scaliger and Sanctius] . . . is simply the result of their not having sufficiently understood the essential nature of the verb, which is none other than the *indicating of an affirmation* . . . we can divide verbs into substantive and adjective. The verbs substantive are those which simply indicate an affirmation . . . The verbs adjective are those which in addition to the affirmation common to all verbs, contain yet another meaning peculiar to themselves; as *amo*, which is the same as *sum amans* . . .[3]

The division of verbs into substantive and adjective was doubtless known to the authors from their reading of Scholastic grammar and

---

[1] *Ibid.* cap, xc. v. p. 68 above.
[2] Though Scaliger rejects *actio* and *passio* from his definition, they play an important part in his discussion of the verb.
[3] p. 458, my translation). This resolution is made by Campanella.

logic. If not, they had a readily available source in Caramuel's *Grammatica audax*, which appeared ten years after the first edition of the *Nouvelle Méthode*, but preceded Lancelot's 1681 edition by a quarter of a century and the *Grammaire générale* by six years.

In any case, this view of the copula was obviously circulating independently at the time, for one may compare the minor grammatical status accorded to the verb in Dalgarno's *Ars signorum* (1661) and Wilkins' *Essay* (1668), neither of which presumably owes anything to Port-Royal theory or exerted an influence on it. What is however capital is that Wilkins acknowledges Campanella and Caramuel as his predecessors, which would suggest that they might be regarded as common sources of both the Royal Society and the Rationalist traditions in universal grammar. Certainly Lancelot's statement that the verb substantive merely indicates an affirmation recalls Dalgarno's expansion *amamus = nos sumus amantes = nos +* present tense + *ita amantes*, where the copula, a 'sign of an act of the mind in judging', can be replaced by the expression of affirmation *ita*. It is considerations such as these in the work of their predecessors and contemporaries – Caramuel's treatment of the verb substantive as a *judicativa copula* (a judgment-forming link), Wilkins' view of it as a consignifying particle 'essential in every compleat sentence' – that parallel or lead to the Port-Royal emphasis on judgment and affirmation, an emphasis which emerges with particular clarity from a reading of the logic:

We call judging that action of the mind by which, joining together various ideas, it affirms that one is the other, or denies that one is the other; as when, having the idea earth or the idea round, I affirm that the earth is round, or deny that it is round.[1]

Since the judgment or proposition – in the Logic the two terms are interchangeable – is indicated by the verb 'to be', it follows that every proposition must necessarily contain the three elements subject, verb substantive and predicate, that *Dieu existe* must be explicable as an abbreviation of *Dieu est existant*. One may suppose that without the precedent of the medieval doctrine of verbs adjective in Latin, it might well never have occurred to the Port-Royal authors to apply this analysis to the French verb. Following the Logic, the *Grammaire générale* defines the chief function of the verb as the indication of 'the link we make in our minds between the two terms of a proposition'.

---

[1] 1662 ed., p. 27 (my translation).

The only verb to retain its pristine simplicity as a signifier of affirmation 'without any difference of person or tense' is the verb substantive.[1] Of some importance here, in view of the Logic's definition of the proposition as the action of the mind in 'joining together various ideas', are again Scaliger's description of the copula as a *nota coniunctionis* and, even more striking, Campanella's treatment of it as devoid of tense and linking 'ideas, not things'.[2] The Port-Royalists' doctrine that the copula binds together 'the objects of our thoughts' (i.e. mental concepts) is quite patently not original to them. Nor is their verb adjective, which in addition to its affirmational component signifies, by changes in mood and inflection, the various 'movements of the soul'[3] – Priscian's *inclinationes animi*, which are indeed long-lived in grammar – an innovation, any more than the doctrine that the verb substantive in non-copulative use is itself a verb adjective, *sum* ('I exist') being resolvable into *sum ens*.[4] The parallels with Dalgarno, the roots of all this in medieval and Humanist theory, the importance as sources of Campanella,[5] Caramuel, and Scaliger, all this need not be laboured. The derivative nature of Port-Royal doctrine on these points has been sufficiently brought out. Even its supposed reintroduction into grammar of the Aristotelian proposition judging a matter as true or false[6] cannot be regarded as an innovation. It was of course no novelty in logic, as witness Thomas Wilson's definition of the proposition, in his *Rule of Reason* (1551), as 'a perfite sentence . . . signifying either a trewe thyng, or a false, without al ambiguitie, or doubtfulness'. In grammar, the first part of this requirement – that an *oratio* constitute a perfect sentence, Priscian's *sententia perfecta* – had been common currency since Dionysius Thrax. The second had already been adumbrated by Vossius' referring his readers to the *De interpretatione* for the 'true' definition of the proposition.

The Port-Royal authors' ultimately medieval approach treats the verb as an abbreviation, the surface manifestation of a deep structure

[1] *Grammaire générale*, p. 96.

[2] *Grammatica*, p. 50: 'notiones, non res'. Cf. Hobbes' definition of the proposition as 'a speech consisting of two names copulated'.

[3] *Grammaire générale*, pp. 90–1.

[4] *Ibid.* pp. 115–16.

[5] *Grammatica*, p. 102: 'Omnia verba resolvuntur in substantivum, *sum* . . . idem ergo valet, ego curro, quod ego sum currens.'

[6] Cf. Aristotle, *De interpretatione*, 4 (H. P. Cooke, *Organon*, p. 121): 'We call propositions those [sentences] only that have truth or falsity in them.'

containing subject, affirmation and attribute. Traditional expansions such as *curro* = *curro cursum* or *curro currere* are however rejected. Just as the adjective *candidus* signifies whiteness and additionally connotes a subject in which whiteness inheres, so the verb *curro* signifies running and additionally makes an affirmation. It follows that it is pleonastic to complete the verb by adding an infinitive or some other noun, for if *curro* implies *currere*, so equally does *candidus* imply *candor*.[1] The treatment of affirmation as a separate semantic component of the verb leads to an interesting analysis of the participle, which is regarded as an adjective equivalent to the verb minus affirmation: *sum amans* = *amo*; *sum amatus* = *amor*. Similarly, the infinitive functioning as a substantive is formed 'by abstraction' from the participial adjective in the same way as other substantives (e.g. *candor*) are formed from other adjectives. The reasoning is as follows:[2]

rubet = 'is red' (affirmation plus attribute, i.e. verb)

rubens = 'red' (verb *rubet* minus affirmation, i.e. adjective)

rubere = 'redness' (adjective *rubens* minus connotation, i.e. substantive).

Not since Campanella's *Grammatica* of 1638 had there been such a closely-reasoned examination of the *rationes* and *causae* underlying the parts of speech. It is a pity that the theoretical treatment in the *Grammaire générale* is so sketchy, reposing for questions of deep and surface structure on much fuller examples of phrase analysis in the *Nouvelle Méthode*, and elsewhere being either frankly derivative or not exploiting fully some fascinating insights.

The second sort of words signifying 'the form and manner of our thoughts' are the conjunctions, which again link mental concepts, carrying out 'the very operation itself of our minds', and include the word *non* as an indication of 'the judgment we make that one thing is not another'. The Latin enclitic particle *-ne* similarly marks a 'movement of the soul' – again we may note the attraction for mentalistic universal grammarians of the long-established tradition of the *inclinationes animi* – in making a judgment. (Hence the analysis of interrogative pronouns into a deep structure consisting of a lexical meaning plus the semantic component signified by this same particle.)[3] In not attributing lexical meaning to conjunctions, which are regarded as performing a purely grammatical function, Port-Royal

---

[1] *Grammaire générale*, pp. 119–20.   [2] *Ibid.* p. 96.
[3] *Ibid.* pp. 137–8.

is heir to a long tradition. Dionysius Thrax, in what is for him an unusually mentalistic definition, treats the conjunction as 'filling gaps in the interpretation', without however ascribing meaning to the word-class itself.[1] Many other early grammarians similarly refuse it independent meaning, Apollonius for example allowing it grammatical consignification, but not full lexical signification,[2] and his disciple Priscian having it consignify the *vis* or *ordinatio* of the word-classes it connects.[3] Finally the interjections, which a long and hallowed grammatical tradition had regarded as natural *voces* (i.e. not *dictiones* or words instituted by arbitrary convention) signifying an *affectum mentis*, are in the Port-Royal system similarly assigned the task of marking 'the movements of the soul'[4] and 'the form and manner of our thoughts'.

Syntax is dismissed in seven pages, of which two and a half treat of the 'figures of construction'. Given that what the authors have to say of real interest centres upon the proposition, it is paradoxical that this section of the grammar should be so slight. J.-C. Chevalier attributes this fact to their inability to exploit on the syntactic level the insights contained in the body of the work.[5] Here again however, one is ineluctably drawn back to the thesis that it is the Latin grammar that constitutes the best illustration of what is specifically *linguistic* in Port-Royal theory, the *Grammaire générale* being conceived as an accompanying explanatory manual. What is merely touched upon in the latter receives full treatment and illustration in the former.[6] But if one treats the *Nouvelle Méthode*, the *Grammaire générale* and the *Logique* as one grammatico-logical work in three volumes, the result is an imposing and coherent body of doctrine and practice. Much of it is however patently derivative, and the short syntax is no exception. The authors note for example that some languages indicate certain syntactic relationships by means of cases, while others use 'particles which take their place'. This leads a commentator such as I. Poldauf to claim that the Port-Royal Grammar 'gives the first impulse to Locke's concern with the various

---

[1] v. H. Steinthal, *Geschichte*, II, 211.
[2] συσσημαίνει, not σημαίνει. v. Steinthal, *ibid.* II, 323.
[3] H. Keil, *Grammatici Latini*, III, 93.
[4] *Grammaire générale*, p. 140. Cf. Donatus' 'Pars orationis significans mentis affectum voce incondita' (H. Keil, *Grammatici Latini*, IV, 366).
[5] *Histoire de la syntaxe*, p. 501.
[6] Cf. *inter alia* pp. 123 and 125 of the 2nd ed. (1664) of the *Grammaire générale*, where the reader is specifically referred to the *Nouvelle Méthode*.

ways of expressing relations'.[1] The *Grammaire générale* may well be Locke's immediate source, but the early grammarians of the vernacular had already illustrated this item of deep and surface structure analysis in their view of certain 'articles' (i.e. prepositions) as *signa casuum* with the same function as the Latin cases,[2] and Port-Royal doctrine is further anticipated in John Wallis' treatment of prepositions in his *Grammatica linguae Anglicanae* of 1653 – no doubt known to Locke – as 'communes affectiones' of substantives. Certainly, in his fifth edition of 1699, Wallis accused the Port-Royalists of imitating him, though their source could equally well be Campanella, who had already noted in 1638 that 'articles' in the vernacular perform precisely that grammatical function which is performed by case in the classical languages.[3] An interesting modern revival of the view of case relationships as present in the deep structure of analytical languages is represented by C. J. Fillmore's positing of a 'universal underlying set of caselike relations that play an essential role in determining syntactic and semantic relations in all languages'.[4] His contention that the notion 'case' is present in the base component of the grammar of every language, determining a 'universal system of deep-structure cases', and that work along the lines he suggests will result in 'a semantically justified syntactic theory',[5] is an indication of how far some present-day linguists have travelled on the road back to the approach of the Port-Royal Grammar and its precursors.

On the level of linguistic analysis, the Port-Royal grammars are derivative. The deep and surface structure treatment in the *Nouvelle Méthode* and the *Grammaire générale* has been conclusively shown to owe a debt to Sanctius and his followers, and most of the theoretical justification provided can be shown to go back to medieval tradition or its continuation in Scaliger, Caramuel and Campanella. The interest of a study of Port-Royal doctrine lies not however in the attempt to show that this or that detail goes back to Sanctius or other authors, but in the situating of the two grammars within a developing tradition which includes them. There *is* in this tradition a decisive movement of thought as compared with representative

[1] 'Problems of English Grammar', p. 159.
[2] Cf. e.g. Linacre's observation (*Rudimenta*, p. 39) that prepositions in the vernacular are *articuli sive notae* of case.
[3] *Grammatica*, pp. 34–5.
[4] E. Bach and R. T. Harms (eds.), *Universals in Linguistic Theory*, preface, p. vii.
[5] 'The Case for Case', *ibid.* pp. 2, 21, 88.

Humanist grammars of the sixteenth and seventeenth centuries, but it begins very early, has roots in medieval practice, and spreads with growing force from about 1540 onwards in the pages of Scaliger, Sanctius, Vossius, Campanella and Caramuel. The movement consists of a growing tendency to apply reason to grammatical analysis, to apply it at the level of the underlying linguistic system (*langue*) rather than at the level of discourse (*parole*), and to seek beneath the details of usage the reasoned framework of *ratio* and *causae*. The mistake has lain in regarding the *Grammaire générale* as inaugurating this movement, rather than simply forming part of it.[1] Its immediate contrast with usage-based grammars of the type produced by Vaugelas caused commentators to regard it, quite rightly, as a great advance on contemporary French vernacular grammars, but at the same time, quite wrongly, and as a result of their ignorance of the Latin tradition on which it rests, to treat it as the great original of eighteenth-century developments in general grammar and in the syntax of the proposition. Thus J.-C. Chevalier, though noting that the philosophical grammarians who preceded Port-Royal laid the foundations, credits the *Grammaire générale* with a 'completely new employment' of logic.

Before Port-Royal, for Chevalier, linguistic analysis takes place at the level of discourse. After Port-Royal, it operates on the level of the underlying logical content.[2] True if one considers only vernacular grammar, this view is too simple if set against the background of the preceding Latin tradition. As V. Salmon remarks, those who fail to take into account the whole intellectual content of developments in grammatical theory can be guilty of serious distortion. To speak, as Chevalier does, of the 'revolution' of Port-Royal insights concerning the underlying logical deep structure is to treat them as original when they simply form part of a developing tradition. It is also to ignore the whole semasiologically-biased trend of Humanist gram-

---

[1] For an example of the perpetuation of this fallacy in a history of linguistics one may cite M. Ivić's *Trends in Linguistics* (*Janua linguarum*, Series Minor XLII, The Hague, 1965), p. 31. Though he duly notes that the seventh-century grammatical tradition was 'permeated by the heritage of the past', the author none the less states that 'it was then, in fact [i.e. with the Port-Royal Grammar] that the rich tradition of normative grammar was initiated'.

[2] *Histoire de la syntaxe*, pp. 490–1, 499: 'jusque-là ... on raisonne au niveau du discours ... à partir de Port-Royal, on raisonne au niveau de la forme du contenu'. F. Brunot (*Histoire de la langue française des origines à 1900*, Paris, 1905–, vol. v, p. 55) similarly speaks of 'la nouveauté et la haute valeur des solutions proposées', solutions which he attributes to Arnauld.

mar, which readily regarded formally divergent structures as semantically identical. Chevalier is however right in seeing that by the late seventeenth century grammatical theory had reached a cross-roads. It had arrived at the point where it had to decide whether to continue with the inherited mixed formal-semasiological approach represented by one strand in grammar, whose analysis confined itself to surface structure, or to follow the path traced by Scaliger, Sanctius, Caramuel and Campanella, and transfer its attention decisively from *verbum oris* to *verbum mentis*, from external to internal discourse. The only other way open was the setting up of a thoroughgoing descriptive formalism of the type initiated by Ramus – a way which had found few adherents and which, by enclosing the analyst within the minutiae of formal features peculiar to a given language, would have led to linguistic nihilism. Here Chevalier's remark that languages are not reducible one to another by the ordinary procedures of formal grammar is indeed to the point. Turning their backs on formalism and on usage-based grammar, the Port-Royal authors found in logic the underlying principle they sought. It is however the contention of the present study that, far from being originators, they brought to the attention of a wider public notions which had been known to Latin scholars for a long time. These notions are that language is a rational phenomenon, whose underlying *ratio* can be stated, and whose *causae* are amenable to logical analysis. For long regarded as the Port-Royal contribution *par excellence* to grammatical theory, these assumptions are all pre-Cartesian, and demonstrably made by several of the Port-Royalists' predecessors, both medieval, Humanist and seventeenth-century, in the Latin tradition.[1]

---

[1] Stephen K. Land's *From Signs to Propositions: The Concept of Form in Eighteenth-Century Semantic Theory*, London, 1974, came to hand too late to be considered, but it perpetuates (p. 77) the erroneous view that Arnauld was the 'prime moving spirit [of the *Grammaire générale*] and may for the sake of verbal convenience be spoken of as sole author'.

CONCLUSION

The Humanist movement in letters was primarily a literary and philological one, bound up with rhetoric and the need to supply a norm of correctness and elegance for the emergent governing classes. In self-conscious reaction against the recent medieval past, its logical approach and inadequate teaching manuals, it is none the less a movement of transition, retaining important features of medieval doctrine and, though ostensibly rejecting Aristotle, basing on him both the reform of the Liberal Arts and the first attempts at 'philosophical' grammar. In the early part of the period, in such monumental works as Linacre's *De emendata structura Latini sermonis*, an immense amount of energy is devoted to the reinstatement of the Ancient grammatical tradition, more especially as represented by Donatus and Priscian. Humanist theory inherits an inability to keep apart formal and semantic criteria, is hampered by the lack of anything approaching morphemic theory, and characterized by an increasingly semasiological bias in linguistic analysis. One important result of the jettisoning of certain aspects of medieval theory is the blurring of precise grammatical distinctions, more particularly the view of the word as a sign with both formal and conceptual facets. The careful medieval separation of *vox* (phonetic form), *dictio* (linguistic sign, i.e. phonetic form plus meaning) and *pars orationis* (linguistic sign in a grammatical function, i.e. lexical item plus consignification) is discontinued, being replaced by definitions in purely lexical terms. Sixteenth-century grammarians tend no longer to take account of the fact that the relation between reality and language is a creation of the mind, that *res* are indicated by intermediary mental concepts before being signified by words. They continue to use the term *significare*, but no longer with the precise meaning attached to it by medieval grammar. The old formula *nomen significat rem* is in effect replaced first by *nomen = res*, and later, as Nominalistic tendencies become ever more strongly entrenched, by *nomen = name*. In spite of sporadic use of a formal approach taken from Varro's

De lingua Latina, grammatical categories are increasingly viewed in terms of Priscian's *conceptus mentis* rather than as signalled by syntactic procedures or by formal elements of structure. The noun becomes simply a name, while the verb is defined solely in the lexical terms, equally appropriate to other parts of speech, of the expression of *actio, passio,* or *esse.* One important strand of sixteenth- and seventeenth-century grammar witnesses the growth of nomenclature at the expense of the more properly grammatical notion of consignification, and results in the complete disappearance of the view that words are signs with formal and semantic facets.

That the impetus to philological enquiry and the restatement of classical values exhausts itself around 1540 is due in part at least to changes in the social and intellectual climate of the times. Society no longer has the same need of an education based on classical norms, and the growing spirit of scientific enquiry, no longer content with the interpretation of a corpus of received knowledge, demands a culture orientated towards discovery. J. C. Scaliger's *De causis linguae Latinae* accordingly attempts to establish philosophical bases for linguistic analysis aimed at revealing the underlying *causae* of language, but his point of departure, at his early date, is still the Aristotelian world-view. His doctrine that language mirrors the universe results in precisely that division of phenomena into *res permanentes* and *res fluentes* which underlies medieval Modistic grammar, while at the same time anticipating the seventeenth-century search for a language that should exactly reflect nature. This is one illustration among many of the fact that what have customarily been regarded as typical seventeenth- and eighteenth-century approaches to language are in fact already present in much earlier work, e.g. the logical approach of certain parts of Nebrija's and Melanchthon's grammars, and the latter's almost total disregard of formal elements in definition. The eighteenth-century universal grammarians' assumption of a reasoned substructure to language is already implicit in Sanctius' insistence on *ratio* and his treatment of ellipse, and before him in an impressive body of medieval and Renaissance precedent which includes Linacre. Even the formalist, structural approach, which is so distinctive a product of twentieth-century linguistics, has an isolated forerunner in the work of Ramus, while the late seventeenth century's tendency to Nominalism, its equating of grammar with logic, its treatment of mental and linguistic processes as virtually identical, has roots not only in earlier work in the two centuries under consideration, but also in medieval theory. To study the grammatical theory of the period 1500–1700 is to be constantly reminded that late seventeenth-century doctrines do not represent a new departure:

Reading these largely unknown Latin texts, one is continually astonished at the relevance of much they have to say to contemporary discussion on the relationship of language and thought, as well as the continuity of ideas from the Middle Ages to the seventeenth century . . .[1]

Thus V. Salmon, and precisely in a context where she insists on the importance of a knowledge of linguistic history as an indispensable preliminary to any discussion of late seventeenth-century, and more specifically Port-Royal, grammatical theory.

Alongside the decline in precise grammatical definition occasioned by the abandoning of medieval doctrine and the growth of Nominalism there exists in sixteenth- and seventeenth-century grammar a second strand of theory, that initiated by Scaliger and continued by Campanella and Caramuel, which represents a return to medieval concepts of signification. The notion of universal grammar, so important for eighteenth-century theory, is medieval in origin, and though Campanella's philosophical grammar is the immediate precursor of the Port-Royal Grammar and of an impressive amount of later theory, it is found on examination to consist very largely of a restatement of Scholastic doctrine. With its emphasis on the consignification of grammatical function as the province of the grammarian it reintroduces notions that, apart from Scaliger and his followers, had long been in disuse. With Campanella grammar is once more *de signis rerum*. Further, insights which were long thought to be the specific contribution to grammatical theory of the Port-Royal authors and such seminal works as Bishop Wilkins' *Essay* (the theory of the copula and the classification of noun and adjective, to mention only two) are found on a closer view to have been anticipated by Campanella, Caramuel and J. C. Scaliger, who in turn have important antecedents in the medieval *Grammatica speculativa*. Even so self-consciously innovative a movement as the campaign for a universal language, with its presupposition of a correspondence between the ontological order of nature and the linguistic order – a presupposition already made by Scaliger and resting on medieval

[1] V. Salmon, review of N. Chomsky's *Cartesian Linguistics*, p. 176.

doctrine – is at least partly dependent on systems of conceptual classification which repose on the Aristotelian world-view and on Scholastic philosophy. As for the prestigious *Grammaire générale et raisonnée* of Port-Royal, its view of words as signs not of immediate reality but of intermediary concepts in the mind not only takes its origin from Scaliger and Frischlin, but is ultimately based on medieval theory, which in turn owes much to Priscian's doctrine of the *conceptus mentis*. The Port-Royal Grammar is however, as befits its universal pretensions, a grammar of concepts, in which *grammatica est de signis rerum* has become *grammatica est de conceptibus*. But even here, its implicit doctrine of a logically determined 'deep structure' underlying the 'surface structure' of individual languages goes back not only to Lancelot's *Nouvelle Méthode latine*, to Sanctius' theory of ellipse and Linacre's syntax, but to Caramuel and a long medieval tradition positing a *verbum mentis* or common mental structure underlying the surface linguistic items of *verbum oris* or discourse. The line of development from medieval grammar, through Scaliger and Sanctius, Caramuel and Campanella, is in many respects, apart from the distorted version of the linguistic sign presented by Port-Royal, an unbroken one down to the end of the seventeenth century. Behind much of modern theory – de Saussure's restatement of the doctrine of the sign, recent interest in a 'deep' and a 'surface' structure of language – there lies a hitherto neglected body of source material, the Latin tradition of the sixteenth and seventeenth centuries, in the light of which a number of commonly made assumptions concerning linguistic history need to be reconsidered.

APPENDIX
ANCIENT AND MEDIEVAL DEFINITIONS
OF THE PARTS OF SPEECH

In view of the importance of Donatus and Priscian for Humanist grammarians, their definitions of the chief grammatical categories are appended here. A few of the more important definitions in the *Grammatica speculativa* are also given.

I. DONATUS (*c.* 350 A.D.) AND PRISCIAN (*c.* 500 A.D.)

(*The letter* (a) *indicates Donatus' definitions,* (b) *those of Priscian.*)

VOX (Phonetic form of the word, i.e. de Saussure's *significant*):

(a) *Vox est aer ictus sensibilis auditu.*[1]
A *vox* is a pulsation of the air perceptible to hearing.

DICTIO or VOX ARTICULATA (phonetic form + meaning, i.e. de Saussure's *significant + significate,* = word):

(b) *Vox articulata est, quae copulata cum aliquo sensu mentis eius, qui loquitur, profertur.*[2]
A *vox articulata* is that which is uttered joined to some sense in the mind of the speaker.
[Cf. Diomedes' *Dictio est vox articulata cum aliqua significatione.*][3]
(b) *Dictio est pars minima orationis constructae.*[4]
A word is a minimal unit of sentence construction.

ORATIO (sentence):

(b) *Oratio est ordinatio dictionum congrua, sententiam perfectam demonstrans.*[5]
A sentence is an ordered arrangement of words in syntactic agreement, making complete sense.

NOMEN:

(a) *Nomen est pars orationis cum casu corpus aut rem proprie communiterve significans.*[6]
A noun is a part of speech marked for case, signifying a *corpus* or a *res* as proper or common.
(b) *Nomen est pars orationis, quae unicuique subiectorum corporum seu rerum communem vel propriam qualitatem distribuit.*[7]
A noun is a part of speech which assigns to every *corpus* or *res* a common or a particular quality.

---

[1] H. Keil, *Grammatici Latini*, IV, 367. [2] *Ibid.* II, 5. [3] *Ibid.* II, 436.
[4] *Ibid.* II, 53. [5] *Ibid.* II, 53. [6] *Ibid.* IV, 373. [7] *Ibid.* II, 56–57.

Appendix

ADIECTIVUM:

(b) [*Adiectiva*] *aliis appellativis, quae substantiam significant . . . adici solent ad manifestandam eorum qualitatem vel quantitatem.*[1]
Adjectives are customarily added to other nouns, which signify substance, in order to show their quality or quantity.

PRONOMEN:

(a) *Pars orationis, quae pro nomine posita tantundem paene significat personamque interdum recipit.*[2]
A part of speech which used in place of a noun has almost the same meaning and receives person.

VERBUM:

(a) *Pars orationis cum tempore et persona sine casu agere aliquid aut pati aut neutrum significans.*[3]
A part of speech with tense and person, not marked for case, signifying the doing or undergoing of something, or neither the one nor the other.

(b) *Verbum est pars orationis cum temporibus et modis, sine casu, agendi vel patiendi significativum.*[4]
A verb is a part of speech with tenses and moods, not marked for case, signifying doing or undergoing.

PARTICIPIUM:

(a) *Pars orationis partem capiens nominis, partem verbi; nominis genera et casus, verbi tempora et significationes, utriusque numerum et figuram.*[5]
A part of speech deriving in part from the noun, in part from the verb; taking from the noun gender and case, from the verb tense and voice, and from both number and *figura* [i.e. simple or compound form].

ADVERBIUM:

(a) *Pars orationis, quae adiecta verbo significationem eius explanat atque inplet.*[6]
A part of speech which added to the verb makes plain and completes its meaning.

(b) *Adverbium est pars orationis indeclinabilis, cuius significatio verbis adicitur.*[7]
An adverb is an indeclinable part of speech, whose signification is added to that of verbs.

PRAEPOSITIO:

(a) *Praepositio est pars orationis, quae praeposita aliis partibus orationis significationem earum aut mutat aut conplet aut minuit.*[8]
A preposition is a part of speech which, placed before other parts of speech, changes, completes or diminishes their meaning.

---

[1] *Ibid.* II, 591. [2] *Ibid.* IV, 357. [3] *Ibid.* IV, 359. [4] *Ibid.* II, 369.
[5] *Ibid.* IV, 363. [6] *Ibid.* IV, 362. [7] *Ibid.* III, 60. [8] *Ibid.* IV, 389.

(b) . . . *pars orationis indeclinabilis, quae praeponitur aliis partibus vel appositione vel compositione.*[1]

An indeclinable part of speech, which is placed before other parts either separately or in composition.

CONIUNCTIO:

(a) *Pars orationis adnectens ordinansque sententiam.*[2]

A part of speech linking meanings and arranging them in order.

(b) *Coniunctio est pars orationis indeclinabilis, coniunctiva aliarum partium orationis, quibus consignificat, vim vel ordinationem demonstrans.*[3]

A conjunction is an indeclinable part of speech, joining together other parts of speech, with which it consignifies, and indicating their semantic force or order.

INTERIECTIO:

(a) *Pars orationis significans mentis affectum voce incondita.*[4]

A part of speech signifying an emotion by means of an unformed word [i.e. one not fixed by convention].

II. THE *'Grammatica speculativa'* OF THOMAS OF ERFURT

VOX:

Vox inquantum vox, non consideratur a Grammatico; sed inquantum signum, quia Grammatica est de signis rerum. (Cap. vi.)

The *vox* [phonetic form] is no concern of the grammarian, except in so far as it is a constituent part of the linguistic sign, for grammar deals with signs of things.

DICTIO:

Dictio est vox significativa. (Cap. vi.)

The word is a meaning-bearing *vox*.

PARS ORATIONIS:

Pars orationis est dictio, ut habet modum significandi activum. (Cap. vi.)

A part of speech is a word, plus [an added grammatical meaning conferred by] the active mode of signifying.

NOMEN:

Nomen est pars orationis significans per modum entis. (Cap. viii.)

A noun is a part of speech signifying by the mode of [static] being [i.e. signifying things in a state of rest and permanence].

SUBSTANTIVUM:

Modus significandi per modum per se stantis . . . constituit Nomen substantivum. (Cap. x.)

[1] *Ibid.* III, 24.   [2] *Ibid.* IV, 364.
[3] *Ibid.* III, 93.   [4] *Ibid.* IV, 366.

Appendix

A noun substantive signifies by the mode of that which is capable of standing alone [i.e. it both signifies substance and has syntactic independence].

ADIECTIVUM:

Nomen adiectivum significat per modum inhaerentis alteri. (Cap. x.)
A noun adjective signifies by the mode of that which [unable to stand alone] inheres in something else. [I.e. it both signifies accident and is syntactically dependent.]

VERBUM:

Verbum est pars orationis significans per modum esse. (Cap. xxv.)
A verb is a part of speech signifying by the mode of [non-static] being [i.e. signifying things in a state of flux and succession].

BIBLIOGRAPHY

PRIMARY SOURCES

(Where appropriate *i* and *u* have been replaced by *j* and *v*, and vice versa. Otherwise the original spelling has been left unchanged. In French titles, modern accentuation practice has been followed.)

Alsted, J. H. *Encyclopaedia universalis*, Herborn, 1630

Alvarus, E. *De institutione grammatica libri tres*, 2nd ed., Milan, 1595

Anon. *An Examen of the Way of Teaching the Latin Tongue to Little Children by Use alone. Englished out of French*, London, 1669

Aristotle *The Organon*, ed. H. P. Cooke, London and Cambridge (Mass.), 1938

Arnauld, A., and P. Nicole *La Logique ou l'art de penser: Contenant . . . plusieurs observations nouvelles propres à former le jugement*, Paris, 1662
Ibid. 1675 ed.
(v. also under C. Lancelot)

Bacon, F. *De dignitate et augmentis scientiarum* (1623), Bk I; in *The Works of Francis Bacon*, ed. J. Spedding, R. L. Ellis and D. D. Heath, vol. 1, London, 1857
Of the Advancement of Learning (1605); *Novum organum* (1620); *De augmentis scientiarum* (1623); in *The Philosophical Works of Francis Bacon, Reprinted from the Texts and Translations . . . of Ellis and Spedding*, ed. J. M. Robertson, London, 1905.

Baker, T. *Reflections upon Learning, Wherein is shewn the Insufficiency Thereof, in its several Particulars. In order to evince the Usefulness and Necessity, of Revelation*, 2nd ed., London, 1700 (first ed. Cambridge, 1699)

Beck, C. *The Universal Character, By Which all the Nations in the World may Understand one Anothers Conceptions*, London, 1657

Brassicanus, J. *Grammaticae institutiones*, Pforzheim, 1510

Brinsley, J. *Ludus literarius: or, The Grammar Schoole; Shewing how to Proceede from the First Entrance into Learning, to the Highest Perfection Required in the Grammar Schooles . . . onely according to our Common Grammar, and Ordinary Classicall Authours*, London, 1612
The Posing of the Parts, or, A most Plaine and Easie Way of Examining the Accidence and Grammar, by Questions and Answers, 2nd ed., London, 1615

Burles, E. *Grammatica Burlesa or a New English Grammar Made Plain and Easie for Teacher and Scholar*, London, 1652

Bibliography

Campanella, T. *Realis philosophiae epilogisticae partes quatuor,* Frankfurt, 1623
Philosophiae rationalis partes quinque. Videlicet: grammatica, dialectica, rhetorica, poetica, historiographia. Pars prima: grammatica, Paris, 1638

Caramuel y Lobkowitz, J. *Praecursor logicus, complectens grammaticem audacem, cuius partes sunt tres, methodica, metrica, critica,* Frankfurt, 1654

Clare, W. *Via naturalis . . . or, the Natural Way to Learn the Latin Tongue,* London, 1688

Colet, J. *Ioannis Coleti . . . aeditio, una cum quibusdam G. Lilii Grammatices rudimentis,* Antwerp, 1537 (First ed. 1527)

Comenius, J. A. *Porta linguarum trilinguis reserata et aperta, sive seminarium linguarum & scientiarum omnium. The Gate of Tongues Unlocked and Opened, Or else A Seminarie or Seed-plot of all Tongues and Sciences,* London, 1631
Janua linguarum reserata: sive omnium scientiarum & linguarum seminarium. The Gate of Languages Unlocked: Or a Seed-plot of all Arts and Tongues. Formerly translated by Tho. Horn: afterwards much corrected and amended by Joh. Robotham, 6th ed., London, 1643
Via lucis, vestigata & vestiganda, h. e. rationalis disquisitio, quibus modis intellectualis animorum lux, sapientia, per omnes omnium hominum mentes & gentes . . . spargi possit, Amsterdam, 1668 (First ed. 1642)
The Way of Light by John Amos Comenius Translated into English, with Introduction, ed. E. T. Campagnac, Liverpool University Press, 1938
Vestibulum linguae Latinae rerum & linguarum fundamenta exhibens, London, 1656
John Amos Commenii Orbis sensualium pictus. Hoc est omnium fundamentalium in mundo rerum, & in vita actionum, pictura & nomenclatura. Joh. Amos Commenius's Visible World. Or, A Picture and Nomenclature of all the Chief Things that are in the World; and of Mens Employments Therein . . . By Charles Hoole, London, 1659
Ars ornatoria, sive grammatica elegans, et eruditionis scholasticae atrium, rerum & linguarum ornamenta exhibens: Cui insuper accessit grammatica eiusdem janualis, London, 1664

Corradus, Q. M. *De lingua Latina,* Bologna, 1575

Dalgarno, G. *Ars signorum, vulgo character universalis et lingua philosophica,* London, 1661

Danes, J. *A Light to Lilie. Being an Easie Method for the Better Teaching and Learning of the Grounds of the Latine Tongue,* London, 1637
Paralipomena orthographiae, etymologiae, prosodiae, London, 1638/9 (First title page dated 1639, second 1638)

Descartes, R. *Discourse on the Method of Rightly Conducting the Reason and Seeking for Truth in the Sciences;*
Meditations on the First Philosophy and *Rules for the Direction of the Mind;* translated by E. S. Haldane and G. R. T. Ross, in *Great Books of the Western World,* 31, ed. R. M. Hutchins, Chicago, 1952
Notes Directed Against a Certain Programme, in *The Philosophical Works of Descartes,* translated by E. S. Haldane and G. T. Ross, Cambridge, 1967

Despauterius, J. *Rudimenta*, 2nd ed., Paris, 1527 (First ed. 1514)
  Commentarii grammatici, Paris, 1537/8 (Dated 1537 on title page, but date
    of printing given at end of vol. as 1538)
Digby, E. *De duplici methodo libri duo, unicam Petri Rami methodum refutantes*,
  1580
Drosaeus, J. *Grammaticae quadrilinguis partitiones*, Paris, 1544
Erasmus, D. *De octo orationis partium constructione libellus*, Louvain, no date
  (Colet's foreword is dated 1513)
Finckius, C., and C. Helvicus. *Grammatica Latina*, 2nd ed., Giessen, 1615
Frischlin, N. *Quaestionum grammaticarum Libri XII*, Venice, 1584
Glanvill, J. *An Essay concerning Preaching*, London, 1678
Hayne, T. *Grammatices Latinae compendium anno 1637. E grammaticis tum
  veteribus, tum neotericis . . . excerptum*, London, 1640
Helvicus, C. *Libri didactici, grammaticae universalis, Latinae, Graecae, Hebraicae,
  Chaldicae*, Giessen, 1619
  (v. also under C. Finckius above)
Herbert of Cherbury, Baron *De Veritate prout distinguitur a revelatione, a
  verisimili, a possibili, et a falso*, [London?], 1624.
  M. H. Carré (ed.). *De Veritate by Edward, Lord Herbert of Cherbury
    Translated with an Introduction*, University of Bristol, 1937
Hobbes, T. *Elements of Philosophy: I. Concerning Body; Leviathan: I. of Man;
  Human Nature: Or the Fundamental Elements of Policy*; in *The English
  Works of Thomas Hobbes*, ed. W. Molesworth, vols. I, III and IV,
  London, 1839–40
  Thomae Hobbes Malmesburiensis Opera philosophica quae Latine scripsit, ed.
    W. Molesworth, vol. V, London, 1845
  *Leviathan or the Matter, Forme and Power of a Commonwealth Ecclesiastical and
    Civil*, ed. M. Oakeshott, Blackwell, Oxford, [1946]
Hoole, C. *The Latine Grammar Fitted for the Use of Schools/Grammatica Latina
  in usum scholarum adornata*, London, 1651
  (For Hoole's edition of the *Orbis pictus*, v. under Comenius above)
Hume, A. *Prima elementa grammaticae in usum juventutis Scoticae*, Edinburgh, 1612
  Grammatica nova in usum juventutis Scoticae ad methodum revocata, Edinburgh,
    1612
  Schola grammatica ad singula capita grammaticae . . . accommodata (Bound in
    one volume with preceding work)
Jones, B. *Herm'aelogium: Or, an Essay At the Rationality of the Art of Speaking.
  As a Supplement to Lillie's Grammer, Philosophically, Mythologically, &
  Emblematically*, London, 1659
Keil, H. *Grammatici Latini*, Hildesheim, 1961 (a reproduction of the
  Leipzig ed. of 1857–74): Vol. I: *Charisii artis grammaticae libri V;
  Diomedis artis grammaticae libri III; Ex Charisii arte grammatica excerpta;*
  II: *Prisciani institutionum grammaricarum libri I–XII;* III: *Prisciani
  Institutionum grammaticarum libri XIII–XVIII;* IV: *Probi Instituta
  artium; Donati de Partibus orationis ars minor; Donati Ars grammatica;
  Servii Commentarius in Artem Donati; Sergii Explanationes Artis Donati*

Bibliography

Lancelot, C. *Nouvelle Méthode pour apprendre facilement et en peu de temps la langue latine*, 5th ed., Paris, 1656 (First ed., 1644)

A. Arnauld and P. Nicole *Nouvelle Méthode pour apprendre facilement . . .*, 8th ed., Paris, 1681

and A. Arnauld *Grammaire générale et raisonnée*, Paris, 1660

Lane, A. *A Rational and Speedy Method of Attaining to the Latin Tongue*, London, 1695

Leedes, E. *Ad prima rudimenta Graecae linguae discenda Graeco-Latinum compendium*, London, 1693

Leibniz, G. W. von. *Nouveaux essais sur l'entendement humain (avant-propos et livre premier)*, ed. E. Boutroux, Paris, 1886

C. J. Gerhardt (ed.), *Die philosophischen Schriften von Gottfried Wilhelm Leibniz*, vol. 4, Berlin, 1880

Lever, R. *The Arte of Reason, Rightly Termed, Witcraft, Teaching a Perfect Way to Argue and Dispute*, London, 1573

Lewis, M. *An Essay to Facilitate the Education of Youth, by Bringing Down the Rudiments of Grammar to the Sense of Seeing*, no place or date of publication (*c.* 1670)

Lily, W. *Ioannis Coleti . . . aeditio, una cum quibusdam G. Lilii Grammatices rudimentis*, Antwerp, 1537. (Identical with the first ed. of 1527.)

S. Blach (ed.), 'Shakespeares Lateingrammatik. Lilys Grammatica Latina nach der ältesten bekannten Ausgabe von 1527 und der für Shakespeare in Betracht kommenden Ausgabe von 1566 (London, R. Wolfius). Neugedruckt von Dr. S. Blach.' (*Jahrbuch der deutschen Shakespeare-Gesellschaft*, Berlin-Schöneberg, 44 (1908), pp. 65–117; 45 (1909), pp. 51–101.)

A Shorte Introduction of Grammar, Generally to be Used in the Kynges Majesties Dominions, for the Bryngynge up of all Those that Entende to Atteyne the Knowledge of the Latine Tongue, London, Reginald Wolf, 1549

A Short Introduction of Grammar Generallie to be Used Compiled and Set Forth, for the Bringyng up of all Those that Intend to Attaine the Knowledge of the Latin Tongue, 1557

(The 1549 edition, which is unpaginated, is imperfect, beginning on what is p. 8 in the 1557 edition and ending on what is p. 116 in that edition. Otherwise, apart from Edward VI's foreword to the 1549 edition, the two are identical. The edition of 1567, not listed here, is identical with the 1557 edition except in minor details)

V. J. Flynn (ed.), *A Shorte Introduction of Grammar by William Lily*, New York, 1945

Linacre, T. *Rudimenta grammatices Thomae Linacri ex Anglico sermone in Latinum versa, interprete Georgio Buchanano Scoto*, Paris, 1533 (First ed. *c.* 1512)

De emendata structura Latini sermonis libri sex, London, 1524

Locke, J. *An Essay concerning Humane Understanding*, London, 1690

Lodwick (or Lodowyck), F. *A Common Writing: Whereby two, although not understanding one the others Language, yet by the helpe thereof, may communicate their minds one to another*, 1647 (Published anonymously, with the initials *F.L.W.* at the end of the preface. No place of publication given)

The Ground-Work or Foundation Laid, (or so intended) For the Framing of a New Perfect Language: And an Universall or Common Writing . . . By a Well-willer to Learning, 1652 (Likewise published anonymously)

Manutius, Aldus *Rudimenta grammatices Latinae linguae*, Venice, 1501

Institutionum grammaticarum libri quatuor, Venice, 1507/8 (Dated 1507 at end of foreword, 1508 at end of vol. First ed. 1501)

Melanchthon, P. *Grammatica Latina*, Paris, 1527 (First ed. 1525)

Syntaxis, Paris, 1528 (First ed. 1526)

Grammatica Phil. Melanchthonis Latina, iam denuo recognita, et plerisque in locis locupletata, Paris, 1550

Mildapettus, F. (=W. Temple) *Admonitio de unica P. Rami methodo*, 1580

From Francis Mildapet of Navarre to Everard Digby of England, an Admonition that the Single Method of Peter Ramus be Retained and the Rest Rejected, 1580

Milton, J. *Accedence Commenc't Grammar, Supply'd with Sufficient Rules, for the Use of Such as . . . are Desirous . . . to Attain to the Latin Tongue*, London, 1669 (Published under the initials *J.M.*)

Nebrissensis, A. (=Antonio de Nebrija or Lebrija) *Ars nova grammatices*, Lyons, 1509 (First published as *Introductiones Latinae*, Salamanca, 1481) Another ed. *Grammatica Antonii Nebrissensis*, Saragossa, 1533

E. Walberg (ed.) *Gramatica Castellana. Reproduction phototypique de l'édition princeps (1492)*, Halle, 1909

I. González-Llubera (ed.) *Nebrija Gramatica de la lengua castellana (Salamanca, 1492)*, Oxford University Press, 1926

Parker, S. *A Free and Impartial Censure of the Platonick Philosophie*, Oxford, 1666

Perottus, N. *Rudimenta grammatices*, 1473

Artis grammatices introductorium . . . ex nicolai Perotti . . . traditionibus: a magistro Bernardo Perger translatum, Basle, 1506 (Simply described on title page as *Grammatica nova*)

Poole, J. *The English Accidence: or, A Short, Plaine, and Easie Way, for the More Speedy Attaining to the Latine Tongue, by the Help of the English*, London, 1646

Ramus, P. (=Pierre de la Ramée) *Aristotelicae animadversiones*, Paris, 1543

Dialecticae institutiones, Paris, 1543

Dialectique, Paris, 1555

Rudimenta grammaticae Latinae, Frankfurt, 1576

Grammatica, Frankfurt, 1576 (First ed. 1559)

Scholae in liberales artes, Basle, 1578 (First ed. 1559)

R. MacIlmaine. *The Logike of . . . P. Ramus Martyr, newly translated . . . per M. R. Makylmenaeum Scotum*, London, 1574

Richardson, A. *The Logicians School-Master or, a Comment upon Ramus Logick, Whereunto are added, His Prelections on Ramus his Grammer*, London, 1657

Bibliography

Sanctius, F. *Minerva: seu de causis linguae Latinae*, Salamanca, 1587

Scaliger, J. C. *De causis linguae Latinae libri tredecim*, Lyons, 1540

Scioppius, G. (= K. Schoppe) *Grammatica philosophica*, Amsterdam, 1659 (First ed. 1628)

Shirley, J. *Via ad Latinam linguam complanata/ The Way Made Plain to the Latine Tongue*, London, 1649

Grammatica Anglo-Latina/An English and Latine Grammar. The Rules Composed in English and Latine Verse, London, 1651

The Rudiments of Grammar. The Rules Composed in English Verse, London, 1656

Manuductio: or, A Leading of Children by the Hand Through the Principles of Grammar, 2nd ed., London, 1660

Siger de Courtrai. *Summa modorum significandi*, ed. G. Wallerand, *Les Œuvres de Siger de Courtrai. Les Philosophes belges, VIII*, Louvain, 1913

Stockwood, J. *A Plaine and Easie Laying Open of the Meaning and Understanding of the Rules of Construction in the English Accidence, Appointed by Authoritie to be Taught in all Schooles of hir Majesties Dominions*, London, 1590

Disputatiuncularum grammaticalium libellus, ad puerorum in scholis trivialibus exacuenda ingenia primum excogitatus, 2nd ed., London, 1598

Sulpitius, J. *Grammatica*, Nuremberg, 1482 (First ed. 1475)

De arte grammatica opusculum compendiosum, Rome, 1490 (First ed. 1475?)

Syms, C. *An Introduction to, or the Art of Teaching, the Latine Speach*, [Dublin, 1634] (Title page missing in copy consulted)

Temple, W. – *v.* F. Mildapettus (pseudonym)

Thomas of Erfurt (pseudo Duns Scotus). *Grammatica speculativa*, ed. M. Doyon, Quebec, 1962 (A reproduction of L. Vivès' edition, Paris, 1891, which in turn follows Wadding's 1639 edition)

G. L. Bursill-Hall (ed.), *Thomas of Erfurt Grammatica Speculativa. An Edition with Translation and Commentary*, London, 1972

Valla, L. *De linguae Latinae elegantia*, Venice, 1471 (First printed in 1471, this work dates from *c.* 1440)

Varro, M. Terentius *De lingua Latina*, in M. Nisard (ed.), *Macrobe, Varron et Pomponius Méla* (*Collection des auteurs latins avec la traduction en français*), Paris, 1850, pp. 477–584

Vossius, G. J. *Latina grammatica . . . in usum scholarum adornata*, 3rd ed., Leyden, 1631 (First ed. 1626)

Latina syntaxis, In usum scholarum Hollandiae, & West-Frisiae . . . adornata, Leyden, 1631

De arte grammatica libri septem, Amsterdam, 1635

Walker, O. *Of Education, Especially of Young Gentlemen*, Oxford, 1673

Wallis, J. *Grammatica linguae Anglicanae*, Oxford, 1653

Ward, S. *Vindiciae Academiarum containing, Some briefe Animadversions upon Mr. Websters Book, stiled The Examination of Academies*, Oxford, 1654

Webbe, J. *An Appeale to Truth . . . About the Best and Most Expedient Course in Languages*, London, 1622

Bibliography

Webster, J. *Academiarum examen*, London, 1654

Wilkins, J. *An Essay Towards a Real Character and a Philosophical Language*, London, 1668

Wilson, T. *The Rule of Reason, Conteinying the Arte of Logique, Set Forth in Englishe*, 1551

SECONDARY SOURCES

Aarsleff, H. 'Leibniz on Locke on Language', *American Philosophical Quarterly*, 1 (1964), pp. 165–88

'The History of Linguistics and Professor Chomsky', *Language*, 46 (1970), pp. 570–85

Adamson, J. W. *Pioneers of Modern Education 1600–1700* (*Contributions to the History of Education III*), Cambridge University Press, 1905

Allen, P. S. 'Linacre and Latimer in Italy', *The English Historical Review*, LXXI (1903), pp. 514–17

Alston, R. C. *A Bibliography of the English Language from the Invention of Printing to the Year 1800*, Leeds & Bradford, 1965– :
  I. *English Grammars Written in English and English Grammars Written in Latin by Native Speakers* II. *Polyglot Dictionaries and Grammars*

Arens, H. *Sprachwissenschaft: der Gang ihrer Entwicklung von der Antike bis zur Gegenwart* (vol. 1:6 of *Orbis Academicus: Problemgeschichten der Wissenschaft in Dokumenten und Darstellungen*), Freiburg–München, 1955

Bach, E., and R. T. Harms (eds.) *Universals in Linguistic Theory*, New York, 1968

Bach, E. 'Nouns and Noun Phrases', in *Universals in Linguistic Theory*, pp. 91–122

Baebler, J. J. *Beiträge zu einer Geschichte der lateinischen Grammatik im Mittelalter*, Halle, 1885

Barrado, S. 'Estudios sobre el Brocense', *Revista Crítica Hispano–Americana*, V (1919)

Bloomfield, L. *Language*, New York, 1933

Bolgar, R. R. *The Classical Heritage and its Beneficiaries*, Cambridge University Press, 1954

Brekle, H. E. Introduction to *Grammaire générale et raisonnée ou La Grammaire de Port-Royal, Edition critique, Tome I: Nouvelle impression en facsimilé de la troisième édition de 1676* (*Grammatica Universalis 1: Meisterwerke der Sprachwissenschaft*), Stuttgart-Bad Cannstatt, 1966

'Die Bedeutung der *Grammaire générale et raisonnée* – bekannt als Grammatik von Port-Royal – für die heutige Sprachwissenschaft', *Indogermanische Forschungen*, 72 (1967), pp. 1–21

Breva-Claramonte, M. 'Sanctius' *Minerva* of 1562 and the Evolution of his Linguistic Theory', *Historiographia Linguistica* II, 1 (1975), pp. 49–66.

Brunot, F. *Histoire de la langue française des origines à 1900*, Paris, 1905– , vol. V

Brøndal, V. *Les parties du discours – Études sur les catégories linguistiques*, translated into French by P. Naert, Copenhagen, 1948 (First ed. 1928)

Essais de linguistique générale, Copenhagen, 1943

Bursill-Hall, G. L. 'Medieval Grammatical Theories', *The Canadian Journal of Linguistics*, 9:1 (1963), pp. 40–54

Speculative Grammars of the Middle Ages. The Doctrine of Partes Orationis of the Modistae, The Hague and Paris, 1971

Bush, D. *The Renaissance and English Humanism*, University of Toronto Press, 1939

Cadet, F. *Port-Royal Education*, translated from the French (*L'Éducation à Port-Royal*, Paris, 1887) by A. D. Jones, London, 1898

Caspari, F. *Humanism and the Social Order in Tudor England*, University of Chicago Press, 1954

Chevalier, J.-C. *Histoire de la syntaxe: naissance de la notion de complément dans la grammaire française (1530–1750)*, Geneva, 1968

Chomsky, N. *Syntactic Structures*, The Hague, 1963

'Goals of Linguistic Theory', *Current Issues in Linguistic Theory* (*Janua Linguarum*, Series Minor, XXXVIII), London, The Hague, Paris, 1964

Aspects of the Theory of Syntax, M.I.T. Press, Cambridge, Mass., 1965

Cartesian Linguistics: A Chapter in the History of Rationalist Thought, New York, 1966

Language and Mind, New York, 1968

Couturat, L. *La Logique de Leibniz d'après des documents inédits*, Paris, 1901

De Mott, B. 'The Sources and Development of John Wilkins' Philosophical Language', *The Journal of English and Germanic Philology*, VII (1958), pp. 1–13

De Wulf, M. *Medieval Philosophy Illustrated from the System of Thomas Aquinas*, Harvard University Press, 1922

Dobson, E. J. *English Pronunciation 1500–1700*, 2nd ed., 2 vols., Oxford, 1968

Donzé, R. *La Grammaire générale et raisonnée de Port-Royal: Contribution à l'histoire des idées grammaticales en France*, Berne, 1967

Duhamel, P. A. 'The Logic and Rhetoric of Peter Ramus', *Modern Philology*, XLVI (1949), pp. 163–71

Faithfull, R. G. Review of P. A. Verburg, *Taal en Functionaliteit*, Wageningen, 1952, in *Archivum Linguisticum*, 7:2 (1955), pp. 144–50

Fillmore, C. J. 'The Case for Case', *Universals in Linguistic Theory* (ed. E. Bach and R. T. Harms), New York, 1968, pp. 1–88

Firth, J. R. 'General Linguistics and Descriptive Grammar', *Papers in Linguistics 1934–1951*, Oxford University Press, 1957, pp. 215–28

Fischer, K. *Francis Bacon of Verulam: Realistic Philosophy and its Age*, translated from the German by J. Oxenford, London, 1857

Descartes and his School, translation of the 3rd ed. by J. P. Gordy, London, 1887

Bibilography

Formigari, L. *Linguistica ed empirismo nel seicento inglese*, Bari, 1970

Fries, C. C. *The Structure of English*, New York, 1952

Funke, O. 'Zum Weltsprachenproblem in England im 17. Jahrhundert. G. Dalgarno's "Ars Signorum" (1661) und J. Wilkins' "Essay Towards a Real Character and a Philosophical Language" (1668)', *Anglistische Forschungen*, 69 (1929), pp. i–v, 1–163

'William Bullokars *Bref Grammar for English* (1586). Ein Beitrag zur Geschichte der frühneuenglischen Grammatik', *Anglia*, LXII (1938), pp. 116–37

'Grammatica Anglicana von P. Gr[eaves] (1594)', *Wiener Beiträge*, LX (1938)

'Ben Jonsons *English Grammar* (1640)', *Anglia*, LXIV (1940), pp. 117–34

'Die Frühzeit der englischen Grammatik. Die humanistisch-antike Sprachlehre und der national-sprachliche Gedanke im Spiegel der frühneuenglischen Grammatiker von *Bullokar* (1586) bis *Wallis* (1653). Die grammatische Systematik und die Klassifikation der Redeteile', *Schriften der literarischen Gesellschaft Bern*, IV (1941), pp. 1–91

'On the Sources of John Wilkins' Philosophical Language (1668)', *English Studies*, 40 (1959), pp. 208–14

García, C. *Contribución a la historia de los conceptos gramaticales: la aportación del Brocense*, Madrid, 1960

Gilson, E. *The Philosophy of St Thomas Aquinas* (translation by E. Bullough of the 3rd ed. of *Le Thomisme*), Cambridge, 1924

Godfrey, R. G. 'Late Medieval Linguistic Meta-Theory and Chomsky's Syntactic Structures', *Word*, 21:2 (1965), pp. 251–6

Grabmann, M. 'Thomas von Erfurt und die Sprachlogik des mittelalterlichen Aristotelismus', *Sitzungsberichte der Bayerischen Akademie der Wissenschaften (Philosophisch-historische Abteilung)*, 2 (1943), pp. 1–103

Mittelalterliches Geistesleben (Abhandlungen zur Geschichte der Scholastik und Mystik, vol. III), München, 1956

Graves, F. P. *Petrus Ramus and the Educational Reformation of the Sixteenth Century*, New York, 1912

A History of Education during the Middle Ages and the Transition to Modern Times, New York, 1914

Green, V. H. H. *A History of Oxford University*, London, 1974

Greenberg, J. H. (ed.) *Universals of Language: Report of a Conference held at Dobbs Ferry, New York, April 13–15, 1961*, M.I.T. Press, Cambridge, Mass, 1963

'Some Universals of Grammar with Particular Reference to the Order of Meaning Elements', in *Universals of Language* (1963), pp. 58–90

Heidegger, M. *Die Kategorien- und Bedeutungslehre des Duns Scotus*, Tübingen, 1916

Hjelmslev, L. *Principes de grammaire générale*, Copenhagen, 1928

Hockett, C. F. 'The Problem of Universals in Language', *Universals of Language* (ed. J. H. Greenberg) (1963), pp. 1–22

Bibliography

Howell, A. C. 'Res et Verba: Words and Things', *ELH A Journal of English Literary History*, 13 (1946), pp. 131–42

Howell, W. S. *Logic and Rhetoric in England, 1500–1700*, Princeton University Press, 1956

Ivić, M. *Trends in Linguistics (Janua Linguarum, Series Minor XLII)*, The Hague, 1965

Jacobson, R. 'Implications of Language Universals for Linguistics', *Universals of Language* (ed. J. H. Greenberg) (1963), pp. 208–19

Jellinek, M. H. *Geschichte der neuhochdeutschen Grammatik von den Anfängen bis auf Adelung*, 2 vols., Heidelberg, 1913–14

Jespersen, O. *The Philosophy of Grammar*, New York, 1965 (First ed. 1924)

Johnson, J. N. *The Life of Thomas Linacre*, London, 1835

Jones, R. F. *The Seventeenth Century: Studies in the History of English Thought and Literature from Bacon to Pope, by Richard Foster Jones and Others Writing in His Honor*, Stanford University Press, 1951:

   pp. 41–74, 'Science and Criticism in the Neo-Classical Age of English Literature', by R. F. Jones, reprinted from *Journal of the History of Ideas*, I (1940);

   pp. 75–110, 'Science and English Prose Style in the Third Quarter of the Seventeenth Century', by R. F. Jones, reprinted from *Publications of the Modern Language Association*, XLV (1930);

   pp. 143–60, 'Science and Language in England of the Mid-Seventeenth Century', by R. F. Jones, reprinted from *The Journal of English and Germanic Philology*, XXXI (1932)

Kelly, L. G. *Twenty-five Centuries of Language Teaching*, Rowley, Mass., 1969

Kiparsky, P. 'Linguistic Universals and Linguistic Change', *Universals in Linguistic Theory* (ed. E. Bach and R. T. Harms), New York, 1968, pp. 171–202

Kneale, W. and M. *The Development of Logic*, Oxford, 1962

Kukenheim, L. *Contributions à l'histoire de la grammaire grecque, latine et hébraïque à l'époque de la Renaissance*, Leyden, 1951

   Esquisse historique de la linguistique française et de ses rapports avec la linguistique générale, Leyden, 1962

Lakoff, R. Review of C. Lancelot and A. Arnauld, *Grammaire générale et raisonnée* (ed. H. Brekle, Stuttgart-Bad Cannstatt, 1966), in *Language*, 45 (1969), pp. 343–64

Loomis, L. R. Introduction to *Plato: Apology, Crito, Phaedo, Symposium, Republic*, New York, 1942

Lyons, J. *Introduction to Theoretical Linguistics*, Cambridge University Press, 1969

   Structural Semantics: An Analysis of Part of the Vocabulary of Plato (Publications of the Philological Society XX), Blackwell, Oxford, 1963

Martinet, A. *Éléments de linguistique générale (Collection Armand Colin no. 349)*, Paris, 1960

McIntosh, M. M. C. 'The Phonetic and Linguistic Theory of the Royal Society School, from Wallis to Cooper', unpublished Oxford University B.Litt. thesis, 1956

Michael, I. *English Grammatical Categories and the Tradition to 1800*, Cambridge University Press, 1970

Mullally, J. P. *The Summulae Logicales of Peter of Spain (University of Notre Dame Publications in Mediaeval Studies, VIII)*, 1945

Ogden, C. K. and I. A. Richards *The Meaning of Meaning*, New York (Undated. First published 1923)

Osgood, C. E. 'Language Universals and Psycholinguistics', *Universals of Language* (ed. J. H. Greenberg), M.I.T. Press, Cambridge, Mass., 1963, pp. 236–54

Pinta Llorente, M. de la *Procesos inquisitoriales contra Francisco Sanchez de las Brozas*, Madrid, 1941

Poldauf, I. 'On the history of some problems of English grammar before 1800', *Prague Studies in English*, LV (1948), pp. 1–322

Prantl, C. *Geschichte der Logik im Abendlande*, vols. III and IV, Leipzig, 1867

Robins, R. H. *Ancient and Medieval Grammatical Theory in Europe*, London, 1951

'Noun and Verb in Universal Grammar', *Language*, 28 (1952), pp. 289–98

'Dionysius Thrax and the Western Grammatical Tradition', *Transactions of the Philological Society*, 1957, pp. 67–106

'Some Considerations on the Status of Grammar in Linguistics', *Archivum Linguisticum*, II (1959), pp. 91–114

'Grammar, Meaning, and the Study of Language', *The Canadian Journal of Linguistics*, 9:2 (1964), pp. 98–114

General Linguistics: An Introductory Survey, London, 1964

A Short History of Linguistics, London, 1967

Rosset, T. 'Le P. Bouhours critique de la langue des écrivains jansénistes', *Annales de l'Université de Grenoble*, XX:1 (1908), pp. 55–125

'Le P. Bouhours continuateur de Vaugelas', *Annales de l'Université de Grenoble*, XX:2 (1908), pp. 193–280

Rossi, P. *Francis Bacon: From Magic to Science*, translated from the Italian (Bari, 1957) by S. Rabinovitch, London, 1968

Sahlin, G. *César Chesneau du Marsais et son rôle dans l'évolution de la grammaire générale*, Paris, [1928]

Salmon, V. 'James Shirley and Some Problems of Seventeenth-Century Grammar', *Archiv für das Studium der neueren Sprachen*, 197:4 (1961), pp. 287–96

'Joseph Webbe: Some Seventeenth-Century Views on Language-Teaching and the Nature of Meaning', *Bibliothèque d'Humanisme et Renaissance*, XXIII (1961), pp. 324–40

'The Evolution of Dalgarno's Ars Signorum', *Studies in Language and Literature in Honour of Margaret Schlauch*, Warsaw, 1966, pp. 353–71

Bibliography

'Language-Planning in Seventeenth-Century England: Its Context and Aims', *In Memory of J. R. Firth* (ed. C. E. Bazell, J. C. Catford, M. A. K. Halliday and R. H. Robins), London, 1966, pp. 370–97

Review of N. Chomsky, *Cartesian Linguistics* (New York, 1966), in *Journal of Linguistics*, 5 (1969), pp. 165–87

The Works of Francis Lodwick: A study of his Writings in the Intellectual Context of the Seventeenth Century, London, 1972

Sandys, J. E. *A History of Classical Scholarship*, vol. II, Cambridge University Press, 1908

Sapir, E. *Totality*, LSA Language Monographs 6, 1930

Selected Writings (ed. D. G. Mandelbaum), Berkeley and Los Angeles, 1949

Saussure, F. de *Cours de linguistique générale*, 5th ed., Paris, 1955 (First ed. 1916)

Shapiro, B. J. *John Wilkins 1614–1672: An Intellectual Biography*, University of California Press, 1969

Steinthal, H. *Geschichte der Sprachwissenschaft bei den Griechern und Römern mit besonderer Rücksicht auf die Logik*, 2nd ed., vol. II, Berlin, 1891

Thurot, C. *Extraits de divers manuscrits latins pour servir à l'histoire des doctrines grammaticales au moyen âge*, Paris, 1869

Ullmann, S. *The Principles of Semantics*, 2nd ed., Glasgow and Oxford (Blackwell), 1957

Semantics: An Introduction to the Science of Meaning, Blackwell, Oxford, 1962

Verburg, P. A. *Taal en Functionaliteit: een historisch-critische studie over de opvattingen aangaande de functies der taal vanaf de prae-humanistische philologie van Orleans tot de rationalistische linguistiek van Bopp*, Wageningen, 1952

Vorlat, E. 'Progress in English Grammar 1585–1735: A Study of the Development of English Grammar and of the Interdependence among the Early English Grammarians', 4 vols., University of Louvain doctoral thesis, 1963

Watson, F. *The English Grammar Schools to 1660: Their Curriculum and Practice*, Cambridge University Press, 1908

Weinreich, U. 'On the Semantic Structure of Language', *Universals of Language* (ed. J. H. Greenberg), M.I.T. Press, Cambridge, Mass., 1963, pp. 114–71

Weiss, R. *Humanism in England during the Fifteenth Century*, Oxford, 1941

Willey, B. *The Seventeenth Century Background: Studies in the Thought of the Age in Relation to Poetry and Religion*, London, 1934

Woodward, W. H. *Studies in Education during the Age of the Renaissance 1400–1600 (Contributions to the History of Education II)*, Cambridge University Press, 1906

Yates, F. A. *The French Academies of the Sixteenth Century*, The Warburg Institute, University of London, 1947

INDEX

Aarsleff, H., 210, 237–8
Abelard, 183
Académie française, 190–221
Accademia Platonica, Florence, 9, 10
accident (philosophical), 37, 39–40, 59–61, 63, 67–8, 72–4, 88, 102, 107, 121–4, 153–4, 167, 171n, 175, 178, 182n, 196–7, 202, 245–8
actio, 45, 47, 50, 56, 59, 68–9, 74, 90n, 116, 126–8, 146–7, 153, 168, 171–2, 182, 197, 199, 200–2, 204, 252, 261, 265
actus, 165, 167–8, 171–5, 178, 199, 201, 204; *a. accidentalis*, 176; *agendi*, 171–2; *essendi*, 171; *existendi*, 171, 176; *patiendi*, 171–2
Adam, 139–40, 147
adjective, *see* noun adjective
adnomen, 173, 206n
adverb, 50–1, 72–3, 86, 91, 99–101, 104, 116n, 117, 122, 129–30, 147, 173–4, 199–200, 203n, 206–7, 244, 249, 251; definitions of, 50–1, 72, 91, 129, 174, 265; as abbreviation of prepositional phrase, 103, 208, 250
advocabulum, 173n
affirmation, 177, 206, 215, 218–19, 229, 251–2, 254–5
Agricola, Rudolph, *De inventione dialectica*, 82
Alexander of Villedieu, *Doctrinale*, 6, 14, 18–20, 23, 52, 84
Alsted, J. H., *Encyclopaedia universalis*, 184n, 216n
Alvarus, Emmanuel, *De institutione grammatica*, 28–9, 41, 44–5, 169n
analogia, 121, 123
analogy/anomaly dichotomy, 121, 123
Ancient grammatical theory, 2, 11–13, 15–16, 18–19, 23, 26, 28–30, 32–4, 36–9, 41–3, 45–8, 50, 66n, 67, 68, 70n, 71n, 72, 85, 87–8, 89n, 90–1, 101n, 105–6, 112, 118, 123, 126, 128n, 129, 150, 154, 164, 168–9, 170, 173, 174n, 175n, 183, 203n, 204, 214, 251, 254, 256, 260–1, 263–6
anomalia, 123
anti-Aristotelianism, 11, 77–8, 80, 82–3, 134, 136, 160, 189, 228, 245, 260
anti-Cartesianism, 210–11
anti-Ramism, 78, 92–6, 178
anti-Scholasticism, 6, 11, 13–17, 27–8, 30, 79, 81, 134–6
Anwykyll, John, *Compendium totius grammaticae*, 18, 23

Apollonius Dyscolus, 16, 21, 23, 44, 50, 66, 70, 101n, 106, 126, 256
appositum, 52, 102, 116, 122n
Aristotle, Aristotelianism, 8, 10–13, 20, 22, 36, 38, 40, 44, 50, 52, 58–60, 61–8, 72–5, 77–81, 83–9, 91–2, 94–6, 98–100, 102, 105, 110–11, 113, 118n, 121–4, 131, 134–6, 144, 148, 154, 158, 160, 165n, 179, 181–3, 185, 192–3, 196–7, 198, 209, 219, 223, 228, 229, 233, 239, 241, 244–5, 248, 251, 254, 260–1, 263; *Categories*, 59; *De interpretatione*, 12, 121, 254; *Ethics*, 10; *Organon*, 11, 82; *Politics*, 10; *Posterior Analytics*, 223, 239; *Topics*, 60, 82
Aristotle's categories, 59, 74, 83, 91, 123, 136, 153, 174, 179, 182, 192, 197, 229; A. causes, 60–1; A. grammatical theory, 11–13; A. predicables, 60, 74, 83; A. predicaments, *see* A. categories
Arnauld, Antoine, 210–11, 219–20, 222, 252, 258n
Arnauld, A. and C. Lancelot, *Grammaire générale et raisonnée*, *see* Port-Royal
Arnauld, A. and P. Nicole, *Logique*, *see* Port-Royal
article, 168, 200, 207, 244, 249; definitions of, 118, 207
'articles' (*hic haec hoc* before nouns in paradigms), 39, 43, 51, 88, 114, 168
artificial language-planners, 45, 64, 131, 139, 145, 153, 157, 161, 180, 184–98, 208–9, 223, 262
Ascham, Roger, 16; *The Scholemaster*, 7
aspect, 68, 89–90, 101, 116
Asper, 19
attributum, 122n
Augustine, St, 99, 180
Avicenna, 234

Bach, E., 225n; and R. T. Harms, 159n
Bacon, Francis, 13–14, 74, 82, 95–6, 131, 133–8, 144, 148–9, 151, 155–7, 160, 178, 185–9, 191, 194–5, 197, 209, 228, 238; *Advancement of Learning*, 135, 137–8, 155, 179, 185–6; *De augmentis*, 96, 155–6, 186; *Distributio operis*, 137; *Novum organum*, 135, 137–8, 149, 151; *Temporis partus masculus*, 81
Bacon's 'idols', 137–8
Bacon, Roger: Greek Grammar, 154n, 216n
Baebler, J. J., *Beiträge zu einer Geschichte der lateinischen Grammatik*, 50n

Index

Baker, Thomas, *Reflections upon Learning*, 197, 245, 249
Barrado, S., 108
Beck, Cave, 191
behaviourism, 35, 180n, 244
being as the root of all verbs, 47, 68, 74n, 105, 172, 205, 219, 252, 254n
being/action dichotomy, 161, 165
Blach, S. (edition of Lily), 25, 26n
Bloomfield, L., 33, 69, 244; *Language*, 12n, 35, 224n, 231
Boehme, Jakob, 139
Boethius, 11
Bolgar, R. R., *The Classical Heritage*, 20n, 83, 95
Bolinger, D. W., 198n
Bouhours, Père, 220, 221n
Brassicanus, J., *Grammaticae institutiones*, 27–8, 31–2, 44n, 50n
Brekle, H., 220n, 245n, 250n
Breva-Claramonte, M., 97n
Brightland, John, 223
Brinsley, John, 124, 151; *Ludus literarius*, 151; *Posing of the Parts*, 119
Brøndal, V., *Essais de linguistique générale*, 108, 156, 163; *Les parties du discours*, 158
Brunot, F., *Histoire de la langue française*, 258n
Buchanan, George, 22, 94n, 112
Budé, Guillaume, 6; *De l'institution du prince*, 5
Bullokar, William, 2, 3
Burles, Edward, 128; *New English Grammar*, 119
Bursill-Hall, G. L., 2, 11, 29; *Speculative Grammars of the Middle Ages*, 2, 29, 60n, 61n, 62n; *Thomas of Erfurt Grammatica Speculativa*, 11, 29
Bush, D., *The Renaissance and English Humanism*, 5
Butler, Charles, *English Grammar*, 93, 95, 112

Cabbala, 133, 139, 141, 189, 226
Calvinism, 94, 178
Cambridge Platonists, 187
Cambridge University, 7, 77–8, 94–5, 112n
Campanella, Tommaso, 65, 133, 157, 160–9, 181, 189, 192, 195, 198–9, 201–6, 208–10, 219–20, 223, 244–5, 247–8, 251–4, 257–9, 262–3; *Grammatica*, 161–2, 164–78, 195, 222, 255
Caper, 19
Caramuel y Lobkowitz, Juan, 157, 179–85, 190, 198, 205–6, 209–10, 219, 223, 244, 250, 252–4, 257–9, 262–3; *Grammatica audax*, 157, 179–84, 195, 253
Carré, M. H., 227
'Cartesian linguistics', 76, 103–4, 107, 215–17, 220, 222, 224–5, 233, 236
Cartesian logic, 228–30
case, 43, 67, 74, 87–90, 100–1, 102, 113, 115n, 116, 125–6, 168, 192, 199, 205, 207, 249, 256–7
Caspari, F., *Humanism and the Social Order*, 7–8, 10, 21
categoremata, 86–7
causae, 14, 60–1, 65, 72–3, 75–6, 98–9, 100, 106, 109, 134, 155, 169, 255, 258–9, 261
Chaderton, L., *see* Chatterton
chain of being, 189
Chalcondyles, 21
Charisius, 16, 36n, 38, 39n, 66n
Chatterton, L., 95
Cherbury, Lord Herbert of, 226–7, 235–7; *De veritate*, 226, 235–6
Chevalier, J.-C., *Histoire de la syntaxe*, 110n, 218, 240–1, 249n, 256, 258–9
Chinese, 172, 180, 185
Chomsky, N., 1, 4, 41, 64, 76, 85, 103–4, 106, 143, 155n, 158, 214, 215–17, 222, 224–6, 230–3, 236–7, 239–40, 242, 244, 250; *Aspects of the Theory of Syntax*, 225, 232, 239; *Cartesian Linguistics*, 1, 4, 103, 209, 215–16, 224–6, 230, 232, 236; 'Goals of Linguistic Theory', 216–17, 224; *Language and Mind*, 103–4
Chrysoloras, Manuel, 5
Cicero, 8, 10, 21, 53, 79, 80, 84, 235; *Epistles*, 9
Clare, William, *Via naturalis*, 127n, 208
Clenardus (Cleynaerts), N., 17n
Colet, John, 6–8, 22–7, 39, 41, 46, 49–50, 79, 141, 187, 200, 208, 245; *Aeditio*, 24–5, 38–9
Collège de France, 5, 15, 78
Comenius, Johannes Amos, 13, 144–9, 152, 159, 188–90, 194, 196, 197n, 236; *Ars ornatoria*, 147; *Didactica magna*, 152; *Grammatica elegans*, 147; *Janua linguarum*, 146n, 184; *Orbis sensualium pictus*, 146–7, 152, 196; *Porta linguarum reserata*, 146; *Vestibulum linguae Latinae*, 146; *Via lucis*, 145, 190
common mentality, 224–5, 231, 236, 263
'common notions', 235–6
'common words', the, 60
competence/performance dichotomy, 217, 225
complex ideas, 165, 176, 189, 198
compositio, 62–3
conceptual classification, 59–60, 73–4, 145–6, 148, 188, 190–3, 196–7, 263
Conches, William of, 61n
concord, 51, 69, 91, 99, 102, 113, 116–17, 175, 218
conformity between Nature and the mind, 226–8, 233, 240
conjugation, 90
conjunction, 12, 72, 86, 91, 100, 122, 129, 174–5, 200, 207, 244, 249, 251–2, 255–6; definitions of, 91, 175, 255, 266
connotation, 40, 130, 169, 176, 246–8, 255

282

Index

consignification, 13, 34, 36, 38–9, 44–5, 48, 50, 56, 65, 71–2, 74, 86, 90, 92, 99–100, 116, 122–3, 126, 129, 165–6, 168–70, 174–5, 183, 199–200, 206, 241–3, 251, 253, 256, 260–2

constructio (see also syntax), 98; constructio justa or legitima, 54, 214n; personalis and impersonalis, 53, 116; transitiva and intransitiva, 53; essential or simple construction, 212, 217; figurative construction, 212–13, 214n, 215, 217, 256

contextual theories of meaning, 163, 180

'converse terms', 246n

Cooper, Christopher, Grammaticae linguae Anglicanae, 208

Copernicus, 133

copula, 47, 68, 74, 171, 183, 200, 205–7, 219, 251–4, 262; judicativa copula, 183, 206, 253

Cordemoy, G. de, Discours physique de la parole, 226

Corpus Christi College, Oxford, 6, 15, 95

Corradus, Q. M., De lingua Latina, 28, 32, 36, 38, 42–3, 48, 50n, 52, 119, 122n

corruption of the arts, 80, 83

creative principle of language use, 64, 158n, 217, 224–6, 230, 232, 244

Dalgarno, George, 157, 191–5, 198–200, 202, 205–6, 253–4; Ars signorum, 191–3, 199–206 passim, 253

Danes, John, 118, 123, 147n; Light to Lilie, 119; Paralipomena, 119, 128

declarativum, 52

declension, 43, 86, 89, 114–15, 125

declinable/indeclinable dichotomy, 38–9, 46n, 50, 87, 123, 172; Varro's genus foecundum and g. sterile, 123

deductive reasoning, 95, 135, 228

'deep' and 'surface' structure, 41–2, 54, 56, 63, 65, 103–8, 109, 122, 127, 143, 155–6, 157n, 158, 177, 183–4, 212–13, 215–19, 221, 224, 231, 234, 237, 249–50, 254–5, 257–9, 263

de la Ramée, Pierre, see Ramus, Petrus

De-Lawne, N., Elements of Logick, 197n

De Mott, B., 190, 194

denotation, 246

derivation, 69, 87, 113, 123, 166–8, 199–202, 204, 207

Descartes, René, and Cartesianism, 76, 82, 92–3, 96, 103–4, 107, 131, 143, 160–1, 164, 187–8, 190–1, 193–4, 209–11, 213, 215–17, 219–20, 222–30, 232, 236–9, 241, 244n, 259; Discours de la méthode, 96, 227–8; Meditations on the First Philosophy, 227, 240; Notes Directed Against a Certain Programme, 232, 237; Rules for the Direction of the Mind, 228; Principia philosophiae, 236n

Despauterius, Johannes, 14–15, 19–20, 31–2, 34, 37–8, 39n, 40, 41n, 42, 47–8, 51–2, 54, 74n, 105n, 112, 128n, 183, 205,

211–12, 214; Ars versificatoria, 20; Commentarii grammatici, 20, 55; Rudimenta, 20, 84

De Wulf, M., Medieval Philosophy, 135n, 144n, 178, 181

dictio, 12, 31–4, 56, 71, 73, 98–9, 121, 140, 162, 180, 241, 256, 260; definitions of, 33, 264, 266

Digby, Everard, De duplici methodo, 95; Theoria analytica, 13

Diomedes, 15, 16, 19, 23, 28, 34, 50n, 66n, 68n, 89n, 113n

Dobson, E. J., English Pronunciation 1500–1700, 25n, 191n

Donatus, 15–17, 19, 23, 26–9, 36, 38, 39n, 45n, 50, 55, 89n, 124–5, 260, 264–6; Ars maior, 15; Ars minor, 15; De octo partibus orationis, 23

Donzé, R., La Grammaire...de Port-Royal, 211n, 219–20, 222n, 244n, 248n

'double articulation' of language, 121

Drosay, Jean, Grammatica quadrilinguis, 28, 42, 46n, 53n

Dryden, John, 25

dualist theories of meaning, 162–4, 180

Dullardus, Johannes, 118n

du Moulin, Pierre, 197n

Duns Scotus, 14, 135n; = Thomas of Erfurt, 162n, 179, 180, 195

ellipse, 47, 54–6, 74n, 101–6, 109, 111, 114, 117, 122, 130, 155, 177, 183, 198, 205–6, 208, 213–15, 217–19, 250, 252–5, 261, 263; nominativus cognatae significationis, 105, 127; accusativus cognatae significationis, 48, 55, 105

Elyot, Sir Thomas, 187; The Boke Named the Governour, 7, 14

emblems, Bacon's theory of, 186

empiricism, 10, 14, 80, 109, 133, 136, 141–3, 145, 148–9, 157–60, 171, 178, 194, 209, 216, 221, 223, 225, 227, 231–2, 239

enallage, 54, 215

ens, 199, 202, 206

Erasmus, 6, 10, 15, 16, 21–4, 58, 79, 187; De conscribendis epistolis, 9; De copia, 9

Erfurt, Thomas of, Grammatica speculativa, 11, 29, 34, 46n, 48, 50n, 51, 53n, 55–6, 62, 63n, 70n, 71, 72n, 73, 75, 104–5, 117n, 129, 150, 155n, 162, 165n, 167n, 171n, 173n, 174n, 175n, 178, 182n, 195, 202n, 208, 218, 241, 242n, 243, 245–6, 249n, 262, 266–7

Erfurt University, 6

essences, 'real' and 'nominal', see Nominalism

essentia, 101, 120, 123–5, 129, 134, 140, 160, 162, 165–75, 177–8, 189–90, 199, 201–2, 204; essentia referendi, 68

Estienne, Robert, 5, 20–1

Eton Latin Grammar, 24–5

etymologia, 53, 84–5, 98, 116, 121, 175, 198

Index

Évrard of Béthune, *Graecismus*, 14, 17
Examen de la manière d'enseigner le Latin aux enfans (1668), 211n
Examen of the Way of Teaching the Latin Tongue (1669), 152–3, 211n
existentia, 169–71, 174, 178
external discourse, *see verbum oris*

Faithfull, R. G., 60–1, 76n
Ficino, Marsilio, 9, 83
figura, 42, 99, 173
Fillmore, C. J., 257
Finck, Kaspar, 113, 157, 162, 164–6, 172n
Finck, K. and C. Helwig, *Grammatica Latina*, 113, 157, 162, 164–6
Firth, J. R., 180; *Papers in Linguistics 1934–1951*, 163
Fischer, K., *Descartes and his School*, 10, 58n
Fisher, John, 6, 7,
Flynn, V. J. (ed. of Lily), 2n, 24–5
forma, 60n, 61, 63, 67, 73, 102, 107, 121–2, 164n, 180, 182, 259–61
formal criteria, 41–2, 45, 46n, 47, 53, 56, 62, 67, 71, 74, 77, 84, 86–91, 99, 101–2, 107–9, 111–12, 115–16, 118, 120–1, 124, 126, 127–8, 155, 165–7, 170, 172, 177, 198, 204, 207, 224n, 231, 241, 246, 249
formatio, 62, 170, 172
Formigari, L., *Linguistica ed empirismo*, 189, 190
Fox, Richard, 6
Frischlin, Nicodemus, 126, 130, 263; *Quaestiones grammaticae*, 76
Fromant, Abbé, 220n
Funke, O., 2, 22n, 24n, 25n, 41n, 84, 91–2, 112n, 187n, 194, 205

Galen, 22
Galileo, 95, 133
Gallup, J., 242n
García, C., *Contribución a la historia de los conceptos gramaticales*, 3, 98, 99n, 108–9
Gaza, Theodore, 5; Greek grammar, 5n, 11, 21–3, 36, 41, 91, 118n
gender, 39, 42, 67, 69, 86–8, 100, 102, 114, 115n, 116, 124–6, 168, 170, 249; *genus compositum*, 125; *g. fictum*, 114; *g. simplex*, 125; *g. usurarium*, 114; *g. verum*, 114
general grammar, *see* grammar, universal
generative grammar, *see* grammar, transformational
genus foecundum and *g. sterile*, *see declinable/indeclinable* dichotomy
gerund, 69, 90
Gil, Alexander, *Logonomia Anglica*, 93, 112
Gilson, E., *Philosophy of St Thomas Aquinas*, 145, 233, 235
Glanvill, Joseph, *Essay Concerning Preaching*, 132
Godfrey, R. G., 154–5, 158, 218n, 242n
grammar, definitions of, 16, 30–1, 62, 75, 84, 98–9, 120–1, 161, 195; 'instituted and particular', 195–6; 'natural and

general', 195–6; revolt against g., 151–2, 184; transformational g., 41, 54, 106–7, 216–17, 221, 224–5, 232; universal g., 2, 45, 121–2, 131, 142, 153–9, 161–85, 191–6, 198–209, 218, 220–5, 230–3, 241–2, 246, 249–50, 255, 257, 261–3; *see also* vernacular g.
grammatica artificialis, 121, 131, 181, 195; *g. civilis*, 161, 195; *g. exegetice* or *historice*, 9, 31, 84, 121, 131, 161, 214; *g. methodice*, 9, 31, 121, 161, 179; *g. naturalis*, 121, 131, 181, 195; *g. philosophica*, 161, 195
Grammatica speculativa, *see* Erfurt, Thomas of
grammatical meaning, 12–13, 34–5, 45, 65, 86, 121, 133, 163–5, 223, 224n, 231, 242, 245–6, 248, 255–6, 260
Graves, F. P., *History of Education*, 8; *Petrus Ramus*, 78, 93, 95
Greaves, Paul, *Grammatica Anglicana*, 2, 84, 93, 111
Green, V. H. H., *History of Oxford University*, 6n, 134, 179
Greenberg, J. H., 158, 196, 231
Grocyn, William, 6, 7, 8, 21, 23

Harms, R. T., 159n
Harris, James, *Hermes*, 62n
Hartlib, Samuel, 190, 194
Hayne, Thomas, 113–15, 117; *Grammatices Latinae compendium*, 22, 93, 111
Heidelberg University, 20
Helwig, Christopher, 113, 160, 162, 164–6, 168n, 172n, 173n, 174n; *Libri didactici* (*Grammatica*), 157, 166
Helwig, C. and K. Finck, *see* Finck and Helwig
Herrera, Fernando de, 98
Hippocrates, 58
Hjelmslev, L., 221, 223–4; *Principes de grammaire générale*, 158, 242
Hobbes, Thomas, 110n, 141–3, 145, 151, 186–7, 228, 237, 254n; *Computatio sive logica*, 186; *Elements of Philosophy*, 141, 237; *Human Nature*, 141–2; *Leviathan*, 141–3, 186, 237; *Opera philosophica*, 142
Hockett, C. F., 155n, 231
Holt, John, 21
homo trilinguis, 15
Hooke, Robert, 191
Hoole, Charles, 146–7, 152; *Latine Grammar*, 119–20, 123n, 124, 127
Howell, A. C., 138n
Howell, W. S., *Logic and Rhetoric in England, 1500–1700*, 59–60, 79, 82, 94–6, 229n
Humboldt, Wilhelm von, 62n, 217
Hume, Alexander, 113–18; *Grammatica nova*, 93, 111–12; *Of the Orthographie and Congruitie of the Britan Tongue*, 93, 112; *Prima elementa grammaticae*, 111–12
Humphrey, Duke of Gloucester, 6
Husserl, E., 159
hylomorphism, 58–9, 60, 75, 76n

284

Index

Index

normative grammar, 9, 16, 18, 21, 26, 30–1, 57, 62, 75, 84, 97–8, 156, 162, 258n, 260

notae notarum (= *notae specierum*), 64–5, 70, 76, 235, 237, 241, 263

notae rerum, 63, 65, 68, 73, 98, 186–7, 200

noun, 35–44, 56, 73, 86–8, 90, 99, 100, 113, 122, 155, 165, 167, 199, 200, 244, 251–2, 261–2; definitions of, 12n, 35–8, 65–6, 88, 100, 113, 123–4, 140–1, 147, 165, 182, 199–200, 208, 264, 266; *nomen absolutum*, 67, 74; n. abstract, 38, 40, 147, 166, 182, 198n, 199, 202–4, 247–8; n. active, 116, 199, 201, 203–4; *nomen ad aliquid*, 71; n. adjective, 37, 39–41, 59, 68, 71, 88–9, 100, 102, 114, 124, 146, 166–7, 170, 174–5, 182, 200–1, 203–4, 245–9, 248n, 255, 262; adjectival comparison, 87, 115, 166, 218; *adjectiva accidentalia et substantialia*, 167, *nomen adulterinum*, 115; n. common, 37–8, 41, 124, 166, 170; n. concrete, 38, 40, 147, 182, 198n, 199, 202–4; *nomen genuinum*, 115; n. neuter, 199, 201–4; *nomen participiale*, 90, 116, 173; n. passive, 199, 201, 203–4; proper n., 38, 41, 124, 166, 169, 170; *nomen relativum*, 67–8, 74; n. substantive, 37, 39, 40–1, 59, 67–8, 71, 74, 88, 100–2, 114, 124, 147, 166–7, 175, 182, 200–1, 203–4, 207, 244–8, 255; definitions of substantive and adjective, 39–41, 88, 100, 114, 124, 166, 200–1, 245, 265, 266–7; substantive present, perfect and future, 207n; *nomen verbale*, 116; n. and time reference, 12, 36, 65, 88, 118, 124n, 183; n. and verb, semantic primacy of, 35–6, 70, 72–3, 122, 155, 165, 244

number, 69, 87, 99–100, 102, 113, 114, 116, 123, 166, 170, 172

numerus nominalis, *n. verbalis*, 87, 88

Oakeshott, M., 142

objets de nos pensées, 243–4, 251, 254

Ockham, William of, 40n, 136, 142, 145, 180n, 234, 247

Ogden, C. K. and I. A. Richards, *The Meaning of Meaning*, 162

'operations of the mind', 150, 228–9, 233–4, 237–8, 240, 244, 255

oral discourse, *see verbum oris*

oratio, 31–2, 35–6, 40, 52, 56, 63, 98–9, 106, 118, 120, 122, 131, 150, 164n, 165, 176–7, 182n, 254; definitions of, 32, 63n, 118, 131, 150, 165, 176, 264; *o. constructa*, 33, 34, 121

original language, 97–8, 139–40, 161

Orleans, 31, 162

orthographia, 85

Osgood, C. E., 159

οὐσία, 125, 129

Oxford University, 77, 95, 134

Padua, University, 22

Paris University, 5, 30–1, 78, 162, 211

Parker, Samuel, *A Free and Impartial Censure of the Platonick Philosophie*, 139–40, 187

pars orationis, 12, 33–5, 56, 66, 74, 85–7, 90–1, 99–100, 113, 121–3, 140, 148, 150, 152–3, 163, 165–6, 175, 198–9, 241–2, 244, 260; definitions of, 34–5, 91, 150, 164, 266

part of speech, *see pars orationis*

participle, 50, 69–70, 90, 99–100, 122, 165–6, 178, 183, 203n, 244, 255; definitions of, 50, 69–70, 90, 178, 265

particle (*particula*), 99, 121, 123, 130, 198, 200, 206–7, 218, 249, 253

Pascal, Blaise, 210, 229

passio, 45, 47, 50, 56, 59, 68–9, 74, 101, 116, 126–8, 146–7, 153, 168, 171–2, 182, 199, 201–2, 204, 252, 261, 265

pedagogy: Humanist, 6–7, 8–9, 14–16, 21–7, 57, 79, 93, 97; Jesuit, 15, 93, 211; Port-Royal, 211–12; seventeenth-century, 143–7, 151; teaching of Latin via the vernacular, 97, 211

permanence/flux dichotomy, 65–6, 69–70, 73–4, 99, 172, 252, 261

Perottus, Nicolas, 17–18, 20, 23, 30–1, 40, 46; *Rudimenta grammatices*, 17, 19

person, 44–6, 53, 66n, 67, 69, 72, 74, 87–90, 101, 113–16, 123, 168–70, 172, 176, 201, 254; definitions of, 45, 66n, 101, 113, 169, Peter of Spain, *Summulae logicales*, 47, 81, 105n, 162, 205n

Petites Ecoles de Port-Royal, 211

Petrarch, 14

Petrus Heliae, 51–2, 129

Petrus Hispanus, *see* Peter of Spain

Philippo-Ramism, 94, 111, 179

philosophical grammar, 75–6, 101, 104, 113, 131, 155–7, 159, 160–85, 191, 193, 195, 205, 207–8, 210, 258, 260, 262

Phocas, 19

phoneme, 34, 121

φύσις/θέσις (νόμος) controversy, *see nature/convention* controversy

pietas literata, 21

Plato, -nism, 8–10, 58, 83, 98–9, 136, 140, 160–1, 187, 233–5, 239

Plotinus, 9

Poldauf, I., 1–2, 52–3, 92, 108n, 244n, 248–9, 256–7

Politian, 21

Port-Royal, 40, 55, 64, 68, 93, 110, 143, 147n, 148–50, 155n, 164, 206–7, 210–25, 228–30, 232–3, 239–59; *Grammaire générale et raisonnée*, 2, 4, 44, 47, 54, 74–6, 85, 103–4, 106–7, 110, 131, 150, 156–7, 205n, 209–10, 214n, 215–17, 218n, 219–25, 229–30, 232–3, 237, 239, 240–52, 253–9, 262–3; Greek grammar, 213, 228; *Logique*, 150, 177, 183n, 210, 220, 222, 228–30, 237, 239–40, 244–5, 247–8, 253–4, 256; *Nouvelle Méthode latine*, 55, 103–4, 106–7, 113n, 119, 176, 183, 211–13, 217–19, 220n, 221–2, 228, 248–50,

Index